PENGUIN BOOKS

THE REAL JAMES HERRIOT

Jim Wight, born in 1943, followed in his father's footsteps at the Glasgow Veterinary College, which by then was part of the University of Glasgow, graduating in 1966. In 1967 he joined the practice of Sinclair and Wight in Thirsk, working alongside his father and Donald Sinclair for the next twenty years when Alf Wight retired. He is still a member of the practice.

Jim Wight is married, and he and his wife Gill have a son and two daughters. They live in a village below Sutton Bank near Thirsk.

D1344394

THE REAL
JAMES HERRIOT

The Authorized Biography

JIM WIGHT

PENGUIN BOOKS

PENGUIN BOOKS

Published by the Penguin Group
Penguin Books Ltd, 80 Strand, London WC2R 0RL, England
Penguin Putnam Inc., 375 Hudson Street, New York, New York 10014, USA
Penguin Books Australia Ltd, 250 Camberwell Road, Camberwell, Victoria 3124, Australia
Penguin Books Canada Ltd, 10 Alcorn Avenue, Toronto, Ontario, Canada M4V 3B2
Penguin Books India (P) Ltd, 11 Community Centre, Panchsheel Park, New Delhi – 110 017, India
Penguin Books (NZ) Ltd, Cnr Rosedale and Airborne Roads, Albany, Auckland, New Zealand
Penguin Books (South Africa) (Pty) Ltd, 24 Sturdee Avenue, Rosebank 2196, South Africa

Penguin Books Ltd, Registered Offices: 80 Strand, London WC2R 0RL, England

www.penguin.com

First published by Michael Joseph 1999
Published in Penguin Books 2000

032

Copyright © Jim Wight, 1999
All rights reserved

The moral right of the author has been asserted

Set in Monotype Minion
Printed in Great Britain by Clays Ltd, Elcograf S.p.A.

ISBN-13: 978–0–140–26881–2

www.greenpenguin.co.uk

To

GILL, ROSIE AND MY MOTHER

who have heard it all before

LIST OF ILLUSTRATIONS

ACKNOWLEDGEMENTS

Many people have helped me with the writing of this book. Two I wish to thank especially; they have shown great patience and understanding in enduring the company of an inexperienced and mono-focused author: my wife Gill, and my editor Jenny Dereham. I also wish to express particular thanks to my agent Jacqueline Korn, at David Higham Associates, whose persuasion it was that I should – and could – write this biography.

I am deeply grateful to my mother, and to my sister Rosie, who have not only supplied so much vital information but have been very cooperative and unselfish in agreeing to my sharing so many details of my father's life with his myriad fans.

Two important people who have been a tremendous source of essential material must be especially thanked: my late Grandmother Wight for saving so many letters and other memorabilia of her son, and Alex Taylor, my father's oldest friend, for his informative and entertaining memories of the countless happy hours spent in my father's company.

I am also particularly grateful to Professor Norman Wright, the Dean of the University of Glasgow Veterinary School and his staff; also Ken Cunningham, Head Master of Hillhead High School and his staff: from these I received invaluable help and vital information.

Many others, among them relatives, friends and colleagues of my father, have provided me with anecdotes, photographs and other such important pieces of information that went to make up the final accurate picture of his life. In particular, I would like to thank: Fred Banks, George Bell, Bertram Bosomworth, Jim Chadwick, John Crooks, Arthur Dand, The Lady Dean of Harptree, Piers Dudgeon, Marjorie Eves, Alan Goldsborough, Janet Grey, Ellen Grout, Audrey Hancock, Robert Hardy, Dr Ken Hibbitt, Professor Peter Holmes, Ken Kilvington, R. M. Major, Martha Nettleton, Eve Pette, Dr Alistair Porter, Ossy Sandy, Peter Shaw, Anthea Sinclair, Bob Smith, Joan Snelling, Jimmy Steele, Eddie Straiton, Chris Timothy, Juliana Wadham.

Without the help and willing cooperation of all these people, the completion of this book would not have been possible.

Photographic credits

The author would like to thank his family and friends for providing many of the photographs which appear in this book. In addition, the author acknowledges the following for permission to reproduce photographs. Every effort has been made to contact all copyright holders: the publishers will be glad to make good in future editions any errors or omissions brought to their attention.

Life Magazine 37, 46, 48 and 52; *Daily Express* 38 and 49; Fay Godwin 39; *Sunday Express* 45; Desmond O'Neill Features 50; *Yorkshire Post* 51; Barratts Photo Press 56; D. N. Wilkinson Productions Ltd 60; Ian Cook/ *People Weekly* 62; Evening Press (York) 64

BIBLIOGRAPHY

IF ONLY THEY COULD TALK Michael Joseph 1970; Pan Books 1973
IT SHOULDN'T HAPPEN TO A VET Michael Joseph 1972; Pan Books 1973
  published together in an omnibus volume
    ALL CREATURES GREAT AND SMALL Michael Joseph 1975; Pan Books 1976
LET SLEEPING VETS LIE Michael Joseph 1973; Pan Books 1974
VET IN HARNESS Michael Joseph 1974; Pan Books 1975
  published together in an omnibus volume
    ALL THINGS BRIGHT AND BEAUTIFUL Michael Joseph 1976; Pan Books 1978
VETS MIGHT FLY Michael Joseph 1976; Pan Books 1977
VET IN A SPIN Michael Joseph 1977; Pan Books 1978
  published together in an omnibus volume
    ALL THINGS WISE AND WONDERFUL Michael Joseph 1978; Pan Books 1979
THE LORD GOD MADE THEM ALL Michael Joseph 1981; Pan Books 1992
EVERY LIVING THING Michael Joseph 1992; Pan Books 1993
JAMES HERRIOT'S YORKSHIRE Michael Joseph 1979; Mermaid Books 1982

Other omnibus editions
THE BEST OF JAMES HERRIOT Michael Joseph in association with Readers
  Digest Association Ltd 1982
JAMES HERRIOT'S DOG STORIES Michael Joseph 1986; Pan Books 1992
JAMES HERRIOT'S CAT STORIES Michael Joseph 1994
JAMES HERRIOT'S FAVOURITE DOG STORIES Michael Joseph 1995
JAMES HERRIOT'S YORKSHIRE STORIES Michael Joseph 1997

Books for children
MOSES THE KITTEN Michael Joseph in association with A & C Black Ltd
  1984; Piper Books 1988
ONLY ONE WOOF Michael Joseph in association with A & C Black Ltd 1985;
  Piper Books 1988
THE CHRISTMAS DAY KITTEN Michael Joseph 1986; Piper Books 1988
BONNY'S BIG DAY Michael Joseph 1987; Piper Books 1989
BLOSSOM COMES HOME Michael Joseph 1988; Piper Books 1991
THE MARKET SQUARE DOG Michael Joseph 1989; Piper Books 1991
OSCAR: CAT ABOUT TOWN Michael Joseph 1990; Piper Books 1992
SMUDGE'S DAY OUT Michael Joseph 1991; Piper Books 1993

PROLOGUE

23 February 1995 was a beautiful day in my part of North Yorkshire. From the top of Sutton Bank on the western edge of the North York Moors National Park, it was possible to see right across the Vale of York to the Yorkshire Dales over thirty miles away. The sun shone brightly out of a cloudless winter sky and I could clearly see the familiar bulk of Pen Hill, standing majestically over the entrance to Wensleydale – the fresh whiteness of its snow-dusted slopes in vivid contrast to the dark green dale below. It was a cold, crisp, perfect winter's day, one that normally would have had me longing to walk for mile after mile in the clean air. It was a day when I should have felt glad to be alive.

The timeless magic of the Dales has always thrilled me but, on that brilliant February day, my mood was one of emptiness as I knew that I would never again gaze across at those distant hills without a feeling of nostalgia and regret. On that day a great friend had died. His name was James Alfred Wight, a father in whose company I had spent countless happy hours. A man I shall never forget.

I was not alone in my sorrow. On that same day, others all over the world were also mourning the loss of a friend. His name was James Herriot, the country practitioner whose skill as a writer had elevated him to the status of the world's most famous and best-loved veterinary surgeon. This incredibly successful storyteller, who sold more than 60 million books which had been translated into over twenty languages, wrote with such warmth, humour and sincerity that he was regarded as a friend by all who read him.

James Alfred Wight, the real James Herriot, was every inch the gentleman his many fans imagined him to be. He was a completely modest man who remained bemused by his success until the end of his life, yet this self-confessed 'run of the mill vet' is likely to be remembered for decades to come. My own memories of him, however, are not of a famous author but of a father who always put the interests of his family ahead of his own.

I think it is true to say that in everyone's life, no matter how happy they may be, there is always a dark cloud somewhere on the horizon.

My own particular cloud had been my father's health which had given the family cause for concern for a number of years; it had assumed threatening proportions in December 1991 when I learned that he had cancer, and the final blow fell when he died just over three years later.

On 20 October 1995, some eight months after my father's death, I found myself seated in the front row of York Minster, surely one of the most beautiful cathedrals in the world. The occasion was the Memorial Service for James Herriot, to which over 2,300 people had come to pay their last respects to a man who had given pleasure to millions. Christopher Timothy, who played the part of James Herriot in the television series *All Creatures Great and Small*, was reading a passage from one of my father's best-selling books and laughter was echoing around the ancient Minster. Although it might have been unusual to hear the sound of such merriment in those magnificent but austere surroundings, I felt that James Herriot's Memorial Service was turning out to be exactly as he would have wished. On that day, we had smiles, not tears.

Alf, as my father was always known to his friends, had always had an intense dislike of funerals, wishing with all his heart that these events could be less solemn. 'Of course, people must be respectful in these situations,' he once said, 'but I feel very sorry for the family and friends on these sad occasions.' I well remember the occasion of one funeral that he had really enjoyed. It happened many years ago when I was still at school, and was the funeral of a Mr Bartholomew, a former associate of one of my father's great friends, Denton Pette (immortalised in the James Herriot books as Granville Bennett). 'Bart', a most likeable but hard-drinking veterinary surgeon, had stipulated shortly before his death that several bottles of the finest Scotch whisky should be provided for those of his colleagues who attended his funeral. My father, Denton and many others were present and afterwards they dutifully carried out Bart's last wishes.

There was a somewhat different atmosphere, however, at home, twenty-five miles away in the market town of Thirsk in North Yorkshire.

'Where on earth is your dad?' my mother exclaimed. 'He set off for that funeral at two o'clock this afternoon and it's now almost midnight! What *is* he doing?'

Knowing how much my father enjoyed the company of his professional colleagues, especially those of the calibre of Denton Pette, it was not difficult to imagine what he was doing. I never heard him return home but he presented a delicate figure seated opposite me at the table the following morning.

He chewed at his dry toast for a minute or two before he spoke. 'You know ... that funeral was not the mourning of the passing of a meaningful and fulsome life,' he said, a gleam of pleasure in his bloodshot eyes. 'It was something else. It was a *celebration!*'

I feel sure my father would have approved of the celebration we were enjoying in York Minster that day, just as he had enjoyed Bart's final farewell all those years before.

Chris Timothy was giving an excellent reading of the passage from *Vet in Harness*, the story where the young James is manfully trying to persuade the suspicious and belligerent Mr Biggins that a veterinary visit to his cow would, despite an ensuing bill, be well worthwhile. It was as I was looking up at Chris and thinking how well the words sounded that I was struck by a stark realisation. In all the years that I had known my father, during all the hours we had spent together discussing our common interests (and there were many of those), I had never once told him how good I considered his writing to be. Indeed, I do not think I had ever told him what I really felt about him. I think he knew but, nevertheless, there is a feeling of regret that I shall carry with me for ever. My father often told me that he was always grateful to the local people for not making a fuss of him. How ironic that his own son should be one of them.

A few months after the Memorial Service, I received a telephone call from Jacqueline Korn, my father's literary agent at David Higham Associates in London. She had a proposition for me. 'How about writing a book about your father?' she asked. 'You knew him better than anyone and the appreciation of him that you gave at the Minster was enjoyed by everyone. I am sure that you could do it.' The prospect of undertaking a biographical work was one that frightened me. I was a veterinary surgeon, not a writer. Why should I be capable of performing such a task? I abandoned English in my fifth year at school and was not, compared to my father, a widely-read man. Jacqueline Korn did alleviate my concerns a little when she explained to me that, on no account should I try to emulate him as a writer but, instead, put down my memories in a readable way. Despite her words of encouragement, I expressed my grave doubts.

I remained indecisive for several weeks but one thing that made me think about the idea seriously was the fact that my father was, without doubt, a world-wide celebrity – one with a massive following. This was vividly illustrated on a trip I made to the United States shortly after Jacqueline Korn's telephone call. I had been invited to speak about James Herriot at a veterinary student convention in Stillwater, Oklahoma, during which time – as part of the trip – my wife Gillian and I were invited to take a few days' holiday in Winter Park, Colorado. One of the highlights was a dog-sleigh ride into the mountains around Winter Park. We were gliding over the snow, with the little Siberian Huskies effortlessly pulling us along, when the team leader, a friendly man who went by the name of 'J.D.', opened the conversation. He had noticed that Gill was wearing an anorak with the words 'Oklahoma State Veterinary School' as the logo.

'You guys veterinarians?' he asked.

'How do you know?' I replied.

'It's on the anorak. You're from England, yeah?'

'Yes, we are.'

'What part of England are you guys from?'

'Yorkshire,' I replied, thinking that, perhaps, he had never heard of the place.

He hesitated before speaking again. 'Say! Maybe you knew that "Doc Herriot" who wrote those books? He was from Yorkshire.'

The conversation was beginning to assume a familiar ring – one I had heard many times before. I said, 'Yes, I knew him.'

'You knew him? You knew him well?' J.D. was impressed.

'Yes,' I continued, 'I knew him pretty well really.'

'Wow! What sort of a guy was he? He sure wrote terrific books! Did you get to speak to him?'

'Yes, actually, I did.' I felt I was getting into deep water and it was time to come clean. 'As a matter of fact . . . he was my dad.'

There was a pause while J.D. took this on board. He then whistled softly. 'You don't say! Boy, wait till I tell my wife! I'm telling you, she is one real fan of your dad's!'

After the ride, Gill and I were introduced to the other dog-team leaders, all of whom seemed to be well acquainted with my father's work. It was obvious that James Herriot's name and fame had thoroughly penetrated into this land of ice and snow, so far from my home in Yorkshire. I began to wonder whether there was anywhere in the United States that the name of James Herriot was not familiar.

The rest of our stay served only to confirm the high esteem in which he was held in that country, with countless numbers of students at the veterinary convention telling me that reading his books had given them the inspiration to take up veterinary medicine for a career. By the time we returned to England, I had almost made up my mind to attempt my father's biography.

Three weeks later, unable to procrastinate any longer, I boarded the train for London to meet with Jacqueline Korn. We had been travelling south for only a short time and I was staring out at the Yorkshire landscape, my mind wrestling with the impending decision, when the loudspeaker system came on.

'Good morning, ladies and gentlemen. This is your conductor, Don Sinclair, speaking. You are travelling on the Newcastle to London King's Cross train, calling at . . .'

Don Sinclair?! The real name of my father's life-long partner, better known to the millions of James Herriot fans as 'Siegfried Farnon', and the pivotal character running throughout his books. I am a sceptic by nature but that extraordinary, almost supernatural episode swayed my decision to accept the challenge of writing the story of my father's life. It was as though something was telling me to go ahead.

The research for this book has been an enjoyable and exciting, as well as an emotional undertaking, but I do not know whether my father would have shared my enthusiasm. He was a very modest and private man – one who insulated his personal life from the rest of the world – and I can only hope that he would have approved.

Some months before his death, I was talking to him at his home in the small village of Thirlby, only one and a half miles from my own. It was a great comfort to him in his twilight years to have his children living nearby. My sister, Rosie, actually lived next door to him and the two of us were regular visitors to his house. Through our sharing of many interests with him, there was always plenty to talk about.

On that particular day, the subject of a book about his life was raised. 'I am not in favour of anyone writing my biography,' he said. 'Biographies, although I enjoy reading them myself, often do not tell the true story. Facts become distorted, with people close to the family being hurt in the process.'

'But I'm sure that many people would love to read the story of your life,' I replied. 'Your books have captured the imagination of millions. A biography would be a fitting memorial to your achievements.'

He moved uneasily in his chair. The crippling pain of the prostate cancer that he had endured stoically for many months was exacting a severe toll. 'Someone has already contacted your mother with a view to writing my biography and I have said "no".'

'They'll probably write it, anyway,' I countered. 'Yours is a fascinating success story.'

'That may be so, Jim,' he continued, 'and there is not much that I can do about that.' He paused for a moment to gaze out of the window and across the garden to the towering Whitestone Cliffs that had been a backdrop to his life for so many years. 'This much I can tell you,' he said. 'If anyone were to write my biography, you should. I don't really want anyone to write it but if you did, I know that you would tell the truth.'

I could see by the distant look in his eyes that he did not wish to discuss the matter further. We went on to talk about subjects of far greater importance to him – such as how the veterinary practice was shaping up or the fortunes of Sunderland Football Club.

One of the most intriguing aspects of the character of James Alfred Wight was that his transition from a relatively unknown country veterinary surgeon into a world-famous author did not change him at all. He steadfastly refused, throughout his years of literary fame, to allow his celebrity status to take over his life, and this was reflected in the admiration and respect felt for him among the local community. As I sat with him that day, I thought to myself, 'What a unique man!' He did not seek praise or flattery. He remained the same, unassuming, down-to-earth father whose company I had enjoyed for so many years.

Time has proved me to be correct in my assumption that books, as well as many articles, would appear following his death. There are many myths and misconceptions surrounding my father's life and these have given me the extra incentive to reveal the truth behind the real James Herriot. One of the most controversial aspects of my father's writing is the veracity, or otherwise, of his stories. Some believe there to be no factual basis behind many of them and he has even been described as a 'writer of fiction'. These statements are very misleading. Ninety per cent of my father's stories are, as he always maintained, based upon fact. Not only did I know the great majority of the characters he described but I heard most of the stories verbally long before they were put into print; in fact, a proportion of them originated from my own experiences. It is true that he deliberately manipulated events and dates to suit his stories but the theme of almost every one is based upon real-life incidents and personalities who really existed. It has been argued that the factual basis of the Herriot stories is unimportant, that they are enjoyed regardless of the fact that they may be works of pure fiction. Does it really matter? I think that it matters a great deal. The ring of authenticity adds a new dimension to the tales and I feel certain that a large proportion of James Herriot's huge following would be very upset to discover that the stories owed little in their origins to factual events. They need not worry.

In conveying to the reader the truth about the real James Herriot, I consider myself to be the best qualified to do so. My father was, first and foremost, a family man who, even during the busiest periods of his life, always found time to spend with his children, with the result that he was a father whom we got to know very well. But it was not only my father, Alfred Wight, whom I knew so well; I spent many hours with his partner – and my godfather – the mercurial, charming, impossible Donald Sinclair. As a veterinary surgeon myself, I worked with both men in the practice of Sinclair and Wight in Thirsk for more than twenty unforgettable years, during which time I was able to observe the true relationship between the two men. There is no one better qualified than myself to tell the story of life in James Herriot's practice as it really was.

During my early years in Thirsk, I experienced the veterinary surgeon's life that James Herriot described, with the greater part of my time spent visiting small family farms that have, sadly, now largely disappeared. It was among these small farming communities, where the day's toil began in the early hours and lasted until dark (and often beyond), that my father met the incomparable characters who were to figure so vividly in his books. I had a taste of that life, not only as a veterinary surgeon, but many years earlier as a small but very proud 'assistant', riding around in my father's car as he drove from farm to farm. From the days when I had barely learned to walk, I watched Alfred Wight the veterinary surgeon, and would continue to do so for more than forty years.

During his years of fame, my father received mountains of fan mail from all over the world. His stories entranced so many of his readers that they felt compelled to write and tell him how much his books meant to them. Many of the letters delivered to his door by the overworked postmen carried a similar theme: his fans sought the real truth behind the stories. They wanted to get to know the real man but, above all, they wanted to join James Herriot in a world that seemed so far removed from their own modern, high-pressure existence. In writing this book, I hope I have answered them.

Much of the material that I needed to fill the following pages, I have in my head but, after beginning, I discovered a mass of extra information. Having asked my mother for permission to go through her house on a fact-finding mission, I found more than I could have hoped for. I had not realised that my parents had kept so much in the way of papers, letters and newspaper cuttings – some of it going back to before the Second World War. For much of this, I have to thank my mother. My father, too, retained copious amounts of paper but making sense of his 'filing system' was difficult. He was never the most organised of men and I spent many hours going over hundreds of scraps of crumpled paper – but it was time well spent.

Another person I have to thank for providing me with invaluable information is my father's mother, dear old Granny Wight. I spent my student days in Glasgow lodging with my grandmother but, in all of my five years there, I had no idea that her house at 694 Anniesland Road contained such a rich store of archive material. She was one of life's hoarders; she threw nothing away. In the summer of 1981, the years had finally established their mark upon this astonishingly independent and energetic lady. Having reached the age of eighty-nine, with her mind (and body) beginning to wander, it was imperative that she be moved closer to her family in Yorkshire. Two or three weeks following her move into a nursing home in Harrogate, I hired a van to travel to Glasgow and collect her belongings. There was a vast amount, including amongst it the contents of the 'glory hole'. This was a tiny room into which Granny Wight had stuffed just about everything she hadn't thrown away. The contents of that little room were transferred to my father's attic in Thirlby and lay there, forgotten, for more than sixteen years until I unearthed it all in 1997. It has provided a wealth of information.

Alf Wight was always a prodigious letter writer and wrote to his parents regularly, right up until the 1980s. His mother had preserved all of these letters, many of which make fascinating reading. Some of them which date back to a time when he was struggling emotionally as well as financially, reveal his feelings during a difficult and exacting period of his life. The dusty, untidy heap of letters from that neglected old den in Glasgow has given me a peep into a part of my father's life that had previously been denied to me. Many people have helped with the research for this book but no one contributed more than the old lady who had so assiduously preserved everything connected with the son who meant so much to her.

Everyone has revelations at some time or other in their lives and I have had a whole bundle of them since I decided to write this biography. Foremost is the realisation that I did not really appreciate my father's work until well after his death. In my defence, this is not surprising as he spoke so little about his literary achievements. I remember in the mid 1970s when his books were hogging the number one spot in the *New York Times* best-seller lists, he would occasionally say, 'I'm in my fifteenth week at the top of the best-sellers in America, isn't that amazing?' 'Great, Dad!' I would reply and the subject would be dropped. That was fine by him; he was really far more interested in talking about other things.

The local people, including the farming community, said very little about their local 'vitinry's' fame but that is not to say they were unaware of it. My father liked it that way and, indeed, he once said to me that he would be surprised if more than a handful of his farming friends had read his books. He may have been wrong.

One day he was operating on a cow and the long, laborious task of suturing the abdominal wound was under way. Such operations on the bovine race are often extremely interesting, especially Caesarean sections where the delivery of a calf 'through the side door' is one of the most satisfying experiences for the country practitioner. Closing up the wound is a tedious business, however, and it is at such times as these that a bit of conversation between farmer and vet can break the monotony.

On this particular occasion, the farmer suddenly said to him, 'Ah've read one o' yer books, Mr Wight.'

This came as a real shock to my father who never expected the local people to show interest in his work, especially busy farmers. He hardly dared to ask the next question. 'What did you think of it? Did you enjoy it?'

The farmer replied slowly, 'Aye . . . why . . . it's all about nowt!'

This was a veiled compliment. The book had been read and enjoyed, despite describing a way of life only too familiar to the reader.

I knew my father as well as anyone but I, too, was one of the many who made little fuss of his achievements. He would have made light of this but now, some four years after his death, I realise that I under-estimated him. His qualities as a friend, father and professional col-league, I have always appreciated; it was his qualities as an author that I did not. That is, until now. Although he and I were always the closest of friends, he was acutely aware of my shortcomings. Organisation was never one of my strong points. 'You're just like me, Jim. You couldn't run a winkle stall!' was a cry I heard only too often, and it was with such encouraging thoughts that I embarked upon this biography.

I have, however, done something right. I decided at the outset to re-read all my father's books and, in so doing, I have at last realised what a great storyteller he was. Others, of course, all over the world, saw his qualities as a writer very quickly but I still think that it is easy to underestimate James Herriot. He had such a pleasant, readable style that one could be forgiven for thinking that anyone could emulate it. How many times have I heard people say, 'Oh, I could write a book. I just haven't the time.' Easily said. Not so easily done. My father, contrary to popular opinion, did not find it easy in his early days of, as he put it, 'having a go at the writing game'. Whilst he obviously had an abundance of natural talent, the final, polished work that he gave to the world was the result of years of practising, re-writing and reading. Like the majority of authors, he had to suffer many disappointments and rejections along the way, but these made him all the more determined to succeed. Everything he achieved in life was earned the hard way and his success in the literary field was no exception.

When I re-read his books, I set out with the idea of analysing them, of trying to pick up some tips from the master, but I always ended up in the same state – the book on the floor and my head back, crying with laughter. I know he would have approved. To have his writing subjected to detailed appraisal was never his wish; he wanted it, quite simply, to be enjoyed. That period of re-reading James Herriot's books has been one of the most revealing and enjoyable times of my life.

The veterinary profession has undergone enormous change since the days when my father qualified from Glasgow Veterinary College in 1939, with great strides having been made in the ongoing quest to conquer animal diseases. Many of the old ailments that my father wrote about have largely been brought under control but others rise up to take their place, presenting continually fresh challenges for the profession. The practice in Thirsk has changed out of all recognition since 'James Herriot's' heyday – a period of his life he described, many times, as 'harder, but more fun'. Gone are the days of driving round the hills visiting little farms, treating a cow with 'wooden tongue' here, a pig with Erysipelas there. As the number of farm visits declined and the small animal work increased, so the practice has now become about fifty per cent pet-orientated.

Thanks largely to my father, however, a window on the veterinary profession of the past has been kept open. Many young people who watched the highly popular television series, 'All Creatures Great and Small', based on the Herriot books, were eager to take up veterinary medicine as a career, but they soon discovered a very different picture from the one displayed on the screen. The world of James Herriot is history.

An American reader wrote to my father's publisher in 1973, in appreciation of his work: 'Herriot seems to possess the quality of being the universal observer with whom the reader can readily empathize. He is one of those individuals who is a natural audience to the quirks and vagaries of the human species.' My father was, indeed, a great observer of human nature but now it is his turn to be put under the spotlight. Throughout his literary career, James Herriot had millions of fans and countless numbers wrote to him. One of his biggest fans is now about to write about him – not just as an author but as a colleague, friend and father. While other veterinary surgeons look to the future, I am travelling back into the past but maybe, as my father would have said, I will 'have more fun'. I will carry the regret to the end of my days that I never told him what I really thought about him, but at least there is one thing I can do. I can tell everyone else.

CHAPTER ONE

Jim Murray, a Scottish cowman working in North Yorkshire, presented a small, wiry bundle of displeasure as he stood, his jaw set like a vice, staring into my face. His sharp little eyes were about an inch from my own. I was still in my early years in Thirsk as a fully qualified veterinary surgeon and thought I had performed a good professional job in delivering a fine calf out of a pedigree Beef Shorthorn cow but I could sense that he did not share my feelings of satisfaction.

'You young vets are all the same!' he growled. 'Always leavin' the soap in the watter!'

Having been so engrossed in my task, I had completely forgotten about the nice, clean bar of soap that the cowman had provided for me; I had left it simmering gently in the bucket of scalding hot water. Jim was now fingering a small, green, glutinous ball that had previously been his soap.

'Yer faither never does this!' he barked. 'He never wastes onything. A guid Scotsman never wastes onything!'

This was not the first time I had been unfavourably compared to my father, but I had an ace up my sleeve. 'I'm sorry about this, Jim,' I replied, 'it won't happen again. But I must tell you that you're wrong about my dad. He's not a Scotsman. He's an Englishman.'

'Awa wi' ye!' was the sharp reply as the little figure stumped indignantly out of the cowshed. Another successful visit from J. A. Wight junior had drawn to a close.

Jim Murray was not alone in his belief that Alf Wight was a Scotsman as he never lost the soft Glaswegian accent he developed over his twenty-three years in that great Scottish city. Long after he had become James Herriot, newspaper articles still often referred to him as the 'Scottish vet who adopted Yorkshire as his home'. Indeed, he is described on the inside jacket of his third book, *Let Sleeping Vets Lie*, as being born in Glasgow and practising all his life in Yorkshire. He was not a Scotsman, nor did he spend his entire life as a practising veterinary surgeon in Yorkshire. He was an Englishman born of English parents in an English town.

James Alfred Wight was born on 3 October 1916 in the industrial north-eastern town of Sunderland. He did not remain there long. Aged just three weeks, he was moved to Glasgow where he was to spend the formative years of his life. Although he left his birthplace as such a tiny creature, he retained close connections with Sunderland and visited it regularly throughout the years when he lived in Glasgow.

Although Alf was an only child, he was, in effect, part of a very large family. Both his parents came from large families so he inherited a host of uncles, aunts and cousins, and he kept in close touch with them throughout his life.

Alf Wight was born at 111 Brandling Street, a modest terraced house in the Roker area of Sunderland. The name of the house was 'Fashoda' and it was owned by Robert Bell, his maternal grandfather who was a printer by trade. His parents, James Henry Wight and Hannah Bell, had married on 17 July 1915 in the Primitive Methodist chapel in Williamson Terrace, Sunderland, where his father had been the organist. Following the wedding they had moved to Glasgow to live, but Hannah Wight returned to the family home in Sunderland fifteen months later, especially to have her baby.

Alf's father, Jim Wight, was by trade a ship plater, like his father before him. The major sources of employment in Sunderland were ship-building, coal-mining and steel-working and in those early years of the century the Sunderland shipyards were booming. The onset of World War One ensured that there was plenty of work, with one third of the adult male population employed in the shipbuilding industry. Despite holding down a steady job in the Sunderland shipyards, Alf's father had left his home town for alternative employment in Glasgow in November 1914 – eight months before he was married. This seems surprising but there were good reasons for his doing so. He enjoyed his work in the shipyards but, unlike the majority of his workmates, Jim Wight was more than just a ship plater; he was also an accomplished musician – one of the qualities that appealed to his future wife during their courtship in the years before the war.

He had been playing in cinemas in Sunderland, partly to supplement his earnings but also to satisfy his great love of playing the piano and the organ. Hannah, too, loved music. Her parents were well known in local Sunderland music circles, within which she, herself, was an accomplished contralto. She sang at many minor concerts but she longed to improve herself, and Sunderland, despite its many good qualities, was not really the cultural centre of the north. Where else in Britain could she go that would ensure that her husband could carry on earning his living in the shipyards, and where both of them could further their musical aspirations? Glasgow fitted the bill perfectly. Hannah always wanted to better herself, and her determination to move in cultured circles resulted in her acquiring the title of 'Duchess' from her more down-to-earth relatives. However, behind the rather 'superior' front she displayed to the world, there were fine qualities. She was a dedicated wife and mother, and this determination to achieve the best for her family would, in the years to come, contribute substantially to the future success of her son.

In 1914, therefore, this forceful young lady sent her future husband off to the big, vibrant city that teemed with cinemas, theatres and concert halls – one that reverberated not only with the clatter of shipyards and steel, but with the sound of music. There, Jim Wight was able to find work among the cinemas and theatres as well as in the great shipyards on the River Clyde.

In a photograph of Jim and Hannah's wedding in 1915, the large families of the Wights and Bells are there for all to see. The quality of the photograph, in which many of Alf's favourite uncles and aunts feature, is still very good despite being taken over eighty years ago. In the back row of the wedding group are two young men, Matt and Bob Wight, both of them brothers of Jim. They were two uncles with whom Alf would spend a great deal of time in his youth. Matthew Wight was barely thirteen years older than Alf who regarded him more as a brother than an uncle. He was an open-faced, jolly man with a mischievous smile, a natural practical joker who spent a large proportion of his life laughing. The other young man, Robert Wight, was far more serious-minded. He shared the same acute sense of humour common to most of the two families but, in addition, he was a deep thinker and a man of great principle. Uncle Bob was an enthusiast and an optimist, one who regarded the world as a place of opportunity. It was these qualities that would appeal so much to the young Alf Wight during his formative years. Robert Wight was the uncle upon whom he would model himself.

Sitting in front of Jim Wight in the old photograph is a young man in army uniform. This was Alfred Wight, Jim's younger brother and the only one of Alf's uncles whom he was never to know. He was a sergeant in the 19th Battalion of the Durham Light Infantry and tragically lost his life on the terrible Somme battlefield only one year after the photograph was taken. The family was devastated by this sad waste of a young life but his name lived on. Alf, who was born fifteen months later, was named after the uncle who had sacrificed his life on that fateful day.

The relatives on the Bell side of the family were a crowd of extroverts; they spoke their minds and did not care what the rest of the world thought about it. Two faces looking out from the wedding photograph, belonging to Stan and Jinny, Hannah's brother and sister, epitomise this effervescent quality of the Bell family. Uncle Stan, a great favourite with Alf, was a small, dapper man with a smiling face that oozed friendliness. In common with Alf's other uncles, he was a fanatical football fan and attended the home games at Sunderland producing a running commentary for all to hear, his head bobbing in every direction whilst giving his forthright opinions. What proportion of the game he actually saw was open to question. Jim Wight (or 'Pop' as he was always called by Alf and the rest of the family) was just the opposite. He was no less a devoted follower of the fortunes of the club but apart from, perhaps, a satisfied smile or an agonised spasm of the facial muscles, he betrayed little emotion.

On later visits to Glasgow, Alf always derived a great deal of amusement from watching his father – a quiet, reserved and very gentlemanly man – attempt to merge into obscurity when in the company of his high-spirited relatives. Pop never forgot a visit to Ibrox Stadium in Glasgow where Stan, despite being surrounded by glowering Glasgow Rangers fans, vociferously delivered his forthright opinion of their team, describing the players as 'Duck Eggs!' This was a common old Sunderland expression and one did not need to be a native of the north-east of England to appreciate its finer meaning. Pop was thankful to leave the stadium alive.

Stan was not the only Bell to send Pop scuttling for cover. He endured many embarrassing situations while in the company of his sister-in-law, Jinny, who would loudly voice her opinion in public places, often instigating an equally noisy response. Jinny was quite happy with this; she quite enjoyed a scene, but she rarely received the support of her brother-in-law. Pop learned one thing quickly following his association with the Bell family – the art of effecting a swift and silent disappearance.

Late in the October of 1916, at the age of barely three weeks, baby Alfred Wight left Sunderland to take up residence in Scotland's largest city –

one that would be his home for the first twenty-three years of his life. His happy and fulfilling childhood days spent amongst the outgoing and friendly people of this big, noisy city, resulted in Alf Wight forever regarding himself as a Glaswegian at heart.

His feeling for the city is displayed in the dedication that is at the beginning of his fourth book, *Vet in Harness*. It reads simply, 'With love to my mother in dear old Glasgow Town'.

He was not alone in his great affection for this charismatic city. Many Glaswegians reminisce about their origins with great pride, despite the city having, over the years, developed something of an unenviable reputation. Between the wars, many of the big cities of Britain had a poor image but Glasgow's was the worst of all. Later on, Alf used to observe, with ill-concealed anger, television programmes portraying it as a sordid mass of filthy slums inhabited by gangs that would slit your throat first and ask questions later. 'No one bothers to speak of Glasgow's finer qualities,' he would exclaim. 'There is no mention of the warm and friendly people, nor of the splendid buildings, parks and art galleries. And what about the wonderful country all around that can be reached so easily?'

Glasgow used to be described as a 'dirty picture in a beautiful frame'. Many parts, admittedly, were not particularly edifying but where else in Britain was there a massive city with such magnificent scenery so close at hand? The residents of Glasgow are fortunate indeed to have such a beautiful playground on their doorstep and this was not lost on the young Alfred Wight. When he was older, he would escape the bustle and grime of the city whenever he could to head out for the hills and glens that were so accessible. Those happy hours he spent in Glasgow's 'beautiful frame' were to instil in him that great appreciation of the wild and unspoilt landscapes about which he would write with such feeling so many years later.

One of the most dominant features of the architecture of Glasgow are the tenements. These gaunt, multi-storey buildings stand over the city streets like giant sentinels and have been the epitome of Glasgow's appearance since well into the last century when huge numbers of immigrants flooded into the city to find work. Glasgow, known at that time as 'The Second City of the Empire', was a booming city, and the tenements provided the answer to the housing problem; they were, in effect, one of the earliest examples in Britain of the high-rise blocks of flats.

Yoker is a suburb of Glasgow, on the east bank of the River Clyde, and it was here, in a ground-floor flat of a tenement in Yoker Road (later re-named Dumbarton Road), that the Wight family had their first of three homes in the city.

The tenement buildings of Glasgow have a terrible reputation of being the embodiment of all that is to do with poverty and squalor. In fact, they varied widely in their degrees of respectability. The black tenements of the Gorbals, on the other side of the River Clyde, were undeniably some of the most depressing buildings imaginable, both outside and in. There was a central passageway, the 'close', through which access was gained to the dingy flats on either side – with dark, forbidding stairways snaking up to the higher levels of the building. These tenements were often damp, dirty and appallingly overcrowded. Many families in the slum areas of Glasgow, like the Gorbals or Cowcaddens on the other side of the city, lived squashed together in one or two rooms. Toilet provision was rudimentary, with up to twenty or thirty people sharing one privy which, commonly, was not even within the building. Poverty and disease were rife. Many children developed rickets through malnutrition and I can remember a young woman who worked for my grandmother, having the bowed legs that betrayed a childhood of deprivation and hardship. No wonder the people living in these awful conditions would often turn to violence and drink to seek some escape from their squalid existence.

However, other tenements, such as the one in which Alf was to spend his earliest years, were in a different category altogether. Although not very prepossessing from the outside, they were perfectly respectable within. To walk inside one was often a revelation. The uninspiring, sometimes grim exterior belied a pleasant, roomy interior with high, sculptured ceilings in the living-rooms and ample space everywhere.

The ground-floor flat in which Alf spent the earliest years of his life, although not exactly the finest example of the Glasgow tenement flat, was perfectly sound and respectable, so much so that the entrance to his home was known as a 'wally close'. These were quite special in that, having tiled walls, one was considered to be a few rungs up the ladder of affluence living 'up' one of these. Each flat consisted of three or four rooms – a large living-room with an adjoining kitchen and one, sometimes two, bedrooms and a bathroom and lavatory. There were recesses set into the sides of the living-room across which curtains could be drawn, thus providing extra sleeping accommodation.

Milk and coal were both delivered by horse and cart. The milk was left in a jug outside the door, and the coalman would clatter into the house to dump the coal into a bunker situated in a corner of the kitchen. The coal was used for heating and, in many flats, it was also the means of fuelling the cooking ranges that were the dominant feature of the tenement kitchens. As well as cooking and heating the home, these imposing black steel fireplaces provided all the hot water the family needed. Alf's first tenement home may not have been a palace but it was comfortable and adequate.

One of the myths that has grown up around Alf Wight and his success is that of his dragging himself up from the 'grinding poverty' of his youth. The fact is that his Glasgow days were exceptionally happy – with the cold finger of hardship rarely felt by young 'Alfie' Wight. The Yoker area of Glasgow – a respectable, working-class part of the city – was one in which many Glaswegians aspired to live. There was certainly heavy industry, shipyards and steelworks – and there were parts of Yoker where faint hearts would fear to tread, especially on Friday and Saturday nights – but much of it was inhabited by solid citizens who were well above the poverty line.

Only a few minutes' walk from Alf's home would take him out into green fields and farmland, backed by the Kilpatrick Hills and the Campsie Fells in the distance – a very different picture from the Yoker of today. The stage upon which Alfie Wight played out the happy hours of his childhood has been replaced by a scene of neglect, dominated by drab buildings and wasteland. Boarded-up shops are a testimony to the crime that, as in most other big cities, seems to be a constant threat. As he played on the streets and in the nearby fields with his friends, young Alf without doubt enjoyed Yoker's better times.

His parents were dedicated workers who ensured that the family was always well catered for. Pop held down a good job as a ship plater in the big Yarrow's shipyard which was close to the family home, and he supplemented his earnings by playing the piano in the local cinemas. He was the leader of an orchestra which provided the sound tracks for silent films as well as music for the intervals between the shows.

Pop took great pride in his musical ability. In the evenings, when most of his workmates were having a drink in the bars of Yoker, Pop would be found seated in front of the beloved grand piano he had brought with him from Sunderland. He would practise happily for hours. I can clearly recall my grandfather seated in front of his cherished piano, eyes closed and with a look of sheer pleasure on his face as his hands danced over the keys. He had lost the forefinger of his right hand when he was a young man but this did not seem to hinder his ability. He used to compose his own music and, in his later years, accompanied a group known as the 'Glenafton Singers' who performed at many concerts in Glasgow. Pop was a truly gifted musician whose enthusiasm spread to his son ensuring that he, too, would discover that the love of music was one of life's greatest joys.

Hannah Wight was as musical as Pop. She and her husband were members of the Glasgow Society of Musicians, performing regularly at concerts in the city. He was the accompanist on the piano while she sang in the choir as a contralto under her maiden name, calling herself 'Miss Anna Bell'. The extra money they earned while performing with this professional organisation must have been a welcome addition to the family budget.

The mid 1920s was a particularly worrying period and parts of Glasgow were grim places to be at the time of the General Strike in 1926. Soldiers were on the streets to maintain law and order, and the windows of the buses and trams were covered in steel netting to protect them from flying missiles hurled by desperate and rebellious mobs. Pop, along with thousands of workers, was made redundant from the shipyards. As with so many others, he had to sway in the winds of depression sweeping the city as work became almost impossible to get. However, he managed to survive through sheer determination and adaptability by turning his hand to other means of earning a living – working first as a joiner and later, when Alf was a teenager, by opening a fish and chip shop. He also had the advantage of having a very resolute and resourceful wife.

Around 1928, Pop's income from playing in the cinemas was ruthlessly cut with the advent of sound tracks which accompanied the films, but Hannah was already earning a living in her own right. Musical ability was not the only talent she possessed; she was adept at making clothes. In the mid 1920s, she set aside one of the rooms of the family home to establish a thriving dressmaking business that she would keep going for almost thirty years. She became so busy that, in the early 1930s, she employed not only several seamstresses but a maid by the name of Sadie. Hannah developed a clientele of many wealthy and influential ladies – something that would be a vital contribution to the family finances.

With two parents who ensured that there was always some money coming into the home, young Alf Wight never knew real hardship. His parents, admittedly, were under financial pressure at times, especially when Alf's education had to be financed, but they survived the years of depression in the city far better than most. Indeed, at that time, there would be few houses in the streets of Yoker that could number a maid and a grand piano among its occupants. Although there were to be times when the spectre of poverty stared Alf in the face, it was not during his childhood days on the streets of Glasgow.

Shortly before he was five years old, Alf Wight began his education at Yoker Primary School. It was a good school and the teachers were well qualified, putting great emphasis on learning the three 'Rs'. The headmaster was a man called Mr Malcolm – 'Beery' Malcolm to the children as he had a florid face that looked as though it was partial to a pint of beer. He was a Master of Arts and a fine headmaster but young Alf's favourite teacher was Mr Paterson who taught History.

Alf loved History and all through his adult years he enjoyed reading books on historical subjects, saying they gave him a stab of excitement to know that he was reading about events that actually happened. Mr Paterson was the man who stimulated this interest through his sparkling and enthusiastic teaching methods. When describing battles, he charged up and down the rows of children, waving a huge cane and spearing his imaginary foes: Robert the Bruce cutting the English to pieces at the Battle of Bannockburn was brought vividly to life, and the laughing children loved every minute of it. Little did the young lad realise that one day many years later he, too, would bring the past alive with his account of the veterinary profession as it used to be. He was to be every bit as graphic with the pen as had been his animated teacher with his cane, leaping around the classroom all those years ago in Yoker.

Alf excelled at English but Arithmetic was a subject he could never fathom and he would stare vacantly at his classmate, Willie Crawford, who could come up with the answer to a problem within seconds. Fortunately, it was not a subject that was essential to his further education, and was one that would forever remain a deep, insoluble mystery.

Yoker School gave Alf Wight an excellent start to his education and he took away many happy memories after leaving. The greatest legacy bestowed upon Alf by his first school, however, was the meeting there of a boy who was to become his lifelong friend. Alex Taylor lived a short distance away in Kelso Street and the two boys struck up a friendship that was to last more than seventy years. Alf would have many good friendships in the course of his life, but none would stand the test of time more steadfastly than that with Alex Taylor.

One amazing character remained forever engraved on Alf's memories of his days at Yoker School – a redoubtable individual by the name of 'Pimple' Wilson. This boy made a name for himself by declaring his intention to leap out of a second-storey tenement window with the sole assistance of an old umbrella. This caused immense excitement among the children and the forthcoming event was awaited with eager anticipation. The great day came, with large crowds of children, Alf and Alex among them, gathering to watch the spectacle. They were not to be disappointed. After a period of tense expectation, the hero of the hour appeared on the window ledge, his 'parachute' in hand, ready for action. There were a few taut moments as the boy fidgeted around on the window ledge, then suddenly, to the sound of gasps from his young audience, he sprang out of the high window, umbrella held aloft. For about one second, all went well, but his plans were to go badly wrong. The old umbrella suddenly turned inside out and, accompanied by the screaming boy, zoomed to the ground. 'Pimple' was taken to hospital and was soon on the mend. It had been a short but dramatic show, and was to remain Alf's most vivid memory of his days at Yoker School.

It was, of course, long before the days of television, and Alf, Alex and the other children made their own amusements. Games played outside in the playground, going by such sophisticated names as 'moshie', 'spin the pirie' and 'cuddie hunch', required no expensive equipment. When not at school, they spent hours kicking a football about, while 'Wee Alfie Wight' often hurtled around the streets on his fairy cycle – the possession of which made him the envy of his classmates. They were happy and carefree days. Despite the poverty and desperation that stalked the streets of Glasgow during the Depression, parents had no fear for the safety of their children. How different it is today.

One of the great entertainments for the children in those days was the cinema. The whole area abounded with picture houses, with the 'penny matinée' one of the most popular occasions. For the princely sum of one penny, or twopence if the upstairs balcony was preferred, the youngsters could see a whole show and many a Saturday afternoon was spent watching comedy or western films. Cowboy films in those days were very popular and the children loved them despite the absence of sound tracks. A favourite hero of the Old West was a wisecracking cowboy by the name of Drag Harlin. This gunfighter did not appear on film, but was a character in some of the popular books of the day. Years later, Alf and Alex would roar with laughter as they recalled their boyhood days reading these 'scholarly' descriptions of life in the Old West. Alex recently recalled an example of the author's peerless style of writing: 'A blue-black hole appeared in the middle of his forehead. An amazed expression crossed his face as he slumped slowly to the floor!' Such passages as these deserved, Alf once said, 'recognition as literary classics!'

Sundays were days for going to church. During his adult life, Alf was not a regular church-goer, but in his primary school days he attended Sunday School each week. His memories of going to church in Yoker were not as vivid as those when he occasionally attended in Sunderland with his uncles and aunts. The Methodist services in those days were conducted with fiery enthusiasm. The minister would frequently be interrupted from the floor with cries of 'Hallelujah!' or 'Praise the Lord!', followed by splinter groups chanting hymns with rhythmic and deafening abandon. It was pure 'fire and brimstone' which young Alf found quite daunting. The services in Yoker Church were not quite so dramatic but one story he told about his Sunday School was rather more intriguing. The small children who were taken out regularly for short walks were taught to spit whenever they passed the Catholic church.

When the history of the city of Glasgow is considered, the spectacle of small children spitting at a church should come as no surprise. Glasgow has had a strong Irish-Catholic population since the middle of the nineteenth century when thousands poured into the city to find work during the boom years. This resulted in Glasgow becoming a city split by religious beliefs, and feelings could run high. In Alf's day (and still now) you were either a 'Proddy' or a 'Papist' in parts of Glasgow and, along with his friends, young Alfie Wight, the little Protestant, was instructed by his teacher to vent his feelings against the Catholic enemy. Fortunately, this sectarian dogma failed to establish a hold over young Alf, and he grew up to be a most fair-minded and tolerant man who could never understand the hatred engendered by these strong beliefs.

Life at Yoker School prepared Alf well for the next step in his education. Most of his schoolmates went on to government-maintained

secondary schools – including Alex Taylor who went to Victoria Drive
School – but Alf's mother had other ideas. She wanted the very best
for her son and decreed that he would go to one of the foremost
fee-paying schools in Glasgow. Alf obtained the grades necessary for
his secondary education and on 3 September 1928, he travelled three
miles into the city to the leafy suburb of Hillhead where he walked, for
the first time, through the doors of Hillhead High School.

CHAPTER TWO

At the time of Alf's admission, Hillhead High School had an excellent reputation, and there was strong competition for places. Alf found himself mixing with many pupils who came from more affluent homes than his own in Yoker. This did not worry him. For the next five years he played his part in applying himself diligently to his work, as his parents played theirs in meeting the school fees and providing a stable family background.

These were difficult times for Pop. Having been made redundant from the shipyards, he was still playing in cinemas and theatres in the city, as well as working as a joiner but his income was certainly not enough to support his family and meet the school fees of around £2–10s per term. Alf, who loved his father dearly, would later reminisce about those days in Glasgow. 'It was a great struggle at that time for poor old Pop,' he said. 'He was bouncing in and out of jobs, with absolutely no guarantee of security in any one of them, but he always held down a job of some sort.'

Although Pop was rarely out of work, it was Hannah, through her thriving dressmaking business, complemented by giving some piano and singing lessons, who was largely responsible for keeping the family finances afloat. Alf Wight was never to forget the support he received from his parents throughout his eleven years of education in Glasgow.

The building in Cecil Street in which he began his secondary education was a solid, but dour, four-storey building within which was a maze of small, overcrowded classrooms. The problems presented by this lack of space, in a school with more than 600 pupils, resulted in its moving, in September 1931, to another building a short distance away in Oakfield Avenue. Here Alf spent the final two years of his time at Hillhead. In the summer of 1997, I visited my father's old school. No longer a fee-paying school, it is now run by the Education Department of Glasgow City Council, but this austere red brick building has hardly changed in appearance from Alf's days there. Inside, the classrooms are still arranged exactly as they were, alongside the once-icy corridors he strode as a boy. The present headmaster, Ken Cunningham, told me that the school was very aware of its connection with James Herriot but, although he enjoyed his time there, Alf rarely referred to his days at Hillhead. Perhaps those days of intense study, combined with iron discipline, did not leave such lasting memories as other more flamboyant periods of his life.

It was during his years at Hillhead, however, that the young Alf Wight was to develop qualities he would carry with him throughout his life – diligence and ambition, together with a love of literature, sport and music. Above all, he acquired attributes that would be the hall-mark of the father I knew – a keen interest in a wide variety of subjects, enthusiasm for everything he did, and a great appreciation of any good fortune that would come his way.

He always assured us that he was a poor pupil, but his school reports tell a different story. His final leaving report is marked 'excellent' for progress, diligence and conduct. His three best subjects were English, French and Latin, with the dreaded Maths trailing far behind. He was well taught. Hillhead, under the headmaster Frank Beaumont, had a reputation for academic excellence backed up by strong discipline. Corporal punishment, so frowned upon today, was a very effective means of maintaining law and order; the school motto was *Je maintiendrai*, 'I will maintain'. The trusted ally of the teachers in upholding discipline was the belt, and Alf was on the receiving end of it many times. This is one part of his life at school that Alf remembered well. One of his teachers, 'Big Bill' Barclay, one whom he remembered better than any, commanded great respect through his physical presence as well as his teaching ability. He did not need to use the belt too often but when he did it was an occasion to be remembered. Some of the teachers would use the belt without hesitation – the slightest misdemeanour being punished with up to six lashes across the hands and wrists. Three thongs at the end of the thick leather strap ensured that there was a thorough distribution of pain.

Alf received a nasty surprise one day when Mr Filshie, his Maths master, expressed displeasure at his pupil's performance. Alf had achieved the remarkable total of 5% in a trigonometry exam and was about to be punished. He recalled this painful incident in his contribution to the Hillhead High School Centenary Year Magazine in 1985.

'Wight,' said Mr Filshie ominously, 'I have always thought that you were just an amiable idiot and have treated you accordingly, but now that I see you have come out top of the class in your English paper, I can only conclude that you have not been trying for me. Hold out your hands!'

Although doing nothing to improve Alf's Maths, this painful means of maintaining control worked and there was a record of excellent discipline within the school. It was this, perhaps, that stimulated the young Alf Wight to keep, for the first time, a diary.

One of the most intriguing aspects of James Herriot's writing was his ability to reproduce incidents that occurred many years before. His attention to detail is so authentic that one would be forgiven for thinking that they happened only yesterday. Many people, when discussing his work, assumed that he meticulously kept diaries to which he referred when he began writing in earnest. Alf often stated, in his many interviews with the media, that he did not keep a diary and that he could remember the old days clearly, right down to the smallest detail. Despite these assertions, he was widely disbelieved, but, in fact, Alfred Wight was not quite the organised and methodical man that many believed him to be. Apart from two brief periods in his life, he did not keep a diary but he was a great observer, especially of anything that interested him, and had an excellent photographic memory. The fascinating vagaries of human nature and the humorous incidents that unfolded before his eyes remained firmly in his mind; this, combined with his gift as a writer, provided a recipe for success.

The first time he kept a diary was from 1933 until 1935 – during his last year at Hillhead School and his first two years at Glasgow Veterinary College. His mother preserved these old diaries, and they have provided an insight into the enthusiastic approach to life that Alf exhibited as a young man.

He used his diary to poke fun at his teachers at Hillhead. 'Miss Chesters (Sophy), endeavours to pump French into us. Chesters is frank and almost boyish and I like her very well. Twice a week, we get Mr (Tarzan) Brookes for Elocution. This bird, tho' probably well meaning, is nothing but a funiosity.' And he wrote about his Latin master: 'Buckie was in a terrible mood today. Roaring and bellowing at us like a rogue elephant. Today, I was amazed to see the length to which his eyes could boggle without falling out.'

As is hinted by these humorous swipes at his teachers, he enjoyed his time at Hillhead. He loved English and Latin, reading widely around both subjects in his spare time at home. He read ancient writers such as Cicero and Ovid, saying later that so well-versed was he in Latin that he reckoned he could carry on a conversation with an ancient Roman. Alf's English, too, benefited from the hours of reading that he put in, and the great enthusiasm he showed for his subjects meant that his school studies were a pleasure.

I always knew that my father was a well-read man. Our home in Thirsk was always bulging with books and almost all of them had been read. His love of reading stemmed from his schooldays – days during which, whenever he had a spare hour or two, he had a book in his hand. He did not just enjoy reading adventure stories; he devoured the classics avidly. By the age of fifteen, he had read the entire works of Charles Dickens, and his diaries substantiate this. Throughout, there are references to Dickens, Scott, Pepys and, on a more lyrical note, Shakespeare and Milton. 'Got Dickens' *Tale of Two Cities* out of the library as we have to read it for school. That suits me down to the ground as I am a great admirer of Dickens.' Dickens gets another mention: 'Dad is smoking Kensitas. They give coupons and I sent away for a catalogue; included is the works of Dickens in 16 superb volumes for 10 shillings. I'm going to get them.'

Sir Arthur Conan Doyle, H. G. Wells and H. Rider Haggard were amongst his favourite adventure writers and he wrote that O'Henry was 'a joy to read'. The Kensitas coupons came in very useful; as well as the complete works of Dickens, volumes of O'Henry and Shakespeare were obtained with their assistance. On the lighter side, P. G. Wodehouse was his number one author, and the *Jeeves Omnibus* his favourite book of all. He read and re-read this book throughout his life, the antics of Jeeves, Bertie Wooster, Young Bingo and others invariably rendering him helpless with laughter.

P. G. Wodehouse must have had a profound effect on young Alf. Some turns of phrase that he used in his diaries smack of passages from Wodehouse's books. While on holiday in West Kilbride in July 1933, he wrote the following about some people he had met: 'David Somerville seems to be crackers over Evelyn, the poor fish! Monty and I regard Dorothy as a fairly decent spud.' This style appears frequently in his diaries, revealing evidence of his admiration for Wodehouse's work.

As a boy, he shared these moments of laughter over Wodehouse with his own father who was also an avid reader and whose home was always full of books. The high quality of the English teaching at Hillhead under 'Johnny' Gibb and 'Big Bill' was a great stimulus but Pop was also very influential in steering Alf towards the joy of reading, deserving a great deal of credit for the encouragement he gave his son in those formative years.

As well as encouraging his son to read, Pop was largely responsible for instilling in him a great love of music. The intense satisfaction his father gleaned from both playing and listening to it did not go unnoticed by the young boy who grew up to appreciate good music every bit as much as his father. Pop loved all kinds of music. During our many visits to Glasgow in my younger days, I used to be fascinated by the old gramophone player that stood in a corner of the house next to the grand piano. This venerable machine had to be wound up by hand, after which the turntable began to revolve and a huge steel arm with a wicked-looking needle would be lowered onto the record. The result was a wild crackling, behind which could be heard some music. It was, however, Pop's pride and joy. One of his favourite operatic records was of the great Caruso singing 'Vesti la Giubba' from *I Pagliacci*. One of Alf's enduring boyhood memories was of his father, sitting night after night next to the old gramophone, listening to this great performer. When Caruso's magnificent voice began to slip into a lower gear, Pop would leap to his feet and crank vigorously at the handle of the gramophone until musical perfection was restored. That overworked record is still in my possession.

Alf's parents first started him at the piano at the age of six. He had years of lessons – his teacher being none other than his father – but he was a poor pupil and practised with little enthusiasm. This became a source of intense frustration for Pop, and many hours of raised voices and discordant notes were endured by father and son before Pop finally conceded defeat. Alf did perform, at the age of thirteen, at a concert in Clydebank Town Hall but that was to be the pinnacle of his piano-playing career.

None of this lessened Alf's love of music. Although he was never to be the accomplished player his father had been, he had inherited his, and his mother's, ear for music – something that would give him untold pleasure throughout his life.

It was not only the academic and cultured side of his schooldays that Alf enjoyed; he loved playing sport and Hillhead had a proud reputation on the playing fields of Scotland. Cricket, athletics and tennis were Alf's favourites and in the 1931–2 year he won an athletics medal, coming second in the Inter-scholastics Sports. His main achievement was in the long jump – known as the broad jump in those days – where he produced a jump of over nineteen feet.

Alf was keen on athletics but the sport at which he really excelled was tennis. In his final year at Hillhead he reached the tennis final only to be narrowly defeated, but he was not discouraged. He had joined Yoker Tennis Club and reached the club's final the following year, only to be beaten once again. However, being beaten in two successive finals did not deter him. He continued to play tennis regularly throughout his remaining years in Glasgow, winning many matches in the West of Scotland Tennis Championships, and when he finally moved to Yorkshire, he played competitive tennis until well into his thirties. His hours of playing when a young man in Glasgow resulted in his becoming a highly proficient performer.

Both the playing of and the following of sport figured prominently in Alf's schooldays, with his boyhood diaries full of references to it. The England cricket team and the fortunes of Hillhead on the rugby field are frequently mentioned but most of the space is allocated to Sunderland Football Club. Despite the fact that his team was 150 miles away, his allegiance to the Red and Whites never faltered. During his years in Glasgow, he watched Rangers and Celtic many times – and he supported Motherwell in the Scottish League – but the fanaticism of his father ensured that it was the team from the town of his birth that remained closest to his heart.

His feelings are exposed on many of the pages, where he wrote quite eloquently of the old team, as on 28 September 1933: 'Oh boy, oh boy, oh boy! What a day! Why weren't these spaces made bigger? Sunderland have defeated Aston Villa by three goals to nothing at Villa Park. Sunderland have never won the cup, despite their magnificent league performances but is this their year? You bet it is! Much as I am tempted to wax poetic about this great event, I'm afraid that, in accordance with the requirements of this volume, I must recount my own doings.' On a more sombre note, he wrote: 'Eheu! I am plunged into the very depths of despondency. Life, to me, is dark and gloomy and the future looms up forbidding and hopeless. Sunderland have been defeated by Derby County at Roker Park.' How passionately he followed the fortunes of the team that was to provide him with a lifetime of both joy and despair.

The diary of 1933 is notable for Alf's positive approach towards looking after his health. He repeatedly commented on how well he was feeling, the reason for this being that the previous year had been a very bad one for him. He had almost died of diphtheria. This disease, caused by a virulent germ, is rarely seen today. It was virtually eliminated in 1946 as a result of the discovery of a vaccine but at the beginning of his final year at Hillhead, Alf contracted the disease – and it very nearly finished him off. In those days, prior to the discovery of antibiotics, he had to fight the disease simply through sheer determination coupled with good nursing from his parents. The standard symptoms were a sore throat and searing headaches, the throat becoming coated in an unpleasant 'cheesy' exudate which made breathing very difficult. In addition, he developed a series of painful abscesses all over his body, and these continued to be a problem for two years after his recovery from the disease. He recalled one particularly gruesome boil at the top of his leg that eventually became as hard as a rock. One evening, having decided that he had had enough of it, he squeezed it with all his might. In his own words, 'A thing like a small cricket ball shot out of my leg and bounced its way across the floor!' It sounds more like something out of a 1990s science-fiction horror story than pre-war Glasgow, but he recovered where many others had died.

This debilitating experience was responsible for a severe dip in his academic results at school, together with a complete cessation of his sporting activities. No wonder he was so glad to be alive. In August 1933, while on holiday in Sunderland, after a particularly exhilarating day playing tennis and bathing in the sea, he wrote: 'When I look at all the fun I've had today and think that, last year, I was a wreck with diphtheria, I thank God for my health. It is the most precious possession anyone can have.'

He emerged from the darkness of diphtheria a new person, brimming with fresh ideas and enthusiasms. He was determined to keep himself fit. One day he was given a book called *My System* by Lieut. J. P. Muller. On the front of the book was a picture of a Greek God and, inside, photographs of a lean, wiry man twisting his body in a multitude of directions. Alf thought this person was the fittest human being he had ever seen and decided that he himself was going to become even fitter. He aimed to transform himself into the second J. P. Muller.

The 'System' is based upon a regime of cold baths followed by exercises – one which my father followed religiously in his youth, and his diary is liberally sprinkled with references to it.

On 20 April 1933, he wrote: 'I'm feeling as fit as the proverbial fiddle.

I put it all down to the exercises and cold baths. I am much brighter and healthier than I was last year before my illness and I seem to be on the upgrade. I'm going to enter everything at this sports – that is the 100 yards, 220 yards, broad jump, discus, javelin, hurdles, cricket ball, and place and drop kick.' He had certainly set himself an optimistic target, his idea being to run off with medals in each one of them. Unfortunately, he got a little carried away with his training, pulled a muscle in his groin, and took no part when Sports Day arrived.

So keen was he on *My System* that he bought me a copy and, during my years in Glasgow as a student, I followed in his footsteps in trying to emulate the indomitable Mr Muller. The cold bath is the worst part. Survival time in the water can be measured in minutes, during which time breathing accelerates alarmingly, while genitalia disappear completely from view. Upon leaping out of the bath, a testing regime of physical jerks is followed by the 'rubbing exercises'; with the help of an abrasive glove, the body is vigorously massaged until it is glowing like a beacon. Loud shouting helps towards the overall feeling of well-being. I did not stick this routine for very long but the young Alf Wight followed it rigorously for years and was taking cold baths right up until the time he was living in Yorkshire.

Alf also subscribed to *Superman* magazine and bought a succession of chest expanders. Not only was he going to be as fit as J. P. Muller, he intended to be twice the size. His best mate Alex Taylor, too, was determined to build a mighty body and the two boys exercised furiously to attain their goal. They measured their bodies regularly but, after several weeks of intense activity, they were no nearer to being supermen than the day they started, and the craze ground to a halt. All that was left as a reminder was a rusty old set of springs that I discovered in my grandmother's home many years later.

Alf considered enthusiasm to be one of the most important of human qualities – one that is both invigorating and uplifting. Throughout his life he was an enthusiast, and he displayed these qualities as a boy at school, as is revealed by many entries in his diaries. Some of the many pastimes which he enjoyed were quite unusual – and whilst a number were short-lived, his eagerness to improve himself shines out from the pages. On 20 February 1933 he wrote: 'I've the notion to make myself a good jazz pianist . . . I think I'll send to Uncle Bob and ask him for a loan of his book on jazz playing.' On 7 March: 'I have started to do a bit of juggling. It's supposed to give you quickness of the eye and the house has resounded to the sound of falling balls.' His ambitions seem to have been limitless: 'Another of my notions. I'm going to read the Bible from beginning to end. Apart from the religious point of view it is a marvellous read!'

He bought books on swimming (he was not good in the water), took up golf, and started woodwork to help fill in the time during the long winter evenings. On a rare visit to a dance, he discovered that he was absolutely hopeless, so he proceeded to have lessons.

Throughout his childhood and school days, the Wight family would frequently return to Sunderland on holiday. Here they would stay with their relatives, all of whom shared the qualities of warmth, humour and generosity.

Warm, however, was not a word to describe the town where they lived. Sunderland has been portrayed as the unhealthiest place to live in the British Isles – a town (although, in fact, Sunderland has recently been accorded the status of a city) of drab, grey buildings and acres of wasteland where, in the winter, freezing easterly winds scream in from the North Sea, while the slightly warmer westerlies carry lung-demolishing pollution from the great industrial areas nearby. In later years, many of Alf's relatives, including Uncles Matt and Bob, and their sister Ella, left the town to live further south, with few of them having regrets about leaving the harsh climate.

It is true that first impressions of Sunderland can be less than appealing, but there are parts of the city that are full of character, especially near the sea front. The Roker and Seaburn areas of Sunderland, and the old fishing village of Whitburn further along the coast, are very attractive places, with their tidy houses and the waves of the North Sea breaking on the beach.

Alf spent many happy days of his childhood in this invigorating playground. During his teenage years, often accompanied by his cousin George Bell – son of Uncle Stan – he would spend hours playing football and tennis in the local parks, walking along the fine beach, and watching cricket at the Ashbrooke Cricket Ground where the local team competed in the Durham Senior League.

One of Alf's fondest memories of Sunderland was the food. The town abounded with 'pork shops' where succulent sandwiches of hot roast pork, often accompanied by that north-east delicacy 'pease pudding' (a tasty concoction made by boiling peas in ham water) could be bought for only a few pence. If he had an extra penny to spare, the sandwich would be dipped in rich, brown gravy to give this culinary masterpiece that final dash of magic. He used to say that the smell issuing from those pork shops would suck him through their doors like a giant magnet.

No matter what else he did when he visited Sunderland, Alf always found time to see his Uncle Bob Wight who lived in nearby Penshaw, a village of grey coal-miners' cottages, from where the two would walk for miles, discussing countless subjects of interest. Robert Wight, an intelligent, well informed and infectiously enthusiastic man, deeply impressed the young Alf who, through his endless quest to better himself, would mirror the qualities of his favourite uncle.

It was a combination of his parents, Uncle Bob and the strong discipline and fine standards Alf experienced at Hillhead that was largely instrumental in developing the young man's optimistic and positive approach to life, and it was during those influential years of his schooling that the first seeds of ambition were sown in his mind. It was one that would, years later, make him famous – the ambition to become a veterinary surgeon.

CHAPTER THREE

At the time of Alf Wight's admission to Hillhead School, Britain was in the grip of a fearsome depression. Glasgow was badly hit. The great shipyards on the River Clyde were laying men off regularly, with the average worker earning little more than one pound per week. Conditions within the veterinary profession – certainly no place for any get-rich-quick character – were little better since very few could afford to pay the vet's fees. Alf, however, early in his time at Hillhead, had made a firm decision to become a veterinary surgeon.

There was little in Alfred Wight's childhood to point him in the direction of a future with animals. Not only did he receive no encouragement from his parents, but his home in Yoker – crowded as it was with his mother's dressmaking business as well as his father's grand piano – had little room for animals. It is difficult to imagine a way of life further removed from that of the country veterinary surgeon than his own city upbringing; the smoke and noise of Glasgow seem poles apart from the hills and dales of Yorkshire that he would describe so vividly many years later.

In 1928, however, a character entered his life who had a profound influence upon his choice of a future career. In that year, partly as a reward for his obtaining the grades necessary for admission to Hillhead School, his parents bought an Irish Setter puppy. There had been cats in the house, but he had always yearned for a dog. Now he had one. This puppy, which was called Don, was the first of Alf's many canine companions and he adored him. A large proportion of his time, throughout his school and college days in Glasgow, was devoted to Don as he walked for miles with the big red dog. He not only walked him day and night around the streets and parks surrounding the family home, but at weekends he would think nothing of walking Don up to twenty miles and more into the nearby Kilpatrick Hills, The Allander, Peel Glen and many other beautiful areas that were on the doorstep.

Don figures prominently in Alf's diaries. He refers to him as the 'old hound' and it appears that almost everywhere that young Alf went, the 'hound' was by his side. One of his great boyhood friends was a lad called 'Curly' Marron, who lived in the same tenement block in Yoker, and walks with Curly and the 'hound' seem to have been a daily routine. Walking remained one of Alf's lifelong passions and that sleek, handsome Irish Setter was the first of many dogs with whom he would share it.

Don was not the easiest of dogs. When in the mood on one of his innumerable walks, he had a disconcerting habit of suddenly bursting away over the horizon. No one worried too much about stray dogs in those days and he usually turned up hours later, tail curled between his legs, worming his way along the floor in abject apology. Nobody in the family had the heart to reprimand the cringing form and he got away with it time and again. He knew how to grovel but he also knew how to growl. Should anyone approach him too closely when in possession of a bone, the ominous rumbling and the quivering lips were a clear warning that Don required no assistance. He was a dog who demanded respect. Despite this, he was a great companion, and a faithful friend who served not only to confirm Alf Wight's inherent love of animals, but to strengthen his awareness of the unique bond that exists between a man and his dog.

However, it was not only the acquisition of a pet that was to influence Alf's decision to become an animal doctor. At the age of thirteen, he read an article in the *Meccano Magazine*. It was one of a series entitled 'What shall I be?', and this particular article was all about veterinary science as a career. As a regular subscriber to the magazine, he had seen several of these articles but it was this one that held a particular appeal for him. As a dedicated dog owner himself, the thought of earning his living through caring for animals gave him a thrill of excitement.

Looking out from the photograph in the centre of the page was the president of the Royal College of Veterinary Surgeons, Mr G. P. Male, MRCVS. He was a distinguished-looking man with neat, well-manicured hair and around his neck hung the glittering chain of office. Young Alf was impressed.

The first paragraph made interesting reading: 'Veterinary Surgery is one of the few professions in which the number of entries has shown a considerable decline in recent years.' How different it is today with thousands of prospective students competing fiercely for the few allotted university places. The article, however, went on to say: 'This decline is probably due to the belief that the expansion in motor traffic has reduced the prospects of success in the profession. The belief is a mistaken one, however, for the decline in importance of the horse is being partially counteracted by the growing demand for the services of the veterinary surgeon in other directions.' This sentence (and how very true it would turn out to be) gave the young schoolboy some encouragement. The first inklings of an idea to become a veterinary surgeon had taken root in his mind.

While the article in the *Meccano Magazine* had stimulated his interest, it was at Hillhead School, a few weeks later, that he became hooked on the idea. The principal of Glasgow Veterinary College, Dr A. W. Whitehouse, was invited to give a talk at the school about a career within his profession. Looking back, it must surely have been a stroke of immense good fortune that these two quite unrelated events occurred so close to each other; they were destined to have a profound influence on Alf Wight's future.

Dr Whitehouse was a kindly and very approachable man with an infectious love for his subject. At the end of his talk, he extended an invitation to any of the boys who were interested to visit him at the college, where they could see for themselves the life of the veterinary student.

Enthused by both the article in the *Meccano Magazine* and the talk, Alf took up this offer and visited the college. Here, Dr Whitehouse, who himself saw the young boy, explained the job in greater detail. He told Alf that he would be unlikely to grow rich as a veterinary surgeon but that he would have a varied, active and rewarding life.

One thing worried Alf – Mathematics. 'Is it terribly important that I pass in Maths to gain admission to the college?' he asked.

'Oh, Maths are very important to a veterinary surgeon,' replied the principal solemnly. There were a tense few moments before his face broke into a smile. 'But only to add up the day's takings!'

Those few reassuring words were enough. Alfred Wight, the school-boy, now had a goal. He knew what he was going to do with his life and he set about his schoolwork with a fiercer determination than ever. His later years as a veterinary surgeon would prove Dr Whitehouse correct in that he would, indeed, have a varied, active and rewarding life within his chosen profession, but the old Glasgow principal was wrong about one thing: the wide-eyed boy seated in front of him that day would also become rich.

*

Throughout his remaining years at school, Alf was a studious and diligent schoolboy, and the excellent marks he attained in his best subjects reflected those happy days. Despite a high work-rate and the time spent playing his favoured sports, he had numerous interests outside the walls of Hillhead School, many of which he would carry with him into his adult years.

He had many friends but his closest was still Alex Taylor. Although after leaving Yoker School they went to different schools, they still saw a great deal of each other during their teenage years. On Saturday afternoons, they stood and shouted support for the football teams, whether in the big stadiums in the city or at the ground of the local junior team, Yoker Athletic. When there was no football to watch, there was the draw of the cinema, and this continued to be a favourite pastime.

There were numerous picture houses in the area around Yoker, so there were not many films that Alf missed. The Tivoli, the Commodore, the Rosevale, the Empire, the Regal, the Bank and many others were all within easy reach. Even after the introduction of sound to accompany the films, Alf's father still found some work in the cinemas, many of which staged singing evenings and variety shows as well. A small orchestra was employed, in which Pop was the pianist. He played regularly at the Commodore and received complimentary tickets which he passed on to Alf; having to pay nothing to see a film added greatly to its appeal. He often wrote opinions in his diaries on the films that he had seen. One such entry is dated 11 March 1933: 'In the evening, I went to see the much boomed film *Grand Hotel*. It was terrible and I was bored stiff. That woman Greta Garbo should be put in a lunatic asylum and kept under close observation!' He had no complaints with the comedies. The films of Laurel and Hardy, who were to remain one of his all-time favourites, appeared regularly and he never tired of watching them.

Young Alf spent a large proportion of his time tramping in the hills around his home. He often camped with Alex Taylor and other friends – notably Jock Davey, Pete Shaw and Eddie Hutchinson – and frequently went off for whole days, sometimes walking over twenty miles. Another great walking friend was Jimmy Turnbull, a deaf boy who was the son of a great friend of his mother. Alf loved to visit Mrs Turnbull's house since her expertise as a cook was unsurpassed. Not only could she elevate a simple meal of porridge into a gourmet experience, but her plates of 'mince and tatties' and succulent cakes were without equal. Those were certainly carefree times – walking for miles in the open air, with the mouthwatering prospect of Mrs Turnbull's cooking to round off the day.

Despite being a city boy, his appreciation of the fine countryside around his home shows on many of the pages of his diaries. 'Spent the whole day in a tramp to the "Whangie" and over the O. K. Hills with Jimmy T. and Jock Davey. It was simply wonderful. I can't find words to describe it.' These expeditions imbued Alf with a love of the great outdoors that was to shine through in the James Herriot books many years later.

Apart from tennis, Alf did not play any serious sport away from Hillhead School but, like many other boys of his age, he spent many hours playing football in the fields and parks, referring to this pastime as 'kicking the wee white ba' aroond'. As well as his friends from Yoker, he often played with the 'gentry of the corner'. The 'gentry of the corner' or the 'corner boys', as they were often called, were terms used to describe a section of the unemployed of Glasgow. During the depression, gangs of men would loiter on street corners, with nothing to do. Spitting, swearing and, when they could afford it, drinking were their main pursuits. With the dole amounting to less than ten shillings per week, these men sometimes resorted to crime as a means of bolstering their meagre allowance. There seemed, however, to be some code of honour among them; although robbery with violence was common-place, molestation of women and children was almost unheard of. When Alf was growing up – in contrast to the serious, often drug-related crime of today – the acquisition of money in any way to get a few decent meals or a drink was the prime motivation for breaking the law.

Many of the 'gentry of the corner' employed other means of earning a little supplementary cash, one way of which was by singing. The term is used in its loosest sense for there was little in the way of melody, there were seldom any words, and the singers were usually well under the influence of alcohol. These characters, however, gave their all, howling and droning away on the bare ground below the tenements. They were known as 'back court singers' and the occupants of the houses would throw down money to them. This was either in appreciation of the quality of music they were hearing or, more commonly, to gain some relief from the long, dreary wails issuing from below. They also 'performed' in the public houses in the city, staring unsteadily into a glass or two of whisky – groaning away interminably with no one taking the slightest bit of notice. It was just part of the scene in a typical Glasgow bar.

One of the corner boys had a unique sideline; he bit off puppies' tails. He was a long, lean character with a patch over one eye, who hung around the Elderslie Bar, a public house in Yoker. One day, Alf enquired after his services as he had heard that this particular gentleman was a master of his craft. The charge was sixpence per pup but young Alf thought that it was half a crown – five times the actual sum. Having spotted him in the centre of a crowd of men on the street corner, he went up and asked nervously, 'Please, sir, my friend has a pup that needs its tail off. Will you do it for him for half a crown?'

The man's eye widened as he gazed down on the young boy. Then he looked around delightedly at his friends before stating his terms. 'Hauf a croon? Tell 'im fer hauf a croon Ah'll bite its fuckin' heid aff!' A chorus of laughing and spitting followed. The future veterinary surgeon did not seek further assistance from the one-eyed man.

During his future years in veterinary practice, Alf developed a gentle, sympathetic approach to his customers and to his patients – a quality, one suspects, that owed little to his experiences on the street corners of Glasgow.

The fulfilling times Alf spent in his boyhood were not confined to Glasgow. He enjoyed vast numbers of holidays. In the summer of 1933, his diary relates that he went away no less than four times – to West Kilbride on the Ayrshire coast, to a guest house on the Isle of Arran, on a camping holiday beside Loch Fyne, and to Sunderland to visit his relatives. The following summer, he went to Llandudno in North Wales, to South Devon to stay with an uncle, to Wiltshire to stay with an aunt, even to stay for a week in a London hotel – and, of course, to see the family in Sunderland.

With so many uncles, aunts and cousins in Sunderland, Alf had a busy time visiting them all, but it was certainly no hardship. When he needed cheering up, his Uncle Matt never failed to brighten the day, as did his cousin Nan Wilkins, daughter of his Auntie Jinny. Nan, who was like an older sister to Alf, was the cousin he saw the most of during his life.

In addition to the time spent with his relatives in Sunderland, there were holidays spent with family and friends in the high Pennine country of northern England, Appleby and Alston being favourite locations. They all stayed in guest houses or small hotels, and photographs taken at that time show the amazing size of these gatherings. They loved the wild but beautiful country of the hills and dales; it provided a relaxed environment which contrasted so much with that around their home close to industrial Sunderland.

Alf's parents were very different in their attitude to holidays. Apart from these breaks in the Pennine country, Pop rarely took a holiday and was quite happy to stay at home with his piano. But Hannah, a dynamic woman who enjoyed travelling, was the opposite. As a result, mother and son spent many holidays with each other.

Alf, who worshipped his mother, was fully aware of the sacrifices she was making for him. Not many women in those days contributed to the family finances but she was an exception; she was the driving force in the family and Alf felt a deep and lasting respect for her. However, their relationship was complex, one that, throughout all the years I observed them together, seemed to fall short of open affection. He rarely appeared to be relaxed when in her company, suggesting an inability to display his feelings fully towards her, whereas with his father there existed an obvious and mutual fondness. Hannah Wight was certainly a force to be reckoned with. She dominated the family home, making many of the important decisions, while Pop seemed content to do as he was told. She was a lady with many fine qualities, but could never be described as a warm person. I, myself, remember finding her difficult to embrace.

There is no doubt, however, that she thought the world of her only son – and he of her. Alf's adulation of his mother shows in some of the entries in his diaries: 'There's Mother laughing just now. It is the world's greatest tonic to me when I know she's happy.' The mature Alfred Wight was certainly not a cold man. He displayed, to a remarkable degree, qualities of warmth and genuine concern for others, and I feel sure that these qualities were apparent in the young Alf, too. Perhaps, as a young man, his reverence towards, and concern for his mother was his way of seeking affection from her – something she was unable to give openly in return.

*

Alf was a boy who packed an enormous amount into his life but he never lost sight of the ambition that transcended all others. He was determined to do well at school and gain the necessary higher grades to qualify for entrance to veterinary college. And this he did. He left Hillhead High School on 29 June 1933, with a Higher Education Leaving Certificate asserting that he had obtained three highers – English (including Literature and History), Latin and French. To his amazement, he also attained a pass in Mathematics at lower level. He achieved results of 67% in English, 53% in French and 48% in Latin. His illness at the beginning of his final year decreed that he did not attain the marks in these examinations that he had worked so hard for, but they were good enough. He had achieved his goal.

He wrote in the diary on 30 June 1933: 'What a day! What a day! I awoke this morning a poverty stricken youth and I am going to bed a rich man. This morning we had the prize giving and I got 4s 6d for being runner up in the championship. I then took my departure from Hillhead for ever. I feel sort of sorry to leave the place and all the pleasant things connected with it but, on the other hand, I am glad to have got my highers at the age of 16 years and 8 months and to be able to get on with my job. I'll join the F. P. (former pupils) Club, of course, and keep up my connection with the school ... Afterwards, Mother presented me with ten bob for getting my highers!'

His parents were extremely proud that their son had gained admission to the veterinary college, and all the relatives in Sunderland and every friend for miles around were posted with the news. One day, shortly after the results came through, the coalman was filling the bunker and Hannah could not resist telling him about her son's achievement.

'We've just had some good news,' she said.

The coalman paused. He looked at her and Pop. 'Aye, that's great, Mrs Wight! Whit's the news?'

'My son is going to go to the veterinary college!' she replied, bursting with pride. 'He is going to become a veterinary surgeon!'

Bright eyes shone out of the grimy face. 'Ach!' he replied, 'some tart'll get a haud o'im!'

In one of the last diary entries written while he was still at school, Alf wrote: 'It's a blinking nuisance having to write this blessed book in the early hours of the morning but mebbe when I'm Prime Minister, I'll sell the copyright for £5000!' Little did the young man realise, as he left Hillhead High School to set out on the next step of his education at Glasgow Veterinary College, that many years later he would have a copyright to exceed all his expectations.

CHAPTER FOUR

The veterinary profession today is enjoying a wave of enormous popularity. At the time of writing this biography, there are three different television programmes currently showing about veterinary activities – all achieving high viewing ratings. James Herriot has been held to be largely responsible for the public's seemingly inexhaustible fascination for all things veterinary. This is a predictable opinion as the television series 'All Creatures Great and Small', first shown twenty years ago, was a runaway success and was enjoyed by millions. James Herriot's books, the inspiration behind that series, are widely believed to have been the main reason for the spotlight that now seems to be permanently upon the veterinary surgeon.

My father, however, repeatedly expressed his opinion that he was not solely responsible for the high profile of his profession and the headlong rush of young people entering the veterinary schools. When I applied for entry in 1960, ten years before the first Herriot book was published, there were, even then, three to four hundred applicants for around forty-five places on the course. With the general public's enduring fascination for animals, a career in veterinary medicine has been a natural choice for an ever-increasing number of young people. The enormous popularity of his books may have inevitably improved the image of the profession, but there are other factors involved and I agree with my father's assertion: James Herriot is only partly responsible. I feel sorry for the youngsters nowadays who aspire to be veterinary surgeons. The competition to enter the veterinary schools is intense, with dauntingly high academic achievements needed – three 'A' Levels in the science subjects, with at least two at 'A' grade. Many listen with envy when I tell them that, back in 1960, I needed only two 'A' Levels to gain entry to Glasgow University Veterinary School. Admittedly, they had to be in the science subjects – chemistry, physics and biology – but an ordinary pass was enough and it was a modest challenge in comparison with the ferocious competition of today. I wonder what they would think of the requirements in my father's day!

*

Alfred Wight gained admission to Glasgow Veterinary College in 1933 with passes in English, French and Latin – hardly ideal subjects for a future scientist, but the situation then was very different. With comparatively few wishing to enter the veterinary profession during the years of the depression, the veterinary schools were only too pleased to welcome anyone to fill the courses. While still at Hillhead School, he had telephoned the veterinary college to tell them that, provided he gained the basic entry requirements, he would like to pursue a career in veterinary medicine.

The principal himself, Dr Whitehouse, had answered the telephone. 'Good!' he had replied. 'When can you start?'

At the time of Alf's entry in 1933, Glasgow was unique among the veterinary schools of the British Isles. It was receiving no financial aid from the government, and its survival depended solely upon the fees received from the students, together with local authority grants and donations from various organisations. A government report of 1925 had decreed that only one veterinary school was needed in Scotland, resulting in the grant upon which the school depended being ruthlessly terminated. Glasgow Veterinary College defiantly carried on functioning through the sheer determination of the chairman of the governors, Professor John Glaister, and the principal, Dr A. W. Whitehouse. As a result, it took a fierce pride in its very existence, and the students emerged from the five-year course feeling a real sense of achievement.

Alf received a Carnegie Bursary of £18 a year together with a Glasgow Education Authority grant of £10 towards his fees, but the real cost was much more. Books, materials and living expenses multiplied the drain upon the students' resources many times over. As at Hillhead, Alf received the full support of his parents throughout the six years he spent at the veterinary college – years that were to provide him with unforgettable memories and life-long friendships.

He began his education at the college on 26 September 1933 and he wrote in his diary at that time: 'A momentous day! This morning I started in the veterinary college. Crowd of new fellows waiting outside – seasoned veterans swaggering in – stamping of feet in lecture rooms – big thrill when I went into a room full of dead animals. There's some queer fish here!'

He was soon to discover that the big difference between Hillhead School and the veterinary college was that, here, no one seemed to

care whether he did any work. In keeping with the regimented discipline at Hillhead School, his teachers had seemed fiercely determined
that he should pass his exams, with the reputation of the school being
at stake. At the veterinary college, however, the whole atmosphere was
almost one of apathy. During his first term, large amounts of time,
especially in the afternoons, were spent playing table tennis in the
common-room, visiting the cinema, or just going home to do exactly
as he liked.

This was not really surprising. The college was only too pleased to
have the students there, paying their fees; if they did not work and took
fifteen years to complete a five-year course, that was their problem. In
fact, there was little incentive to qualify since there were very few jobs
waiting for them when they eventually achieved their goal. For the
student whose parents were wealthy and willing enough to continue
their support, the way of life at Glasgow Veterinary College was an
attractive proposition. To some of the students, money did not seem a
problem and they did, indeed, take up to ten, twelve or more years to
complete the course. Some of them never made it at all, finishing up
in a variety of jobs. In the years following his qualification, Alf used to
see some of his old college chums during his visits to Glasgow; one he
saw serving in a textile shop, and he was startled to see another of his
old pals directing the traffic at Charing Cross. Some of these long-serving
students became such a part of the establishment that when they
eventually took their leave, Dr Whitehouse and his staff bade them
farewell with a tear in the eye. In the introduction to his book *James
Herriot's Dog Stories*, published many years later, Alf described the
professor's reaction to the departure of one of these 'permanent
students':

One chap, McAloon by name, had been there for fourteen years but had
managed to get only as far as the second year in the curriculum. He held
the record at the time but many others were into double figures ... The
fourteen-year man was held in particularly high esteem and when he finally
left to join the police force, he was sadly missed. Old Dr Whitehouse, who
lectured in anatomy, was visibly moved at the time. 'Mr McAloon,' he said,
putting down a horse's skull and pointing with his probe at an empty space,
'has sat on that stool for eleven years. It is going to be very strange without
him.'

*

The building in which Alf received his veterinary education was an uninspiring one, situated on a steep hill on the corner of Buccleuch Street in the Cowcaddens District of Glasgow. This old establishment, formerly a pumping station for Glasgow Corporation, was built of dull stone with rows of tired-looking windows, and bore more resemblance to a high-security prison than a recognised seat of learning. Gloomy tenement buildings looked down on the college from all sides, and there was not a sign of any greenery for as far as the eye could see.

Despite its forbidding appearance, there was a warmth and friendliness within those grim walls. Alf felt a great affection for his old college, but one of the interesting things about the James Herriot books is the absence of stories about his life there. In the years following publication of *The Lord God Made Them All* in 1981, he swore that he was not going to write another one. This disappointed me, as I knew it would his fans, and I often reminded him that he still had plenty of material left, including his years as a veterinary student. Apart from a handful of people, everyone was under the impression that he had written nothing about those days apart from the section in the introduction to *James Herriot's Dog Stories*. This is far from the truth.

In the early 1960s, when he first began writing in earnest, he wrote a series of stories, some of which were based on his experiences at Glasgow Veterinary College and which he pieced together into a novel. The abandoned typescript, which lay forgotten for many years, has been very valuable in nudging my memories of the veterinary college experiences that he so often recounted to us. In this novel, which was written in the third person, he called himself 'James Walsh'.

After only three weeks at the veterinary college Walsh knew his life had changed. He had thought that learning to be a vet would be a kind of extension to his schooldays with the same values holding good and the same scholastic atmosphere. True, it would be rather a slummy extension because his first sight of the college had been a shock: a low, seedy building covered half heartedly in peeling, yellowish paint crouching apologetically amongst grime blackened, decaying apartment houses. In Victorian times the district had been the residential quarter of the prosperous city merchants and many of the houses had imposing frontages and pillared entrances but now, it was a forgotten backwater, the haunt of broken down actors, purveyors of dubious trades and pale, stooping women.

It was rumoured that the college had once been the stables for the horses which drew the first tram cars and there was no doubt that the outside appearance of the place lent weight to the theory. A single arch led into the yard around which the classrooms and laboratories were grouped, rather like a lot of converted stables and it was under this arch that Walsh first met his fellow students. His first impression was that they did not look like students at all, at least he couldn't see any fresh faced young men with blazers and bright scarves around their necks. Later, he found that many of them were countrymen, farmers' sons, some from the valleys of Forth and Clyde and a large sprinkling from the Northern Highlands and it probably explained the tendency towards dun coloured hairy tweeds and big, solid boots. Two turbaned Sikhs provided an almost violent contrast and the first year intake was completed by a solitary, frightened looking little girl.

There were no frills. No cool cloisters to pace in, no echoing, picture-lined corridors, no lofty, panelled dining hall. There was a common room with a few rickety chairs and a battered grand piano which was mainly used as a card table and a hatch in the corner which served tea, meat pies and the heaviest apple tarts in Scotland. This was the social nerve centre of the whole building and all functions were held there.

But still, Walsh gradually became aware of a pulsing life, warmer and more vivid than anything he had known before. The dilapidated little college was an unlikely stage for the host of colourful characters who thronged it but they were there all the same: rich, vital, outrageous and beguiling.

The college was indeed full of fascinating and often unruly characters. In 1949, it became affiliated to Glasgow University, but in Alf's day it was not answerable to such a high authority – a fact displayed more than adequately by its high-spirited students. He appeared surprised at the character of his fellow students. A few weeks after he began his veterinary education, he went to the college 'smoker' – a kind of introductory welcome for the new boys – and wrote about it in his diary. 'The boxing was a new experience and very interesting. The lightweights were especially natty. I was a bit amazed at the character of the various songs and anecdotes which were rendered on the platform. There was a good violinist doing his stuff. They are a queer crowd here, all types and kinds, but decent enough.'

Up until this time, Alf had been brought up in a home where drinking and swearing hardly existed, and some of the songs he heard that night must have come as a bit of a culture shock. A more vivid example of the unruly students of his day occurred at the annual prize-giving that November. Prize-givings are usually well-ordered and dignified occasions, but this one was different.

This remarkable ceremony was reported the next day in the *Glasgow Evening Times*:

A human skull decending suddenly on a cord from the ceiling to within a foot or so of his face was one of the shocks sustained today by the chairman at the prize-giving of the Glasgow Veterinary College, Buccleuch Street. The platform party was met by thunderous applause and banshee shrieks when they entered the hall in which the students were assembled. The opening remarks of the chairman, Mr Alexander Murdoch, were punctuated by loud interruptions and the speaker was threatened with early hoarseness. He was diffident, however, about having recourse to the water carafe because it looked suspiciously like an aquarium – a goldfish having been inserted there by some 'person or persons unknown'. After his first half-dozen sentences, he raised his head and was confronted by a dark brown skull revolving slowly on a cord in front of his face. After a 'look round' at the platform party, the skull slowly rose to the ceiling again, from which it descended, 'spider fashion' at intervals, finally dropping with a loud bang on the table much to the alarm of the chairman. The students seemed to enjoy the command performance.

Alf had obviously appreciated the occasion, as his diary entry shows: 'The prize-giving. What a rag! They hissed the unpopular profs, cheered the doctor, and sang 'For he's a jolly good fellow', and bawled remarks at the big-wigs as they entered. I enjoyed it, I can tell you!'

Alf threw himself willingly into this new way of life. A few weeks after the prize-giving, he went, in the company of seventy other students, to the Empress Theatre in St George's Road. The students, already having had a drink or two, were intent on having a good time. The police were soon on the scene. One student kicked in the door of the theatre as he left, later receiving a fine of two guineas – a punishing sum for a student in those days. Alf made good his escape by running into the jungle of nearby tenements; his athletics training at school stood him in good stead that evening.

Riotous behaviour was not confined to 'extra-curricular' activities outside the walls of the college. Some of the lectures within bore more resemblance to wild parties than periods of study and in those early weeks at the college, James Alfred Wight was beginning to realise that life at Buccleuch Street was going to be a little different from that at

Hillhead. In his unpublished novel, he later wrote about the teachers whose lot it was to teach these tearaway students:

Some of the staff were old men snatched from retirement and forced to spend their declining years in an unequal struggle with boisterous youth. Others were veterinary surgeons in practice in the city who combined their daily work with lecturing and, in the process, imparted a practical and commonsense slant to their instruction which stood their pupils in good stead in later years. They, like the older men, had a detached, fatalistic attitude to their job and took the view that if the students paid their fees it was up to them whether they gathered knowledge or acted the fool.

Professor Andy McQueen, who taught biology in the first year, read his notes out from papers in front of him and if he ever turned over two pages at once by mistake, he just carried on as if nothing had happened. Alf later wrote about one of his lectures in his novel and it illustrates the atmosphere at the college very accurately. He gave his old teachers varying *noms de plume*, and refers to Andy McQueen as 'Professor King'.

The difference from school life first became apparent in the lecture rooms. Professor King, who taught biology, was an incredibly old and frail man who conducted his classes with total detachment. Stooping over a sheaf of yellowing notes, he mumbled almost inaudibly down at his desk and whether the students listened or not, was a matter of no concern to him; it was entirely up to them.

The class took their cue from the considerable number of failed men left over from the last year and stamped and cheered as though they were at a football match. This rowdiness started right at the beginning of the lecture when the roll was being taken. When the name of the only female was being called, there was an uproar of shouts and whistles while the poor girl, who was naturally shy by nature, coloured deep red and sank lower in her seat.

The other outbursts came at the jokes. Professor King, at the beginning of his teaching career in the later years of the nineteenth century, had decided that his lectures would be racy and full of wit, so he had pencilled in a comical allusion for each lecture. For nearly fifty years, he had not changed a single word of his lecture notes, so that successive generations of students knew exactly which joke was coming and where.

For instance, when he was discussing the snake Dasipeltis shedding its skin, he would clear his throat, pause and say 'for Dasipeltis always returns the empties'. This was the signal for more stamping, wild yells and hysterical laughter from the class.

The only time he ever looked up from his papers was at the end of his lecture when he invariably drew a large watch from his waistcoat pocket, gazed around the students with a smile of childlike sweetness and said, 'I see by my gold watch and chain that it is time to stop.' Pandemonium then broke out again.

Another of the elderly teachers was Professor Hugh Begg who taught parasitology. He was a well-liked man, full of good advice to the students, but he was hard of hearing and so was only dimly aware of the tumult that characterised his lectures. He would raise his head, peer around him and say, 'Wha' . . . what's that noise?' One would need to be totally deaf not to hear the response from the assembled students. Hugh Begg did, however, have a piece of advice one day that Alf never forgot. He was a wise old man, with many years of experience behind him, and he was talking about the kind of life that awaited the veterinary surgeons of the future. On this occasion he had the ears of the class, and his theme – a vitally important one – was that they would learn by their mistakes.

'Gentlemen,' he said solemnly, 'ye'll never make veterinary surgeons until every last one o' ye has filled a forty-acre field full o' carcasses!' Prophetic words.

When I talk to some of the young graduates in our practice in Thirsk, hearing of the pressure they were under at University, I cannot help casting my mind back to my father's stories of his student years. The card games in the common-room, the time spent sitting happily in the cinemas rather than in lessons, and the riotous scenes in the lecture theatres when they did attend, paint a very different picture of veterinary education from that of today. However, despite the rather unorthodox lectures, the material given to the students was sound and, providing they worked and read the text books, they had every chance of qualifying within a reasonable time.

My father, well aware that the cost of his education was being borne largely by his parents, was determined to do well. He bought the necessary text books such as *Sisson's Anatomy* and *Animal Husbandry* by Miller and Robertson, and spent many hours studying in the huge Mitchell Library which was near the college. He obviously found the atmosphere in the big library somewhat daunting and wrote in his diary: 'That place depresses me. You can almost hear the brains throbbing.'

He was taught Animal Husbandry, Chemistry and Biology in the first year, and made a steady start. He passed his Chemistry and Biology, although he only just scraped through in Biology, attaining a mark of 46%. This led to a conversation with a fellow student that he repeated to me many times.

'What's the pass mark?'

'45%.'

'What did you get?'

'46%.'

'You've been working too hard!'

Another of his friends used a different approach in following this rather risky attitude to study. He was being examined in Anatomy and was presented with a large bone. 'What is this?' asked the examiner.

'A femur,' replied the student.

'Correct,' continued the examiner, 'a femur of what species? Is it the femur of a cow or a horse?'

'It's all right,' said the student dismissively, 'you can forget that one. I'm not looking for honours!'

During that first year, Alf's teachers seemed quite pleased with him. His chemistry teacher, Professor Duncan, wrote in his report: 'Is quite a fair average, not likely to be brilliant but I expect him to be steady.'

In his next year, 1934–5, he started to slip back. He failed his Physiology and Histology examinations, together with Animal Husbandry. Very poor marks of 36%, 25% and 37% respectively were attained and his teachers were not pleased. Remarks such as 'not in attendance' and 'does not work; very poor' are evident in his report.

This is rather surprising. Alf was a responsible and ambitious young man. He wanted to get out into the world, earn his living, and cease to be a burden upon his parents. In addition, he was not one of the band of students who played cards in the common-room all day with the intention of extending their carefree college life well beyond the allotted five years. After a few sessions round the card table in his first year when he lost heavily, the appeal of that enjoyable but expensive pastime died very quickly. In his report of Autumn Term 1935, Dr Whitehouse wrote that he was 'not in attendance' for his Anatomy classes. This seems strange behaviour for a well-adjusted young man. While Alf was never a brilliant student, carrying off little in the way of distinctions during his time at the college, this does not fully explain his poor showing.

There was, however, a serious reason. In his last year at Hillhead School, he had experienced severe pain in his rectum that developed into a discharging anal fistula. He recovered from the initial attack but this debilitating condition, which resurfaced in his second year at the college, would be one that would dog him intermittently for the rest of his life. He was so ill in the summer of 1937 that he was admitted to hospital where he underwent a minor operation to clean up the affected area. It was a failure and he was back in the Western Infirmary in 1939 for another attempt at resolving this persistent complaint but, as before, it was not successful.

This acutely painful affliction, inevitably, affected his ability to concentrate fully on his studies. Without the help of antibiotics in those days, it was not only the pain of the condition that weakened him, he had to endure bouts of severe septicaemia brought about by multiple fulminating abscesses. The only treatment was to go to bed, often with a raging temperature, and bathe the area with hot water in an attempt to keep the infection under control.

Alf was very philosophical about this blot on his otherwise good state of health and always managed to put a humorous slant into any discussions about it. 'I may not be an expert on many things,' he was to say years later, 'but I consider myself to be an authority on the subject of "Arsology!"' He spoke from bitter experience, going on to say, 'I've had several operations on the old posterior, all of them agony, but I've had enough! No one else is going to have a go at remodelling my backside. This lot is going into the "box" with me!'

By the summer of 1936 at the end of his third year, he had passed his Physiology and Histology exams, but failed yet again in Animal Husbandry. He sat that examination for the fourth time in the December of that year. This time, he received a little help. One of the assistant lecturers in the department was Alex (Sandy) Thompson – a man who also taught me twenty-six years later. He was a pipe smoker who, during the examination, was seated behind the examiner, in full view of Alf, contentedly puffing on his pipe.

'How many orifices are there in the teat of a cow?' the examiner asked.

Alf hesitated, then noticed that one forefinger, accompanied by a puff of blue smoke, was pointing into the air behind the examiner's back.

'One,' he replied.

'Correct. How many in the teat of a mare?'

Two smoke-enshrouded fingers appeared, still caressing the pipe.

'Two,' Alf responded. The rest was easy.

In 1937, Alf did much better and in July, he passed his Anatomy, Pharmacology and Hygiene exams although his marks were modest; he achieved 45% in Anatomy, which was just enough.

Anatomy was taught by the principal himself, Dr Whitehouse. Alf found the subject interesting but, at the same time, it was a hard, grinding slog. With so many facts to assimilate, he felt at times that his brain was reaching saturation point. The students had to learn the detailed structure of several different domestic animals and the subject was not only hard work, it could also be very boring. Alf enjoyed Dr Whitehouse's practical sessions in the anatomy labs where the students worked in groups dissecting an assortment of dead animals, mainly horses and cows, but the Anatomy lectures were a different proposition. These were much quieter than the riotous sessions under the elderly teachers. Instead of the wild shrieks and paper missiles that characterised Professor Begg's lectures, a different sound predominated – the rhythmic and contented drone of sleeping students.

This was understandable. Dr Whitehouse worked from the huge tome called *Sisson's Anatomy*, the forbidding contents of which every student was expected to assimilate. The following extract is typical: 'The great sciatic nerve (*N. ischiadicus*) . . . is derived chiefly from the sixth lumbar and the first sacral roots of the lumbo-sacral plexus, but usually has a fifth lumbar root and may receive a fasciculus from the second sacral nerve. It turns downward in the hollow between the trochanter major and the tuber ischii over the gemellus, the tendon of the obturator internus, and the quadratus femoris. In its descent in the thigh it lies between the biceps femoris laterally and the adductor, semimembranosus, and semitendinosus medially, and is continued between the two heads of the gastrocnemius as the tibial nerve. Its chief branches are as follows . . .' There is little wonder that in the face of such a bombardment, the students' minds either wandered on to subjects of greater interest or, more commonly, just descended into insensibility.

In the Autumn term of 1937, at the beginning of his fifth year, Alf progressed to Pathology, Medicine and Surgery. With his failures in

several subjects necessitating re-sits, he had fallen behind and was
resigned to the prospect of taking more than the statutory five years to
complete the course. He was not too downhearted. Not only were many
of his friends in a similar position but, having reached a stage of his
education where he felt that he was entering the nuts and bolts of his
future career, he was more determined than ever to do well. Pathology,
the study of disease: this was what it was all about. Pathology was a
subject that both fascinated and frightened him, and at this stage of his
education, a man entered his life who would remain vividly in his
memory until the day he died. A man who would figure in his dreams
for years to come – someone he told us about so many times that I
almost felt I, too, had sat next to my father, quivering in the supercharged
atmosphere of his Pathology lectures. A man by the name of Professor
J. W. Emslie.

I am not one who is prone to nightmares. Once settled beneath the
sheets, I spend, in general, a pleasant several hours in another world. I
dream vividly and my dreams are usually a pleasant variation on my
life's activities. I do, however, suffer a recurring and disturbing dream.
The orchestrator of these unnerving experiences is a nameless and
shapeless individual who persistently informs me that I am not a
qualified veterinary surgeon at all. I do not know this person but I have
grown to dislike him intensely over the years. 'You haven't passed your
Physics and Chemistry and you'll have to take them again!' he repeatedly
tells me. I shrug this off, asserting that I shall re-take the exams and
pass them without any problem, but he has his doubts – and so do I.
As the dream progresses, I do nothing about swotting for the exams
until finally I face the prospect of cramming the whole of the Chemistry
and Physics syllabus into one day. At this point, to my intense relief, I
wake up.

My father, too, suffered a similar dream throughout his life but it
was not Chemistry and Physics that were to frighten him in his nocturnal
wanderings. It was a subject that he loved but found difficult to grasp,
and one whose exam he failed at veterinary college. That subject was
Pathology and, as with me, an alarming individual presided over his
dream, bombarding him with bad news. There was one big difference:
Alf Wight knew his tormentor well. He was none other than his old
professor of Pathology, the menacing and unforgettable John W. Emslie.

My father spoke to us at great length about his college days, and we heard much about the many friends he made there but, without any doubt, the number one character we remembered best was Professor Emslie. Quite simply, he frightened my father out of his wits.

A rude shock was in store for the students when they began Pathology. The days of noise and laughter in the lecture theatres became a thing of the past as Professor Emslie burst into their lives and presided over the trembling students like the Demon King. He left such a deep impression on Alf that he was later to appear in Alf's early attempt at a novel in the guise of a formidable professor by the name of 'Quentin Muldoon'.

Muldoon. The name was like a knell, like the tolling of a great bell in an empty tower and the students heard its warning echoes from their first days. . . . Quentin Muldoon, professor of Pathology, was a dedicated and, in many ways, brilliant scientist in the prime of life and though he may have questioned the justice of divine providence in selecting him to disclose the breathless secrets and supreme wonders of his subject to the shaggy creatures who shambled before him through the years, he did his duty as he saw it. That duty was to teach Pathology and anything or anybody getting in the way of his teaching was mercilessly crushed. Pathos Logos, the science of disease, the answer to all the questions, the brilliant light bursting suddenly on total darkness, the steady pointing finger of truth and hope. That was how Muldoon saw Pathology and he made some of his students see it too. The others just learned the facts of it or he crucified them.

Walsh learned about Muldoon in whispers from the older students. He hadn't been at the college for a week before the mutterings started. 'Aye, it's all very well just now but wait till your fourth year, wait till you get Muldoon. Don't worry, he'll know all about you before you get into his class. Mark my words, every single thing you do, good or bad, from the day you enter this college, Muldoon knows. He's got you taped, laddie, right from the word go. Every mark in every exam in every subject. Every time you skipped out of the anatomy lab to go to the pictures, every time you got drunk at the dances, it's all there in that big black head!'

When the first three years went by and Walsh's class finally filed into the Pathology classroom, the tension was almost unbearable. Muldoon was late and the minutes ticked by as the class sat looking up at the empty platform, the desk and blackboard, the rows of specimens in glass jars. Then the door at the back clicked. Nobody looked round but a slow, heavy tread was coming down the central aisle. Walsh was half way down the class at the end of the row and a dark presence almost brushed him as it passed. He had a back view of a bulky figure in a creased, tight fitting, slightly shiny navy blue suit. The head, massive and crowned with abundant black hair, was sunk broodingly between the shoulders. The feet, splayed and flat, were put down unhurriedly at each step and under one arm was a thick wad of notes. Muldoon mounted the platform and moved without haste to his desk where he began to lay out his notes methodically. He took a long time over this and still he hadn't even glanced up. Still looking down at the desk he straightened his tie, adjusted the handkerchief in his breast pocket then he raised his head slowly and gazed at the class.

It was a broad, fleshy, pale-jowled face and the eyes, black and brilliant, swept the students with a mixture of hatred and disbelief. After a trial run, the eyes started at the beginning and began to work their way slowly along the packed rows in an agonising silence. Muldoon, having finally finished his scrutiny, thrust his tongue into his cheek – a characteristic gesture with a 'God help us, this is the end' touch about it – sighed deeply and began to address the class.

He began suddenly, with an abruptness which made some of his charges jump nervously, by throwing out one arm and shouting, 'You can put those away for a start!' The students who had been fumbling with notebooks and pens dropped them hurriedly and Muldoon spoke again. 'I'm not going to lecture to you today, I'm just going to talk to you.' And he did talk for over an hour in a menacing, husky monotone. He told them what he expected them to do during the coming year and what would happen to them if they didn't do it. The end of the lecture came and went but nobody moved a muscle.

When it was over, Walsh went down for a cup of tea. He felt as though somebody had drained a few pints of blood from him and realised that, for the first time in his life, he had had contact with an overwhelming personality.

One of Alf's clearest memories of Professor Emslie was that of his picking on certain students he thought (or should one say, knew) were shirking. There were few of his lectures that were not enlivened by a human sacrifice with one of his choice victims, a student called George Pettigrew. On one occasion, while discussing the family of bacteria known as the Clostridia, the Professor decided to have a little sport. He began benignly. 'We now come to rather an abstruse point, gentlemen, so perhaps we had better consult one of our more advanced and enlightened students. Now, who shall it be?' The black eyes darted among the silent students, finally coming to rest on the quivering figure of Pettigrew. 'Ah yes, of course, Pettigrew!' The student responded by sitting bolt upright and staring straight at his tormentor.

Professor Emslie's attack began quietly. 'Mr Pettigrew, perhaps you would be so kind as to tell us the sequence of events following upon the invasion of a tissue by Clostridium Septique.'

'A gas is formed, sir,' answered the student swiftly, a thin film of sweat upon his brow.

An agonised silence followed. Everyone had feared that Pettigrew's reply would be an inadequate one. The silence deepened. The professor slowly shook his head from side to side before quietly beginning to speak. 'A gas is formed ... A gas is formed? A GAS IS FORMED?' he suddenly shouted, rounding on the cowering Pettigrew, jabbing his finger almost into his face. 'Yes, damn you, you useless clown! Every time you open your mouth, that is what happens, A GAS IS FORMED!'

Pettigrew was not the only one to feel the lashing tongue of Professor Emslie. The inadequacy of the entire class was ruthlessly exposed until finally, as abruptly as it had exploded, the voice returned to ominous normality. Alf could never help feeling that somewhere along the line the stage had lost a great tragedian, Emslie's ability to switch from berserk rage to glacial calm particularly impressing him.

Professor Emslie was not just a frightening character. He was also a man of mystery which added to the sense of awe in which he was held by the students. Not one of them ever saw him either arrive at or leave the college; how did he get in and out of the building? Various interesting theories arose. One student claimed to have seen him flash through the wall of the Pathology lab leaving a strong smell of brimstone behind him. Another was positive he had seen him with a briefcase and a bowler hat emerging from a hole at the bottom of Buccleuch Street. Yet another was convinced that he flew into the college down one of the chimney pots.

This extraordinary man was certainly feared by the students but, above all, he was respected – and he was a good teacher. Always having considered the professor to be a fair man, Alf actually grew to like him. Those who worked diligently were treated accordingly.

In July 1938, Alf scraped through his professional Parasitology exam but he failed Pathology, achieving only a mark of 40%. He re-sat Pathology in December 1938, passing with 49%. He certainly had not distinguished himself in the subject and, upon graduating one year later, he did not expect a glowing report from Professor Emslie. All the teachers had a dossier on their pupils which could be read by them on graduation day and Alf Wight was not looking forward to Emslie's considered opinion of him. He received a pleasant surprise.

'Wight, James Alfred. Lacking in brilliance but showed a perception of the subject which I personally found rewarding. A pleasant-mannered, likeable boy of transparent integrity.'

Alf did mention that he occasionally considered writing about his days at the Glasgow Veterinary College and, had he done so, I suspect that Professor Muldoon – a man about whom he spoke more than any other when recalling his student days – would have become another character to stand alongside Siegfried, Tristan and all those other famous creatures great and small.

CHAPTER FIVE

During Alf's time at the Glasgow Veterinary College, the classes were in a continual state of flux, with students failing their exams with monotonous regularity and sliding backwards, while other more dedicated students forged ahead. There is little wonder that the faces of his colleagues in his final few years bore little resemblance to his first year at the college. Some had given up altogether while others were lodged down the ladder, either desperately trying to make some progress or just happily playing cards in the college common-room.

During his school years at Hillhead, Alf had made friends but none with whom he would keep in close touch after he left. His years at the Glasgow Veterinary College, however, provided him with friendships that he would never forget. Unlike school, where the pupils had been helped along their way with excellent teaching and strong discipline, the students at the college held their destiny very much in their own hands. This generated an intense feeling of comradeship within the bleak old building in Buccleuch Street.

Alf's closest friend at the college was a good-looking, open-faced young man called Aubrey Melville, an ebullient character who rarely missed a good night out and was frequently accompanied by a pretty girl and a laughing crowd. He epitomised the sort of flamboyant, extrovert character Alf was pitched amongst at the start of his veterinary career.

Two of Alf's friends had to raise the funds for their beer money in rather different ways. Andy Flynn bolstered his financial state by playing in an orchestra – although it was to no avail since he failed his veterinary exams time and again before giving up altogether – while Pat O'Reilly relied on gambling at the dog tracks in the city; he too failed a huge number of exams but eventually qualified. There was Dominic Boyce who, when drunk, invariably resorted to solitary singing, just like the renowned 'back court singers', Jimmy Steele, a born entertainer and storyteller, and Bob 'Ginger' Smith who played alongside Alf in the college football team.

There was one college friend, however, who would come in and out of Alf Wight's life more than any other. His name was Eddie Straiton – a small, compact, dark-haired man who came from Clydebank, a district very close to Alf's home in Yoker. Eddie was a fitness fanatic and possessed incredible energy. He was a dedicated and very able student who achieved high academic results at the veterinary college through sheer hard work. Although neither a smoker nor a drinker, he participated fully in the many wild nights that the students enjoyed. Large quantities of alcohol were consumed on these occasions and Alex Taylor, who sometimes joined Alf among his veterinary friends, remembers Eddie standing beside the sinks in the toilets as the swaying students lined up to be sick, methodically twirling his fingers around the plug-hole to disperse the stomach contents of the last 'customer'. After cleaning the sink to his satisfaction, he would shout, 'Next please!' Business was always brisk.

Eddie played in the college football team alongside Alf, and his energy on the field was legendary; he just ran and ran. At the end of the game, in contrast to his hard-drinking, heavy-smoking team mates, he appeared to be totally unaffected by the exercise. He was to carry this incredible vitality with him throughout his entire life. Alf and Eddie were good friends at veterinary college and this friendship continued long after they both bade farewell to Glasgow. In the years to come, Eddie would, many times, cross the path of both Alfred Wight, the veterinary surgeon, and James Herriot, the world-famous author.

Alf's transition from schoolboy to veterinary student was a vitally important part of his life. The enthusiastic, but studious and well-behaved boy, had discovered a totally new world. The social life of the Glasgow veterinary student was a vibrant one, liberally laced with wild nights of carousing and drinking, and Alf found little difficulty in adapting to it. He was a major participant in the social functions that the students enjoyed; indeed, he was much in demand at parties where his natural ability to thump out tunes on the piano contributed in no small way to the memorable nights they all had. His popularity on the piano extended to Buccleuch Street itself, where he could frequently be seen happily playing his favourite tunes – 'Stardust' or the old Duke Ellington classic, 'Mood Indigo' – on the battered piano in the common-room. It is no surprise that Alf regarded his veterinary college days as some of the happiest of his life.

But one thing had not changed – his deep respect for his mother.

After an evening of serious drinking with his friends, he would walk for miles through the streets around his home, making sure that he was thoroughly sober before returning to the house. Even in later years when visiting his mother in Glasgow, he would never have a drink in front of her – instead, he kept the odd secret bottle of gin around to fortify himself when the need arose.

Whether his actions were out of respect for, or fear of his mother, is debatable, but I remember a wry smile flitting across his face one day, after I had recounted an incident during my days at veterinary school in Glasgow when I had endured the wrath of my grandmother who had observed with disgust my unsuccessful attempts at climbing the stairs after a particularly enjoyable night on the town. I certainly saw a stern side to my grandmother on that occasion. She was then in her early seventies but she came at me like a force ten gale. I can only imagine what a strong personality she must have been as a younger woman.

Alf, however, by adopting a far more subtle approach, never experienced her wrath during his college years. She remained totally unaware of his nights of revelry until the end of her days, believing her son to be a virtual teetotaller. The many James Herriot fans were to hear little of Alfred Wight's memorable days as a veterinary student, but he would often recall those far-off days in Glasgow – and with good reason. That sudden invasion of his life by so many varied and interesting characters, many of whom were as colourful as any he would make famous through his writing years later, impressed him so deeply that he never forgot them, even down to the smallest detail.

The making of so many new friends at the veterinary college did not mean that Alf neglected his others. His great friend Alex Taylor, after leaving school, had not pursued his further education. Instead, he got employment at Drysdales, a big engineering firm where he worked in the wages department, but he and Alf still saw a great deal of each other.

At around this time, Alex and Alf met a young man from Yoker called Eddie Hutchinson. Eddie, like Alf and Alex, was a member of the Yoker Tennis Club where the three played for many an hour through the long summer evenings. Eddie was one who introduced a new level of ferocity into the game, venomously thrashing the little white ball around the court. Off the court, he was a different man, with an attractive, slow, easy-going manner. He just went through life at his own pace. This likeable man, whose company Alf found both enjoyable and relaxing, became one of his greatest friends; photographs taken of Alf, Alex and Eddie clearly reflect the happy times the three young men enjoyed during their years together in Glasgow.

Hiking and camping in the hills around Glasgow was another pastime shared by the three friends, often accompanied by other chums, notably Pete Shaw and Jock Davey. Alf's love of spending days in the hills was just as strong during his college years as it had been throughout his days at school, but now he had to combine work with pleasure. He would frequently take his books with him and set off for several days at a time to do some studying alone; then, his friends, who were working in Glasgow, joined him at weekends. A great deal of his time attempting to absorb the vast amount of material necessary to pass the veterinary exams was spent under canvas.

Favourite camping sites were near Fintry, in the Campsie Fells – rolling, heath-covered hills to the east of Glasgow – and the village of Rosneath on the Firth of Clyde. This village is situated on a pretty peninsula of quiet woods and fields, overlooked by the big mountains of Argyll, and it was here that Alf was able to work in total peace. Although only a short distance from Glasgow, once he had pitched his tent in one of the green fields that ran down to the seashore, he felt himself to be in another world. In later years, a large naval base was constructed near to Rosneath and some of its charm was lost, but even now it is still a most attractive village.

Despite his ambitions to explore further afield, Alf rarely ventured north to the big mountains of Scotland. They beckoned to him from his camp sites at Fintry and Rosneath but he climbed very few mountains, despite his youthful aspirations to do so. He did, however, undertake one major expedition into the Scottish Highlands in July 1938, shortly after having sat and failed his dreaded Pathology exam at the veterinary college. With his good friends Eddie Hutchinson and Pete Shaw, he 'conquered' the towering mountain called the Streap, near Loch Arkaig. The effort, in boiling hot weather, ensured that this was to be the last mountain Alf would climb for many years, and was an experience he would never forget.

Alf had been very unfit on that foray into the mountains, having just spent weeks shut away, studying for his exams but, in general, during his college years, he kept himself in pretty good shape. As well as regular games of tennis, he endured his cold baths and exercises most days, and walked miles with his dog, Don.

From the age of twenty, he began to play tennis more regularly, joining the nearby Scotstounhill Tennis Club. Although tennis acted as a great antidote to his hours of study, he took the game very seriously and won a number of key matches in the West of Scotland Tennis Championships. His partner in these matches, and one with whom he practised for hours, was a young man called Colin Kesson, a fine player who taught Alf a great deal about the game. Alf could never get the better of him and would joke with his college chums that, apart from finally qualifying as a veterinary surgeon, his other great ambition was to be able to say that he had – just once – managed to beat Colin Kesson.

More relaxing games of tennis were played at the Boys' Brigade Camps, usually at St Andrew's or North Berwick. The Boys' Brigade was a church organisation of which Alex Taylor and Eddie Hutchinson were also members. Together with other friends, the young men had happy, carefree days walking, bathing in the sea and playing tennis.

Another sport he began to play in his college years was football. While at Hillhead, he had played rugby but, apart from kickabouts in the park with his friends and the 'gentry of the corner', he had not played the game seriously, despite being, in common with thousands of other citizens of Glasgow, a fanatical follower of the game. The city pulsated with football and he did not have to venture far to see it. Very close to his home, in Dumbarton Road, was the ground of the local Junior League football team, Yoker Athletic. He was a great supporter of this team and was overjoyed when they won the Scottish Junior Cup Final in the 1932–33 season. Such was the following that this team enjoyed, more fans sang on the terraces of Yoker than on those of the neighbouring Scottish Football League side, Clydebank. Alf and Alex sang and shouted with the rest of the crowd while watching Yoker play teams with singularly Scottish names like Duntocher Hibs and Kirkintilloch Rob Roy.

It was while watching this team that the first ideas of playing the game properly entered his head. Whilst many players in the Junior League went on to play professional football in the Scottish League, Alf did not aspire to play at that level, considering that his studies were too demanding. He decided to play instead in the Juvenile League. Although not playing football to the standard of the Juniors, the Juveniles took their game very seriously, with each team carrying its own dedicated gang of supporters.

One grey February day, Alf made his debut for the Juvenile side, Yoker Fernlea. He scored the only goal of the game on a quagmire of a pitch. The games were fiercely contested, with Alf playing to such calls from the touchline as, 'Get intae him, ye big feartie!' or 'Awa hame, ye mug ye!' There are references to some of these games in his diaries: 'Played Ettrick Thistle today – fiasco. Two of our lads sent off and one carried off. We lost 2–1 in front of a big crowd.' 'Played Tweedhill and drew 3–3 ... got a wallop on the shin which has stiffened me up.' Conditions could be primitive. With pitches often composed of ash and gravel, sliding tackles frequently resulted in sharp stones being driven deep into the wounds of battle.

The games were watched from the touchline by the 'support'. This collection of largely unemployed individuals followed the team wherever it went, gleaning great satisfaction from the games by shouting and swearing at both the players and the referee. They were a motley collection, some fat, but most of them thin and sallow-complexioned, usually with cigarettes dangling from their mouths and beer bottles bulging their coat pockets. They could, on occasion, contribute dramatically to the outcome of a match and, more than once, Alf observed the abrupt cessation of progress by a member of the opposing team, brought about by the timely intervention of a leg darting out from the touchline.

Sometimes, however, their enjoyment could be rudely punctured. It was not uncommon for the team to be short of players at the start of a game, leaving only one course of action open to the manager – that of making up the numbers by procuring the assistance of one or two of the supporters.

'Are we all here, Hughie?' Alf asked one day before the start of a game.

'One man short,' replied the manager. He was a small, dark man with sleek black hair, who looked like a friend of Al Capone – and the club was his life. He was not only the manager, he was the secretary, the treasurer, the physio; in fact, he ran the club almost single-handed. He looked towards the line of shambling characters eagerly awaiting the start of an afternoon of shouting. 'We'll ha' tae strip the support!' He cupped his hands and bawled in the direction of the assembled supporters. 'We're a man doon! One o' ye, get yer kit on. Come on noo!'

'Strip the support' became a regular cry at Yoker Fernlea. The man who drew the short straw usually had an uncomfortable afternoon. These men were not prepared for the rough and tumble of the games and Alf had vivid memories of white, skinny legs and baggy shirts flapping on scrawny torsos as the 'support' was thrust unmercifully into battle. They soon discovered that watching was considerably less exacting than playing, as heaving, sweating forms bludgeoned into their pale bodies.

In the mid 1960s when Alf was starting to write, he produced several short stories which failed to reach publication. One of these was about a timorous, downtrodden little man whose only escape from his aimless life was on a Saturday afternoon when he gave vent to his feelings by screaming at the players on the football pitch from the sideline. It was the only time he felt powerful. His world collapsed around him one day when he himself had to turn out and perform on the field – his frail body almost destroyed by the conflict. This story was based on Alf's own observations of the uncomfortable afternoons experienced by the 'support' on the raw football parks of Glasgow. It was another of the many vivid memories he committed to paper, but one that was never published.

Alf played his last game for Yoker Fernlea on an ash pitch one afternoon at Govan, a hard and uncompromising part of the city. His team committed one serious error that afternoon. They won. The referee for the game, intimidated by the crowd, did his utmost to sway the game their opponent's way, but Yoker Fernlea still won. The local supporters vented their displeasure by attacking the players who barricaded themselves in a shed while hooligans tried to break down the door. It was a frightening experience and one which made Alf think twice about continuing to play. He was going to enter a rough and sometimes dangerous profession but there was no point in getting himself maimed before he started. He would play for Yoker Fernlea no more.

That unnerving experience in Govan, however, was not his last game of football in Glasgow. He played several games for Old Kilpatrick Amateurs in the West of Scotland Amateur League, as well as turning out regularly for the veterinary college team. There was not so much pressure playing in this team. Games often took place on a Saturday following the Friday night dances at the college, with many of the participants in no condition to start charging around a football field. The exercise was good, however, and helped to dispel the hangovers induced by the previous night's revelry.

He played alongside many of his friends, including Bob Smith, Eddie Straiton, Donald McIntyre, Adam Farrell, Johnny Ogg, George Mcleod and V. J. (Pat) O'Reilly. During one weekend spent visiting Dublin to play the veterinary college there, they all had such a rubustuous weekend that Alf wrote an essay about their experiences. Although having by now abandoned the conscientious keeping of his diary, the urge to preserve his memories to print had not been lost.

In 1936, the Wight family had moved from their home in 2172 Dumbarton Road to take up residence, about two miles away, in a semi-detached house at 724 Anniesland Road, Scotstounhill.

One of the reasons the family were able to move to a more salubrious area was that they had inherited some money. Alf's grandfather, James Wight, died in Sunderland in November 1934, and he had left a tidy sum. The estate was valued at £7,366 which, in those days, was quite a fortune. He had been a frame-turner in the shipyards but also a bit of a property speculator. He had owned no less than six houses which, after his death, were distributed among his offspring – bequeathing to Pop his house in 65 Fulwell Road, Sunderland, together with a share in the residue of the estate.

Their new house was on a relatively quiet road, commanding fine views of the hills surrounding the city. Although close to their previous home, it was very different – more like a leafy suburb, in contrast to the tenement-lined streets of industrial Yoker with their whining tram-cars and noisy public houses. Here Hannah had more room in which to carry on her thriving dress-making business, while Pop was still within easy reach of the fish and chip shop that was now providing him with an income. Not only did the move to the new house mean that Alf had the advantage of a quieter environment in which to study but, as he worked, he could pause occasionally to gaze happily from his bedroom window at the sweet places that had given him such pleasure, the Campsie Fells and the Kilpatrick Hills.

In September 1938, he was beginning, what he fervently hoped would be his final year, and he needed plenty of encouragement. Having failed his Pathology exam just two months previously, he realised that, although he was enjoying some great times with his friends, he must never lose sight of the most important objective of his life – to qualify as a veterinary surgeon. In that month, he got his head down; he knew that there was still a lot of work to be done.

CHAPTER SIX

For the Glasgow Veterinary College students, their studies took on some real meaning when they began to study Medicine and Surgery – the diagnosis and treatment of disease. They had the thrill of trying their hand at surgical procedures, getting a feel for their future lives as veterinary surgeons.

In their study of Pathology, they had been introduced to diseases like tuberculosis, liver-fluke, anthrax and 'wooden tongue' as well as micro-organisms with imposing names such as *Fasciola hepatica, Corynebacterium pyogenes, Dictyocaulus viviparus, Fusiformis necrophorus* and many others. Now they were learning how to combat these adversaries and it was a hard but fascinating challenge. When studying Medicine and Surgery, the students had to master text books on these subjects – assimilating the knowledge from such revered tomes as Udall's *Practice of Veterinary Medicine*, Dollar's *Veterinary Surgery*, and Caulton Reeke's *Colics in the Horse* – but the practical side of their education had to be learned outside the college. The students were assigned to various veterinary practitioners in the Glasgow district, in order for them to acquire some hands-on experience.

A number of these outside vets also lectured at the college. Professor Willie Robb, who taught Medicine and Surgery in the final year, ran a thriving practice in Glasgow, assisted by his son Harry, and was one of the most respected practitioners in the country at the time. Willie Robb, a highly-skilled surgeon, gained a great reputation as a horse specialist, having lived through the great days of the heavy draught horses when the City of Glasgow was full of them. His experience with horses was second to none, and Alf learned a great deal from him.

Another whom he held in great esteem was Bill Weipers, a veterinary surgeon who ran a small animal surgery in the West End of Glasgow. The animal receiving most attention from the teaching institutions in those days was the horse, followed by the cow, pig and sheep, with the smaller animals, dogs and cats, receiving far less consideration. Bill Weipers could see, even during those years of the depression, that the small animal could become a very important part of the future veterinary surgeon's life. X-Ray machines, microscopes and all the best up-to-date equipment littered the premises of this skilful surgeon, who was performing operations that others only dreamed about. He was a man years ahead of his time and the Glasgow students were incredibly fortunate to operate under his guidance. Bill Weipers later became the principal of the Glasgow Veterinary College, integrating it into the city's university system in 1949. This industrious and dedicated man, who was to receive a knighthood in recognition of his services to the profession, was one whom Alfred Wight held in the highest regard, not only in his student years but throughout his life as a veterinary surgeon.

Donald Campbell of Rutherglen was another distinguished veterinary surgeon with whom Alf spent some time. He learned much from this go-ahead practitioner, but his fondest memory of him – one that he would never be able to recall without tears of laughter – was at the end of evening surgery when Donald Campbell would telephone his wife, informing her that he was on his way home. An unvarying ritual was performed so often that Alf became almost hysterical in trying not to laugh every time he listened to it.

Donald Campbell had an ancient telephone system by means of which, when the day's work was over, he would contact his wife by cranking vigorously on a black handle attached to the phone. Having completed several energetic twirls on the handle, he would shout loudly into the mouthpiece, with a piercing and distinctive drawl, 'Calling the ha-ouse, calling the ha-ouse!' There would then be a tense pause while Donald waited for a response, followed by a faint ping from the other end and a low chattering noise while he listened intently. Having received the necessary information that he was through to the ha-ouse, he would then inform his wife that he was on his way home. 'I'll be na-ow, I'll be na-ow!'

This set piece, which never varied, put enormous strain upon Alf's powers of self-control. He enacted the ritual for his friends at the college, which so intrigued Aubrey Melville that he requested a day seeing practice at Donald Campbell's surgery. At the end of that particular day, Alf and Aubrey were in a state of high tension waiting for the famous telephone ritual. Aubrey was so charged up that the slightest nudge would have been enough to send him over the edge. When Campbell moved over to the black handle, the pressure was really on, and once the cranking began, Aubrey was at breaking point. True to form, Donald's voice pierced the silence with, 'Calling the ha-ouse, calling the ha-ouse!' Aubrey Melville was nowhere to be seen. He had disappeared into a nearby cupboard, his head buried deeply into an old curtain. By the time, 'I'll be na-ow, I'll be na-ow!' came over the airwaves, he was writhing on the floor.

Despite being such an unconscious source of amusement to the students, Donald Campbell was held in high regard. He was a first-class veterinary surgeon and the students gained tremendous experience while under his care.

Alf saw plenty of small animal work with Bill Weipers, while Donald Campbell gave him a taste of life with the large animals as well as the small, but he wanted next to spend some time with a specialist country veterinary surgeon. At this point in his life, he thought that he would probably become purely a small animal veterinary surgeon. Nevertheless, he wanted to get among cows to observe the life of the large animal veterinarian for himself. He had already worked with some cows. Not far from his home in Scotstounhill was a dairy farm run by a man called Mr Stirling, and Alf was a regular visitor there in his final two years at the college. He had the opportunity to observe the cows, milk them by hand, assist during calving and examine any that were ill.

During the vacations in his final two years at the college, he went further afield to gain this experience, first seeing practice at Dumfries in the south-west of Scotland with a veterinary surgeon called Tom Fleming. He soon discovered that life among the large animals was very different from that among the clean and orderly small animal surgeries in Glasgow. This part of Scotland is the home of the Galloway cattle and, although they can be very docile animals if left to get on with their lives, they respond spectacularly to any hint of interference. The veterinary surgeon is often an unwilling participant on these occasions.

Alf and Tom Fleming visited a farm one day to remove an afterbirth from a Galloway cow of uncertain temperament which, miraculously, the farmer had managed to tie up in an old hen-house of dubious construction. On entering the dark little shed, the men received a hostile glare from their patient who further showed her displeasure by savagely switching her tail from side to side, propelling liquid faeces in every direction. The prospect of making any sort of contact with this animal was not an appetising one.

Alf, following Tom Fleming's generous gesture in allowing him the privilege of removing the afterbirth, soaped his arms in a bucket of water, advanced towards the cow and gave a gentle pull at the mass hanging from her rear end. The following few seconds were lively ones. The cow burst forward with a deafening bellow, and as the chain around her neck sprang open she saw her line of escape. There was a small window in front of her and she charged straight for it. Her head smashed through the opening as she plunged forward, taking one end of the old hen-house with her. The remainder of the 'building' collapsed on top of the men as she catapulted away over a large field, her rate of progress seemingly unhampered by the splintered remnants of the shed still around her neck.

As the three men watched the ruined hen-house thunder over the horizon, the farmer displayed the qualities of a man who could make an instant decision in a crisis. 'Let the bugger go!' he yelled.

'*What* sort of a cow was that?' thought Alf. It bore little resemblance to the docile creatures he milked on Mr Stirling's farm in Glasgow. At that moment, he had no inkling that unplanned rodeos among the bovine race were to figure prominently in his future life.

Some more surprises were in store. One of the more unpleasant aspects of a veterinary surgeon's life is the wide range of amazing smells that assails the nostrils – smells taken for granted by the experienced veterinary surgeon but which can come as a considerable shock to those who are unused to them. Alf had experienced plenty of challenging smells in the small animal clinics in Glasgow, but he was unprepared for the fresh olfactory experience that awaited him as he and Tom Fleming walked into a large knacker's yard near Dumfries.

These establishments, now no longer in existence, disposed of fallen stock and unfit meat; being full of dead and decomposing animals, they were not the most edifying of places. Young Alf Wight had not been inside this one for more than a few seconds before he, quite spontaneously, vomited his breakfast straight out onto the floor. The smell that had hit him was quite unlike anything he had experienced, a mixture of decaying organs and the sickly sweet smell of fresh blood. Mountains of skins, bowels and bones loomed over him while a bright green piglet lying at his feet did little to ease the situation. His reaction was watched with mild interest by a slaughterman who was sitting on a carcass, happily munching at a large sandwich, a fat-smeared, blood-stained teacup in his hand. This man, wallowing amongst, possibly, every pathogenic organism known to mankind, was the picture of health.

His pink, shining face broke into a smile. 'Dae ye no like the smell?' he laughed. 'Ah widnae worry, they all dae that when they first walk in here!'

Many years later, as a qualified veterinary surgeon, Alf would watch, with equal amusement, other young students struggling to come to terms with the bombardment of smells from a knacker's yard that he himself by then regularly entered with nonchalance.

There was another veterinary surgeon with whom Alf saw practice during his final two years at the veterinary college. J. J. McDowall, a vet in Sunderland, was someone who played a very influential part in Alf's life, both before and after his qualification from Glasgow Veterinary College.

During his regular visits to his relatives in Sunderland, he would stay in Beechwood Terrace with his Auntie Jinny Wilkins. Not only was her home very close to J. J. McDowall's practice, but she used to attend his surgery with her dog, Bonzo. Alf, at her suggestion, enquired whether it might be possible to obtain some practical experience with him. This request, which was readily agreed to, began a friendship between the two men which would last for many years.

These were the days before the Veterinary Surgeons Act of 1948 which prohibited the practising of veterinary medicine and surgery by non-qualified people. Prior to this, students could work unsupervised among animals, and McDowall often left Alf to run surgeries single-handed. He wrote a letter to his parents in 1938 from Sunderland:

'Down at the clinic (where Wight is in charge) I had to remove a tumour from a dog aged 12 years and after hacking away for a bit found it was attached to a testicle – so I had to remove the testicle too . . . a bigger job than I had ever tackled. I can tell you, I wished Mac had been by my side. I sent the dog away with a horrible wound and never expected to see it alive again. But, strange to say, it turned up for dressing two days later, bright and frisky and the wound beautifully clean. I felt immensely bucked up about it.'

At this stage of his life, while still only a student, he was experiencing the pressures and emotions that typify the veterinary surgeon's day: the anxious waiting to know whether your patient is going to survive; the joy and satisfaction of a job well done. There can be no doubt that the Veterinary Surgeons Act is a necessary one. It is wrong that inexperienced people should work on animals without adequate supervision, and the Act was passed to protect the interests of the patient. Nevertheless, students in those earlier years certainly gained wonderful experience from being thrown in at the deep end.

Back in Glasgow, Alf spent most of his time studying. He was now in the 'home straight', with only the passing of Medicine and Surgery standing between him and a career as a veterinary surgeon. But it was not all work; some recreation was essential to break the long sessions of swotting he put in, secreted up in his little bedroom in Anniesland Road. He went walking and played tennis as much as he dared, but it was on Saturday nights that he and his friends would go to the cinema or go dancing in the big Glasgow ballrooms.

On a more cultural note, he frequently went to the theatre with his mother. Glasgow boasted a huge number, and the Regal, La Scala, the Playhouse and the Alhambra were theatres that Alf got to know well. It was here that he acquired not only an appreciation of classical music but, also, considerable knowledge of the subject. One of his greatest memories as a young man was hearing Rachmaninov play his Second Piano Concerto in a Glasgow concert hall. He and his mother who were seated very close to the stage, watched, spellbound, as the great man, crouching like a bear over the keys, played some of the most wonderful music they had ever heard.

Music a few rungs down the ladder of culture was to be heard at the veterinary college dances at Buccleuch Street on most Friday nights, and Alf regularly attended these throbbing sessions. The governing body of the college needed to turn a blind eye to the dances; if they had not done so, those riotous functions might well have been terminated.

Alex Taylor heard about the dances and asked if he could attend one. It turned out to be an evening he was never to forget. When Mrs Taylor learned that her son was going to the next vet college dance, she asked Alf, 'I've heard that these occasions can be a wee bit rough, Alf, and I've heard that some rather odd women attend them. Now, Alex won't get into any trouble, will he?'

He was quick to reassure her. 'Oh goodness me, no, Mrs Taylor. It's just a wee bit of a get-together with a few of the lads and then we just stroll up to the college to have a few dances before going off home. Don't you worry yourself. Alex will be fine, just fine.'

He did not think it necessary to tell Mrs Taylor that this was also 'freshers' night' which added that little extra spice to the evening's activities. It began, as usual, in a public house in Glasgow. The place was bulging with students and Alex was soon enjoying himself. The noise was stupendous, with everyone laughing, including Alex, who seemed to be surrounded at all times by red, sweating faces. Any semblance of intelligent conversation soon melted away as the rate of consumption of beer and whisky accelerated.

Eventually, closing time was rung, and they were evicted noisily onto the city streets. Alex can vaguely remember Alf carrying aloft a lifesize cardboard figure of 'Johnny Walker', as the swaying column of students ascended the hill to Buccleuch Street. By this time, Alex's mouth was hanging open and everything was a blur; it seemed that the whole of Glasgow was revolving before his eyes. The students decided to crash past the officials at the gates of the college to avoid paying the modest entrance fee. This was only partially successful as, in the ensuing fracas, Alex received a massive blow on the chin which laid him out.

This posed a dilemma for Alf. Here was his best friend whom he had brought to the vet college dance for the first time. It was meant to be a good night out with the lads but, instead, he was pole-axed. What was he going to do with him? It did not help that Alf was in a high state of intoxication himself and in no real condition to help anyone. The serene expression upon Alex's face led his friend to suspect that the blow he had just received was not entirely responsible for his present condition – but he still had a crisis on his hands.

Suddenly, he had a burst of inspiration. The dance, as always, was taking place on the upper floor of the veterinary college and, in the yard below, he saw several long boxes filled with wood shavings. These seven-foot long containers had carried a supply of new microscopes and other laboratory equipment. 'The very thing!' thought Alf. 'Let's put Alex in one of those. He will be comfortable in among the shavings and I can keep an eye on him from up here.'

With the dubious assistance of several inebriated friends, he dragged the limp form of Alex down the steps to the yard below, his heels drumming rhythmically on the steel stairway. When they reached the chosen box there was a snag – Dominic Boyce was already inside, deeply embedded in the shavings. He was wearing a flat cap, his face a ghastly bluish tinge. One of the students, on seeing the staring, sunken eyeballs, said that Dom must be dead. 'Don't worry,' replied another, 'he always goes that colour.'

The second box was also occupied; another student was comfortably in residence, a peaceful half-smile on his sleeping face. Alf began to wonder whether every box would contain a moribund student, but he was in luck. An empty one was eventually found and Alex was lowered gently inside. Having made sure that his old friend was comfortably tucked up amongst the shavings, Alf gave a final glance at the rows of boxes, each containing its silent occupant, before heading to the pulsating noise above on the dance floor.

Alf remembered little about the rest of the evening, save that he thought the police were involved at some point. Somehow, he and Alex, who had spent the remainder of the evening at peace with the world, found their way home. Alex was relieved that his mother was away at the time but, when she returned a day or two later, she said to him, 'I believe that you had a good night at the vet dance, Alex.'

'Yes, I had an excellent evening, thank you,' he replied.

'I know,' she went on, 'I read all about it!'

Not for the first time, the Glasgow veterinary students had made the pages of the press.

Alf took a number of young ladies to dances in Glasgow but one thing he spoke very little about was his experiences with members of the fairer sex, and consequently there is precious little information about his youthful romances. He definitely had several girlfriends but he had no steady relationships until his final couple of years at college, and these were soon forgotten after he left Glasgow.

While he still lived in Yoker, he had a soft spot for a young lady called Jean Wilson and went out quite regularly with her during his time at Hillhead, but he was very young and it was never really serious. Charlotte Clarke was a girl he met while on a Boys' Brigade weekend, and he kept in touch with her for about a year. He appeared really keen on her, describing her in his diary as 'The sweetest thing I have ever known.' This friendship, however, was terminated when Charlotte decided to give him the elbow during his second year at veterinary college. Young Alf was quite upset; he was always a sensitive person and capable of becoming extremely emotionally involved.

While on one of his camping weekends at Rosneath, he met a girl called Marion Grant. He went out regularly with her throughout his college years, and kept up a correspondence with her after he left Glasgow; in fact, he was still writing to her during his first few months as a qualified veterinary surgeon in Yorkshire. He did not regard this relationship as a particularly serious one, however, as he was seeing someone else at the same time. She was called Nan Elliot and came from Knightswood, not far from where Alf lived in Scotstounhill. This young lady also continued to correspond with Alf long after he left Glasgow.

He certainly enjoyed female company during his time at the veterinary college but there would be only one deep and lasting relationship in his life, and it was not during his years as a young man in Glasgow.

In July 1939, Alf Wight sat his final qualifying examinations in Veterinary Medicine and Surgery. He was longing to finish being a student and begin his chosen career but it was not to be; he passed Medicine but failed his Surgery exam. He would have to wait a while longer before leaving the veterinary college.

This came as a severe blow but it was not that surprising. His anal fistula had struck again and he was very ill in the months preceding the exams. The condition became so painful that he underwent a second operation in the Western Infirmary in Glasgow and, in his words, 'Had my backside rearranged again!' He did well to pass in Medicine while carrying such a debilitating condition.

His friend Jock McDowall, the vet in Sunderland, was full of admiration for him, and wrote to Alf in August 1939: 'I fully expect you will have had your operation by this time and you're possibly not feeling too good. I expect the surgeon would make what is commonly called a few heroic gashes in your tender spot. You were unfortunate in getting asked all those questions about the Corpus luteum and Graafian follicles in your oral. I couldn't have said much myself about the subject. However, it says a whole lot when you sailed through Medicine. By Jove, you must have put in some graft despite not feeling too well; you deserve a medal.'

His father was very upset when Alf failed his final exam in Surgery. Pop, the eternal pessimist, had never encouraged his son to enter the veterinary profession. He had always believed that Alf was taking a big chance entering a profession where one of its main sources of revenue, the heavy draught horse, was rapidly being replaced by mechanisation, but he still shared his son's deep disappointment when he failed to qualify.

For Pop himself, the outlook was better. Although his fish and chip shop business had failed around 1936, he soon found alternative employment, working as a shipyard clerk for Yarrow's down by the

Clyde. Unlike his son, Pop had a good head for figures, with a neat hand and an organised mind; an ideal man for such a job. With the threat of possible war with Germany, the fortunes of the Glasgow shipyards were beginning to pick up as the demand for ships grew, and Pop was enjoying a more secure financial position than he had for many years.

As Alf began to study for his re-taking of the Surgery exam in December, Pop had even more reason to hope that his son would pass. When Britain and France declared war on Germany in September 1939, Pop knew this could mean his son having to serve his country in the armed forces. The veterinary profession was regarded as a 'reserved occupation' – one whose services would be needed at home – and Pop had no desire to see Alf risk his life on foreign fields.

Alf had few qualms about serving his country if needs be. The recent involvement of the International Brigade in the desperately fought Spanish Civil War, where thousands of young men from Britain and other countries had voluntarily given their lives in the fight against Fascism, had stirred the patriotism of many, and Alf was no exception.

However, to achieve his full qualification as a veterinary surgeon was his number one priority. Apart from wanting to start work properly, his perpetual dependence upon his parents also worried him. Although their financial position was by no means parlous, he wished to be a burden upon them no longer.

During that Autumn term of 1939, he felt a little better and worked feverishly to pass this last obstacle. After the exam, he thought he had done well enough, but he still awaited the day of the results with rising tension. That day duly arrived, with Alf one of a large crowd of students jostling for position in front of the notice board, eyes desperately scanning the list for the names of those who had passed. The name of James Alfred Wight was not there. At that moment, he felt only one emotion – despair. Deep, deep despair. He had done his best but he had failed again, and he wondered for how many more years he would have to remain anchored to Buccleuch Street.

He was about to return home to give his parents the shattering news when a door opened and an official of the college walked out to stick another piece of paper onto the notice board. 'My apologies, gentlemen!' he said. 'There has been a clerical error. Another name is to be added to the list.'

That name was J. A. Wight.

As the shaken but immensely relieved young man walked through the streets of Glasgow that day, he felt as if the old college, reluctant to lose another student to the outside world, had made a last despairing snatch at him.

On 14 December 1939, Alfred Wight officially qualified from Glasgow Veterinary College as a fully-fledged Member of the Royal College of Veterinary Surgeons. He had taken six and a quarter years to complete a five-year course but, compared to some of the other semi-permanent students, he had attained his goal with admirable speed. He did not leave the college without a twinge of regret. In his introduction to *James Herriot's Dog Stories*, he expressed his feelings for his old seat of learning:

When I qualified and walked out of the door of the college for the last time I felt an acute sense of loss, an awareness of something good gone forever. Some of my happiest years were spent in that seedy old building and though my veterinary course was out of date and inefficient in many ways, there was a carefree, easy-going charm about that whole time which has held it in my mind in a golden glow.

The young Alf Wight emerged from Glasgow Veterinary College a much wiser man. He had absorbed a huge amount of information but his learning curve had only just begun. It was one that would never end.

CHAPTER SEVEN

During that final term, Alf had had an incentive to work extra hard. For many of his friends who had qualified with him, their troubles were only just beginning as the daunting prospect of trying to find a job loomed before them. For James Alfred Wight MRCVS, however, things were a little different. He had a job waiting for him. The town of his birth had beckoned him back; he was to be assistant to J. J. McDowall MRCVS of 1 Thornhill Terrace, Sunderland.

It is a widely-held belief that the real James Herriot launched out on his professional career as assistant to 'Siegfried Farnon' in the York-shire Dales. Indeed, the author himself leads us to believe this; nowhere in his books is there any reference to his being employed anywhere other than in that magical part of Yorkshire that he would make so famous.

His first job, in fact, was in Sunderland and, although he spent barely six months in the employment of McDowall, it was an eventful period in his life, so much so that several chapters in the early Herriot books are based upon people and incidents from that seminal stage of the young man's career.

Alf learned a great deal in that time, much of which he was never to forget. J. J. McDowall was an experienced and clever man, well-versed in the 'art' as well as the 'science' of veterinary medicine, and Alf soon realised that the 'art' was every bit as, if not more important than, the 'science'.

As he travelled south to work in his first position as a qualified veterinary surgeon on that day in January 1940, he knew for certain that he was an extremely fortunate young man. He was walking straight into a job while many of his friends had either failed their exams or, having qualified, had little prospect of employment for the foreseeable future. These were awful days for newly-qualified veterinary surgeons. The depression had meant that jobs were scarce, and working conditions primitive. Those applying for what jobs existed were regarded as lower forms of life to whom prospective employers could dictate their own terms. For those managing to obtain employment, poor pay with long hours was all they could expect; indeed, in many cases, time off work was unheard of.

The situation was so dire that some young men advertised in the *Veterinary Record*, the official journal of the British Veterinary Association, offering their services free of charge. 'Fit, strong, able young man. Will work for keep' became a common sight in the advertising pages of the journal, and many of Alf's friends 'worked for their keep' in those hard days. For an employer, it was an attractive proposition: feed a man, put a roof over his head and he'll work for you for nothing.

The prospective assistant today faces a vastly different picture. With plenty of jobs available, the new graduate can afford to be selective. Good pay, civilised working conditions with ample leisure time – in some cases with no night duties to be undertaken at all – go towards presenting the young veterinary surgeon with an enviable choice. What a stark contrast to those bleak conditions years ago.

Alf wrote in a letter to his parents while in Sunderland: 'I had a very funny letter from Bob Smith. He is still working on the land, poor lad, and is fed up but still maintains his dry humour. He says that when he puts his height in when applying for the jobs advertised in the Record, he adds an inch every time, but though he is now 6 ft 8 ins it doesn't weigh the scales!'

At least Bob Smith had qualified. It was worse for some of Alf's other friends, still trying to pass their exams at the veterinary college. The failure rate was to remain high, as Alf revealed in a letter written some months later: 'Poor Aubrey is down in both subjects and so is Tom Black. Sickening, isn't it? But they hadn't a fair break because Eddie Straiton wrote and told me there was nearly a 70% plough; they won't let them through when there is a shortage of jobs. Poor Andy Flynn is down in both Pathology and parasites for the fifth time. Thank the Lord I'm out of that business.'

There is little wonder that Alf was counting his blessings as he began his employment with Jock McDowall. He received a salary of £3 3s per week which was roughly the going rate at the time. This sum won't even buy a gallon of fuel today but he was thankful that he was, at least, receiving a salary. He had the additional advantage that he could stay at his Auntie Jinny's house in Beechwood Terrace. He paid £1 per week for his board and lodgings – good value considering his aunt's reputation as an excellent cook. Malnutrition would not be one of his worries in the weeks ahead.

Alf's position at McDowall's was, however, a tenuous one. The reason that J. J. McDowall was able to offer Alf a job was that he had a contract at the nearby South Shields Greyhound Racing Stadium where he was the 'veterinary surgeon in attendance'. However, the track at the time was in a questionable financial state and Jock had warned Alf that should it become insolvent, his position at McDowall's could be terminated. McDowall had, in fact, offered the job to Alf at the end of 1938, and the young man had seized the opportunity with both hands. Plans had been thrown into confusion in July 1939 when he failed his final examination in Surgery, but the Sunderland vet held him in such high regard that he was prepared to wait until the following year, keeping the position on hold for him.

Alf, despite being fully aware that his employment could be terminated at a moment's notice, embarked upon his job full of enthusiasm. This was fortuitous as he had a stern baptism. Only a day or two after his arrival, his employer took to his bed with a severe attack of influenza, and remained there for two full weeks. Alf had to run the practice single-handed – great experience but emotionally and physically exhausting. A further problem was that, since he still had not passed his driving test, not only had he to fit driving lessons into his already crowded schedule, but a qualified driver – an elderly friend of the McDowalls – had to accompany him on his rounds.

Alf always referred to McDowall as 'Mac' who, in return and for some unknown reason, addressed my father as 'Fred'. I suspect that he did not like the name Alfred and decided to use the back half instead. This was no hardship for Alf as he never liked his name anyway; even as a young child, I was aware that he regarded the name Alfred as a cross he had to bear.

He never forgot Mac's opening words to him as he began his first day's work. 'Welcome to Sunderland, Fred! You'll see a bit of everything here, but I like my dog and cat work best of all. These small animals are the things that pay. The folk around here will rush their pet to me at the drop of a hat. They're in through that door if it coughs, sneezes or farts!'

J. J. McDowall was a small, red-faced man whose rich, imposing voice and impressive moustache bestowed a military air upon him. His florid complexion owed much to a regular consumption of alcohol and he never missed an opportunity of a good night out provided it was liberally laced with drink. Mac was only one of countless veterinary

surgeons in Alf Wight's day who jousted on the frontiers of alcoholism.
There is no doubt that, at the end of a hard day, the world becomes
far more attractive after one or two drinks, but many of his colleagues
turned this pleasant antidote to the day's labours into a crusade. Tales
of the hard-drinking vets of that time are legion and Alf was to spend
many hours with them, both at work and at play.

In a letter in which he describes a night out with Mr and Mrs
McDowall, he refers to Mac's weakness for the bottle: 'The "do" was
held at the Rink which, as you know, is an unlicensed premises, so I
wondered how Mrs McD had persuaded Mac to go. However, I had
reason to repair to the gent's lavatory and there found Mac with the
inevitable bottle of whisky dishing out measures to his pals – various
notable solicitors, Rotarians etc, all in their tails.'

Alf was to appreciate the fragility of his position only too soon. In
mid January, less than two weeks after he had arrived in Sunderland,
he received the news he had been dreading. Mac had been informed
that the greyhound stadium was faced with closure and he had no
alternative but to advise his young colleague to look elsewhere for a
job as he could no longer afford to employ him.

This news marked a grim period in Alf's life. He heard there was a
job in Guisborough, a town on the edge of the North York Moors
about twenty-five miles south of Sunderland; he applied at once but
was turned down. With no money and little prospect of a job, he began
to wonder seriously whether he had made the right decision in becoming
a veterinary surgeon. He felt pitched into the same hapless situation
facing so many of his college friends – no job, no prospects and no
money. A letter to his parents dated 14 January 1940 gives an insight
into the parlous situation facing the young veterinary surgeons of the
day.

My dear Mother and Dad,

I'm afraid I have some bad news and I may as well get it over with. I don't
get the job at Guisborough. McDonald, the vet there, received an application
from a man from Skye and as he is from Skye himself that was that. Don't
be too despondent about this; it's a big disappointment but remember that
fellows like me are being turned down all over the country. Mac's ill and won't
be up for another few days so I'll be OK for another week's pay, but after that,
what?

If it's all the same to you folks I think it would be better if I stayed on here even though I get no more pay. You see, I get free driving practice, I'm in touch with veterinary affairs and, most important of all, I would get no chance to get rusty and stale as I would at home with nowt to do. Here, I'm learning every day and there is just a chance that Mac might slip me something now and again towards my board. Don't be too upset about the job, something may turn up.

As to recreation, I have had none and haven't seen any of my friends and relatives. I get home just in time for a game of cards with George and then early to bed. Mac hasn't given me my pay yet but he slipped me a quid on account at the beginning of the week so I was able to get Auntie Jinny a bottle of lavender water for her birthday.

Love Alf

P.S. Feeling fine!

Alf did not want to worry his parents but he was, in fact, far from fine. The painful effects of the operation on the anal fistula in Glasgow the previous year had shown a stubborn reluctance to abate, with the result that he suffered constant discomfort and at times he endured excruciating agony. The effects of the 'old fist', a term he frequently used when referring to his omnipresent affliction, were so severe while he was in Sunderland that there were days when he wanted to 'just lie down and die'. Those very first days of his professional career – ones that should have been full of excitement and optimism – were actually some of the darkest of his life.

A mere ten days later, however, his fortunes took a sudden turn for the better. Mac, after being drawn into consultation with the National Greyhound Racing Board over the future of the South Shields Stadium, was offered the job of veterinary adviser at the track, part of a team set up to revitalise the stadium. He could now afford to keep Alf on as his assistant with, as the icing on the cake, a salary soaring to £4 4s per week. To add to this upturn in his fortunes, Alf passed his driving test at the end of January. Fate was smiling once again on the young man.

After that turbulent beginning to his first professional job, Alf felt determined to make the best of his time in Sunderland by learning as much as he could. This he certainly did, and it was here that he received a lesson in the 'art' of veterinary practice which would remain with him forever.

One morning, after a hard night on the town, Mac was feeling particularly delicate. His blotchy face and bloodshot eyes were evidence that his system had received another searching examination. There was a call to a calving and Mac was in no mood for a trial of strength in an icy cow byre. He looked blearily at his young colleague. 'Fred,' he said, 'there's a cow calving over at Horden. They've been trying to calve her for over two hours and they're beat. Just slip over and do it, will you?'

Alf, eager to impress, set off in his rattly old car. He arrived at the farm to find a pair of dejected-looking farmers standing beside a cow. There was no sign that she was calving save for a few inches of a small tail hanging from her vulva. Alf removed his shirt, soaped his arms thoroughly, and gently inserted a hand into the cow's vagina. He soon discovered that the calf was abnormally presented. It was coming backwards with the legs folded underneath, its rump blocking the birth canal. This presentation – known as a 'breech' – can be tricky, but the young vet had done one or two as a student. He was going to enjoy this; here was a chance to create a really good impression.

Working quickly and smoothly, he produced a live calf within fifteen minutes, followed by another five minutes later. It was a job well done but there were no words of gratitude from the farmers, no pats on the back with a cry of 'Well done, young man!' He received only a stony silence and a terse wave of farewell.

When he got back to the practice, he went to find Mac. 'They're a miserable lot out there, Mac,' he said, recounting the morning's work. 'What do I have to do to please them? If I'd conjured up a few more calves they still wouldn't have been happy.'

Mac had had a while to recover from the previous evening's festivities and was feeling chirpier. He thought for a while and stroked his moustache. Then he looked at his unhappy young colleague. 'Well done, Fred!' he barked. 'Don't worry, you've done a good job – but tell me, how long did you take to produce those two calves? About fifteen to twenty minutes, you say?'

'Yes,' Alf replied. 'It was a good fast job although I say it myself.'

Mac thought for a moment. 'Do you know what I think, Fred? You got 'em out a bit too quick!'

'I beg your pardon?'

'You just think about this. Those two farmers have been struggling on for two hours or more and you come along and the whole show is over in a few minutes! It makes them look a bit stupid! And another thing. They're paying us good money to calve that cow and you have made it all look a bit too simple! If I had been there, I would have made

1. Hannah Bell

2. James Henry Wight

3. The formal family photograph following the wedding of Hannah and James Wight, July 1915. The two young men in uniform in the front row are, *left*, Alfred Wight, after whom Alf was named and, *right*, Stan Bell, Hannah's brother; between them are Pop's two sisters, Jennie and Ella. Bob and Matt Wight are on either end of the back row; below Bob is Auntie Jinny and her husband, George Wilkins

4. A typical tenement building in Yoker where Alf spent the early years of his life

5. Pop (at the piano), with some of the members of the Glasgow Society of Musicians

6. Alf, on right, with young friend
Lawrence Tyreman, in Sunderland

7. Jim and Hannah Wight, with young Alfie

8. Alf on holiday with his parents at Inverbeg by Loch Lomond:
one hopes they did not have far to walk

9. Alf with Jack Dinsdale

10. Alf between Auntie Jinny and his mother and, behind, George, Nan and Stan Wilkins

11. Several holidaying families gathered together near High Force

12. (*Top*) With Don as a young puppy

13. (*Left*) Alf with Stan Wilkins and hairy friend

14. Alf while he was at Hillhead School

15. Ready to turn out for the Glasgow Veterinary College football team

16. The Glasgow Veterinary College football team. Alf is in the centre row on the left with Bob Smith in fifth position and Eddie Straiton third from right. Aubrey Melville is in the front row, on the far left, predictably with a girl next to him

17. With his mother in Llandudno, *c.* 1937

18. Alf and Peter Shaw beside Loch Ness, their bare legs fair game for the midges

19. The Boys' Brigade relaxing on the beach at North Berwick.
From left to right: Alf, Eddie Hutchinson, Pete Shaw and Alex Taylor

20. Alf with Donald Sinclair and Eric Parker, in the garden at 23 Kirkgate

the job appear very difficult. I would have shown them that they were getting their money's worth. Never make a job look too easy, Fred.'

Alf listened in silence. He was receiving one of his first lessons in the art of veterinary practice.

Mac gave his young assistant a pat on the shoulder. 'Cheer up, you've done a really good job!' He paused and a half-smile played across his face. 'Do you know, Fred,' he continued, 'there have been many occasions in the past where I have been manipulating calves inside cows, with the sweat pouring off me, holding the bloody things in!' Mac finished his little lecture with a statement that Alfred Wight would never forget; something that he, himself, would repeatedly drill into the many young assistants who would work under his guidance in the years to come. 'Remember this, Fred! It's not what you do, it's the way that you do it!'

Alf was beginning to realise, very quickly, that the acquisition of knowledge was, in itself, not enough to guarantee success in veterinary practice, but he was a willing listener, and he was learning fast. In those few months working in Sunderland, he learned a great deal about human nature, too, observing Mac's many moods as well as those of a great variety of people who came to the surgery in Thornhill Terrace. He also learned that he could easily be brought down to earth with a jolt, just as he was beginning to think that he was one of the finest vets in the land. With Mac, he learned that the life of a veterinary surgeon was one long, unpredictable succession of triumphs and failures.

One day, while operating on a horse with Mac, and feeling a bit low after a day of little success, he was gratified to learn that even the most respected members of his profession can lose their cloak of dignity at times. They were being helped by a local man who was telling them that, at his last place of employment, the great Professor Mitchell had been called to operate on a couple of young horses. Willie Mitchell was regarded as one of the finest horse surgeons in the land, and Alf was deeply impressed.

'It must have been a great experience to see him at work,' he said, wishing that he could have had the opportunity to observe such a revered and dignified figure. 'He must be a very impressive man.'

'Aye,' came the reply, '\'e's a clever feller, all right. 'E laid out them 'osses on the ground wi' chloroform an' 'e operated on 'em, smooth an' fast as yer like.'

'It must have been wonderful to see,' Alf continued, 'to watch a real artist at work, someone totally in control of the situation.' The man thought for a second or two, before leaning forward. His face broke into a grin. 'Mind yer, one o' them 'osses stopped breathin' – an' yer should 'ave seen 'im dancin' on the bugger's ribs!'

Alf may have been lucky to have a job but he had to work for his money. He worked almost every night with only an occasional Sunday afternoon off. He once had to summon up the courage to request a day off at Easter as his mother was coming down from Glasgow to visit her relatives. Mac nearly had a fit. One whole day! He was so taken aback by such an audacious request that the wish was granted.

As well as mediocre pay, the young veterinary surgeons of the day were given cars of very dubious reliability in which to travel to their visits. Alf Wight's car was no exception. To climb into his first car, a tiny Ford, was an adventure – a journey into the unknown. Each time he sat in its spartan interior, he weighed up the chances of arriving at his destination. On one occasion, he dented the wing of the car in a Sunderland street. Two men, who came to his assistance, lifted the whole car on to the pavement, gave the bodywork a mighty heave, and the damage was straightened out in a matter of seconds. The future James Herriot would have been just another statistic had he ever had a head-on collision in such a vehicle.

He gave a good description of life behind the wheel in one of his letters to his parents: 'The car, using the word in its broadest sense, makes a colossal din and, in the country, the birds rise from the hedges in fright and the cows and horses in the fields look definitely startled. The vibration is terrific over 35 mph and my liver will be in splendid condition after a month or two at it.'

Alf would go on to spend a large proportion of his life behind the wheel of a motor car. Those very first days on the road ensured that he was always the first to appreciate the comforts of modern motoring, comforts that he would not experience until very many years later.

The thrill of savouring his first job in veterinary practice received some added but not entirely welcome impetus from several visits by the German Air Force. In these early days of the war, the Sunderland area received many such attacks, with the big shipyards on the River Wear being the prime targets. Alf described, in a letter dated 30 January 1940, the frightening experience of treating a cow in the middle of an air raid: 'The enemy planes are giving our coast a lot of attention. Mac and I had a grandstand view of the whole show as we were at a farm on the water's edge in South Shields, just opposite the ships over which the enemy planes were diving and swooping. We saw all the firing from the AA batteries and the ships, and the Nazi being chased off by our fighters. The poor old cow didn't get much attention as we dashed out of the byre after every bang and left her!'

Nazi Germany may have removed a little of the gloss from Alf's enjoyment of his days in Sunderland, but there was one aspect of his work that he thoroughly hated. Although he realised that it was the dogs' very existence that had enabled him to keep his job, visits to the greyhound track at South Shields were ones he dreaded. His task of checking the animals before each race was an unenviable one. In those days, the track seemed to be patronised by many strange, furtive people who would stoop to any trick to win a race. Young Alf Wight, who had been brought up in such an honest and upright home, and could not identify with such devious behaviour, faced a barrage of abuse when he, rightly, would not allow dogs to race as the result of illness, or such practices as doping and overfeeding. He did not mind working hard for his money, but this was like threading his way through a minefield, with deceit and dishonesty shadowing his every move.

Many years after he became famous, with his financial status somewhat improved, he would recall those days at the dog track when he was a young vet with hardly a penny in the world. At the end of one of the meetings, he was downing a welcome cup of tea, seated opposite a bookmaker who was counting the takings for the day. Alf had never seen so much money in his life as the bookmaker continued to arrange notes and silver into huge piles on the table. He suddenly paused, taking in Alf's frayed shirt and raggedy trousers. He raised one eyebrow, grinned, gave a curt nod and casually flicked half a crown across the table before returning to his counting. As Alf would write in *Vets Might Fly*, in which he transposed his experiences at the dog track from Sunderland to Yorkshire, he felt grateful to the man, not just for the money, but for the rare experience of a gesture of friendship towards him.

Those impecunious days, however, provided the future James Herriot with many rich memories that, years later, he would recall in his books, and Mac would be one of the earliest of his veterinary acquaintances to be portrayed in them – albeit loosely. In the first two books, an unpleasant character called Angus Grier appears, and some of the incidents involving this man were based upon Alf's experiences in Sunderland. To be fair to Mac, he was in no way the disagreeable character that Angus Grier was. My father liked Mac and the two men developed a close friendship, but he was undoubtedly capable of displaying many different moods. He was not a man to be crossed and, when in a temper, it was wise to adopt a low profile.

Mac and his wife often invited Alf round for an evening meal, which was frequently followed by a game of table tennis or Monopoly. The sessions round the Monopoly board could be serious engagements. If Mac started to lose, tension soon sprang into the atmosphere, with any further deterioration in his fortunes inevitably leading to raised voices and the children running upstairs in tears to bed.

Alf would always remember this explosive but clever man with great affection and as yet another of the great characters who have graced the veterinary profession.

The insecurity of his position at McDowall's was never far from Alf's mind. With the ever-present threat of dismissal should the practice fall upon leaner times, he regularly scanned the *Veterinary Record* for alternative employment. Mac himself had assured Alf that prospects of his obtaining a permanent post within the practice were remote. Not that he relished the idea of going into partnership with Mac: he was a delightful man in many ways but one who enjoyed the high life a little too much. Alf envisaged years of slavery stretching ahead.

There was another reason for casting his net in more distant waters, and this was a reluctance to spend his future in Sunderland. The north-east of England had been hit especially hard during the depression and there was little money about. Although he had great affection for the place of his birth, Sunderland could be a grim place in which to work. During the winter months, which seemed to last for half the year, the north-east winds screamed into the town and roared along the streets, often accompanied by sleet, snow or freezing rain. Huge waves smashing onto the roads on the sea front, and the rows of drab, terraced houses standing defiantly against the elements epitomised the aura of depression that hung over the town. It was a dismal place to begin a professional career.

There were very few positions advertised in the veterinary journals but one day, while leafing through the pages of the *Record*, he noticed that there was one available in Thirsk. He had never heard of the place.

Where was Thirsk? Upon perusing a map, he discovered that it was in Yorkshire, only about fifty miles south of Sunderland. The job was described as 'Mainly agricultural work in a Yorkshire market town', with the principal of the practice being a veterinary surgeon by the name of D. V. Sinclair.

Although the majority of the work in Sunderland had been with dogs and cats, he was interested. He had enjoyed his taste of work with the larger animals and the thought of spending more time with farm animals intrigued him. Yorkshire held no particular appeal for him. He knew little about it – having an image of the county as a flat, industrial wasteland, full of smoking factory chimneys – but it was not far to go for a look. He wrote for an interview and, to his surprise, he received a reply. On a sunny day in June 1940, he set off to see Thirsk for himself.

Many people who have read the James Herriot books have their own particular favourites. My father's family and his close friends have little hesitation in nominating the first book, *If Only They Could Talk*, closely followed by the second, *It Shouldn't Happen to a Vet*. These two books, which were later combined into one volume under the title of *All Creatures Great and Small* for the American market, are full of the episodes that were already familiar to us since we had heard my father tell the stories so often.

The authenticity of the narrative added extra appeal. In these books are to be found many of the most colourful characters who entered his life at this point. Nowhere is his ability to manipulate the reader's emotions more brilliantly illustrated than in that first book which quietly appeared on the bookshelves of Britain in 1970. Here, the whole foundation of the Herriot saga is laid, upon which successive best-sellers were built. The scene is set as the reader is introduced first to the stage upon which his show would be performed – the town of Thirsk, to be immortalised in the books as Darrowby, and the Yorkshire Dales, among whose green pastures and high, windswept moorland he determined that his stories would unfold. The main characters that run through James Herriot's books appear in the pages of these early works – his partner Siegfried, Siegfried's younger brother, Tristan, and James Herriot's future wife, Helen. The reader is also introduced to many of the most colourful Yorkshire people among whom he worked. For any book – or television series – to be successful, rich and varied characterisation is essential. James Herriot's books radiate with unforgettable characters.

He did not have to invent them; they were all around him, contributing towards making his first years in Thirsk among the hardest but happiest of his life. Many of the incidents that James Herriot recounted in *If Only They Could Talk* were reproduced just as they happened. His first meeting with Siegfried was no exception.

When Alf Wight knocked on the door of Donald Sinclair's surgery, at 23 Kirkgate in Thirsk, he was about to experience the first of a lifetime of surprises with his future partner. Donald had completely forgotten that the young vet from Sunderland was coming for the interview and was not at home. The housekeeper, Mrs Weatherill, did not seem particularly surprised that her employer had overlooked the appointment; she apologised, gave him a cup of tea and told him to make himself at home. I am not in the least surprised that Donald forgot that appointment. After joining the practice myself, over twenty-seven years later, it was not long before I realised that whenever Donald was involved in the organisation of anything, confusion and disarray inevitably followed. Little had changed in the passing years. By the time he finally returned home that day back in 1940, Alf had fallen asleep under an old acacia tree in the garden. He woke to find Donald standing in front of him. He staggered hastily to his feet.

'My name is Donald Sinclair. You must be Alfred Wight!' he said, as the two men shook hands and, at that moment, the association between Sinclair and Wight was born. It would have a very shaky beginning, and there would be times when Alf would doubt his judgement in hitching his life to such a singular man, but it would survive.

The description of Donald in the first Herriot book fits him perfectly: 'He was just about the most English-looking man I had ever seen. Long, humorous, strong-jawed face. Small, clipped moustache, untidy, sandy hair. He was wearing an old tweed jacket and shapeless flannel trousers. The collar of his check shirt was frayed and the tie carelessly knotted. He looked as though he didn't spend much time in front of a mirror.'

James Herriot's last sentence of that paragraph is very true. Donald was the archetypal gentleman, very much the ladies' man, but over many years in his company, I never saw him comb his hair, let alone admire himself in a mirror. Perhaps he had become bored of the image of himself, as he seemed to remain unchanged with the passage of time. Alf said once, describing his partner, 'When Donald was thirty he looked fifty and when he was seventy he looked fifty.'

Donald exuded charm. Everyone liked him, but he was also a most erratic and unpredictable man. 'Eccentric' is almost too mild a term to describe him but, above all, he was a warm, humorous and interesting person. As 'Siegfried', he would be the pivotal character in the Herriot books, and a heaven-sent personality around which Alf was to set so many of his stories.

Many people believe that the character of Siegfried was grossly exaggerated in the books. 'Surely he was not really like that?' is a question that has been put to me many times.

'You are right!' is my usual reply. 'He was not like that at all. His character was considerably toned down.'

This opinion was shared by those who knew him best, specifically the Yorkshire farmers who observed him for years, hurtling impatiently into and out of their farmyards. 'By gaw, yer Dad's got old Sinclair right in them books!' was something I heard more than once during the early years of my father's literary success. There was never a man quite like Donald Sinclair and no one knew him better, or portrayed him more vividly, than that great observer of human character, James Alfred Wight.

Alf first observed Donald's impulsive nature during the course of that interview in 1940. Donald suggested they should go to see a few of the farms in the practice. He allowed Alf about two seconds to get into the car before hurtling off down the road. The two men roared round the country roads at breakneck speed while Alf concentrated on maintaining his composure in a seat that moved freely backwards and forwards on the floor of the car. They were accompanied on this hair-raising ride by six dogs who seemed to enjoy every minute of it.

It was not only the speed that alarmed Alf as they shot round the practice; Donald had a rather unorthodox method of holding the steering wheel – steering with his elbows while his chin remained cupped in his hands. This disturbing habit, which he maintained until his old age, was one that was observed with disbelief by many more rigid passengers.

Alf soon realised that he was in the company of a man very different from the average human being and he was to receive another surprise when, after a lightning tour of the surgery premises at Kirkgate, Donald offered him the job. There had been other applicants but this impulsive man, who had taken an instant liking to the young vet, did not wish to waste any time. Not only was he about to join the Royal Air Force himself, but his then assistant – a young man called Eric Parker – had informed Donald that he, too, would soon be leaving the practice to join the Air Force. Donald, who urgently wanted someone to run his practice while he was away, warned Alf that it would be hard work as he would be running the business single-handed for an indeterminate length of time. His head reeling, Alf thanked him and returned to Sunderland to ponder his future.

Events had moved so fast he could hardly believe his luck. He had been offered a job while hundreds of other hopeful applicants were being turned down all over the country, but what would the future hold for him in Thirsk? Donald Sinclair was quite obviously an extraordinary man and he had only had a glimpse of the practice on the whirlwind tour. An unknown world with a different way of life lay before him, but there was one aspect of Donald's offer that he knew he could not refuse.

In those difficult days for young veterinary surgeons, the acquisition of some job security was, for most of them, little more than a dream. Alf was, astonishingly, offered a salaried partnership before he had even accepted the job. Rather than receiving a salary while Donald was away in the Royal Air Force, Alf would receive five-eighths of the profits of the practice – helping himself to any cash that he could generate in the course of his work. After Donald's return, Alf was promised a salary of four guineas per week in addition to a share in the profits made while doing extra work for the Ministry of Agriculture.

Alf knew he would have a busy time ahead if he accepted. As well as doing the work of two men while Donald was away, he would also be balancing the books and running the Kirkgate premises, but it all added up to a tempting financial carrot for a penniless young man.

Money, however, was not everything. Alf knew he wanted to work in an environment that he could enjoy, and his first glimpse of Yorkshire had been an eye-opener. Instead of a drab, industrial landscape, he had seen rich, green fields and attractive little villages nestling at the foot of the Hambleton Hills. The thought of working in such pleasant surroundings appealed to him. Thirsk, with its collection of uneven buildings clustered around the cobbled market place, had an atmosphere of friendliness and charm. It was in marked contrast to the grey, windswept streets of Sunderland.

The unusual character of his prospective employer did not mar these positive thoughts. Donald Sinclair may have been a little eccentric in his behaviour but Alf had instinctively liked him from the moment they had first shaken hands. He had an honest and open face, together with a sharp sense of humour and an appealing personality.

The dearth of available jobs in 1940 decreed that Alf needed to make his mind up quickly, and he did. He informed McDowall of Donald's offer and then wrote immediately to Donald advising him that he would accept the job.

Mac was sorry to lose his young colleague, but he knew that Alf would not have stayed in Sunderland for long. He understood why the ambitious young man had been looking for a permanent post, with better prospects than he could ever offer him.

Alf travelled down to Yorkshire with his meagre belongings, arriving in Thirsk on 18 July 1940, and took up residence in one of the upstairs rooms of 23 Kirkgate. After spending a few days travelling round the practice with Donald and Eric Parker to acquaint himself with the area, he signed his contract as a salaried partner on 24 July, and began work two days later. As he set off on his rounds on that July day, little did he know that, many years later, he would turn Donald Sinclair's business at 23 Kirkgate into the most famous veterinary practice in the world.

CHAPTER EIGHT

In the early years of his literary success as James Herriot, Alf Wight wrapped a cloak of secrecy around the true location of Darrowby, revealing to no one the identity of the people on whom his characters were based. His portrayal of Darrowby was deliberately altered and is described in the books as being in the High Dales country, surrounded by wild fells and green valleys, with drystone walls snaking down towards the little town. His efforts to insulate himself, his friends and this area of Yorkshire from the explosion of publicity in the early 1970s were not very successful. It was not long before the media publicity had revealed that he lived in Thirsk, and it was his experiences in this Yorkshire market town that provided the greater part of the material for his books.

The vast majority of the incidents recounted within the stories happened in and around Thirsk, not in the Yorkshire Dales over twenty miles away. Thirsk was Darrowby and Alfred Wight, despite his enormous love for that area, could never be described as a Dales veterinary surgeon.

A postcard from Thirsk, sent by Alf to his parents on the day he arrived there in July 1940, shows that the town has not really changed a great deal in appearance over the years. There is a refreshing absence of motor vehicles in the old picture, but the unevenly roofed buildings surrounding the cobbled market place are very familiar. It was in this rural environment, far removed from his city upbringing, that he was to lay the foundations of a successful career as a veterinary surgeon. 23 Kirkgate, that he would years later make famous as 'Skeldale House', would be his home for the next twelve years, and his practice premises for the whole of his professional life.

Alf's feelings for the house and garden are clearly expressed in chapter 2 of his book *If Only They Could Talk*, where he describes seeing it for the very first time:

I liked the look of the old house. It was Georgian with a fine, white-painted doorway.... The paint was flaking and the mortar looked crumbly between the bricks, but there was a changeless elegance about the place....

I was shown into a sunlit room. It had been built in the grand manner, high-ceilinged and airy with a massive fireplace flanked by arched alcoves. One end was taken up by a french window which gave on a long, high-walled garden. I could see unkempt lawns, a rockery and many fruit trees. A great bank of peonies blazed in the hot sunshine and at the far end, rooks cawed in the branches of a group of tall elms....

Sunshine beat back from the high old walls, bees droned among the bright masses of flowers. A gentle breeze stirred the withered blooms of a magnificent wistaria which almost covered the back of the house. There was peace here.

Although there may have been peace at 23 Kirkgate, he had little time to sample it. During those first months in Thirsk, Alf discovered that the life of a country veterinary surgeon was fascinating, challenging and extremely hard. The 'free' salaried partnership into which he had entered with Donald Sinclair was a two-edged sword. Although he did not have to find the money to buy his partnership, he repaid Donald's gesture with something he had in abundance – a willingness to work hard – and his repayments got off to a flying start during that summer of 1940.

Donald left to join the Royal Air Force within days of Alf's arrival and Eric Parker departed four weeks later. Alf was left to run a strange practice entirely single-handed in an area with which he was almost totally unfamiliar. Having had most of his experience with small animals, he now had to transform himself into a large animal vet – and pretty quickly, too. The days were long and tiring but he managed to enjoy them as well as learning an enormous amount.

It is interesting to study the old practice ledgers which reveal how different the nature of the work was from the present day. Much of Alf's time was spent visiting individual animals on small family farms and, of course, his patients received very different treatment in those days before the arrival of modern drugs. He was continually drenching bovines with strange concoctions such as 'Stimulant Stomach Powders' or 'Universal Cattle Medicine'. He washed out cows' stomachs with these quaint mixtures, and irrigated their genital tracts and their udders with Acriflavine to combat infertility or mastitis. Acriflavine, an anti-septic, was a great standby for the veterinary surgeon; it was syringed up just about every available orifice that needed cleaning. In those days, the veterinary surgeons spent many long hours mixing medicines to their own 'recipes'. These seem so outdated now but many of them were actually quite effective. The more dramatic side of the work was never far away – the calvings, foalings, castrations and various stitching jobs that have always punctuated the veterinary surgeon's day.

The enjoyment of tackling his new job was heightened by the surroundings in which he found himself. Thirsk is situated in the Vale of York on some very fertile, flat arable land, but a few miles to the east is the western boundary of the North York Moors. At the foot of this great escarpment are numerous picturesque villages and Alf derived great pleasure from driving around this beautiful area, revelling in his visits to Boltby, Thirlby, Kilburn, Coxwold and other charming places. He was equally entranced when he coaxed his little car up to the top of the Hambleton Hills, where he would spend a large part of his working life in the years to come. This area of the practice, 800 feet above the flat land around Thirsk, was the domain of the hill farmer and the sparse landscape was dotted with grey, stone farmsteads, standing defiantly in the face of the howling north-east winds that whipped across the plateau in winter.

In the colder months, he experienced a harsh and forbidding place with no protection from the elements, but in the summer he saw a land of sunlit heaths and moorland, bisected by deep wooded valleys, the silence broken only by the bleating of sheep and the plaintive cries of curlew and golden plover. It was a wild and unspoilt area, the type of country that Alf always loved, and he felt at home in those airy surroundings.

The access to this high land is via a steep hill, Sutton Bank, from the top of which there is a fine panorama across the Vale of York to the distant Pennines. Alf, who always called this view 'the finest in England', never tired of stopping at the top for a moment or two to drink in the scene laid out before him. A mile or two further east, he could look across thirty or forty miles of unbroken moorland towards the Yorkshire coast and the towns of Whitby and Scarborough.

He had not been many days in Thirsk before he knew that he would be happy here, and he was to develop a lasting love for the surrounding countryside in which he was to spend his entire working life. Many times, he and Donald would remark that they considered themselves to be lucky men, driving around such a lovely area – and getting paid for it, too.

Alf was not only sampling a new sort of work. He was getting to know a different community of people, a way of life far removed from his urban upbringing. He was beginning to mingle with the Yorkshire country folk about whom, one day, he would write with an authority born of half a century in their company. At first, he was very unsure of them. The average inhabitant of rural Yorkshire could be difficult to get to know, and he had to work hard before he was finally accepted into the community. He was an incomer, a 'furriner', one to be regarded with suspicion until he had proved himself. It would be years before he felt he was completely accepted in the local area, as an extract from a letter to a friend illustrates: 'For some reason, the local farming community regards Wight with some asperity. I cannot understand the reason for this as I have a most charming method of approach!'

He found their attitude towards him very different from that in Glasgow. In the big city, everyone aired their opinions openly, while in Yorkshire, people kept their feelings to themselves. He did not know whether they liked him or thought him a complete idiot. They remained inscrutable. Another great difference between city and country life was that, in the country, everyone seemed to know all about him. Stripped of the comparative anonymity that he had enjoyed in Glasgow and Sunderland, he had the feeling that he was under the microscope. He felt that he was being watched.

Another obstacle was the learning of a new 'language'. Words like 'felon', 'garget', 'marra' and 'wick' bombarded his brain as he attempted to unravel the mysteries of the Yorkshire dialect. This old way of speaking is less common today but it was a problem for anyone new to the area in those days. He used to tell a story about a visit to a farm at which he had to attend a young heifer with a growth on her teat. The farmer was worried that the growth, if not treated, would cause severe inflammation of the udder, probably leading to mastitis. The farmer was not one to speak in hushed tones; a life among bellowing cattle and squealing pigs meant that a loud voice was often a necessary aid to communication on a Yorkshire farm.

'Na then, Mr Wight!' he bawled, his red face about six inches from Alf's.

'Good morning, Mr Musgrove,' he replied, his ears ringing.

'Ah 'ave a beast wi' a waart i' ya pap!' shouted the farmer.

'Oh, I see.'

'Aye! Thow'd better gitten tiv'er afower she's segged i' yower! Ah doubt she'll a' cripple felon afower long!'

Alf had shown a gift for learning foreign languages but it was severely put to the test in his early years in Yorkshire.

Alf particularly liked the Yorkshire country people's honesty and fairness. They were hard-working, lived a tough, exacting life, and while some of them could be dour and unsmiling, they were just in their attitude to anyone who did their best for them. This Alf did, and he soon made many good friends among the farming folk. His accounts of that country community are affectionately written, and with good reason. He was fascinated by the ways and traditions of the people, uncovering warmth, humour and other qualities that belied the impenetrable front they often displayed to the outside world. The country folk around Thirsk may have been studying the young Alf Wight but he, in turn, was studying them – and he was going one better. He was filing it all away at the back of his mind until, years later, he would reproduce it in print for thousands the world over to share.

Donald Sinclair had bought the practice from an elderly veterinary surgeon, Mr Wood, and although he had greatly improved the profitability, it was still not a very lucrative one at the time of Alf's arrival. The farmers were very reluctant to call the vet; money was in short supply, and extracting it from them required a mixture of firmness and diplomacy. Some of the entries in the old practice ledgers seem to indicate that working as a veterinary surgeon was not a formula for becoming a rich man. A typical entry is as follows:

To: Mr Smirthwaite, Topcliffe Parks, Topcliffe   *25 November 1940*
          Visit, calve cow   6 hours
          Pessaries, 1 bottle UCM, 1 injection strychnine
          £2 0s 0d

Unlike today, there was limited small animal work to help maintain cash flow through the practice. Alf learned a little about the financial side of life in the practice in those first months, Donald having asked him to keep an account of all the money coming into the business. At the end of every day, he had to sit down to write up the books. He soon began to see where the most lucrative work lay. Driving around the countryside attending to various sick animals was certainly not going to fatten his employer's purse but Tuberculin Testing herds of cattle presented a very different picture.

One of the veterinary profession's greatest achievements has been the virtual eradication of tuberculosis from the national herd. This disease was the scourge of the dairy industry in the 1930s and 1940s. Very few young veterinary surgeons today have ever seen a cow infected by TB, thanks to the efforts of the profession fifty years ago but, in those days, stricken animals presented a sorry sight – gaunt, emaciated creatures, with the giveaway soft cough that Alf got to recognise so well. It was not only cows that succumbed; countless people died through drinking the milk from these infected animals. Jean Wilson, his old girlfriend from his Yoker days, died through contracting it as a young woman, and Donald Sinclair, who had married while still a student at Edinburgh Veterinary College in the early 1930s, lost his young wife to the disease. Veterinary surgeons were paid to help eradicate the disease by carrying out intradermal tests on the animals, after which any reactors would be slaughtered. It was tough and tedious work, involving the injection of many thousands of uncooperative beasts, but it was a lifeline to cash-strapped practices.

A typical day's work in Donald's practice ledger at that time would amount to around £2–3 per day whereas a couple of days' TB Testing could earn the practice £20–30. No wonder veterinary surgeons snatched eagerly at any testing that came their way.

There was one notable exception to this. He was a veterinary surgeon who lived in Leyburn, twenty-five miles from Thirsk, in the Yorkshire Dales – a beautiful area which teemed with cows. This vet did not want the tedium and paperwork associated with TB Testing; the acquisition of money meant less to him than the preservation of his steady, enjoyable lifestyle. His name was Frank Bingham, an unambitious but very capable Irish vet, described by Alf as one of the finest veterinary surgeons he ever knew. It was Frank's easy approach to life that was largely instrumental in introducing Alf to the Yorkshire Dales.

Donald Sinclair's practice, at that time, covered a very large area. Within the part of Yorkshire which stretches some sixty miles from Helmsley in the east to Hawes, a town at the far end of Wensleydale in the west, there were very few practices and Donald's and Frank Bingham's were two of them. Frank, having no desire to undertake the TB Testing work, offered it some years later to Donald who, naturally, grabbed it with both hands. They entered into a tenuous partnership, one which for a few years was known as 'Bingham, Sinclair and Wight'.

When Alf first started work in Thirsk, his days were very long. He travelled across to Frank Bingham's Leyburn practice in the mornings to test endless cows before returning to Thirsk in the afternoons to deal with the work that had accumulated there. He covered vast distances but in doing so he had a wonderful introduction to the Dales, an area that was a revelation to him the first time he set eyes upon it. He was totally captivated by the wild majestic fells sweeping down to the green valleys, with the stone walls winding down from the high tops to the sturdy grey villages and farmsteads. He loved the sweet, clean air punctuated with the sounds of birds – curlew, lapwing, skylark and grouse. It is no surprise that, many years later, he would set his books in the Dales; he would see many beautiful places in his lifetime but there was nowhere he would love more than the Yorkshire Dales.

Another bonus resulting from this arduous regime was that he became well acquainted with Frank Bingham. Frank, a distinguished-looking man with fair hair and blue eyes, was almost twenty years older than Alf, and was a man who had travelled widely. He had been a Mountie in Canada and had spent time in Australia riding the rabbit fences, enduring many long hours in the saddle, with the result that he was an artist when it came to dealing with horses. This elegant and soft-spoken man was someone to whom Alf Wight took an immediate liking. He and his Swiss wife, Emmy, enriched his first years in the Dales with their wonderful kindness and hospitality.

Alf was always hungry in those days. He would set out from Thirsk in his basic little car, with just a pack of cheese sandwiches to last him the whole day, but there was more than cheese waiting for him whenever he walked into the Binghams' house in Leyburn. Emmy was a magnificent cook, and she fed him like a king. Delectable stews, apple pies and cakes passed his willing lips, while Frank would sit back and talk quietly as though there were all the time in the world.

Frank, who went about his work calmly and methodically, was one who would never be hurried. His great saying was 'Always set your stall out first', and he would never embark upon any job unless he was thoroughly prepared. To a young, eager-to-learn veterinary surgeon like Alf Wight, he was a joy to watch. Some of the principles to which he adhered in his work – great care combined with scrupulous cleanliness – are just as valid today as they were fifty or more years ago. Alf used to be amused when he saw Frank boil up his instruments and wrap them in clean brown paper before every operation, but he noticed that Frank's surgical wounds always healed rapidly and cleanly.

He was a real horseman who could rope and throw wild colts with effortless ease, and on one remarkable occasion, Alf watched fascinated as Frank cast an unbroken young horse with one hand while rolling a cigarette with the other. He was equally at home when dealing with cows. One of the most daunting challenges to a veterinary surgeon is the replacement of a prolapsed uterus in the bovine. This involves the returning of an enormous pink mass of tissue through the vagina, a task rather like trying to stuff a large cushion up a drain pipe. It can be a demoralising and exhausting job. Frank, as usual, made little of such a challenge, and young Alf Wight watched in amazement on a Dales farm one day as he covered the huge mass with sugar before rolling the cow onto a small stool to stop her straining the uterus back out. The sugar sucked the moisture out of the tissues, reducing it to a fraction of its size, while Frank, gently, replaced it – a freshly rolled cigarette dangling from his lips as he worked. As the young vet watched, he reflected that such things are not taught at veterinary college; they are acquired over years of experience.

Frank Bingham appears in the third of James Herriot's books, *Let Sleeping Vets Lie*, under the name of Ewan Ross, and the admiration Alf felt for the man shows clearly in his writing. Perhaps not everyone shared his opinion, however. Frank was regarded by most as a fine veterinary surgeon – when he made himself available.

Frank Bingham had a problem common to many veterinary surgeons of the day. He liked a drink – and he liked more than one. Numerous are the tales of his long sessions in the inns and public houses of the Yorkshire Dales, sessions that could last for days. Frank worked only when he felt like it, and once he was comfortably seated beside a warm fire with a drink in his hand, it was a persuasive man who could winkle him out. As many of the Dales folk were from strict Methodist families, such drinking habits may well have been frowned upon, but it was not this aspect of his character that Alf remembered. The warm friendship that this easy-going and charming man had extended to him, ensured that Alf's early days in the Yorkshire Dales were ones that he would always recall with happiness and nostalgia.

I hardly remember Frank Bingham, since I was only eight years old at the time of his death in 1951, but I do have a recollection of a visit to a café in the Dales shortly after he died. The waitress was none other than Emmy Bingham who was working there to earn a little extra money. My father, deeply upset to learn of her financial misfortune, could not finish his food. He was unable to come to terms with the situation of being waited on by the lady who had been so kind to him during those first years in the Yorkshire Dales.

It was not unusual in those days for veterinary surgeons to die leaving their wives in penury. They worked so hard that survival was a priority, with thoughts of pensions and insurance policies hardly crossing their minds. In due course, the profession became aware of the number of veterinarians' families who were struggling financially, and a fund known as the Veterinary Benevolent Fund was established, its aim being to provide such families with assistance. Alf Wight contributed generously to this fund during the years when he was making money as a writer, but he was in no situation to help Emmy Bingham all those years ago, at a time when he, himself, had to account for every penny.

During those first four months in Thirsk, the practice was fully stretched. He wrote to his parents about the kind of life he was leading.

Dear Folks,

I've been trying to find time to write for ages but just recently I have been working harder than I've ever done in my life. There is far too much for one man to do and, frankly, I don't know how I ever get through all the work. I've been rising at 6.30 am and working till dark for ages and then there's all the writing to be done on top of that. And bills! Oh boy, I never realised how things could pile up and how much it would cost to live. I can't believe I've been here for four months. Time slips past when you're working and, apart from my weekend in Sunderland at the beginning, I've never had a day off, never been out with a girl, never played a game. It's enough to age anybody!

Today, the young veterinary surgeon leads a far more civilised life, with better working facilities, an arsenal of modern drugs to combat disease, and comfortable cars to ride around in – but whether they are happier than those slaves of yesterday is debatable. The modern veterinary surgeon is beset by rules and regulations while the demands of his clients become ever more exacting. The stress associated with the job is high, both financially and emotionally, with threats of litigation lurking around every corner. Young Alf Wight worked hard, but it is likely that his unbridled, outdoor way of life, set in one of the most beautiful parts of the country, is one that is now looked on by many with more than a touch of envy.

*

Following Donald's and Eric Parker's departure for the Royal Air Force, a deep sense of isolation began to descend on Alf. He was not only trying to establish himself in a new job in an unfamiliar environment but, apart from Frank Bingham in Leyburn, he had no one to turn to for advice, nobody with whom to share his hopes and fears as he drove the long and lonely miles. The Yorkshire farmers did little to bolster his confidence; many had developed a great deal of faith in Donald and Eric, and few could conceal their disappointment upon beholding the unknown and inexperienced vet driving on to their farms. Never had Alf felt the need of moral support as fervently as he did during those first few weeks in Yorkshire.

It was not long before he did something about it. He suspected that his friend Eddie Straiton, having recently qualified, may not have got a job. He was right; Eddie was desperate to find some work and when Alf offered him the chance to join him in Thirsk, the young man leapt at the opportunity. Alf could not pay him but he would put a roof over his head and feed him, in return for which Eddie would be able to gain some practical experience while helping Alf in his everyday work. Eddie was doubly grateful, as he knew, when applying for jobs elsewhere, that to be able to say that he had had some weeks working in practice, would stand him in good stead.

Eddie was a great help to Alf in more ways than one. Not only was he good company during the long drives up into the wildest reaches of the Dales, but he was an able assistant. He was put to work early almost every morning as the old Ford car often needed a good push before it could be persuaded to start, but it was up on the bleak hill farms, helping to catch the animals, that Eddie came into his own. The TB Testing was tough work as the two young vets were thrown about by rough, hairy cattle who had no intention of making the job any easier. Eddie was not a big man but he was strong and fearless, and Alf had abiding memories of the small figure with the jet black hair bobbing around in a throng of angry, steaming cows and being hurled around like a cork on the ocean. Once Eddie had his fingers in a beast's nose, he hung on like a terrier.

Many years later, Eddie Straiton would reminisce about the time he spent working with his old college friend in the hills and dales of Yorkshire. He went so far as to say that they were among the happiest weeks of his life – hard and penniless, but carefree and full of fine memories.

As well as the TB Testing in the Dales, the practice at Thirsk was always busy and it was here one evening that Alf and Eddie received a lesson in the up-and-down fortunes of the veterinary surgeon's life that they were never to forget.

They were called to a calving at Knayton, a village near Thirsk, and arrived full of enthusiasm. A calving is a dramatic event, with success boosting a new veterinary surgeon's reputation. On the other hand, should things turn out badly, the vet could have a mountain to climb, re-establishing his image.

Alf stripped to the waist and inserted his arm into the cow. His confidence drained away within seconds. He could feel only a large mass of hair and bone. There were no legs, no feet and no head. Was this a calf? What else could it be? He explored the mysterious depths of the cow, trying desperately to find something that was familiar, but there was only the huge hairy ball of tissue lodged firmly within the pelvis of the cow. He grappled with the nameless lump for a while longer before turning to his friend. 'Edward, would you care to feel this for me?'

'Certainly, Alf,' replied Eddie, stepping forward confidently.

Alf's expectations of a successful calving began to sink even lower as he watched the wriggling figure behind the cow, the face set in grim determination. Eddie, too, was obviously finding this a challenge. He eventually withdrew his arm and spoke.

'I think you had better have another feel, Alf,' he said. 'It is a rather strange case.'

Alf resumed the struggle, his mind in a turmoil. Whatever this thing was, it was not going to come out. These were the days before Caesarean section was an option; the 'calf' – or whatever else it might be – had to be extracted out of the passage that nature intended. There was no other route. What was he to do? An important quality of a good veterinary surgeon is the ability to make a firm decision; it is of little use procrastinating in periods of crisis. He had to do something, and he did.

He turned to the farmer and said in as steady a voice as he could muster, 'I am afraid that what we have here is the uncalvable cow. It could kill her to take this huge calf out of her but if you slaughter her as quickly as possible, she will dress out well and you should receive a reasonable price for her carcass.' Such confidently spoken words belied his inwardly seething emotions.

The farmer was staring blankly at Alf when suddenly a voice broke the oppressive silence in the gloomy cow byre. 'Ah'll 'ave a go!' Another man had silently drifted in to observe the proceedings, a heavy-set, lugubrious individual who had been observing the contortions of the two young men with apparent indifference. The farmer seemed agreeable, and Eddie and Alf were in no position to argue. The man rolled up his sleeves, took out an old knife and, with it carefully covered by his hand, inserted his arm in the cow's vagina and set to work.

To the two young vets, the next hour or so seemed like days as this man produced a decomposing calf, bit by bit, out of the cow until, finally, the result of his labours lay in shreds on the cow byre floor, relieving the exhausted cow of her unwanted burden. He had succeeded where the veterinary surgeons had failed.

Eddie and Alf muttered their thanks before slinking out of the byre and rattling off down the country road back to Thirsk. The shame was overwhelming. They were so demoralised that nothing was said for a long time, but eventually Eddie broke the silence with a remark that my father would never forgot.

'The ruin of two promising careers, Alf!' he said, staring gloomily out of the old cracked windscreen.

'Aye, Eddie, you're probably right,' he replied. 'News travels fast round here – especially bad news. Oh, they're going to love this! The farmer had to do the vet's job! They'll be shouting it from the roof tops! This'll be all over Yorkshire by tomorrow!'

The following few days were misery as they waited for some reaction from the farming community – but there was none. They began to think that the whole episode had been just a terrible nightmare, but they still dreaded a call to anywhere within a mile or two of the disaster. They soon got one. They were called to a neighbouring farm to see a cow and they braced themselves for an uncomfortable visit.

It was not long before the farmer resurrected the painful incident. 'Me neighbour was tellin' me about you two young fellers,' he said.

'Oh yes?' replied Alf, ready to hear the worst.

''E's right upset about that calvin' job 'e 'ad done t'other night, Ah can tell yer!'

'I bet he is!'

'Aye, 'e's right brassed off about it, like.'

There was an embarrassing silence before the farmer spoke again.

''E should never a' let that daft bugger kill 'is cow wi' cuttin' that calf away wi' that knife!'

Alf and Eddie stared at the farmer. Alf broke the silence. 'I beg your pardon?'

'Aye,' continued the farmer. ''E wished 'e'd listened to you lads! If 'e'd 'ad't cow slaughtered like you said, 'e'd a' made a bit o' money on't carcass. Cow died afore you lads were out o' t' yard. Now 'e 'as nowt. 'E's right upset ower't job Ah can tell ther! 'E thinks a bit about you lads! 'E'll listen to't vet in future!'

A warm feeling began to flow over the two young men. They had had a taste of the fluctuating emotions experienced by every veterinary surgeon. They both told me that story in my student years, and each gave me the same words of encouragement. 'Whenever you think that all is gloom and despair, never forget that there is always another day!'

The ability to make a decision was one of Alfred Wight's strengths as a veterinary surgeon. He made the right decision in that cow shed all those years ago, and he would continue to make many more throughout his professional life.

In November 1940, Sinclair and Wight were reunited. Donald suddenly returned from the Royal Air Force which meant that Eddie had to leave but, before he did, Alf wrote, on his behalf, letters of application for various jobs that were advertised. Even way back in those early years, Eddie was grateful for his friend's flair as a writer of letters; he was offered a job in Colne very soon afterwards.

Eddie Straiton was immensely grateful and the opportunity to repay his friend's generosity would, in fact, arise more than twenty years later.

Although Donald had, in fact, been thrown out of the Royal Air Force, he had half expected it. In order to join, he had lied about his age, but it was his less than satisfactory reflexes while undergoing flying instruction that had been his undoing. When the authorities discovered he was approaching thirty, they reviewed his case and decided to send him home. The fact that he was a veterinary surgeon, a profession regarded as a 'reserved occupation', had done little to help his cause.

His response to this rejection was to attack the work in the practice like a man possessed. It was as well that he was in this mood as the practice was becoming busier by the day, with both men working flat out. Some 'help', however, was soon to be on the way.

Eddie Straiton's father had a car for sale which Donald decided to buy. He turned to Alf one day. 'Alfred, I want you to go up to Glasgow to get that car. While you are there, take a day or two off to see your mother and father and, on the way back, will you pick up my brother from the veterinary college and bring him here for the Christmas vacation? The young bugger is in his third year now and has probably failed his exams again! God help him if he has!'

Alf Wight was about to meet Brian Sinclair, a man who would become a dear and lifelong friend. The man he would immortalise, many years later, as Tristan Farnon, was about to enter into the life of Alfred Wight.

CHAPTER NINE

Brian Sinclair strode into Alf Wight's life like a breath of fresh air. Photographs taken of him in the 1940s reveal a lively, humorous face, one that must have been a great tonic to the over-worked and poverty-stricken young vet. Alf had been in Thirsk only a few months but already he was beginning to feel like a veteran; Brian's arrival added a refreshing twist to his daily routine.

Brian was not at all like his elder brother in appearance. He was shorter and plumper with an oval face that looked as though it was about to crack with laughter at any moment. This open and honest face portrayed the true character of the man behind it; Brian Sinclair spent a large proportion of his life laughing and Alf would spend many an hour laughing with him.

The descriptions of Brian and his escapades in the early James Herriot books give a vivid account of life in 23 Kirkgate at that time. Alf, Donald and Brian, when he was on vacation from veterinary college, all lived together in the Kirkgate house, placing Alf in the company of two of the richest characters he had ever met. The ongoing love-hate relationship between the brothers would provide wonderful material for his books, with the antics of the pair of them figuring prominently in the early volumes.

It was all the funnier as Donald very rarely saw the amusing side of the tense exchanges between himself and Brian – and with good reason. He felt a responsibility towards the welfare of his younger brother. This included the funding of his education, but Brian was not the world's most diligent student; he failed his exams regularly, leaving Donald severely out of pocket. The explosive and, in many cases, justified blasts at Brian from his frustrated brother, are accurately chronicled in the early Herriot books.

When Alf was writing his first book in the 1960s, he consulted with Brian at length to ensure that these incidents were authentically reproduced. A draft typescript of the first book, *If Only They Could Talk*, contains several inserts and rough scribblings on many of the pages, one chapter of which caught my eye.

It was the one describing the episode when Tristan wrecked his brother's car, despite dire warnings to be careful from Siegfried who was prostrate in bed with flu. Tristan eventually summoned up the courage to explain to Siegfried that his beloved Bentley had had a 'minor' accident, resulting in a smashed wing and the complete absence of two of its doors. There was a terrible silence while the elder brother absorbed the bad tidings. Suddenly, and with a superhuman effort, he sat bolt upright and screamed wildly into Tristan's face, before collapsing back exhausted on the bed.

On the relevant page of this manuscript, Brian's unmistakable scrawl is next to my father's description of the incident. It reads: 'He said, "You bloody fool! You're sacked!"'

When Brian returned from Glasgow on that day in December 1940 to break the news to his brother that he had failed Pathology and only 'done all right' in Parasitology, he received the verbal battering from Donald that he was expecting. Brian's fun-loving and carefree approach to life continued unabated despite suffering considerable discomfort while under the lash from Donald who treated him at times with complete disdain.

Alf remembered seeing a curt message on the mantelpiece once that simply read, 'Brian! Go home! Donald.' On another occasion, Alf and Brian walked into the kitchen one morning where Donald was frying three eggs for breakfast. He turned casually to his brother with the words, '*Your* egg's broken!'

Shortly after meeting Brian Sinclair for the first time, Alf began to wonder what his contribution would be towards the running of the practice. Donald, who tried repeatedly and unsuccessfully to instil the work ethic into his young brother, took it out on Brian by giving him all the worst deals that were going. It soon became clear that he was a factotum – somebody who was supposed to dispense and deliver medicines, wash the cars, dig the garden, answer the phone, keep the books and even, in an emergency, go to a case.

At least, this was how Donald saw his function, but Brian had other ideas. He devoted his whole time to enjoying himself, regarding all kinds of physical activity with abhorrence; in fact, his whole life seemed to be geared to the cause of doing as little as possible. This, he largely achieved – spending many long and happy hours sitting in a chair doing crosswords, smoking interminable numbers of Woodbines, or simply snoozing peacefully. He was rousted into activity by his brother on occasion but, by and large, Brian had a pretty easy time in the old house. When not reclining in his favourite chair, he could be found conversing effortlessly in the local public houses or carrying out practical jokes on anyone who was unfortunate enough to be in the vicinity at the time. This frequently happened to be Alf and very few weeks went by without his being the victim of one or two mischievous pranks.

Brian, who could imitate a wide range of different voices, frequently brought beads of perspiration to Alf's brow as he mimicked farmers calling him out to horrendous cases – always, of course, on a dark and filthy night. Alf never forgot the classic call from a farmer with the rough Yorkshire voice growling down the phone. 'Is that t'vitinry? This is Keel, Hesketh Grange. I 'ave a big 'oss as wants stitchin' up. Cut 'isself right bad on't back leg. 'E's a nasty devil an' all!' Brian allowed Alf to sweat a while before laughingly revealing his true identity.

Many times, Alf would attempt to turn the tables on Brian. He would go to great lengths to disguise his voice, ringing him at all hours of the day or night, but the young joker was almost invariably too clever for him. One night, having just returned home from a late call, Alf received one of the worst frights of his life. There was a bright moon shining into his bedroom and, as he started to undress he saw, to his horror, the naked figure of a man silhouetted against the window. The moonlight shining behind the apparition added to the terrifying effect.

'Who, in God's name, is that?' he croaked, his heart thumping wildly.

The figure took an eternity to reply. Eventually, there was a sinister and sepulchral response, 'B–r–i–a–n!'

It is surprising that the young Alf Wight managed to carry out his daily work with such a prankster at large, but he was not the only one to feel the sharp sting of Brian's many jokes. Although renowned for his ability to exist happily doing nothing, Brian could throw his heart and soul into anything that interested him, and he certainly put everything into developing the reputation of the 'Pannal Ghost'.

This eerie figure, clothed in white sheets, was famous at the time and on moonlit nights could be seen gliding across the road at the top of Pannal Bank near Harrogate. Terrified motorists would perform lightning U-turns in the road before speeding away in the opposite direction – to the glee of the laughing ghost, none other than Brian himself.

One night, however, two motorcyclists, rather than fleeing, decided to give chase. This unexpected turn of events, which took the ghost completely by surprise, resulted in his taking off at high speed over a succession of ploughed fields with the motorcyclists in hot pursuit. Unused as he was to hard physical exercise, this desperate chase – in which he was encumbered by yards of flapping white material – was a most disagreeable experience. He made his escape by hiding in a huge drainage pipe that stank of tom cats, and it was while he was lying trembling in his refuge, with an icy wind screaming down the pipe, that he came to a firm decision: the 'Pannal Ghost' would be seen no more.

One of the chapters in *Let Sleeping Vets Lie* is about the 'Raynes Ghost', and is based on this incident.

Brian had a repertoire of party tricks which, when in the mood, he would perform with wild abandon. His favourite was the 'Mad Conductor' – also well described in one of the Herriot books – but another, that was not so well known but equally dramatic, was his imitation of 'Donald drinking the Universal Cattle Medicine'. Alf would often recall this incident as a prime example of the erratic behaviour of his senior partner.

When returning late from a call one evening, Alf was walking down the long garden behind 23 Kirkgate. It was very dark, the rain was pouring down, and he was just about to enter the house when he heard a soft rustling from the bed of nasturtiums at the side of the path. On closer inspection, he saw in the dim light what appeared to be a pile of sacking. As he tentatively poked it with his shoe, the shadowy mass twitched and groaned. Something, or someone, was deep in the flower bed.

'Who on earth is that?' he asked, peering down at the shapeless heap. There was a moment of silence save for the drumming of the rain. There then followed another groan as the mysterious form began to writhe in the darkness.

At this point, the door burst open and Brian appeared. 'Thank goodness you're back, Alf,' he said. 'Give me a hand and let's get him inside!'

'Who?'

'Donald!'

'*Donald*?' The mysterious heap was none other than his senior partner. 'What the devil is wrong with him?' he asked. 'He sounds as though he is dying!'

'He deserves to!' went on Brian. 'He has just swigged about half a bottle of Universal Cattle Medicine.'

Brian was laughing but Alf was more than a little alarmed. He could hardly believe his ears. Universal Cattle Medicine (U.C.M.) was a savage concoction that was used to combat a wide range of bovine diseases and supposedly had stimulant properties. It consisted, among other things, of arsenic and ammonia, with the dose for a large cow, about two dessertspoonfuls. It was a brave man who sniffed the top of the bottle, let alone sampled its contents. Cows, on being drenched with this mixture, coughed and spluttered for several minutes, but it seemed to work in many cases. This venerable liquid was indicated to be for the treatment of 'coughs, chills, scours, pneumonia, milk fever, garget, and all forms of indigestion'. Whenever the veterinary surgeon was mystified by a case, there was always good old U.C.M. to fall back on. The early practice ledgers are full of references to it; Sinclair and Wight sold gallons of the stuff.

It was a stimulant, without doubt, and it had certainly stimulated Donald Sinclair. The two men carted him inside and laid him on the sofa in the living-room. Brian then gave Alf an account of what had happened.

Donald, on returning from a night out and in an inebriated condition, had decided that some 'medication' might make him feel a little better. He had swaggered into the little dispensary, seized a bottle of U.C.M, and bitten off the cork. He had turned to his brother with a devilish smile and, before Brian could stop him, had gulped several mouthfuls of the powerful liquid. There had been a brief, still moment as the dark mixture scorched its way down his gullet. Donald then leapt convulsively into the air with his hands clasped tightly round his throat. Staggering out into the garden, he had collapsed with a hoarse cry into the huge bed of rambling nasturtiums, his legs twitching rhythmically. It was after the jerking body had become still that Brian had decided to run inside to call the doctor.

Donald, happily, recovered but Brian made the most of this incident, with his graphic imitation of his brother drinking the U.C.M. becoming an integral part of his repertoire. Many customers in the drinking establishments of Thirsk were to observe the spasmodically twitching figure with the goggling eyes. Needless to say, these dramatic performances were never to be seen by his elder brother.

One old farmer said to Alf many years later, 'Aye, Ah've seen "Young

Sinclair" doin' one of 'is turns. He ended up lyin' on't floor o't Golden Fleece, fickin!' This was an old Yorkshire term for 'twitching' and, indeed, most of Brian's party pieces resulted in a prostrate figure convulsing its way around the floor.

Another demonstration – one which Alf found most unnerving – was Brian's 'maniac laugh'. It began with a low, sinister chuckle which gradually increased in intensity before finally ending in wild shrieks of laughter. To Alf's embarrassment, he would frequently launch into this maniacal howling at a moment's notice, often following a session at the local pub; the dark streets of Thirsk reverberated many times with Brian's demented cries.

From the moment that Brian Sinclair came into his life, Alf Wight realised that he was in the company of a unique personality. Never before had he encountered someone with such an insatiable appetite for humour; at times he wondered whether Brian could ever be serious.

It was not only Alf who found Brian Sinclair such a stimulating personality. An official of the Ministry of Agriculture was talking to Alf one day, after spending the previous evening with Brian in the Golden Fleece Hotel in Thirsk. 'What a delightful man that young Sinclair is,' he said. He paused a while as though reflecting upon that evening's activities. 'Don't you think, however, that his sense of humour is a little *over*developed?!'

An extraordinary personality he may have been, but Alf enjoyed every moment of his company. As well as sharing a similar sense of humour, the two men enjoyed other common interests. They spent many evenings escorting young ladies to the cinema or to dances, and they both loved the atmosphere of a friendly public house where numerous pints of beer would be consumed.

It was when in the company of the foaming brew that Brian really came into his own. Brian remained a dedicated beer drinker until the final years of his life and, for a smallish man, it was amazing how much he could put away. In all the years Alf knew him, he rarely seemed the worse for wear following a night at his favourite pastime. As a beer drinker, even as a young man when he and Alf were enjoying their nights of alcoholic revelry, he had the assurance born of years of practice.

Both Alf and Brian had very fertile imaginations which they put to full use, roaring with laughter as they fantasised about Thirsk and the surrounding area. The town has a small, meandering waterway, the

Codbeck, running through it, and the two young men would imagine it as a great river, with Thirsk, a thriving seaport, at its mouth. The opening of one of Brian's letters began, 'And as the fully-rigged sailing ship *Cryptorchid* sailed into the harbour ...' When recalling the story, Alf could get no further than that first line. The high land at the top of Sutton Bank, a part of the practice that Brian regarded as 'The Lost World', was another focus for their imagination. The two men dreamed up images of swaying columns of vets and sundry other people trekking across the barren landscape on their way to a dinosaur in distress. A letter written by Alf to Brian, when Brian was in the Army Veterinary Corps in India in August 1944, reveals how much he missed his company, as well as referring to the fantasies the two men shared together:

How now, old China! I hereby take up my pen to write to you which is more than you did when I was languishing in the R.A.F. but, as you see, I am still the sweet natured and forgiving youth you knew of old!

The old town is much as usual, but I confess life is not the merrier for your absence. Hancock, the new 'horse leech', acquitted himself well on his first visit to Cold Kirby. He was called to a crop-bound pterodactyl and severe downfall of the udder in a dinosaur. Some of the natives with blow pipes peppered him rather severely on his journey but he won through, left his gross of U.C.M.s, and returned with great credit.

We had an excellent Gymkhana more recently in aid of the Red Cross and some of the results of the contests were very interesting. Alan and 'Leedle Jas' [Brian's pseudonym for me] finished first in the three-legged race for teething infants while in the married man's egg and spoon race, Donald carried a magnificent egg and won a popular victory. Myra Hugill was a game second in the septaguanarians' hundred yards dash and the gents' bicycle and sack of potatoes trundle was, of course, a gift for Jim Barley.

Here we must end, old comrade. Try to send a line south of the border down Sowerby way.

Yours aye,
Alf.

Brian certainly found something to laugh about every day but there was one occasion that stands out above all the others – one that reduced the young man to a helpless, weeping shell. It was the day that Donald's dogs chased the local dustbin men out of the old garden at 23 Kirkgate.

Alf recounted this incident to his family many times and, in fact, wrote it down, but before James Herriot was 'born', and the story was never published. The two brothers in the story were called not Siegfried and Tristan, but Edward and Henry.

On another peaceful August afternoon, Henry and I were sitting in the lounge waiting for the phone to ring. The french windows were open and, outside, the lawns and rockery and flowers slept in the sunshine. At our feet lay the dogs, draped over each other and breathing heavily. Then, we noticed the dustbin men coming through the little door at the far end of the garden.

The dustbin men had always fascinated Henry and me. There was one very tall, thin, lugubrious one, a very small, sad looking one and a fat one who always wore a black beret pulled down over his ears. We never saw any of them smile and they never seemed to speak to each other.

But the most striking thing about them was the slow pace at which they moved. The first time we saw them, we decided that one or all of them must be ill, so snail-like was their progression down the garden path. The tall and the short one used to appear first at the top of the garden. The fat one always walked behind. They would trail with incredible slowness down the path, heads down, unspeaking. They would disappear into the little yard where the bins were and reappear after an interval with the tall and the short one carrying a bin between them, dragging it listlessly along at arm's length. Behind would be the fat one, carrying a box or some other small article of loose rubbish. The sorrowful procession would then shuffle painfully, foot by foot, up the path until it disappeared through the far door. After a minute or two, they would reappear, deployed in the same order and carrying the empty bin. Then they would start their weary journey back to the yard, dragging languid feet, their eyes fixed to the ground in hopeless resignation. When they gained the yard, they would repeat the process with another bin.

The garden path is a long one, all of eighty yards and dead straight. The high wall borders it on one side, and on the other lie the lawns, two tall apple trees and the vegetable garden. It always took a long time for the dustbin men to walk the full length of it and I suppose this may have had something to do with their disconsolate appearance.

On this hot afternoon, they seemed to be going even more slowly than usual and Henry and I watched, spellbound, as they laboriously made their way towards us. They had travelled about three quarters of the way and were just about to turn into the yard when the lurcher, Joe, spotted them. Some small noise had awakened him and he lifted a sleepy head, but at the sight of the dustbin men, his aspect changed suddenly. His neck stiffened and his head reared up, alert and watchful. The hairs along his back began to rise and a deep growl rumbled in his throat. The trailing, shuffling group seemed to hold a strange menace for Joe. Without taking his eyes away from them he rose slowly to his feet, and the other dogs, who were augmented by a waddling little Scottie and a large, long-haired animal of doubtful parentage, stirred into wakefulness.

Everything happened rapidly. Joe walked to the open french window with a stiff gait, every hair on his back and neck erect and bristling. His lips flickered back from his teeth and with a tremendous baying howl, he hurtled out onto the lawn, closely followed by the other five dogs in a solid mass. I can only imagine how those poor men must have felt when, out of nowhere, in the sunlit peace of the old garden, they suddenly saw this screaming horde bearing down on them. I must say this: they showed not the slightest sign of hesitation or indecision at this critical moment. In less than one second they had dropped the empty bin and were legging it back up the path like Olympic sprinters.

This electrifying transformation seemed to paralyse our faculties and we stared, open mouthed, at the scene. The tall, thin man got off to the best start and went away with his arms working like pistons. It was soon apparent, though, that his energy was being largely dissipated by faulty leg action. He had very long legs and he ran in an extraordinary high-stepping manner, his knees seeming to reach his chin. The little man had a whirlwind style, throwing his arms across his body and tossing his head about and taking tiny, rapid steps which made his legs look like a flickering blur. The real stylist of the three was the fat man. He set off with a beautiful, slightly rolling lope, his body straight and his arms moving in the classical manner. His pace over the first twenty yards was a revelation but he was obviously lacking in stamina and, his action becoming laboured, he began to fall behind. He showed remarkable resource here because, looking back and seeing the baying pack almost on his heels, he swung himself effortlessly into the branches of one of the apple trees.

It was a wonderful effort deserving of the highest praise and served not only to save his own skin, but also to divert the pursuit momentarily from his friends. Joe faltered in his stride and the other dogs, coming up at terrific speed, knocked him over. For about three seconds there was a snarling, fighting heap and then they sorted themselves out and went after the other two men. These latter were still going well with never a backward look, all their faculties intent upon their goal – the little green door at the top. It did not seem they could possibly make it. The dogs, with Joe in the van and the little Scottie bringing up the rear, were closing the gap at an alarming speed.

But over the last few yards the two runners made a supreme effort and stepped up their pace by the vital fraction. For a sickening moment it seemed they would jam together in the doorway, but then they were through with the door banged behind them and the dogs leaping up at it and howling in thwarted rage.

I ran up the garden to rescue the fat man up the tree. Henry did not come with me; he was lying on the floor, pulling at his collar and making strange, moaning sounds. By yelling savagely and throwing stones, I managed to get the dogs rounded up and locked safely behind the french windows.

I then, apprehensively, approached the apple tree. The fat man was slowly climbing down. He wheezed and groaned and when he gained the ground he leant back against the trunk of the tree gasping for air. He said not a word in reply to my stammered apologies. After a minute he pulled his black beret more firmly down over his ears and tottered painfully up the path and through the door. I could not recognise him as the lissom athlete of a short time ago.

This lively little interlude was followed by a problem that persisted for several weeks. The dustbin men, not surprisingly, had no desire to revisit the old garden and the refuse in the back yard soon assumed mountainous proportions. Donald eventually solved the dilemma by firmly pressing a pound note into one of the dustbin men's hands outside the Black Bull in Thirsk, with the assurance that his pack of dogs would be kept under firm control in future.

Brian Sinclair visited Thirsk not only during his vacations from veterinary college, but whenever the practice became impossibly busy. He would then 'secure' leave to come to Thirsk where he would help by going on farm visits, making up medicines, acting as a receptionist, or assisting with any other tasks Donald set him. This rather elastic arrangement with the veterinary college contributed to Brian taking over ten years to pass his examinations. He had, in fact, begun his veterinary education at the Royal Dick Veterinary College in Edinburgh when he was seventeen, but repeated failures in his examinations resulted in the college suggesting to Donald that his brother should carry on his studies at an alternative centre of learning.

He moved to Glasgow Veterinary College for just one year – where he was thrown out of the terrifying Professor Emslie's class for laughing (something that was completely beyond Alf's comprehension), before Donald, now at his wit's end, returned him to Edinburgh.

Dire warnings from Donald, together with a realisation that the funding of his education could possibly cease, resulted in the young man pulling himself together and finally qualifying as a fully-fledged veterinary surgeon in December 1943.

Alf could never look back on those early days with Donald and Brian without a smile stealing across his face. They were, in reality, days of toil and hardship, but they were also ones of humour and excitement, spent with two of the most entertaining men he had had the privilege of knowing. Many years later, through the books of James Herriot, those hours of laughter along the stone corridors of 'Skeldale House' would be shared by millions more.

CHAPTER TEN

In 1941, Brian Sinclair was involved in a very important event in Alfred Wight's life. The two young men were friendly with a cattle dealer in Thirsk called Malcolm Johnson, a likeable worthy of the town who met Brian and Alf regularly over a few pints of beer. This sociable fellow, a mine of information on the local population, enjoyed not only male company – he knew numerous young ladies, one of whom was a girl called Joan Danbury.

He approached her one day. 'There's a dance in the village hall in Sandhutton tomorrow night,' he said. 'I'm thinking of going with a couple of friends of mine and wondered if you and a few of your friends would like to come along?'

At the time, Joan was already involved quite seriously but she was always interested in a lively night out. 'Who are these friends of yours? Do I know them?' she asked.

'Oh, a couple of young veterinary fellows – Alf Wight and Brian Sinclair. They're a good laugh and they have a car so we could all drive out to the dance.' Wisely, Malcolm decided not to describe the car in too much detail; he was all too aware of its condition. It was a typical Sinclair car, featuring holes in the floor, a symphony of rattles, and the rich, unmistakable aroma of the farmyard.

Joan agreed to go. On a wet night in March 1941, Alf, Brian, Malcolm, Joan, her friend Doreen Garbutt and another young woman set off from 23 Kirkgate in the direction of the village dance in Sandhutton.

Joan Danbury, on whom the character of Helen in the Herriot books is based, was not the daughter of a farmer as the reader is led to believe. She was a secretary at Rymer's Mill, the corn merchants in Thirsk, and her father was an official in local government who was working at that time in York. Her family came from Winchcombe, a picturesque little town in the Cotswolds in Gloucestershire, and they moved to Thirsk when Joan was eight years old. At the time of her meeting with Alf, she had quite a string of boyfriends, her number one suitor being a wealthy farmer from the Harrogate area.

It is not surprising that she had her admirers; photographs taken of her in her younger days reveal a very attractive girl. Some of the descriptions of Helen in the first books describe the young Joan Danbury vividly: 'The small, straight nose' and the mouth 'that turned up markedly at the corners as though she was just going to smile or had just been smiling. The deep warm blue of the eyes under the smoothly arching brows made a dizzying partnership with the rich black brown of the hair.'

Alf's first evening with Joan in the company of their friends did not go smoothly. In appalling weather, the little Ford car ground to a halt on a flooded road with water pouring in through the floor. The men leapt out, pushed the car onto drier ground, restarted it and returned to 23 Kirkgate in order to dry themselves out. They finally made the dance, then returned once again to the old house where they spent the remainder of the evening chatting, drinking and listening to Brian's endless string of humorous stories. He threw in a couple of spectacular convulsions for good measure.

From that very first meeting, Alf decided that Joan Danbury was worth pursuing, although he acknowledged there was plenty of competition. He summoned up the courage to ask whether he could see her again and, to his delight, she agreed. If she was looking for someone with money, she certainly was on to a loser with Alf Wight. He may have been a professional man but, in common with many young veterinary surgeons of his day, he was a financial nonentity; he was worth little more than the clothes he stood up in, with his capital in the bank standing at around five or ten pounds.

She saw other qualities in him. He was an attractive young man with a sincerity and honesty about him that appealed to her. Most importantly, they shared a similar sense of humour and she enjoyed his company – vital ingredients in the recipe for a long and happy relationship.

Their courtship was not an extravagant one. As Joan, too, had little money, visits to the cinema (romantically seated at the back in the 'one and nines'), trips to village dances and walking in the hills were enough to stretch their budget to its limits.

Joan, when time off from her job allowed, often accompanied Alf on his TB Testing trips up into the Dales, helping him by writing the numbers of the cows in the book. Although he loved the Dales, the TB work was boring and repetitive, but to have a young lady, to whom he felt so attracted, accompany him on his long and usually solitary journeys, put a completely different complexion on the working day.

The village dances were a prominent feature of country life. They have largely disappeared today but, fifty or more years ago, there was a dance every Saturday night in one of the local village halls with throngs of people, young and old, attending them. A few drinks in a nearby pub, followed by an energetic fling on the dance floor and a good feed from the vast tables groaning with good Yorkshire fare, made for a great night out.

These events, at which he had a chance to observe the huge appetites of the Yorkshire country folk, were a revelation to Alf. The food, usually prepared by local housewives, was of the highest calibre, even during the austerity of the war years. Pork pies, brawn, piles of sandwiches, apple pies, trifles, cakes and pastries were all consumed with effortless ease. He was a willing participant in the duty of demolishing the delicious mountains of food – and, in Joan, he had an able assistant. Over his many years working among the farming community, Alf never ceased to be astonished by the farmers' ability to put away staggering quantities of food. He was always a good eater himself, but these people were in a league of their own; they worked hard and they had appetites to match.

I remember, many years ago, attending the silver wedding celebrations of one of our farming clients in a small village hall. The place was teeming with laughing faces, there were vast amounts of food, and very soon a buzz of satisfaction pervaded the atmosphere, dominated by the noise of the scraping of plates and happy chatter. People filed up to the serving tables for second and third helpings, and I was taking my turn when I felt a tap on my shoulder. It was an old client of my father called Herbert Megginson who was a regular at the village dances in the days when he used to visit them. He especially used to enjoy dancing with my mother – on one evening, when heavily under the influence of drink, whispering unsteadily into her ear, 'Ooh! You 'ave such a supple form!'

'Supple form', as he was always known from that day onwards, was enjoying himself on this occasion, surrounded as he was by food, drink and women. 'Hey, vitin'ry!' he said, with a knowing smile.

'Hello, Mr Megginson,' I replied. 'This is a good "do". Plenty to eat!'

'Aye, ye're right there!' He plucked at my sleeve. He was obviously impressed by the speed with which the food was being shovelled out of sight. He nodded in the direction of a group of busy, sweating faces. ''Ave yer got yer instruments with yer in case someone gets blown?'

It was at these village functions, which formed such an enjoyable part of their courtship, that Alf and Joan met many people who would become lasting friends, but there was a serious side to Alf's courtship, too. He was a great letter writer and pursued Joan with the written as well as the spoken word. Some early letters in the summer of 1941 reveal his fluency as a writer, together with more than a dash of the romantic to his nature:

Joan my dear,

Why on earth should I be writing this when, if the Gods are kind, I'll be seeing you tonight? I believe it is because something, a very trivial something, has been fermenting in this funny, analytical mind of mine and now demands an outlet. It is just that a succession of little thoughts have resolved themselves into a brooding sense of injustice that so many fellows seem to be writing love letters to young Danbury while Wight, with all his music within him, as it were, never puts pen to paper.

Anyway, Joan, now that I am sitting down to the job, I find myself rather up against it because I realise now that I have never written a love letter before. But how difficult it is when it should be so easy. Somehow, the feeling I have for you is not one that bubbles up and froths over in a mass of endearing terms and neatly turned compliments. It is such a very quiet thing like a wide, deep running river and so completely sincere that I, who have always shunned sincerity with its way of laying one open to all the hurts and disappointments that are going, am rather scared. It is only when I sit down to write that I realise the hopeless inadequacy of words to come near to expressing my thoughts; or maybe I am just tired.

Yes, that's it. How can I make a go of this very important letter when my head is nodding and my arms are aching? But I am going to stagger out with this unfinished fragment so that tomorrow you'll know that I did make an effort anyway. I'll be thinking of you till Tuesday – all the time. Goodnight, Joan.

     Just yours,
     Alf.

His sincerity and quiet determination were to pay dividends. In July 1941, he proposed to Joan and she accepted. Overjoyed, he felt that this was the happiest moment of his entire life as he looked forward in anticipation to spending the rest of his life with the girl he knew was the right one for him. There was, however, a blot on the landscape; it was a large one and it was two hundred miles away in Glasgow.

Alf's mother, a most strong-minded and formidable lady, was not pleased that her son was considering getting married before he had achieved any lasting security. Shortly after he had mentioned the subject to her, she made her feelings known during a tense and bitter telephone conversation. She considered that no one was good enough for her only son, stating, very emphatically, that Joan was taking her place in his affections. His father, too, did not approve, but his objections were of a more practical nature. Pop, the eternal pessimist, worried that his son would be unable to support a young wife at such an impecunious stage of his life and he expressed his feelings strongly, though not quite so forcefully as his wife.

Alf's feelings are best illustrated by reproducing excerpts from letters written to his parents during this difficult time. The first was dated 21 July.

Dear Mother and Dad,

I'd like to tell you how I am feeling just in case you think I am airily dismissing your side of everything. No son ever had more wonderful parents than I have and I have lain awake at nights marvelling at the things you have done for me and worrying about how I could ever repay you. I often thought that there was nothing that I could do for you that would ever make up for your wonderful kindness and self sacrifice. . . .

You asked for some particulars, Mother, about Joan and said you would be a severe critic. You frighten me a bit there because if you are out to criticise you'll find plenty of faults because she's just an ordinary girl and no paragon of all the virtues. . . . But just one thing, Mother; never talk again about anyone 'taking your place'. Nobody will ever do that. You have a compartment all to yourself in my mind.

Alf, although deeply hurt and disappointed by his parents' reaction, would not be put off marrying the girl he loved. In August, he took his somewhat apprehensive fiancée to Glasgow to introduce her to his parents. His mother, although civil to Joan, reiterated her objections to Alf who, in turn, reaffirmed his intention to marry. Pop, who liked Joan immediately, was far more welcoming, but he was overshadowed by the considerably more determined figure of his wife. The visit heralded an especially difficult period in the relationship between Alf and his mother.

One of Hannah Wight's objections to her only son's choice of future wife was that she did not come from a good enough family. Hannah, through her successful dressmaking business, had been mixing in some highly influential social circles. She had made elaborate dresses for several society weddings, and the thought of her only son marrying someone with very little money was too much to bear. Even worse, Alf told her that he and Joan were planning to be married quietly and unceremoniously, thus denying her the prospect of participating in a grand white wedding – one for which she certainly would have expected to have been asked to provide the dresses. She was not in any way rude to Joan during the visit, but her intense disappointment was something she could not fully hide.

Joan was certainly not frozen out by the rest of Alf's family; they both received enormous support from the relations in Sunderland. Both his uncles, Bob and Matt, after meeting her for the first time, were quick to pass their vote of approval back to Hannah. Uncle Stan and Auntie Jinny felt similarly, as did Alf's cousin, Nan. During this difficult time, these warm gestures of friendship and acceptance from Alf's relatives would never be forgotten by Joan. She made many lasting friendships with those open and friendly people of Sunderland.

Hannah, however, continued to voice her disapproval right up until the wedding day in November. Alf's feelings are adequately revealed in a letter written only three days before the wedding:

My dear Mother and Dad,

It was nice to hear your voices the other night and it alleviated to a certain extent the black misery which has been periodically descending on me lately. I may as well tell you how I feel. If you folks were financially secure, I would be happier now than I have ever been which would be natural since I am going to marry the girl I love and who loves me.

You know, never in my life have I felt closer to you two; I seem to have grown up suddenly and life has taken quite a different aspect. I can see, now, everything in its proper place and with its proper value, and right on top of everything stand my father and mother surrounded by thousands of memories that have suddenly grown much clearer and more dear than ever. And yet, at the very same moment, I feel that you folks think I am letting you down and it is a horrible thought which has haunted me ever since that bad session we had on the phone....

It is queer, the things that pass through my mind, streams of little memories that are as clear as day to me now. I see you, Dad, coming in from Yarrows when I was playing with my new meccano. And you, Mother, washing my lip after I'd tried to knock that lamp post down. Dad teaching me how to ride my fairy cycle or me watching the back of your head when you were playing the piano in the 'Alex' and I was perched in the front row. Sunday school and the musical nights with Gus. Mother carting me in a shawl through railway barriers so that I could go for less fare and Dad exasperated over my music lessons. And those two years of pain I had; what would I have done without you when I often felt that I was finished with being strong and healthy?

All through those thoughts there is one thing stands out like a beacon; the wonderful way in which you put me first and gave me a chance to be something in the world. At this moment, I know that what I have and what I am, I owe entirely to you and never did any son appreciate the fact more.... And for goodness sake don't think that you are losing me. You have got me more firmly and closely at this minute than you ever had when you were putting little silk blouses on me. And it will always be that way. And if you're worried about my choice, you don't need to. Joan isn't the perfect creature and has her faults as we all have but I couldn't find a better wife if I looked for the rest of my life.

She worries like mad over her folks too, as she does a lot to support them. They haven't any money except what her old man is making and he hasn't much of a job. When he was clerk of the council here, they had lots of money but now they are broke. Joan does a lot towards the running of their house apart from her wages. She does the shopping and a lot of cooking and general housework.... She could have married money several times over but she has chosen to come and share a bed-sitting room with me which proves a few things.

Now it is very late and my eyes are closing so I really must stop. Remember, as they say about here, 'It'll be right!'

This was an immensely difficult time for Alf, with his loyalties split between the girl he loved and his parents to whom he owed so much. His mother should never have worried about her son's choice of wife, one who would look after him superbly all his life. Joan's greatest pleasure was looking after people and it was not only Alf, but his children as well, who would benefit from this admirable quality. From the earliest days of their marriage, when she would cook, keep a clean home and faithfully answer the telephone for the practice, right up until the final months of his life, when she helped to nurse him through his incurable illness, she would be a totally dedicated wife. The determination to marry Joan Danbury in 1941 was never to be regretted for a moment.

Happy though he was at the prospect of marrying the girl of his choice, the stark response by his parents to his engagement – and, later, marriage – to Joan Danbury, threw Alf into an emotional turmoil. The debt which he felt he owed his parents was one he considered he could never repay, one which preyed on his mind to such an extent that it was partly responsible for a severe breakdown he would experience twenty years later. It was a debt he would, in fact, repay many times over.

James Alfred Wight and Joan Catherine Anderson Danbury were married at 8 o'clock on the morning of 5 November 1941 in the church of St Mary Magdalene in Thirsk. It was a bitterly cold day, and the sum total of five people attended. The best man was none other than his senior partner, Donald Sinclair, while Joan was given away by her employer, Fred Rymer, from the mill in Thirsk. The elderly Canon Young, who conducted the marriage ceremony, shivered with cold throughout and could hardly get through the proceedings fast enough.

At my parents' Golden Wedding celebrations held at the Black Bull Inn near Richmond in 1991, my father reminisced, during an amusing speech, about his quiet little wedding all those years ago. His abiding memory was of Donald standing next to him, his teeth chattering with cold, and mumbling a long succession of 'Amens' at regular intervals, while Canon Young droned on in the icy church. At one vital point, the Canon asked Alf, 'Will you take this woman to be your lawfully wedded husband?!' He corrected himself upon receiving a blank stare. Alf would never forget his feelings on that happy day as he walked out of the church with his new bride. He wrote later, 'I'll always remember that sight – the cold frosty morning, the empty street facing us and the slanting beams of sunlight.'

It was an amusing experience for Joan and Alf to watch, many years later, the wedding of James Herriot and his bride in the television series 'All Creatures Great and Small'. The occasion portrayed was a substantial one, with the bride wearing white and many notable people in attendance. The reality was so different; although not uncommon during the war years, few people will have had a more modest wedding ceremony.

Somewhat surprisingly, Joan's parents, both of whom thoroughly approved of Alf as a future son-in-law, did not attend the wedding of their only daughter, despite living only a mile or so away from the church. However, they had their reasons. Apart from Joan's father, Horace, being very ill at the time, they were aware of the problems between Alf and his parents and, knowing that Alf and Joan wanted a very quiet wedding, they decided to stay at home. With Alf's parents having stated their reluctance to attend the wedding, together with difficulties presented in travelling around Britain in wartime, the result was a complete absence of both sets of parents on that unpretentious, but nevertheless, important day.

Alf and Joan had every justification for such a small and secretive occasion. A larger wedding, to which they would have felt compelled to invite many people, was, quite simply, beyond their financial horizons. Joan Danbury was in no better financial state than her husband: the sum total of her wedding dowry was a half-share in a pig which she owned in partnership with a man called Bob Barton. This big strong man, who drove the delivery lorry for Rymer's Mill, could throw eight-stone sacks around as though they were tennis balls, but there was a soft streak to his nature. When the time came for the pig to be killed, Alf remembered the big man leaning on his shoulder, his eyes full of tears. In the course of many months looking after her, he had become deeply attached to this appealing creature.

'Mr Wight,' he said, his voice cracking with emotion, 'that pig – Ah'm tellin' yer, she were a Christian!'

There was some consolation, however. Not only was the meat from that pig, when roasted, some of the finest Alf had ever tasted, but Joan made some magnificent pork pies from some of the choicest cuts. Alf's Uncle George Wilkins, who considered himself an expert in the art of pork-pie tasting, came down from Sunderland one day and asserted that he had never eaten anything finer. That wonderful pig had not died in vain; Joan's dowry may have been a modest one but it provided an unforgettable gastronomic experience.

After the wedding ceremony, Alf and Joan had a champagne breakfast with Donald at 23 Kirkgate before setting off on their honeymoon in the Yorkshire Dales. They stayed in the Wheatsheaf Inn, in the village of Carperby in Wensleydale. This small village inn is so proud of the fact that the future James Herriot spent two nights of his honeymoon there, a plaque on the wall describes it as 'James Herriot's honeymoon hotel'. The inn was famed for its good food all those years ago and the young couple, who were both tremendous eaters, made the most of it – wading into kippers, as well as bacon and eggs, for breakfast, with plenty of locally-made Wensleydale cheese and butter always available.

For the first two days of their honeymoon, Alf spent his time T.B. Testing cows in the hill farms of Wensleydale. This seems a rather unusual activity for such an important holiday but, with the practice becoming busier, he had insisted to Donald that he would combine work with pleasure.

In the event, those few days turned out to be very enjoyable. The farmers and their wives, amazed that the young couple were spending a working honeymoon, treated them to real Dales hospitality in the form of delicious farmhouse meals followed by gifts of ham, eggs and cheese – a real bonus in wartime when such delicacies were severely rationed.

One farmer's wife, Mrs Allen of Gayle, situated at the head of Wensleydale, had repeatedly teased Alf about his marriage prospects. To her astonishment, he said to her just one day before his wedding, 'I've taken your advice, Mrs Allen. I'm going to get married!'

'Eeeh,' she replied, 'Ah'm right pleased! When?'

'Tomorrow!'

'Termorrer? But ye're comin' 'ere to read't TB Test in a couple o' days' time.'

'That's right!'

What a surprise she received when she duly met his brand new bride, dressed in old trousers and scribbling down the numbers of the cows in the book.

The weather was kind and the sight of the Yorkshire Dales in their best autumnal colours enhanced their enjoyment of that unconventional holiday.

On the Saturday morning, Mr and Mrs Alfred Wight left the Wheatsheaf to spend a short time with Alf's relatives in Sunderland – although the entire staff of the hotel was needed to push Alf's old car before it could be persuaded to start. Once in Sunderland, they were treated to some wonderful north-east hospitality, with Alf's happiness tempered only by the deafening silence from his parents in Glasgow. He wrote to them, on the last day of his honeymoon in Sunderland.

My dear Mother and Dad,

This is really the first chance I have had to write since the big event as the first part of our little holiday has consisted of work. I have tried in vain to phone you. But I am worried that you have sent no word – not even a wire on the day. I really am upset about it as I hurried back to Thirsk on Saturday expecting to find some word from you. I only hope nothing is wrong and I'll be relieved when I hear from you. . . .

It is lovely here among the Wilkins and I only wish you folks were sitting in the room with us all. One thing I hope is that there will be a letter from you waiting for me at Thirsk.

Despite his happiness at such an important period of his life, Alf worried continually about the parents to whom he felt so attached. He was, however, convinced that he had made the right decision in standing up to his mother, and hoped that the passage of time would ease her strong feelings about his marriage to Joan. One thing was certain; he was not going to allow this to come between himself and his wife.

There were other important matters to be addressed, not least his future as a veterinary surgeon that stretched before him. After only three days in Sunderland, he was back at work in Thirsk, jumping once again on the treadmill that was veterinary practice. His honeymoon had lasted exactly six days, two of them working ones. His holidays away from the practice would be few and far between for the next ten years of his life.

CHAPTER ELEVEN

Alf and Joan Wight's first home in Thirsk was the upper reaches of 23 Kirkgate, from where they looked out over the old high-walled garden down to the outbuildings, behind which soared the huge elm trees with their permanent residents, hundreds of noisy rooks. Donald had readily agreed to Alf's request to let himself and Joan live in part of the big house. This caused no disruption to Donald as the top floor of the house up until that time was unused, while there was still plenty of space on the lower levels.

Alf and Joan's 'kitchen' at the top of the house differed from the modern equivalent in one notable respect; it had a sink but no water. Every drop had to be brought up in jugs from the ground floor, an excellent form of exercise that did wonders for Alf's circulation. All the cooking was done on two gas rings, with a square tin perched on top of them serving as an oven. Despite these primitive conditions, Joan produced excellent food, something she would continue to do for the rest of her married life. On the first floor, below the kitchen, was their bed-sitting room. This had a fireplace around which they used to sit on cold winter nights, listening to the radio, reading, or playing their favourite card game, Bezique.

Furnishing these two rooms was not a problem. There were no big decisions to be made, their financial status leaving them little choice but to buy the cheap but durable furniture that was available at the many salerooms and house sales in the surrounding area. Alf bought a table from Leyburn for six shillings, and a pair of chairs for five shillings each from a farm client, while Joan's mother provided them with a bed. They also received many useful items as wedding presents from friends in Thirsk.

There was one item they bought new. It was an oak coffee table made by a local woodcarver, Robert Thompson of Kilburn, a village close to Thirsk which is overlooked by the famous White Horse carved into the nearby hillside. This great craftsman's work was, and still is, sold all over the world. When Alf and Joan bought the table, Mr Thompson told them he had some work on display in Westminster Abbey and that he had set his sights on Buckingham Palace next. His trade mark was a little mouse carved on to the wood, and this table is in my mother's sitting-room to this day. I can picture my father, just three days before he died, his arm resting on the fine old table that he bought with his last few shillings, fifty-three years before.

Being married transformed Alf's life. Although the young couple had to divert every penny into the upkeep of their home, they enjoyed their new lifestyle. Joan loved keeping the place in order, housework being a pleasure to her, while Alf's work continued to fascinate him. It was also tiring, and he returned to his wife at the end of each day with no great desire to 'go out on the town', which was just as well considering the state of their bank balance. He bought a wireless called a 'Little Maestro' and the two of them would sit for hours listening to it. Alf was fascinated by the wireless, considering it to be a wonder of modern technology, and hardly able to believe that he could listen to people all over the world, their distant voices issuing from the little plastic box as though they were there with them in the old house in Thirsk.

With Brian Sinclair away at veterinary college, Alf did little socialising, but he still managed to enjoy the odd pint or two, notably with his father-in-law, Horace Danbury. Alf got on well with his parents-in-law from the very beginning. They were both quiet, easy-going people who approved of Alf from the moment they met him. Unfortunately, Horace was not a well man; he suffered from a severe chest complaint that was to be the cause of his death only a few years after meeting Alf. In the meantime, however, the two men enjoyed many a drink together, often before a monumental Sunday lunch prepared by Joan's mother, Laura.

To Alf's intense relief, his own mother soon began to take a more relaxed attitude towards Joan. He took Joan occasionally to Glasgow for the weekend and this had the effect of easing the tension that had previously existed between the two women. His mother, able to see that Alf was extremely happily married, would never again express her feelings so vehemently, although there would, for the first few years of his married life, still be an air of slight unease whenever he took Joan north to Glasgow. Alf, satisfied that things could only go on improving, did not let this upset the happiness of his first year as a married man.

Reading was one of his greatest pleasures and he read for many an hour during the long winter evenings. In the summer months he developed a new interest – gardening. It was an activity he would always enjoy, but he would never have a finer place to follow this pastime than the old walled garden behind 23 Kirkgate. The soil was of the finest quality and, with the high walls around the garden ensuring that the plants were protected from the cold winds, it was capable of growing almost anything. Soon there were neat rows of onions, lettuces, potatoes, peas, beans and other healthy-looking greens, while outdoor tomatoes flourished against the walls, and apple and pear trees stood proudly above the packed rows of vegetables. There was a huge bed of asparagus at one end of the garden while, at the other, a thicket of rhubarb grew at a furious rate, developing stalks like tree trunks. Strawberries were grown in the summer and at one point Donald, who was sporadically enthusiastic about the garden, even grew some melons. The place was a gardener's paradise.

After Alf and his family left Kirkgate, the garden gradually fell into disuse and, many years later, when thronging fans visited the surgery, they would look out over the garden from the french windows in the waiting-room, but there was little for them to see. Two apple trees, the wonderful wistaria and the old walls that still stood as steadily as ever, were all that remained of the garden James Herriot described so lovingly in his books. They would have seen a different picture could they have looked out at the garden when my father was in charge fifty or more years ago.

The reason for the rich soil was twofold. There was always a plentiful supply of manure from the local farms, and this was assiduously dug into the soil – sometimes by a very unwilling Brian but more often by Alf with the assistance of an elderly man called Wardman.

Wardman was a general factotum employed by Donald to look after the property, the garden, the cars and anything else that needed attention. He also cared for the hens and pigs that Donald and Alf kept at one time in the buildings surrounding the yard at the bottom of the garden. Wardman had come through the Great War of 1914–18 and there was nothing he liked better than to reminisce about his experiences to anyone who could spare an hour or two in his dark little den, a converted stable in the yard where he lovingly stored all his tools.

Wardman appears in the Herriot books as 'Boardman' and, as the author wrote, he found a willing listener in Tristan. Brian certainly used to sit for hours down there, smoking a long succession of Woodbines and convulsing old Wardman with his inexhaustible store of jokes. The old man looked forward eagerly to Brian's holidays from veterinary college.

Another reason for the rich soil was that it contained the deeply-buried bodies of innumerable dead animals. One of the problems for the veterinary surgeon in those days was the disposal of carcases. This is not a worry for the modern vet – all bodies are now cremated cleanly and efficiently – but, years ago, there existed only the doubtful services of the knacker man who not only picked up fallen stock from farms, but would call in at the surgery as well to pick up the bodies of animals that had been post-mortemed, died naturally, or had had to be put to sleep. When the knacker man failed to arrive at the surgery – which was frequently – the vets had to roll up their sleeves and dig the bodies deeply into the ground. The garden gradually turned into a giant cemetery, one that grew giant vegetables.

One evening, around twenty years ago, I was with my father in an Italian restaurant in Yarm (he always loved pasta dishes) and, as so often, he was reminiscing about old times. The subject of the garden, and life with Donald, came up. I thought that I had heard all the astonishing exploits of Donald Sinclair, but my father had another one or two up his sleeve.

'Donald is an amazing man, and I have written about him at length in my books, but there are some stories about him that I would never print,' he said.

'Why not?' I asked.

'Well, Donald is a bit sensitive about the way he has been portrayed as Siegfried in the books. He doesn't consider himself to be an eccentric and I don't wish to make matters worse by telling everyone about some of his more bizarre behaviour.'

I was surprised. I knew that Donald was a very unusual person but I thought I had heard all the stories.

'Did I ever tell you about the "hot bones"?' continued my father with a sidelong glance.

This sounded an interesting one. He then proceeded to recount an episode that illustrated, perfectly, the impulsive and chaotic nature of his partner.

One day, in the early years of his employment in Thirsk, Alf had to put a little dog to sleep. He understood the owner's grief and performed the sad task with great sympathy and respect for her feelings. He thought that this was the end of the matter but, about three weeks later, she came in to the surgery to thank him for his kindness, and to ask him a very delicate question.

'Mr Wight,' she said, 'you were so kind to me and I am very grateful to you but I have been haunted by something since that sad day.' There was a pause as she composed herself before continuing. 'Could you tell me what happened to the body of my poor little dog?'

Alf's brain shot into overdrive. This was a difficult one. How could he tell the owner that the knacker man had probably picked it up and that his body could be anywhere? Suddenly, he was aware of a presence at his right shoulder. Donald had walked into the room and was in one of his confident and effusive moods.

'I'm so sorry about your dog,' he said, oozing charm, 'and you have no need to worry. He was cremated!'

The lady was overjoyed. 'Oh thank you so much!' she said. 'That is exactly what I hoped you would say. If you will excuse me for a moment, I'll just pop out to my car. I have a cloth to put his ashes in.'

She walked out of the door to a profound silence from the two veterinary surgeons. Alf felt a sudden tightening in the pit of his stomach.

'She shall have them!' Donald cried suddenly, springing out of the room.

There were a few tense moments as Alf tried to guess his partner's next move. He steeled himself for his return. He did not have to wait long. Donald swept back through the door within two minutes, brandishing a dustpan in which was a heap of grey ashes and bones. Down in the old back-yard, Wardman kept an outside boiler, used for heating swill for the pigs, underneath which piles of ash and old bones collected; it was to here that Donald had just executed a speedy visit. The owner, who had returned, held out the cloth and Donald poured the ashes onto it. Alf stared at his partner. He could not believe this was happening, but the charade was not yet over. Suddenly the lady gave a loud shriek and threw the cloth high into the air; within seconds, the room was thick with smoke. The little dog may have died weeks ago, but his 'ashes' were still hot.

Alf might have had a fairly quiet life during the first years of his marriage but, with a partner like Donald Sinclair, there was never a dull moment. One evening the two of them were having a drink in the Golden Fleece. After a hard day's work, it was a pleasant place in which to unwind – the good beer, pleasant chatter and the roaring fire all helping to make the world seem a better place. (This pub is called the 'Drovers Arms' in the Herriot books.)

With them on this particular evening was a man called Scott Inglis. He was working for an organisation known as the W.A.R.A.G. This was established during the war to give advice to farmers, helping them produce food for the nation as efficiently as possible. Scott Inglis was a mild, gentlemanly person who later became a professor of Animal Husbandry at Glasgow Veterinary School – and who taught me in the early 1960s. I remember him, during one lecture, saying, 'Nine times seven. Let me see now, that's approximately sixty-three.' He could be a little vague at times and was a most charming and inoffensive man.

He was carrying a round steel helmet in his hand on that occasion and Donald was extremely interested in it. 'What's that, Scott?' he asked abruptly.

'It's my safety helmet,' he replied.

'What's it for?' continued Donald.

'It protects me from such things as falling bricks when I am, for example, going round damaged buildings.'

'Is it any good?'

'Oh yes, it's very strong.'

'How strong?'

'Well, let me see. If you hit me with that poker there, by the fire, it would protect me from injury very effectively.'

'Can I test it out?'

'By all means, Donald. You can hit me over the head with the poker and you will see that it protects me very well,' continued Scott confidently. He placed the helmet firmly onto his head.

Donald moved over to the fire, grasped the poker and swished the air with it a couple of times. Alf felt a stab of tension. He was aware of his senior partner's unusual behaviour but was unprepared for the next move. Suddenly, Donald raised the heavy poker and, with every ounce of his strength, brought it down on to Scott Inglis' head with a terrifying crash. A huge dent appeared in the helmet and the little man sank silently to the floor.

Alf stared with horror at the motionless figure. 'My God!' he thought, 'he's killed him!'

After an agonising few moments, Scott delicately regained his feet, but it took more than one restorative draught to effect his complete recovery. His helmet had just passed its most severe examination.

I remember Professor Inglis, many years later in Glasgow, asking me how everyone was in Thirsk. 'How is your father?' he asked.

'Very well, thank you,' I replied.

'Good! Do please give him my regards.' Professor Inglis paused for a moment before speaking again. 'And Mr Sinclair?'

'He's well too.'

He paused again. 'An interesting man,' he said, a distant look in his eyes.

Alf was not alone in finding Donald Sinclair a source of amusement. Many others, farm clients included, were unable to mention his name without introducing a humorous slant into the conversation.

Many years later, my father was highly amused to hear of a visit that I had made to Sir Hugh Bell's farm at the village of Ingleby Cross. Sir Hugh appeared in the Herriot book, *Vets Might Fly*, as a character called Lord Hulton, and was a most open and likeable man. I had been to see some pigs and Sir Hugh, who was friendly with Donald, was asking after him.

'How is Donald these days?' he said, with a mischievous grin.

'Very well, Sir Hugh,' I replied.

'Pleased to hear it,' he continued. His boyish face then broke into a wide smile and his sharp eyes danced before me. 'An entertaining man,' he chuckled, 'and only *slightly* insane!'

Alf may have had an extraordinary employer for whom he had to work very hard, but his good fortune in having a job at all was never far from his mind. Some of his friends from Glasgow Veterinary College were not so fortunate. In a letter to his parents in July 1942, he wrote:

I heard some remarkable things about some of the lads I knew. You remember McIntyre who was in my year? Well, he's still there, poor devil, sitting surgery for the umpteenth time. And Andy Flynn is still sitting pathology. Isn't it amazing! Aubrey couldn't stick it any longer at Cornwall, describing his employer as a miserable old 'get', and is now in Sussex, while Eddie Straiton seems to be the only one who is doing well. Jimmy Steele says Eddie works from 6 am to 9 pm every day and will have a nervous breakdown if he isn't careful. The wages, I hear, are awful, too, and though I sometimes grouse at my lot, I feel I am a great deal better off in most respects. There are too many miserable devils and slave drivers in this profession. Jimmy has to do most of his jobs on a bicycle.

I laughed till I cried at Jimmy's description of his last billet with one Benjamin P. Boyle in Staffs. He had to cut the lawn and hedges, chop wood, collect coal, but when they told him to clean the chimney, he left!

Jimmy Steele had, in fact, been receiving the princely salary of £100 per year. Although the availability of jobs in the veterinary profession was gradually improving, primitive working conditions for recently qualified assistants were still commonplace. Alf, considering himself to be a lucky man, was determined to make the most of his position in Thirsk. He had soon realised that treating farm animals, especially cows, was what interested him most. In some of the letters to his parents, he expressed his feelings for his job:

It's funny how one gets a reputation in certain branches of the work. Nowadays Donald is the horsey man and I the cow doctor. I am also firmly established as the small animal surgeon of Thirsk. All the ladies now ask for Mr Wight to see to their dogs and cats. Donald can't be bothered much with them and my Sunderland training stands me in good stead – but in my heart I am a cow man. When I started this game, I thought I'd never get to like those seemingly dull and uninteresting creatures, but I really have a great interest and affection for them now.

My dream of the future is a practice of my own in a nice country town, bigger than Thirsk, with enough to provide a decent small animal practice and, outside the town, a good dairying district with cows for ever. Of course, it seems impossible ever to save enough dough to buy a practice.

This illustrates Alf's ambitions – ones which he was to realise in the years to come. His work never failed to enthral him and, even in the wondrous years of his world-wide fame as an author, he would repeatedly maintain that he was 'ninety-nine per cent vet and one per cent author'. This statement might be hard to believe, but there is absolutely no doubt that he was one of those who was blessed with a genuine love for his job throughout his working life.

Although James Herriot endeared himself to so many of his fans through his caring and thoughtful approach to his small animal cases, the real man – Alfred Wight – was, first and foremost, a large animal veterinary surgeon. It was not until well into the late 1960s that the treatment of family pets would become an important contributor to the practice finances.

That is not to say that he was disinterested in the small animal work; he enjoyed it. During those early, tough years when he was tuberculin testing, castrating and dehorning, when he was spending long hours stripped to the waist, calving cows and lambing ewes, the treatment of dogs and cats made a welcome and civilised variation to his day's work. He also realised, from his earliest days as a qualified vet, that the establishment of a thriving small animal side to the practice would become ever more important as the years rolled by.

In the 1940s, however, with the large animal work dominating the veterinary surgeon's day, Alf used to gaze longingly westwards to the green dales of Frank Bingham's practice. They contrasted sharply with the prime arable land around Thirsk, with its fields of sugar beet, barley and potatoes outnumbering those full of grazing animals. He regarded the Dales as the veterinary surgeon's paradise – no ploughed fields, just grass and cows everywhere. He relished his frequent trips to do the TB tests for Frank Bingham. He loved the work but it was hard and, in the winter, it was cold.

One of the first things Alf noticed about Yorkshire was that it was much colder than Glasgow. There is very little shelter on the vast Vale of York, and howling north winds were commonplace, bringing with them heavy falls of snow. Just getting to cases could be a feat in itself. With his primitive little car adding to the discomfort, by the time he had driven the thirty or so miles up into the Dales, he was often numb with cold. On arrival, he had the near stupefying prospect of handling frozen syringes with fingers that had lost all feeling. The first item he put in his car in preparation for these comfortless journeys was a shovel. He was continually digging his car out of huge snow drifts but this, at least, had the effect of thawing him out. He considered himself to be an expert in the art of digging – the garden in summer, and the snow in winter. In a letter to his parents he wrote:

The snow has dominated everything for the last few weeks. What weather! I performed great deeds in battling round the Dales for the first two weeks of the storm and it was some experience, believe me. In the mornings, by the time I had driven to my first farm up in the hills at the top of Wensleydale, I was literally frozen stiff and had to thaw out over the farmer's fire before starting. Then away up the hillsides from barn to barn, trudging through the snow with head down against the blizzard. And so on all day. The first week was a bit too much for me and I found I couldn't eat my dinner when I got home at night – just frozen miserable. But the second week was OK; I must have got tougher.

Last week, however, capped everything. We woke up on Tuesday morning to find snow about four feet deep even on the main roads. It took Donald and me over an hour to dig the cars out of the garages and even then we couldn't get to our local cases.

The Dales were notorious for snow in those days but the high ground of the Thirsk practice was just as bad. When it was raining in Thirsk, villages such as Cold Kirby or Old Byland on the top of the Hambleton Hills could be experiencing sweeping blizzards. Alf got to know, only too well, the high-pitched buzz of his car tyres as they spun wildly on the frozen roads, or the sight of the exquisitely shaped snow drifts sweeping across the road, beautiful but deadly as they relentlessly erased his tracks in the snow. Many times, as he struggled with tough cases on remote farms, Alf would wonder whether he would be able to return home safely over the white, snowbound roads. The less severe winters in Yorkshire today bear little resemblance to those weeks of freezing blizzards that Alfred Wight experienced so many years ago.

His introduction to the county that he would grow to love was, indeed, a cold one, but the summers in Yorkshire could be as sublime as the winters were unrelenting. During those long hot days, as Alf drove from call to call with his car windows and sunroof open, he would continually marvel at his good fortune in working in such a beautiful area of Britain.

However, summer or winter, he had to contend with one of the major difficulties facing veterinary surgeons years ago – the dearth of effective drugs with which to combat disease. Alf, Donald – and, when he was present, Brian – spent many hours concocting mixtures like colic drinks, bloat drenches and stomach powders. Some of the names of the ingredients, such as sweet spirits of nitre, sublimated iodine and flowers of sulphur, had a magical ring to them. Today's drugs do not have the same charisma but there is no doubt that they represent a tremendous advance in the treatment of disease.

When presented with a cow suffering from acute toxic mastitis, the modern vet has an armoury of drugs with which to treat the overwhelming shock to the system. In those early days, before the discovery of antibiotics and anti-inflammatory drugs, the vet survived on his wits. A common treatment was to cut the cow's teat clean off to allow the infected material to drain away. Large sacks were put over the animal to keep her warm and she was drenched with an exotic variety of stimulants. For cases of pneumonia, mustard plasters were slapped onto the animal's chest, while skin conditions received gruesome attention in the form of liberal application of such substances as tar and diesel oil.

A very serious condition in young cattle at pasture was parasitic bronchitis, or 'husk' as it was commonly known. This was caused by a worm that invaded the lungs of the unfortunate animal, and often resulted in death. Nowadays, there is a vaccine to prevent this disease, and modern drugs to treat it, but the old vets had to resort to the only treatment of the day – injections of turpentine and other savage liquids directly into the windpipe in the hope of destroying the worms. Some animals dropped dead on the spot while others, with a bit of luck, survived.

It is not surprising that the farmers in those days developed a stoical approach to treatment of their ailing stock; in many cases, it was an acceptance of the inevitable. 'Only them as 'as 'em can lose 'em!' was the final epitaph for many an animal – and one that Alf heard many times. Some of the old Yorkshiremen may have been dour, which is unsurprising considering the hard, unyielding life they faced, but a dry sense of humour was never too far away.

One of Alf's favourite stories concerned two old farmers who met one day at the cattle market. One of them, Albert, was a man of few words.

'Now then, Albert,' said his friend, 'Ah 'ave a beast wi' husk.'

'Oh aye?' replied Albert.

'Didn't thou 'ave one wi' husk a while back?'

'Aye.'

'Didn't thou inject it wi' turpentine inter its windpipe?'

'Aye.'

'I think Ah'll try summat like that.'

'Oh aye?'

The two men met again a week later.

'Hey, Albert,' said the farmer to his friend, 'yer know that beast o' mine Ah told yer about last week?'

'Aye.'

'That one that 'ad husk?'

'Oh aye.'

'Well, Ah injected it wi' that turpentine, just like thou did wi' thine.'

'Aye?'

'Aye, Ah did – an' it died. Right on't spot!'

'Aye? So did mine!'

What strides the profession has made in its fight against disease. Alf often stated that it was more fun in those old days, but it must also have been very frustrating. Today, it is sometimes possible to diagnose a condition without even touching the animal. Blood samples, X-rays, ultra-sound and other ancillary aids have made the job easier, but the modern vet must never lose his ability to use his basic clinical skills. Alf did not have these modern advantages in his formative years as a vet; he had only his eyes, his hands and his brain. Perhaps this fact contributed, in no small way, to his emergence as a first-rate clinician. In all the years that I worked with him, he seemed to have a natural ability to accurately diagnose and treat his cases. Those hard, early days had stood him in good stead.

To survive his physically demanding job, Alf needed to be well 'fuelled'. In Joan, he had a wife who made sure that his energy levels were well maintained as a succession of fine meals kept heading in his direction. One of the big differences about married life was the superb variety of sandwiches he discovered each day when he was away working in the Dales. Formerly, he had survived on an interminable succession of cheese sandwiches but now it was different. To open every lunch pack was a gastronomic adventure as he bit into succulent pies, delicious cakes, and sandwiches made with homemade bread. As Alf tasted the wonderful food produced by Joan (the deprivations induced by wartime rationing seemed to have little effect upon her ingenuity as a cook), his mind would frequently stray back to his bachelor days in 23 Kirkgate when he, Donald and Brian often had to cook for themselves. On the occasions when the housekeeper, Mrs Wetherill, was away, Donald would roast huge pieces of mutton which would last the men for days. Alf, who was never keen on either lamb or mutton, experienced a dull, leaden sensation in his stomach as he remembered those endless slices of cold, grey meat, with their thick white slabs of fat.

It was not only Alf who realised that he was on to a good thing in his early married days. His college friends, Jimmy Steele and Bob Smith, who had procured jobs in the nearby towns of Knaresborough and

Boroughbridge, visited Alf in Thirsk on several occasions. The three men not only had the enjoyment of swapping their tales of triumphs and disasters, but they had the pleasure of sampling Joan's cooking. Jimmy assured Alf that the experience had convinced him that it was time he looked out for a wife for himself.

The daily consumption of such culinary delights had its downside. Alf, for the first time in his life, began to get fat. His intake of food was so high that even the hard exercise up and down the hillsides in the Dales, or the energy-sapping calvings, rolling about on cow byre floors, were not enough to burn away the calories. Donald was the opposite. He was built like a string bean, with long thin arms and a spare waistline. As one client commented: 'Ah've seen more fat on a fork shaft!' Another client, Jim Fletcher, remarked to me one day, while recalling Messrs Sinclair and Wight of years ago: 'When your dad stripped off we used to say, "Where's 'e come from?" and when Mr Sinclair took his shirt off, we'd say, "Where's 'he gone?"'

One thing, above all others, that benefited from Alf's life as a country veterinary surgeon was his health. The active outdoor life – calvings, foalings, the miles of exercise hiking to the high barns in the Yorkshire Dales – made him feel better than he had done for many years. Alf was deeply appreciative of his good fortune in this respect. He looked back to those pain-wracked days in Sunderland, hardly able to believe that, in so short a space, the healing hand of time, together with the clean, fresh air of Yorkshire, had effected such a remarkable transformation.

Alf's happy state of mind reached new heights in July 1942 when he learned that Joan was expecting their first child. He was soon to be a father as well as a husband, and the idea of becoming a family man was one that thrilled him. He had a job that he loved, a wife with whom he was exceptionally happy, and a baby was on the way.

There was something, however that loomed over him like a gathering storm. Some sixteen months earlier, just a week or two after meeting Joan for the first time, Alf had signed up to join the Royal Air Force. As a qualified veterinary surgeon – a profession rated as a reserved occupation – there had been little pressure on his serving in the armed forces, but at the time, fired up by the wave of patriotism that had been sweeping Britain, he had looked forward enthusiastically to serving his country at a time of need. As the months had flown by, with Alf beginning to wonder whether he would ever be called up for training, he and Joan had seen no point in delaying starting a family. When his call-up papers did eventually arrive on his twenty-sixth birthday in October 1942, they filled him with gloom. He was now in a vastly different position to that of the carefree young bachelor vet of sixteen months ago. He was a married man with a pregnant wife and responsibilities. Also, having begun to establish himself in the practice, he looked on his forthcoming call-up as potentially damaging to both his career and to the practice.

Just over seven weeks later, on 16 November 1942, Alf Wight boarded the train at Thirsk railway station on the way to serving his country in the Royal Air Force. He was to assume a new identity – 1047279 AC2 Wight, J. A. On that day, he had graduated from the status of an insignificant specimen of the veterinary profession to that of a tiny pawn in the turmoil of the Second World War.

CHAPTER TWELVE

Quite apart from wanting to serve his country at a time when Britain was virtually standing alone against the might of Nazi Germany, there was another good reason why Alf joined up. In March 1941, the German Luftwaffe had launched a savage air raid on the city of Glasgow. The area of Clydebank was a prime target, with the big shipyards on the River Clyde receiving special attention; hundreds of people had been killed. It had been an intensely worrying time for Alf because his parents lived very close to Clydebank. They survived but their house at 694 Anniesland Road, into which they had only recently moved, was badly damaged. Alf had been given leave by Donald to visit Glasgow to see his parents, from where he wrote a letter to Joan giving her an account of the grim conditions there.

My dear Joan,

I suppose you'll have heard that my house was blitzed. After some searching around, I've found that there is no chance at all of finding another place around here as everyone is in the same boat. So, there's nothing for it but to try to make the battered remains of the old house more or less habitable and to get a good shelter built in the garden in case of a second visit.

Number 694 looks rather like Rievaulx Abbey on a smaller scale but we have managed to make two rooms at the back sort of half safe though it's dangerous to bang the doors in case the ceiling comes down. It is all rather sickening but I am too pleased that my folks are safe to worry about material things. Mother sleeps at one of the few comparatively sound houses in the district and Dad and I kip down on the floor under a dining table, just in case the ceiling gets tired of staying up. We have reached the stage of laughing at everything so we aren't so bad. My beloved grand piano had a leg blown away but I've managed to get it shored up and, much to my delight, it still plays. I bet it's queer for people outside to hear strains of music emanating from the ruins!

Infuriated by this affront to his beloved city, Alf had signed up to join the Royal Air Force. Little did he realise that it would be a full twenty months before he would begin his training. One reason was that there was no shortage of young men applying to become fighter pilots; it was in maintaining the supply of planes, not those who could fly them, where the RAF felt its most pressing need. Moreover, the authorities did not regard a man in a reserved occupation to be high on the call-up list: veterinary surgeons were needed at home to contribute towards the well-being of British agriculture and the all-important food production line. To further add to the problems he faced endeavouring to serve his country, that old bugbear came back to haunt him – mathematics.

He had to pass some fundamental mathematics exams before he would be accepted, and he attended night school in Thirsk to brush up on his slender knowledge of the subject. After a number of failures, he finally gained the necessary grades and was therefore clear to go when his call-up papers arrived.

He described that day in November 1942, as he left Thirsk to begin his training, as the 'blackest day of my life'. Driving away from 23 Kirkgate, and seeing his pregnant wife waving tearfully from the window, was a scene he would never forget.

Alf's time in the Royal Air Force was not particularly eventful, and he was only there for just over a year before being invalided out but, ironically, there is a mass of information about that disappointing part of his life. He and Joan wrote to each other almost every day while he was serving, and she kept literally hundreds of the letters that passed between them.

On his very first day away from Joan, he wrote to her:

My Darling Joan,

I have just a few minutes before lights out to write this and I'm feeling very tired after a day of tremendous activity. I feel heaps better than I did this morning; I thought it was the cold that made me feel so rotten, but it wasn't. It was leaving my little wife that did it. Honestly, Joan, I've never felt so completely lousy in my life and believe me, it has been a lesson to me; I'll never leave my little wife again. It's funny, I haven't known you so very long and yet you have become my whole life to me and when I left Thirsk I felt I was leaving a part of myself behind.

He was certainly at a low ebb – but no more so than Joan. Like many other young wives, she was terrified that her husband might be killed while on active service, not a happy thought for a young woman carrying her first child. She knew that she would only see him very rarely, and it certainly didn't help that his pay was to be a paltry three shillings per day – a big step down from the £4–5 per week he had earned in the practice. He sent as much as he could afford but it amounted to very little. With her parents having none to spare and her husband almost penniless, Joan was supported by a wartime benefit and maternity allowance amounting to about £2 10s per week.

The multitude of letters that passed between Alf and Joan carried a similar theme – Alf, despite the pain of being away from his wife, displayed a determination to do well in the RAF, while Joan wished desperately that he could return home. It was a very sad young woman who waited expectantly each morning for the letter from her husband that would help to lift her spirits.

Alf's first month was spent at Regent's Park in London where he was examined, inoculated and trained in preparation for his assignment to an initial training wing. He drilled and marched for hours in all weathers. He attended courses on maths, navigation and meteorology which were followed by test papers. To his surprise, he passed the basic maths exam quite easily.

The standard required was not very high which, of course, suited Alf very well but it was a stern test for those who had had little education; for these men, the sitting of examinations was a frightening experience. Later, when he moved to Scarborough, he was amazed to observe the effect this had on some of his fellow trainees. Men came out in boils, some hardly slept and there were long queues for the lavatories just before the exams.

Alf was older than most of the other men, with the experience of many years of exams behind him and, at the ripe old age of twenty-six, he was looked upon by his comrades as something of a father figure, with many of his mates approaching him for advice.

In one letter home, he gives an indication of the intellectual level of some of the new recruits. When visiting Westminster Abbey, one young airman saw a floor-plate with the words, 'Here lies an Officer and a Gentleman.' The young man remarked, 'Queer idea, burying two guys in one grave.'

Many others, however, were well educated – with doctors, teachers and accountants amongst those who made his group of fellow trainees a true cross-section of society.

While at Regent's Park, he had one of his teeth pulled out; the RAF was very keen on keeping the men's teeth in good order, as any problems could cause great pain while they were in the air, affecting their concentration. This particular dentist, however, was of doubtful assistance, yanking out the wrong tooth with a huge pair of forceps that bore a strong resemblance to those used on heavy draught horses. Alf had had few problems with his teeth before he joined up; his service days changed all that.

Not knowing where he would be posted for his initial training, Alf applied for a posting to Scarborough on the Yorkshire coast. This was granted and, on 19 December 1942, he moved there, attached to No 10 Initial Training Wing, No 4 Squadron, No 2 Flight. His spirits soared; he would be a mere forty miles away from Joan in Thirsk.

Alf was in Scarborough for five months and it was here that he spent his happiest times in the RAF. He trained very hard and soon became extremely fit, with long runs along the beach and up the sea cliffs, endless marching, drilling and gymnastics, all turning him into a lean, ten-stone machine. The men were billeted in the Grand Hotel where the windows were nailed open to allow the freezing north-east wind to roar around the dormitories. Far from succumbing to terminal pneumonia, he suffered few coughs and sneezes under this hard regime and felt fitter than he had ever been in his life.

As well as the physical training, he studied navigation, morse code, armaments, hygiene and law, in addition to being taught to understand about engines and to develop basic mechanical skills. Alf passed the exams easily and began to feel that he was acquitting himself well. He looked forward to the next step in his training; he wanted to climb into an aeroplane and get into the air.

Alf's most enjoyable times at Scarborough, however, were when he visited Joan in Thirsk and this is a part of my father's life that I find intriguing. He was always a man who played everything by the book; the idea of breaking the law in any way was unthinkable. Throughout his years as a veterinary surgeon he never pocketed a single penny away from the eyes of the Inland Revenue, nor did he smuggle as much as a thimbleful of wine through customs during his holidays abroad. As far as the law was concerned he was a total conformist yet, during the months of January and February 1943, he went absent without leave several times to visit his wife.

He must have been desperate to see her as the consequences, had he been found out, could have been very serious. The need to see Joan was heightened by the strange fact that he experienced odd pains in his stomach as the birth of his first child approached. His letters to Joan at this time refer to these weird pains.

He 'deserted' for the third time on 13 February 1943, to visit her on the day that I was born. As he later wrote in *Vets Might Fly*, he received a severe shock on seeing his son for the first time. He was used to gazing upon new-born animals – usually most attractive and appealing little creatures – but the sight of a freshly-minted human being presented a vastly different picture. His surprise was greeted with waspish indignation by the midwife, Nurse Bell, who promptly showed him another equally grotesque little form in the next room. It was only then that he felt a little calmer.

Shortly after the birth of her son, Joan returned to live with her parents in Sowerby, a village adjoining Thirsk. Alf visited her whenever he could, reminiscing in his later years about the delectable meals she prepared for him. His favourite was egg and chips.

One of the privations of the war years was, of course, rationing. Such staples as eggs and butter were in short supply but Joan had connections with some local farmers while Donald would sometimes slip a little butter and a few eggs her way. Alf was always a man who loved his food – and, in the far-distant future, would eat in some of the finest restaurants in the land – but he would experience nothing that could beat the memory of savouring those plates of fresh eggs and home-made chips.

There were some enterprising individuals in the Thirsk area who made the most of this war-time rationing, with thriving businesses springing up, especially in the farming community. Eggs, butter, bacon and ham were there in plenty, if you knew where to look – and were prepared to pay. As Alf remarked later, 'Aye, it was a black day on some of the farms round here when peace was declared in 1945!'

Following the birth of his son, Alf felt much happier, but he was soon to be posted further away from Joan to begin his flying instruction. On 20 May, with a swollen face – the RAF dentists having raided his mouth again, hauling out two wisdom teeth and filling several others – he arrived at Winkfield aerodrome near Windsor. By now, he had graduated to the rank of Leading Aircraftsman, second class (LAC2) and his pay had shot up to seven shillings per day. Not only was he looking forward to flying, but his financial status was healthier; he had the sum of £9 in the bank and, even better, Joan had £14. Although Alf did not like heights and invariably experienced severe vertigo when perched on the top of a cliff, his days in the air at Windsor held no fear for him. He learned to fly in small single-engined planes, Tiger Moths, and he loved it. Out of fifty men, he was one of only four who were allowed to fly solo after less than two weeks. His first solo flight was on 7 June, and he managed to land successfully first time, while the others made repeated attempts, watched with rising tension by the instructors on the ground.

Alf was making a real success of his RAF career, the only blot being his constant state of homesickness and worry about his wife who, he knew, was still missing him desperately. In addition, Joan's only brother, Joe, of whom she was extremely fond, was serving in Gibraltar and she worried about him, too. Alf tried continually to raise her spirits, exhorting her to think of the happy times that they would have when he returned to civilian life. A letter written from Windsor, just prior to a day or two of leave, illustrates very eloquently his memories of life at home.

Joan my darling,

Tomorrow will be the first of June and it brings back memories of the last two Junes. Two years ago this time, I had just realised I had met the only girl and was walking on air and living in a land of beautiful dreams. Country dances and long nights under the moon, a little print dress and a yellow Laburnum tree. Days of sunshine and longings and jealous frettings, the most wonderful ecstasies and the most dreadful glooms. What a summer that was! And the next year, quiet happy days in our little room, tomato growing, little fights and 'not speakings', trips to York, broccoli on Sundays and over everything a wonderful sense of peace and happiness.

I must away to bed now. I wish my wife was here to cuddle but it won't be long now! Goodnight sweetheart.

If Alf's time at Windsor represented the high spot of his Air Force career, his days of success and achievement were numbered. Henceforward, they would be ones of frustration and disappointment.

From Windsor, he was posted to Salford, near Manchester, where he was due to be classified as a pilot and it was there that his Achilles heel struck. The anal fistula began to give him such pain that, reluctantly, he had to seek medical advice. Despite the doctors showing considerable concern about the condition, he managed to persuade the authorities that he still felt fit to progress to the next stage of his training. He remained keen to do well but his optimism was misplaced; with the RAF adamant that anyone going on to fly combat aircraft had to be one hundred per cent fit, he was now a marked man.

He was posted to Ludlow in Shropshire where the men were subjected to a 'toughening up' course – digging ditches, erecting fences, constructing a reservoir, and helping the local farmers with their harvest. The exercise instilled a sense of fitness and well-being once again, and he soon began to feel as fit as he had been in Scarborough. His hopes of continuing his flying career were dashed, however, when he was summoned to see a specialist in Hereford in July. Three days later, he underwent an operation on the anal fistula in the RAF hospital at Creden Hill, Hereford.

Alf, who remembered the pain of those operations all too well, often used to wonder whether he could have progressed further in the RAF had the Air Force surgeons just left him alone. The operation in Hereford was a disaster; far from curing his condition, it merely added to the pain and he very soon realised that a fulfilling career in the forces was never going to be possible. As he watched his trainee comrades depart without him for Canada to continue their instruction, he felt deep disappointment and failure.

He was sent to a convalescent home, Pudlestone Court Auxiliary Hospital near Leominster, where he had a pleasant but rather aimless existence. Pudlestone Court was a fine old country house, and he was told by the old matron in charge that he should relax as much as possible, taking a little exercise by walking in the beautiful parkland, playing clock golf, tennis or croquet, or just lounging in the deck chairs on the lawn. The food was excellent, he reported to Joan, and he was able to have a hot bath each night.

During his two weeks there, he occupied his time teaching some of the other men to play the piano and spending many hours tending the garden. The hours of working the soil behind 23 Kirkgate had turned him into a very capable gardener and the matron was extremely impressed with his work.

His gentle existence at Pudlestone Court was in marked contrast to the exacting regime in Scarborough but his spirits were sinking lower with every passing day. Still in a great deal of discomfort, he was examined at the hospital at Creden Hill where, to his despair, he was operated upon yet again. The operation was another pain-racked failure. To further compound his feelings of misery, it was discovered that the tooth that had been pulled out eight months before still had some of the root left embedded in his jaw. Realising that, in the eyes of the RAF, he was an invalid, he knew that he would never progress further in the quest to serve his country. He had had enough – he wanted to go home.

On 23 August he was sent to Heaton Park, Manchester, where he was assigned to 'stores'. Here he was put in charge of the stocks and distribution of mountains of clothing and footwear. It was a mercifully brief assignment. In *Vet in a Spin*, he sums up his feelings perfectly, writing: 'Somewhere in the back of my mind a little voice kept enquiring how James Herriot, member of the Royal College of Veterinary Surgeons and trainee pilot, had ever got into this.'

While he was at Heaton Park, he went before the Medical Board again, and this time it was decided that he was to be 'grounded'. He was declared, officially, as 'unfit for aircrew', and on 28 October he was sent to Eastchurch in Kent. This was a discharge camp, a great 'filter tank' of the RAF, from where, in a letter to Joan, he described his feelings about it: 'All the odds and sods of the RAF are here and there are plenty of scroungers and hard cases but plenty of laughs going on too, I must say.'

Despite shafts of humour from his assorted comrades, with whom he spent most of his time playing football or going to the pictures, he was by now thoroughly depressed. As a final insult, his pay was clawed back to three shillings per day after which, having taken stock of his financial position, he reckoned that he had the sum of four pennies to his name!

His feelings of despair at that time were not helped by the news of the death of his beloved old dog, Don. Don had remained in Glasgow when Alf went south to earn his living as a vet; although it was a wrench to leave him, he decided it would be kinder to leave him at the home he knew. Alf's parents had looked after him so well that he had reached the age of fifteen before finally succumbing to renal failure. Alf, who had rarely failed to ask after Don in his many letters home, learned of the news with great sadness as his mind strayed back to the countless miles the 'old hound' had run by his side.

As he looked out across the flat, grey landscape of Eastchurch, Alf reflected upon those happier days he had spent in the green dales of

Yorkshire and on the fine mountains of Scotland. He was at a low point of his life; one that seemed to be going nowhere.

Wondering how long he would be condemned to his futile existence, Alf applied for discharge from the RAF. To his dismay, this was rejected. He was so desperate to re-start a life of meaning and hope, he re-applied. His requests were finally heeded and on 10 November 1943, to his profound relief, he left the Royal Air Force. LAC2 Wight, J. A. had completed his war service for his country. It had lasted for just under one year.

In his books, Alfred Wight wrote amusingly about those final weeks in the Royal Air Force but, in reality, they were some of the most miserable of his life. He was a reject – something that was hard to accept for an ambitious man who took a great pride in all he did.

The reading of his old letters has been a moving experience. Those to his parents during his courtship were like a cry for help and understanding, while those to his wife during his time in the RAF displayed the soul of a man torn apart by conflicting emotions. His early days in the RAF were full of expectation but, as his Air Force career began to crumble, his feelings of hopelessness became more apparent with every letter. Through no fault of his own, his attempts to serve his country in its time of need had failed but he left feeling that, at least, he had tried.

His time in the forces contrasted sharply with that of his old Glasgow chums, Alex Taylor and Eddie Hutchinson. Both had been called up into the army, and both spent years abroad – Alex in North Africa and Italy, while Eddie served his time in the Far East. They would look back on their army days with pride and satisfaction but Eddie paid a price for his. His experiences fighting the Japanese in the jungles of Burma left scars that were never to heal, and he would never again be quite the carefree lad with whom Alf and Alex had spent so many happy times in Glasgow.

His Air Force career, frustrating though it had been, left no scars on Alf; indeed, the affectionate and amusing accounts of his Air Force days that appear in his books hint that he did not consider them a total waste of time. He had met many interesting people from all walks of life and had experienced that feeling of great comradeship common to so many who have served their country in times of war.

Had he not been invalided out, his whole life could have been so different. I remember him saying to me, years later, 'Who knows, much as I have cursed that fistula, it may have saved my life!'

On his return to civilian life, Alf still had a job. He had maintained correspondence with Donald who, with the help of Brian – albeit *still* unqualified – had managed to keep the practice going and now welcomed Alf back. His days of marching, drilling and playing football were at an end. Many years of hard work stretched before him but they would be times of happiness and achievement. No longer an unwanted man, he could now restart his life as a veterinary surgeon – the life that he loved best.

CHAPTER THIRTEEN

After his discharge from the RAF, Alf Wight travelled straight up to Glasgow. His parents were still living at 694 Anniesland Road, which had been rebuilt after the German air raid of almost two years before, and Joan, baby son and Auntie Jinny, from Sunderland, were staying there with them. By this time, Alf's mother had mellowed towards Joan who had visited her in-laws twice during her husband's time in the forces. The proud presentation of her baby to the grandparents contributed greatly towards improving the relationship between Joan and her mother-in-law, one that would become easier as the years passed by.

Alf, although so happy to be reunited with his family, was not at all well. The stress of his final weeks in the RAF, together with the pain induced by the thorough overhaul of both ends of his digestive tract, had left him in a state of mental and physical exhaustion. But he could not stay long in Glasgow; he was broke, and needed to get back to Thirsk and begin building a secure future for his family. On returning to Thirsk, he soon found that the practice had become much busier. Years later, when recalling the pain and weariness at that time, Alf remarked, 'I had the simplest and most effective of therapies – work!'

Alf had a job in Thirsk to return to – but no home. In June 1943, while he was still serving in the RAF, Donald Sinclair had remarried and was living with his wife at 23 Kirkgate. Unable to return to live in the top rooms at Kirkgate, Alf joined Joan and her parents at their home in Sowerby.

This was no hardship for Alf. The house, Blakey View, was situated on the tree-lined front street of this attractive village whose appearance has changed very little to this day. Blakey View was not only comfortable, with a pleasant walled garden at the back, but it was conveniently positioned next to the Crown and Anchor pub and many were the pints of beer that Alf shared with his father-in-law and friends in its welcoming interior.

Donald's marriage had come as a shock to Alf, as he had always considered his senior partner to be the archetypal ladies' man who would never settle down. The James Herriot books depict Siegfried as full of charm and attractive to women, while Tristan is portrayed as the girl-chaser, but as an expert in the art of pursuing the fairer sex, the elder brother stood alone.

Siegfried's housekeeper is described in the books as repeatedly telling visitors to Skeldale House that her employer was in Brawton visiting his mother. James Herriot based this fictional town on Harrogate, which was where Donald's mother lived, but there is little doubt that she was not the only lady who enjoyed the company of the real Siegfried Farnon on his regular absences from the practice.

Donald, however, married well. His bride was Audrey Adamson and they were to remain happily married for over fifty years. She had an entirely different temperament to her husband; where he was impulsive and impatient, she was the embodiment of calm. Many considered her to be the perfect foil for the mercurial Donald.

The new marital status of his senior partner – and thus the changes at Kirkgate – was not the only difference Alf found when he returned to work. He soon discovered that the practice in Thirsk was busier than ever. One of the greatest contributors to the rejuvenation of British agriculture was Adolf Hitler, the war years having ensured that the country needed food. With both arable products and livestock becoming more valuable, farming fortunes took an upturn and, with them, those of the veterinary profession.

Alf found himself working harder and harder, and although enjoying his work despite the long hours, he soon began to feel that a major decision about his future would have to be made. As a salaried partner, he was not only working harder than Donald, but doing virtually all the night calls, and he felt that he deserved his fair share of the profits. In addition, he had no lasting security. He wanted to have a full partnership. With Donald benefiting from the increased revenue from the practice, a large gulf had opened between the fortunes of the two men and it was widening by the day.

Alf would often recall those days. 'My overwhelming ambition was to work for one man – J. A. Wight. Much as I liked Donald, I needed more security. I was simply working myself to the bone and filling his pockets.' In January 1944, he approached Donald with a view to acquiring a full partnership. Donald, although having a genuine affection and respect for his younger colleague, had no intention of relinquishing undisputed control over his practice, and Alf's request was flatly refused.

Alf found he had easily re-established himself in the practice, and felt that he could have enjoyed a long and happy future in Thirsk; he liked the farmers with their hard and honest approach to life, and he got on well with his senior partner, despite his unpredictable ways. Desperately disappointed at Donald's rejection, he began to consider his options.

He would not attempt to establish a business in opposition to Donald; not only did he regard him as a friend but his contract as a salaried partner precluded such a move within a radius of ten miles of Thirsk. He discussed the situation with Joan who, although not wanting to leave a town that had been her home for so many years, was fully prepared to go where her husband could find security which, for a man in his perilous financial position, was of paramount importance. He had no alternative but to begin to look elsewhere.

Many conflicting opinions about Donald Sinclair have been expressed over the years. Articles have been written accusing Alfred Wight of being too hard on Donald, claiming that his portrayal of Donald as Siegfried Farnon was unfair and that he was not simply an eccentric and unusual man, but one full of fine qualities – ones that the books failed to convey. Others, however, have hinted that James Herriot was much too kind towards the character of Siegfried, saying that the real Donald severely exploited his younger partner throughout his professional career.

The truth lies somewhere in between. Above all, Donald was a humorous and warm personality, someone whom it was utterly imposs-ible to dislike and there is no doubt that James Herriot portrayed him as such. The fan mail that Alf received over the years substantiates this; to millions of readers, Siegfried Farnon is a most engaging and fascinating man. In this respect, James Herriot's readers have not been misled, but Alf hid the other side of his partner from his fans. Donald may have been a most interesting and entertaining person but he was also one of the most difficult, with many being of the opinion that the partnership survived thanks only to the patience and good nature of Alfred Wight.

Regular work was something to which Donald would never submit. He was not a lazy man – in fact, he was on the go all the time – but his erratic personality dictated that he could not discipline himself to work regular hours. In the early years when there were only the two of them in the practice, Alf worked almost every night, Donald looking after night duties only when his partner was away on his short and infrequent holidays. The constant and tiring grind of veterinary practice was not for Donald Sinclair.

This fact was only discussed among his close associates and, in his later years, my father used to amuse us with his memories of Donald's reluctance to work. 'There is a subtle difference in our approach to night work between Donald and myself,' he told me, many years ago. 'I dislike night work, but I do it. He loves it, but he doesn't do it!'

Donald regularly told me how much he, himself, loved out-of-hours work and often he would reprimand me gently should I be a little short-tempered in the morning following a night of feverish activity on some farm while everyone else, including Donald, was asleep. 'You should count your blessings, Jim,' he would say to me patiently. 'It's a privilege to get up in the early hours on a summer morning and drive around this beautiful countryside. It's like a holiday with pay!' Strangely, he very rarely enjoyed this attractive aspect of the veterinary surgeon's life.

'Call out the boys!' was a cry we often heard. Such was his pride in our provision of a prompt twenty-four-hour service, he would repeatedly inform our clients, 'If you have any doubts, do not hesitate to telephone. Day or night, call out the boys!'

The 'boys', of whom I was one, did not advertise their services with quite the same enthusiasm. Over the twenty-five years that I worked with Donald, I never saw him perform any night duties at all, save during one period in the mid 1970s. He decided then, for some inexplicable reason and at the age of well over sixty, to begin regular visits to farms at night – something he had *never* done previously. Was this because he was feeling a little guilty? I do not think so. I am sure it was just another example of his unique and unpredictable personality.

Donald's avoidance of regular work throughout his professional life has been a source of great amusement, not only for Alf Wight, but for the many young veterinary surgeons who worked in our practice. A gentle smile would always crease my father's face whenever he produced the classic phrase which summarised his partner's attitude perfectly. 'Willing to work . . . but won't!'

Alf not only worked harder in the practice than his partner, he shouldered almost all the responsibilities of running it. He had no one to share this burden as Donald steadfastly declined to take on any additional partners. Many young veterinary surgeons sought partnerships in Thirsk but all were refused, myself included. Donald did not want the hassle of partnerships, considering them a potential source of bad feeling within the practice. There may be some truth in this, but it also resulted in the practice of Sinclair and Wight lacking any real stability, with the paying customers having to keep adjusting to a long procession of different veterinary assistants driving on to their farms.

James Herriot was very loyal in the portrayal of his partner in the books, revealing little of the difficult side to his character but, in fairness to Donald, his many good qualities would always far outweigh his less appealing ones.

When I was refused a full partnership in 1976, I did not worry too much. I had some security – knowing that, one day, I would inherit my father's share – but for him, back in 1944, the situation was very different.

At the time Alf was not short of offers. He was in regular touch with his first employer, Jock McDowall in Sunderland, while he saw a great deal of Frank Bingham in Leyburn during the course of his work. Not only did both men, having heard of Alf's dissatisfaction with his situation in Thirsk, express their interest in his joining them, but his old Glasgow college friend, Eddie Straiton, who was building up a large practice in Staffordshire, wrote to Alf as early as November 1943 suggesting the possibility of a partnership.

In February 1944, Alf visited Stafford to have a look round and he liked what he saw. Eddie was well organised and his practice was booming, with a busy small animal branch as well as the large animal work. There were cows everywhere; Staffordshire, with its endless green fields full of bovines, was exactly what Alf was looking for. He returned to Thirsk to think things over and discuss a possible move with Joan. There was no urgency to join Eddie straight away, which suited Alf as he wanted time to consider; a big decision lay ahead. Staffordshire, although an attractive county, could not take the place of Yorkshire in Alfred Wight's heart; he desperately wanted to remain in the county that he loved. Over the next few months, he could think of little else but his future. In the rare time off that he had, he visited other parts of the country where there were opportunities to set up in practice.

One place he visited was Whitby on the Yorkshire coast. As there was no veterinary surgeon there at that time, Alf considered it had potential. One afternoon, he stood on the high ground near Whitby Abbey and looked out to sea. As he watched the waves crashing onto the shore, with a bitter north-east wind slamming into his face, he

thought to himself, 'It can be cold in Thirsk, but this is something else!'
He looked out to sea again before turning round in a full circle. Another
thought struck him: 'There's only half a practice here!' No money was
to be made out of the North Sea, and Whitby was crossed off the list.

He visited a practice in Cumbria where there was a possible partnership but he did not take to the veterinary surgeon there; a future with
someone he did not particularly like was not an appealing prospect and
that opening too was jettisoned.

His brain boiled with possibilities. He still had offers from both Jock
McDowall and Frank Bingham but did not consider them seriously.
He did not fancy going back to work in Sunderland. Not only had he
grown to love the beauty of the countryside around Thirsk but he did
not want to return to mainly small animal work, having tasted the life
of a country vet. He realised he would also have to work very long
hours unless old Mac changed his drinking habits. Frank Bingham's
offer had the attraction of a life among cows in some of the finest
scenery in England but, much as he loved Frank, he could not accept,
knowing that he would be doing almost all the work. Frank could spend
vast amounts of time with a glass in his hand and Alf knew him well
enough to know that he would never change. There was no one he
liked more than Frank Bingham, but the easy-going Irishman and the
young, ambitious Alf Wight would form a very one-sided partnership.

Eddie Straiton's offer, too, worried him. Knowing Eddie well, he was
aware of his machine-like work rate. How long could he keep pace with
him? Some letters he received from Eddie in 1944 gave him food for
thought.

'I have been trying to get time to answer your letter, Alf, but this last
fortnight has been something of a nightmare. Ten days ago between 7
and 8 a.m. one morning we received 14 phone calls – all large animal
cases and three of them were calving cases.' In another letter, he wrote:
'I have now finished my colts [castrations], thank goodness. I did seven
last Sunday morning. I have been wanting to get a car with some power
in it for you because this is a widespread area and these small horsepower
cars just don't stand up to the work.' In yet another, he wrote: 'My
wife only sees me once per day at around 6–7 am. One man can only
do so much but two men can attain three times as much.'

Eddie Straiton was extremely keen for Alf to join him. With his
dream of forming a partnership of Straiton and Wight, he not only
offered Alf an immediate and equal share of the practice profits, but

he was prepared to allow him an extended period of time over which to buy his share in the business. This was enough to sway Alf's decision. Despite fully realising that he would be plunging into a fermenting cauldron of work, he could not refuse this opportunity to establish himself in a practice with enormous potential. In the spring of 1944, he accepted Eddie's offer. Never one to be frightened of hard work, he made preparations to join his workaholic chum in Stafford.

Having informed Donald of his decision, he assured him that he would stay on until an assistant was appointed to take his place. Several weeks elapsed before one arrived and it was Alf who had arranged it. While in the Air Force in Scarborough, he had met a fellow veterinary surgeon called Jim Hancock. The two of them had worked together in the Grand Hotel's basement where Jim had remarked that it was an unusual sight to see two qualified vets shovelling mountains of coke. The Air Force authorities must have considered them a good team as they were promoted to mucking out stinking piggeries together later in their RAF careers.

Alf and Jim Hancock had become friends, and when it was agreed that he was leaving Thirsk, Alf contacted Jim, suggesting that there may be a job for him there. Jim accepted and arrived in July 1944.

It was then that all Alf's plans were, quite suddenly, blown clean away; the deal with Eddie Straiton fell through. Eddie wrote to Alf with some disturbing information. With the war still in progress, he said that, despite veterinary surgeons being in a 'reserved occupation', he had been informed that should Alf join him as a partner in the Stafford practice, there existed the possibility of one of them being called up into the armed forces.

This unexpected turn of events presented the two young veterinary surgeons with a very serious situation. Eddie, having built up his practice through months of unbelievably hard work, could not take the chance of being called up; the effects on his thriving, but still young, practice could have been catastrophic. With a heavy heart, he wrote to Alf suggesting that their plans would have to be shelved until after the end of the war – an unknown period of time. Eddie's letters to Alf at that time display genuine, deep-felt sorrow, but he had no alternative.

Alf, now unemployed, with little money and a wife and child to support, had to find work somewhere – and fast. But he was not too downhearted. British agriculture was in a healthy state which meant that there were well-paid jobs available. He began to study the *Veterinary*

Record for vacancies, but could see little that really appealed to him. Despite the problems over a partnership with Donald, he really wanted to remain in Thirsk. He saw little chance of achieving this but, to his astonishment, he was wrong.

Within days, the opportunity arose to restart his career in the town he felt was home, and it was his friend, Jim Hancock, who was largely responsible for providing it. Jim had worked in Thirsk for only a week or two before he realised that such a life was not for him. Not only did he find it impossible to adjust to Donald Sinclair's erratic running of the practice, but he nurtured an ambition to enter the world of teaching and research. When he learned about Alf's predicament and understood that Donald would accept Alf back into the practice readily – the two men were still friends despite the difficulties of the preceding few months – he generously offered to leave quickly, thus providing Alf with the opportunity to start again in Thirsk.

This unselfish and providential gesture from Jim Hancock marked a turning point in Alf Wight's fortunes. From that time on, he established a toehold on the ladder of financial security and consolidated his position through years of hard work and common sense. He was to have periods of financial worry ahead of him but never again would he stand in front of his family as a man who owned . . . nothing.

After Jim Hancock's departure, Alf felt that the finger of fate was pointing to his future in Thirsk. He still could not acquire a full partnership with Donald but, with every passing day, his love of the Thirsk area grew and, with it, the realisation that this was where he wanted to make his home and bring up his family.

Donald was someone he still could not help liking. He had come to know him well and could see beyond his awkward side, discerning qualities he considered vitally important in a colleague – a sense of humour and not so much as a trace of underhand behaviour. The only remaining problem lay in persuading Donald to accept him as a full partner.

Donald's lifestyle, through his marriage to Audrey Adamson, had undergone a remarkable transformation. Audrey, who came from a wealthy shipbuilding family, bought a fine, elegant country house, Southwoods Hall, and she and Donald moved there in 1945. Having married into money, he could indulge in some pleasurable pastimes – shooting, hunting, fishing and walking around his country estate which was finely situated in the hills a few miles east of Thirsk. With the persistent nudge of financial worries no longer being felt by Donald, he did not really have to put in too many hours at 23 Kirkgate. It helped, too, that in Alf Wight he had a willing worker as a colleague.

As 1945 progressed, however, Alf decided, in his own words, 'to be a sucker no longer'. With his standing in the farming community now much stronger, and feeling in a solid position to demand a fairer deal from Donald, he approached him again.

This time, Donald, although still refusing to grant him a full partnership, agreed to Alf having an equal share of the practice profits from 1946 onwards, resulting in a tremendous boost to Alf's finances. He had received a total of £464, about £9 per week in 1945 but, after sharing the profits equally with Donald, he grossed £1229 at the end of the financial year in 1946, a leap of 265%. He had to work like a Trojan to earn it but he didn't mind. He was on his way.

A lot of nonsense has been talked about the exploitation of Alf Wight throughout his years as a veterinary surgeon, describing his earnings as paltry and his attitude to his senior partner as one of a mixture of fear and servility. His earnings in 1945 of around £9 per week were certainly not those of a poor man, while to receive well over £20 per week in 1946, placed him in the bracket of a high earner. In 1946, at the time when Alf was earning £20, a fully qualified chartered accountant, for example, was earning less than half that amount.

On 2 May 1949, Alf Wight's roots in Thirsk were finally anchored when he received a full partnership from Donald. He did not have to pay a single penny for this but he had to earn his share of the partnership in other ways, as one part of the agreement reveals: 'Para. 11. The said James Alfred Wight shall devote his whole time and employ himself diligently in the business of the partnership and use his utmost endeavours to promote the interests thereof and the said Donald Vaughan Sinclair shall give such time as he may desire to the partnership affairs.'

Donald, quite obviously, had no intention of working his fingers to the bone, but the next paragraph reveals that the partnership was not quite so one-sided after all: 'Para. 12. The said Donald Vaughan Sinclair shall be entitled to two-thirds of the fees paid to him or the partnership in respect of professional services rendered by him in connection with the said practice or one-third of the net profits of the said practice whichever shall be the lesser amount and the said James Alfred Wight shall be entitled to receive the balance of the net profits of the partnership.'

This meant that Alfred Wight was to earn more than Donald Sinclair – and so it would turn out to be for the rest of their professional lives. Alf would always work harder in the practice than Donald but, in return, he would earn more. He had displayed patience and determination in achieving his goal of a partnership – two qualities that were to resurface more than twenty years later in his pursuit of success in a very different field.

The arrangement must have been broadly agreeable to both parties as they remained friends and partners for another forty years.

Alf always considered himself fortunate to have known such a fascinating man as Donald Sinclair but Donald, in return, was blessed throughout his professional career with an honest and hard-working colleague. Alf was to be a selfless and loyal partner for Donald and later, as James Herriot, he would be equally generous in his portrayal of Donald as the unforgettable Siegfried Farnon.

CHAPTER FOURTEEN

When Donald and Audrey Sinclair moved out of 23 Kirkgate in the summer of 1945 to live in Southwoods Hall, Alf and his family moved from Blakey View in Sowerby to live, once again, in the old house in Thirsk, staying for the next eight years. Alf's mother-in-law, Laura Danbury, accompanied them. His father-in-law, Horace Danbury, had died in January of that year and Laura did not want to continue living alone at Blakey View. 'Lal', as she was always known, was to live with us for the next thirty years.

Lal was not the typical 'music hall' mother-in-law. She was a quiet, sweet-natured lady with whom we never had a cross word. She was no trouble – in fact, she was a great asset since she was always a willing baby-sitter when Alf and Joan wanted to go out. She was also of great assistance to Joan in the big house, helping her daughter with both the housework and the cooking.

Despite Lal's help, Joan found the burden of keeping 23 Kirkgate clean an exhausting one. Alf worried constantly as he saw his wife slaving day and night in the big rambling house. Through her obsession with housework, she fought stubbornly to keep everything sparkling and geometrically neat and tidy. 'For God's sake, Joan! Stop scrubbing these stone floors, will you?!' was a cry that we heard almost every day. Aware that his pleas were falling on deaf ears, he realised that the only way to stop his wife destroying herself with work was to find another home and leave 23 Kirkgate. My mother's 'domestomania' would be a major factor in our eventual departure from the old house in 1953.

All three storeys of the house were available to the family. The top storey, which had been Alf and Joan's first home, was little used. There were three bedrooms and a bathroom on the middle floor, while downstairs were the sitting-room, dining-room, kitchen and scullery.

In those days, with very little dog and cat work, the waiting-rooms and consulting-rooms were virtually non-existent. People just marched in to have their animals attended to on a little wooden table – either in the drug store or just in the old passageway – very often by the veterinary surgeon in wellington boots.

The extensive and well-stocked surgeries shown in the television series and films of the Herriot books were greatly exaggerated. The real 'Skeldale House' never looked so impressive, with the family rooms doubling up as rudimentary consulting-rooms and waiting areas. The house certainly had plenty of charm with its long winding corridors and the fine walled garden, but it was really quite basic. It was also extremely cold.

The modern large animal veterinary surgeons still have a demanding life, and have to wrestle with difficult cases in cold conditions, but at least they usually return to warm, centrally-heated premises. This luxury was not available to the young Alf Wight. He returned to 23 Kirkgate. We spent many happy years there, but the old house certainly did not wrap us in comfort. The winter winds probed its every corner, with draughts blasting up and down the long stone-flagged corridor. As I spent my youth attired in short trousers, I frequently complained of the cold, whereupon my father used to say, 'Run, Jimmy, run!', and I would hurtle up and down the length of the house to keep warm.

The winters in Yorkshire nowadays are positively tropical in comparison to the iron-hard days we endured when I was a boy. Snow fell regularly throughout the winter months, while huge icicles hung from the gutters for weeks. With the windows often white with frost, my most vivid memories of 23 Kirkgate are of the beautiful wintry patterns on the glass – something we rarely see today in our warm, centrally-heated homes. The only sources of heat in the entire house were two coal fires downstairs and an infuriatingly temperamental anthracite stove in the office.

Most things were done at high speed; to linger resulted in severe hypothermia. On winter mornings, my father, having leapt out of bed into the freezing air of the bedroom, would run downstairs and along the passageway into the kitchen to light the fire. He could never even loosely be described as a handyman and was virtually useless at performing household tasks. His attempts at putting a picture up on the wall would invariably result in its crashing to the floor within minutes; to ask him to change an electric plug was followed by what seemed hours of intense concentration, followed by sparks and the house invariably being plunged into darkness. The job of lighting fires came no easier to him and there was little comfort to his family when they came into the kitchen in their search for warmth each morning. My overriding memories of his tiny fires are of black, smoking mounds from the depths of which occasionally appeared a small, white flame that quivered and spluttered for a few seconds before disappearing as suddenly as it had arrived.

My mother's fires in the living-room were a different proposition. She could have a roaring inferno going within minutes and we sat round this oasis of warmth in high-backed chairs and sofas, the perpetually moving curtains bearing testimony to the draughts coursing around the room.

Although I will never forget the cold of 23 Kirkgate, those days of frost and snow were ones that instil warm and nostalgic memories. Snow has always fascinated children and I was no exception. My father felt somewhat differently about it. Snow meant sledging and snowball fights to me but it spelt trouble for him, preventing his reaching many of the outlying farms. The massive snowfall of 1947, when it snowed almost every day from January until April, often confining him to the house for days, meant a loss of revenue that he could ill afford.

If Alf had little comfort in his home, he had even less in his car. The smooth, modern motor cars of today, with their warm and comfortable interiors, bear scant resemblance to the harsh little machines that Alf drove. Lengthy journeys to farms during those winter days and nights were ones of sheer endurance. The cars had no heaters and, in the severest of weather, with the windscreen white with frost, he would travel with his head out of the window to make sure he was still on the road. With virtually non-existent brakes, and tyres as smooth as glass, these journeys were not only uncomfortable, they were dangerous. Mercifully, there was far less traffic on the road than today.

As a very young boy, I have painful memories of winter journeys in my father's cars in which I used to suffer agonies of cold. I was always a rather noisy little boy and, in response to my cries of discomfort, he would urge me to wiggle my toes in my wellingtons or clap my hands to get the circulation going.

The lack of a heated windscreen was an enormous handicap but, one day, I remember my father proudly showing me his latest acquisition. It was a piece of wire that attached to the windscreen inside the car with two rubber suckers. The ends of the wires led from the car battery and after flicking a switch, an area of melted frost, about six inches square, eventually appeared on the windscreen. 'Look, Jimmy!' he said, peering forward through the tiny field of vision. 'I can see! Isn't it wonderful!'

It was not only the discomfort of his early cars that Alf had to contend with; it was their lack of power. His old Austin Seven had a top speed of around 50–55 miles per hour but to approach such a speed resulted in a colossal noise accompanied by stupendous vibration. At 50 miles per hour, he felt as though he were breaking the sound barrier.

These small horsepower engines were a great disadvantage for anyone working in a hilly district. One of the worst hills in the practice was Sutton Bank, a steep gradient of 1 in 4 that presented a formidable barrier to anyone needing to reach the high ground of the Hambleton Hills. The modern motor car sails up the bank in high gear but, all those years ago, it was a feat of engineering to reach the top. Alf's little cars just could not cope with Sutton Bank but he soon developed a technique to overcome this difficulty. The small, rear-wheeled cars – like his old Austin Seven – were lower geared in reverse so, on approaching the foot of the hill, he used to perform a three-point turn in the road before crawling up backwards.

Although life at 23 Kirkgate could never be called comfortable, Alf was happy; he was working in a part of the country that he loved, and in a practice that he could call his own.

Alf's happiness was enhanced in 1946 when his oldest friend, Alex Taylor, returned from the war and came to live in Thirsk. Having spent the war years in the African desert and the mountains of Italy, he had left the forces without a job, hoping to find employment near to his old friend in Yorkshire. He was engaged to an American girl, Lynne, whom he had met in Rome, and who was soon to join him in Thirsk.

Alf was delighted to see Alex again. He had always had a special affection for his great friend from Glasgow. He wrote to him in Africa at the time of my birth in 1943, asking him to become my godfather. I was christened James Alexander, after the man whom he regarded as his oldest and dearest friend.

When he returned to Britain, Alex was young, fit, about to be married, and was ready to embark on a new life back home. There were only two minor problems; he was completely broke and had not the slightest idea what he was going to do. At this point, Alf stepped in to help him. Alex stayed at 23 Kirkgate for several weeks, during which time he accompanied Alf on his farm visits. He enjoyed the open-air life so much that he decided to make a career for himself in farming.

Alf contacted one or two local farmers, and Alex and Lynne, who married in May of that year, were soon in lodgings with Tommy Banks of Oldstead, a fine and well-respected farmer with a good herd of dairy cows. Farm workers were very poorly paid but Alex received his keep as well as gaining some invaluable practical experience.

At the time before mechanisation, with many tasks having to be performed by hand, every farm employed large numbers of men. Such jobs as hay making, harvesting and mucking out the fold yards were completed by hours of hard physical labour. The old term 'farm labourer' meant just that. The men developed bodies as tough as teak and although Alex reckoned that he was fit and strong – during his five years in the army, he had trekked countless miles through the mountains of Italy – he was ill-prepared for the Yorkshire farmer's typical working day.

One of his first jobs at Tommy Banks's farm was to carry 16-stone sacks of corn up the granary steps. Tommy's sons, Fred and Arthur, could run up the steps with the sacks on their shoulders but when the first sack was put on Alex's shoulders, his knees buckled and he collapsed on the floor, his arms and legs thrashing beneath the huge sack like a stranded beetle. It was a welcome piece of light entertainment for the farm lads.

After leaving Banks's farm, Alex and Lynne found lodgings in Thirsk where they remained for three years. Alf was able to find more work for Alex with a number of farmers who were good customers of the veterinary practice.

Following his time with Tommy Banks, his next job was with Bertram Bosomworth, and it was no easier there than it had been at Oldstead. It was harder. In his heyday, Bert – who is still alive to this day – was the epitome of the rugged Yorkshire farmer, a man whose life was one of work. He worked 'all the hours God sent' and expected his men to do the same. A hard but fair man.

Alex remembers wryly how, during the biting winter, he would set out at six o'clock in the morning to ride the three miles to Bert's farm on Joan's old rusty bicycle. Here, as well as the regular back-breaking chores of milking the cows, feeding and mucking out, he would pick frozen sugar beet out of the iron-hard ground for hours. He returned home each night in a state of complete exhaustion. He would stagger into the house and collapse onto a chair, his head bowed and his arms dangling by his sides. As Alf looked at the limp form with its cracked and bleeding fingers, he often wondered whether he had done his friend a good turn in introducing him to the life of a farmer.

Bert Bosomworth said to Alf one day when he was making a farm visit: 'Aye, I do like Alex. He's a grand bloke. You know, I don't think of him as a worker, he's a companion!' Alex Taylor, Bert's 'companion', laughs heartily when we talk about those old days now, but he wasn't laughing fifty years ago.

There is an old proverb, 'hard work never killed anyone'. This is debatable. Many farmers and veterinary surgeons were crippled by hard labour but men such as Bert Bosomworth are, perhaps, testimony to some truth in the old saying. There is little wonder that my father respected the Yorkshire farmers of his day; some of these men seemed to him to be almost indestructible.

Although the sapping work on the Yorkshire farms almost destroyed Alex Taylor, it provided the first step on the young man's road to a successful career in estate management that was to take him all over the United Kingdom. He would never forget the help he received from his friend Alf Wight during those tough, unrelenting days in Thirsk.

9 May 1947 was a memorable day for Alf and Joan. It was the day they became parents for the second time as their daughter, Rosie, came into the world. Alf, Donald, Alex and several other friends decided to celebrate the birth in style. This they did in the Black Horse in Thirsk (a public house, like many others in the town, that no longer exists) and Alf was later to write about the riotous evening in his seventh book, *The Lord God Made Them All*.

With drinking after hours being strictly forbidden, the carousing was brought rudely to a halt when the local policeman suddenly burst into the room, threatening everyone with an appearance in front of the magistrate in the morning. The officer of the law, however, after a period of gentle diplomacy on the part of Alf and his friends, decided to share in the celebrations and was still in the pub hours later. Dawn was breaking when Alf's car eventually wound its unsteady way through Thirsk market place. Alex was in the back seat, desperately attempting to quieten the obscene chants of the intoxicated policeman who was hurling abuse at the police inspector's car parked near to the town clock.

Rosie's birth marked the beginning of a period during which Alf spent increasing amounts of time with his family. Despite his high work rate, he always found time to spend with us, especially during the summer months when the practice was not so busy. As well as taking us to the seaside, or on trips into the hills around Thirsk, we both travelled miles with him in his car around the farms. This was a time of his life he would repeatedly recall as 'one of the happiest of my life'. Alf Wight was not only a dedicated veterinary surgeon but a truly devoted family man.

The years 1945–50, however, were ones dominated by work. Having gained his full share in the partnership, he dedicated everything towards the prosperity of the practice. They were not only years of hard work, but ones of tremendous change within his profession as new technology and drugs began to sweep away the old techniques. Although this made the veterinary surgeon's life just a little less physically demanding, it was still no job for a weakling.

One day, in the years when I was still at primary school, my father was seated opposite me at the table. His face was drawn and weary. He had been up half the night at a calving case and he looked even more tired than usual.

'You look exhausted, Alf,' my mother said.

He laid his head back, looked up and took a deep breath. 'I am,' he replied. 'What a bloody awful shambles we had this morning!'

It was not surprising that he was tired. Following an exhausting night in a cow byre, he and Donald had endured another of the stress-packed episodes that so typified the veterinary surgeon's life. They had visited a farm near Bedale to castrate a big horse. In those days, Donald and Alf did the job 'standing' – operating on the animal solely under local anaesthesia. This method required great care and expertise; many a veterinary surgeon suffered serious injury, and even death, after receiving fearsome kicks from their patient.

Not surprisingly, the loss of his testicles had not figured in this animal's plans, and he had proved to be a difficult patient. Donald had hardly begun when he felt what he thought was a gentle rush of air past his face. The knife that had been poised in his hand was nowhere to be seen; the lightning kick that had removed it from his grasp had missed his head by inches. It was after this that the show had really begun.

With Donald thankful to be still alive, the horse had been led into a field, at which point a chloroform muzzle had been applied to its nose, the idea being to perform the operation under full anaesthetic. This had sparked a dramatic response and the horse had taken off like a bullet across the field, with Alf hanging on grimly to the head rope. It must have been an entertaining sight but the animal had soon dispensed with his services. As the chloroform took effect, the big horse had crashed through a fence into a garden, flattening an ornamental flower bed in the process. The operation had been finally completed with Alf sitting on the horse's head while Donald operated speedily among the flowers at the other end.

This spectacular variation to his daily routine had been observed by the unsmiling owner of the garden; legal proceedings could well be on the agenda.

I remember my father saying to me when I was very young, 'It's dead easy to remove the testicles from a horse. The real skill lies in persuading him to part with them!' He thought for a few seconds before he spoke again. 'One day – I don't know when, but one day – someone will invent an injection given in a small syringe and the horse will collapse quietly to the ground. The vet will walk up and do the job – no shouting, no flying hooves, just a calm, professional procedure!'

Prophetic words! Nowadays, in our practice, we inject a small volume of anaesthetic into the patient before performing our task safely and quietly; very different from the tumultuous days that Alf 'enjoyed' in his heyday. He was quoted as saying in 1992: 'I enjoy writing about my job because I loved it and it was a particularly interesting one when I was a young man. It was like a holiday with pay to me. The whole thing added up to a lot of laughs. There's more science now, but not so many laughs.' As the many readers of the James Herriot books have learned, there were a lot of laughs – and numerous events were amusing to recall – but they were not quite so funny at the time. As a small boy, I remember laughing loudly on being told of that escapade with the horse, but I do not remember my father sharing in my delight.

Alf Wight experienced more than half a century of enormous transformation within his profession. As a full-time working vet for more than forty years, no one could write with more authority about the changing face of veterinary practice than he. In those days, it was a much more physical job. It was a man's job and the tougher you were, the better. As well as the rough obstetrical work with cows and horses, the vet's day was occupied with jobs such as foot trimming, TB Testing and dehorning and, while the veterinary surgeons of today still have many hard physical tasks to perform, they have more effective drugs and modern equipment to assist them.

In the 1950s, the farming industry decided that cattle would be better without horns and Alf spent many an hour sawing or guillotining them off. It was hard work. The horns were often the consistency of concrete, with the work more akin to butchery than surgery. It was, however, a task that had to be done properly, and many veterinary surgeons took great pride in executing a good, professional job. Alf used to purr with satisfaction upon seeing the fruits of his labours six or eight weeks later – a smooth even slant on each side of the head where once there had been a pair of wicked-looking horns.

Whilst dehorning work was rough, some of the calvings and foalings of these big animals were worse. Farm animals – never having been noted for their cooperation when receiving veterinary attention – seem, most unreasonably, to exhibit a preference for giving birth during the hours of darkness. This meant that Alf's early days as a veterinary surgeon were characterised by many hours of work when most of the country was asleep. To add to the discomfort, stripping off to the waist was frequently a necessity. This harsh existence, with rasping winds playing around the naked torso, took its toll. His respiratory system went through a regular cycle each year; he began coughing every November before finally stopping the following May.

It is more than coincidence that the opening chapter in his very first book describes a calving case. Some of his experiences struggling in cold cow byres remained his most vivid recollections of the hard old days.

One of the lowest points of his career occurred one New Year's morning. He had crawled delicately into bed at 2 a.m., his Scottish connections having ensured that he had celebrated Hogmanay to the full. At six o'clock sharp, the bedside telephone blasted into his ear. He groped for the receiver, to be greeted by the flat voice of a Yorkshire farmer. New Year meant little to these men and there was no need to waste time with season's greetings.

'This is Stanley Duffield, Kilburn Parks. I 'ave an 'eifer calvin'. Don't be ower long!'

Stan Duffield was a faithful client of the practice, one who typified the honest and hard-working Yorkshireman Alf liked and respected, but he felt an intense desire not to see him that morning.

As well as the physical strain on the system, one of the greatest problems for the vet, years ago, was the limited availability of drugs to combat infections. May and Baker's Sulphonilamide, which appeared around the early 1940s, was the only standby, and the old ledgers of Sinclair and Wight were full of references to the widespread use of 'M & B'. This came in powder form which, when mixed with water and poured down the throat, saved many lives.

A great advance, in the mid 1940s was the appearance of sulpha drugs in injection form. One, known as 'Prontosil', was much more effective than the drenches down the throat, but the greatest leap forward in the treatment of infection was the emergence, a year or two later, of antibiotics. In the early years of their use, results were often spectacular – animals with huge temperatures appeared to be miraculously improved the next morning, following one simple injection in the rump. This period of his professional life, during the late 1940s and early 1950s, not only gave Alf enormous satisfaction but his customers were hugely impressed. The vet, armed with a needle and a syringe, attained the status of a magician in the eyes of some of the older farmers.

Modern intensive farming has resulted in the emergence of diseases that were unheard of years ago – ones that often respond poorly to antibiotic injections. The vet is no longer the 'magic man wi't needle', but Alf was one of those lucky enough to experience the golden years of antibiotics, savouring the wonderful results following the simple 'jab in t' arse'.

Donald Sinclair was not slow to exploit this situation. One day he visited a pig with Erysipelas, an acute infectious disease that responds dramatically to an injection of penicillin. The pig belonged to a small-holder called Tommy Barr and Donald decided to make a bit of a name for himself. He always believed in 'painting a black picture' about every case that he saw. 'Never say anything is going to get better,' he used to tell the young assistants in the practice. 'If you say it's going to be all right and it dies, you're sunk! If you say it is going to die and it does, well, you have been proved right. But if it lives, you're a hero!' This particular pig was very ill. It was lying flat out and covered with purple spots but Donald knew that she would be a different pig after his injection. He gave a grim prognosis but the pig, true to form, was eating everything in sight the following day. Little Tommy Barr was staggered.

One week later, Alf was seated at the desk when Tommy came into the surgery to pay his account. He spoke in revered tones as Alf receipted it. 'Mr Wight,' he said, wide eyed, 'Ah'm tellin' yer, it were a miracle!'

Alf was both gratified and a little surprised. It was unusual to hear the work of the veterinary surgeon described in such glowing terms. 'I'm pleased to hear it, Mr Barr,' he replied.

The little man continued. 'Aye, Mr Sinclair came into't pig 'ouse and there she were, all covered wi'spots. Ah thowt she were goin' ter die, an' so did 'e.' Tommy paused for breath. ''E looked at me, an' Ah looked at 'im, an 'e looked at't pig! Ah could tell by't look on 'is face as he thowt it were a bad job. Then 'e shook 'is 'ead an' said, "By gaw, Tommy! Ah doubt we're ower late!"' Tommy's eyes became even wider. 'But we weren't, Mr Wight! 'E capped that pig wi' that injection! It's a miracle, Ah'm tellin' yer!' That example of applying the art as well as the science to the everyday work of the veterinary surgeon resulted in Tommy Barr regarding Donald as a god.

Apart from the arrival of antibiotics, Alf received very little assistance during those long days around the farms, but at least he had some company. I travelled extensively with him from the age of two years, my main jobs being gate-opener and carrier of equipment, tasks that I seriously regarded as of paramount importance. I am sure that those early days, right up until I attended secondary school, 'helping' my father on his daily rounds, were responsible for my following in his footsteps. His great love and enthusiasm for his job could not fail to impress a young mind such as mine.

My sister Rosie, too, was soon to become a seasoned traveller in his car. She, like me, was later to express a desire to become a veterinary surgeon like her father, but he did not share her enthusiasm; he regarded the job as far too rough for a woman. There were few women in veterinary practice in those days, although it is very different now. The majority of graduates are women, and those that enter large animal practice manage very well, but I can still understand his feelings. The thought of his daughter driving lonely miles at night to attend to a hostile, half-ton cow in a muck-spattered byre did not appeal to him. He knew well, from experience, that the bovine race had scant respect for any human being, male or female.

My father had no such worries about me, and was pleased that I showed an interest in his work at such an early age, but he needed to be very patient with me. Much of my 'assistance' in the car was of dubious value. I kept up a fairly non-stop conversation, asking such meaningful questions as, 'Dad, what's the fastest? A magic train, or a phantom motor car . . . Dad? . . . *Dad*? . . . DAD?!'

The pressure of answering these sophisticated questions must have been considerable as he had a great deal on his mind. I can remember him driving around, glassy-eyed, as his overworked brain wrestled with details of difficult cases, as well as mounting problems such as wondering how he could further develop the practice or how on earth he could manage to conjure up enough money to buy his own home? Those loud punctuations from his noisy little son must have been trying, but he usually managed to come up with a satisfactory answer, only to receive many more searching questions as the day wore on.

Rosie and I journeyed widely with my father but he had another passenger in the car who rarely missed a visit. A faithful companion who accompanied him day and night for more than ten years – a dogged traveller who would sulk for days should my father ever have the temerity to leave him at home. His name was Danny.

CHAPTER FIFTEEN

'Alf, where's Danny?' Joan Wight stared at her husband, a ring of tension in her voice.

'Danny? Oh my God! I've left him at Aysgarth Falls!'

Alf, who had just returned from another day's TB Testing in the Dales, was looking forward to relaxing at home but within seconds he was back in his car and screaming through the darkness to Aysgarth, some twenty-five lonely miles away. He had had so much on his mind, he had completely forgotten about his little companion; he just hoped that he would be able to find him.

Throughout the years of his literary fame, Alf, as James Herriot, was repeatedly asked, 'What is your favourite animal?' He invariably gave the same answer, 'Most definitely the dog.'

Dogs figured prominently throughout his life. From his earliest days in practice, a variety of four-legged hairy friends accompanied him on his daily rounds. His books abound with so many stories about dogs that, in 1986, *James Herriot's Dog Stories* was published, an anthology taken from his other books.

During his busy days in veterinary practice, he would always find some time to stop the car and walk his dogs. This pastime, strolling amongst the hills and dales with his favourite animals by his side, provided shafts of delight and relaxation in his demanding days. No matter how busy he was, he always found time for his dogs.

For the first year in practice he was without a dog, but this was soon to change. Joan brought more to the marriage than her half-share of a pig. She owned a dog who was to become the first of a line of canine companions that was to ride thousands of miles with her husband, and walk hundreds more. It was this small, white creature, of mystifying parentage, that he drove frantically up into the Yorkshire Dales to find on that dark night about fifty years ago.

Danny was a compact bundle of muscle and hair who had been presented to Joan by one of her boyfriends. His uncertain origins meant that no one really knew to what breeds of dog he belonged; we always thought of him as mainly West Highland White Terrier but the rich blood of many obscure breeds coursed through his veins.

Danny, whose character radiated self-assurance, was totally devoted to my father. His whole existence was geared to accompanying him everywhere he went; to leave him at home was the ultimate insult. On these rare occasions he sulked very effectively; a small nose peeping from under the bed, exuding waves of hurt and indignation, never failed to consume my father with guilt.

At 23 Kirkgate, the cars were garaged at the bottom of the long garden and Alf would have to walk the length of it when called out at night. He never had to call Danny from his bed; he knew that the small bristly form would be already trotting by his side. Arriving at the dark garage, he would automatically hold the car door open for a second and the little dog would flit silently inside. Alf was never alone during those countless night calls of his early career.

Alf was mortified as now he hurtled along the road to Aysgarth Falls to retrieve his dog; how could he have done such a thing to his faithful ally? He need not have worried. As his car drove onto the bridge over the river, the headlights picked out a small white creature sitting patiently at the roadside; Danny had seemingly not moved since my father had left him there hours previously. After jumping into the car, he sat haughtily on the seat all the way back to Thirsk; to his ordered little mind, this was simply a puzzling deviation from the daily routine.

Danny did not look to be a thin dog; in fact, he appeared to be rather well-rounded. His dense mass of white hair, however, belied the sinewy body beneath. On the few occasions that he was bathed, we were horrified to observe the skeletal figure that emerged from the tub before he disgustedly disappeared up the garden to dry himself off.

In those days it was accepted that dogs roamed freely, and Danny was familiar with every dark alleyway of Thirsk, which resulted in his becoming a veteran of many fights. Here, his thick coat of hair was a great advantage. He never seemed to instigate a fight – he was always being picked upon by large dogs – but he knew how to look after himself. To observe Danny in action was a lesson in tactics. His assailant often appeared to be having the better of the affray, but was managing only to grab huge chunks of hair while his little opponent, having dived underneath the bigger dog, was wreaking havoc from below. These short, frantic fights usually ended with the larger dog limping away, bleeding, while little Danny, covered with saliva, would casually shake himself before trotting off to carry on with his day.

He was not only an expert pugilist, he was also an accomplished ratter, a sport he indulged in gleefully in the yard at the bottom of the garden. My father used to keep battery hens in an old stable which was plagued by rats. They climbed up into the batteries and ran among the hens, eating all the feed – something my father could ill afford to waste. He, Danny and I would work as a team. I would shine a torch while my father blocked off the rat holes around the floor of the stable to prevent their escape, following which, with the aid of a long stick, he would poke at the rats among the battery cages.

Rats would shoot out of the batteries onto the floor where the quivering little dog was waiting; one quick bite was all that he needed. I have a clear childhood memory of Danny, his eager face shining in the torchlight, as he waited for his next victim.

On our visits to Glasgow, where this confident little dog accompanied us on all our holidays, my memories are of the small figure trotting away on his own along the streets surrounding my grandparents' house. The alien city seemed to hold no fears for him.

His wiry little frame was sustained by a Spartan diet. He was never a greedy dog, sniffing disdainfully at succulent plates of meat that other dogs would demolish in seconds, but there was one thing that he loved – pancakes, sugar and milk. Joan fed him this for years and, apart from the odd gristly bone, this unusual dish maintained Danny to a ripe old age. The manufacture of dog food is now a huge industry, with special diets scientifically formulated to help dogs live healthily into old age. I do not know what the modern nutritionist would have made of his diet but it certainly suited our little friend.

Another friend was soon to come back into Alf's life. Towards the end of 1949, he was delighted to learn that Brian Sinclair was returning to live in Yorkshire.

Following his eventual graduation from Edinburgh Veterinary College, Brian had joined the Royal Army Veterinary Corps, during which time he was posted to India where he was, in his own words, 'involved in studies of infertility and spent a large part of my time with my hand up the backsides of water buffaloes'.

Despite the hours he spent exploring these dark and pungent recesses, he developed an interest in infertility which he continued to pursue in his next job working for the Ministry of Agriculture in Inverness in the north of Scotland. He remained there for three years, before returning to work in Yorkshire, again for the Ministry of Agriculture, in the veterinary diagnostic laboratories in Leeds. He was to remain there until his retirement.

Since Brian and Alf now had young families, the wild and carefree escapades of ten years before were fewer, but with Brian having bought a house in nearby Harrogate, he and Alf were able to meet regularly, a refreshing injection in Alf's hectic life. The two friends would never lose touch from that time on.

At about the time that Brian returned to the area, Alf's other great friend, Alex Taylor, left. Alf had heard of a vacancy for an assistant district officer with the Ministry of Agriculture and Alex applied for the job and got it, he and Lynne then moving to Whitby on the Yorkshire coast. Soon he was on his way to passing exams which qualified him as a land agent, managing farms for big estates. Alex was to leave Yorkshire in 1954 but although he then worked in several far-flung corners of the British Isles, he always maintained regular contact with his old friend.

Years later, Alex recalled how much he owed Alf in getting him set up with a job, as well as providing support at a perilous financial period of his life. 'Not only was he responsible for setting me on the right track,' he said, 'but he was, in so many other ways, such a great friend to me.'

During the years immediately following the war, Alf faced a demanding routine. He worked a seven-day week, being on call almost every night and weekend, but he still found time to follow his many interests.

One of these was music. Although not an accomplished performer on any musical instrument – save for his ability to turn out tunes by ear on the piano – music always formed an integral part of his life. He loved all varieties of music and was just as much at home listening to the voices of Bing Crosby or Frank Sinatra as he was sitting in a concert hall, drinking in the enthralling music of a Puccini opera.

Around 1949, he bought a radiogram. This most elegant piece of furniture – for which he saved diligently – was a wireless and record player combined, in front of which he would sit for hours on long winter evenings, listening to the music of his favourite composers, among many others, Beethoven, Mozart, Brahms and Tchaikovsky. He used to listen enthralled, night after night, to the lyrical voice of his favourite tenor, Beniamino Gigli – just as his father had sat, listening interminably to the great Caruso on his old gramophone in Glasgow.

Alf's passion for sport, too, provided therapeutic breaks from work. His football team, Sunderland, was too far away to visit regularly but he could watch first division football at the nearest league team, Middlesbrough. With fellow supporters, Cyril Dale, Bill Spence, Maurice Peckitt, Ray Hart and several others, he travelled regularly to the stadium at Ayresome Park and soon became an avid Middlesbrough fan.

His Uncle Stan, however, ensured that he never forgot his allegiance to the red and white stripes of Sunderland, despatching to Thirsk every week during the season the *Sunderland Football Echo*. After Uncle Stan died, his son-in-law, John Eves, carried on the tradition, the bulletins always being essential reading for Alf.

Through his love of football, he met a man who was to become a lifelong friend. Guy Rob, a farmer from the village of Catton near Thirsk, travelled thousands of miles with Alf to watch football. Guy, who was considerably older than Alf, was an intelligent and humorous man and provided Alf with many hours of welcome conversation along the well-travelled roads to the football grounds.

Guy was a good horseman and hunted regularly but, rather unusually for lovers of field sports, he was also a fanatical follower of cricket and football. This real gentleman was equally at home at the local hunt ball, a glass of fine wine in his hand, as he was on the rain-swept terraces of Sunderland Football Club, clutching a cup of watery Bovril while chatting with the flat-capped supporters around him.

Guy's sister, Kitty, who was also a good friend of Alf, was a respected breeder of Pembroke Corgis and was a client of the practice. She was, however, very different from Guy. She was a small, rounded lady who smoked prodigious numbers of cigarettes, drank steadily, and cared little what she said or to whom she said it. Where Guy was quiet and reserved, Kitty was open in her views.

She was a highly intelligent lady whose sharp wit would provide Alf with many entertaining moments during his visits to her breeding kennels. Alf's favourite memory was of her entering into a heated discussion on the topic of healthy living with a doctor – a tall, lean man who, unlike Kitty, neither smoked nor drank but lived frugally on only the healthiest of foods.

The argument came to a head when he finally took a long look at the chunky little figure before him. 'Miss Rob,' he said, 'I must confess

21. Market day in Thirsk, around the time Alf arrived in Yorkshire

ALF AT WORK

22. In the vegetable garden at 23 Kirkgate

23. TB-testing in the Yorkshire Dales

24. Alf, in RAF uniform, with his baby son

25. Joan on the beach at Llandudno, 1951, with Danny

26. Pop and Alf with Rosie and Jimmy in the garden at 23 Kirkgate

27. With his mother in the Campsie Fells

28. Alf with Jimmy and Rosie, Alex Taylor with Lynne

29. Picnic time with Pop and Granny Wight

30. Alf and Jimmy Youth-Hostelling near Reeth in the Dales, 1957

31. A postcard of Kirkgate in Thirsk, looking up to the parish church
– and, by coincidence, Alf's car outside the surgery

32. A farmer has helpfully cleared a path
through the desperate snow drifts that
were all too common

33. Brian Sinclair *c.* 1948

34. The garden at 23 Kirkgate, not as well tended as when Alf was in charge

SOME OF THE ASSISTANTS AT 23 KIRKGATE

35. Brian Nettleton, t' vet wi't badger

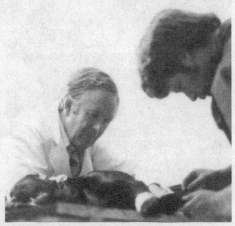

36. The author, with his father, 'always a comforting presence'

37. Hector the Jack Russell almost seemed to want to drive the car himself, while Dan was content to be passenger

38. Joan was as fond of the dogs as Alf

39. Walking up onto Sutton Bank with Hector and Dan, Gormire Lake and the Vale of York below

40. Bodie, the border terrier, Alf's last dog

41. Rosie with Bodie and her dog Polly at Sanna Bay on the Ardnamurchan Peninsula

42. The Whitestone Cliffs on Sutton Bank that Alf loved so much

43. The brass plate outside 23 Kirkgate: Mr D. V. Sinclair and Mr J. A. Wight, Veterinary Surgeons

44. The brass plate outside Skeldale House, announcing S. Farnon and J. Herriot, Veterinary Surgeons

that, should you ever come to my surgery, I would feel compelled to put you on a very strict diet!'

Kitty stared frostily at his spare frame before replying swiftly, 'Doctor, should you ever come to my kennels, the first thing I would do is worm you!'

Alf, like Guy Rob, was a great cricket fan and, whenever he could, would travel to Headingley – the home ground of the Yorkshire Cricket Club – or to the annual cricket festival at Scarborough.

Alf not only managed to watch sport; he played the one at which he had excelled since his boyhood – tennis. He was a regular at the Thirsk Athletic Club, playing for the club in the local tennis league. Alex Taylor, during his few years in Thirsk, was also a member and he and Alf formed a formidable doubles partnership that won many matches for Thirsk. Joan, too, was a good player. She had always been an excellent hockey and tennis player in her years at Thirsk Grammar School, and her keen eye for a ball ensured that she and Alf had many challenging matches together on the club's courts.

One half-day per week, every Thursday, was Alf's only regular break from work for the first ten years of his professional life. These hallowed few hours were spent in the town of Harrogate. This elegant spa town, referred to in the Herriot books as 'Brawton', was one for which he and Joan developed a lasting affection. Right up until the final years of Alf's life, they followed the tradition of visiting Harrogate every Thursday with, in the early days, these visits following a set pattern. Eating was the number one activity.

Alf and Joan always enjoyed their food but their performance with the knife and fork was particularly impressive at that time. Thursdays opened, as usual, with a good breakfast, after which Alf built up an appetite around the practice in the morning while Joan whetted hers, scrubbing at the already clean Kirkgate stone floors. They then departed for Harrogate, stopping en route at the Red Lion at South Stainley, a famous inn noted for its good food. After a substantial three-course lunch, they drove on to Harrogate and spent the next couple of hours browsing around the shops, before hunger pains drew them through the doors of Betty's Café. What followed then was the effortless consumption of hors d'oeuvres, fish and chips and a tasty dessert. The clean and friendly café, with the smiling waitresses and the gentle chink of fine china, was a wonderfully relaxing contrast to the rough and tumble of the cold Yorkshire farmyards.

The next stop was the cinema, after which, upon emerging from its dark interior, they were assailed by the irresistible aromas issuing from Louis, a nearby restaurant. Louis was a small, volatile Italian gentleman, a masterful chef who ran a small café that provided a satisfying end to the Wights' day as they swiftly put large plates of spaghetti, or other delicious Italian dishes, out of sight. Harrogate was a sweet retreat for Alf and Joan – a place where they could forget the clamour of 23 Kirkgate with its relentlessly ringing telephone. He writes affectionately in 1979 about the town in his factual book, *James Herriot's Yorkshire*: 'I love my work but it is stressful, and the sense of escape as Helen and I roamed the streets of this lovely town was unbelievable. Even now, when I step from my car in Harrogate, I can feel myself relaxing, feel the tensions and the pressures growing less.'

One day, Alf and Joan were in Betty's when Alf was approached by a man who said to him, 'Excuse me, but are you George Donaldson?'

'No,' replied Alf. 'Why do you ask?'

'You look just like George Donaldson,' he replied. 'He was at school with me at Strathallan.'

'The only man I know of who comes from Strathallan is Gordon Rae, the vet from Boroughbridge,' continued Alf. 'But I've never actually met him.'

'Now you have,' said the man. 'That's me!'

Gordon Rae began laughing – something that he and Alf would continue to do together for many years to come. This meeting began a lasting friendship between Gordon and his wife Jean, and Alf and Joan, during which time they would meet regularly in Harrogate almost every Thursday afternoon for the next twenty-five years.

If I had to count the very best friends of my father on the fingers of one hand, Gordon Rae would be among them. Originating from north-east Scotland, he ran the veterinary practice in the town of Boroughbridge, not far from Thirsk, and was just the sort of man that my father liked. Gordon was a man with no 'side' to him – someone you felt that you knew well after a very short time in his company, with honesty and decency shining out of his friendly face.

Although in a far stronger financial situation than my father, he had little time for life's fineries. He was happiest spending hours tramping through the mountains and camping with his children. I have clear memories of Gordon, whistling tunelessly away to himself while throwing his boots and rucksack into the back of the car, his smiling face a picture of contentment. Unlike my father, he had little interest in sport or music but, as well as sharing a sense of humour, they both loved the wild uplands of Britain, where they would spend many hours together walking and laughing. This cemented their friendship in such a way that Jean and Gordon, with their three sons, Alastair, Martin and Douglas, would spend several family holidays with us in the years to come.

With Gordon, like Alf, a slave to general practice in those days, he had many amusing tales to tell. It was an especial comfort to Alf, as he laughed at Gordon's stories of triumph and catastrophy, that his exacting life as a veterinary surgeon was one that was shared by so many of his colleagues. Alf Wight would never tire of the company of Gordon Rae.

In 1949, with the veterinary practice in Thirsk becoming impossibly busy for the two vets, Donald and Alf acquired their first employee, a retired railway clerk called Harold Wilson. Up until this time, Joan, as well as being on almost permanent telephone duty, had helped in keeping the practice books but, with her growing family and house to attend to, the work load had become too much for her. Some neat and tidy organisation was badly needed. Bits of paper covered with Donald's spidery writing littered the office, and spare cash bulged out of drawers and over the top of the old pint pot on the mantelpiece that James Herriot was to describe in his first book.

Harold Wilson who, unlike both of his employers, possessed a remarkable head for figures, soon had things in better shape but he had an uphill task in receiving full cooperation from Donald. In *If Only They Could Talk*, James Herriot describes the first secretary in the practice as a 'Miss Harbottle' who had a running battle with Siegfried in trying to balance the practice books. This character was, in fact, based very loosely upon Harold Wilson, and is one example of Alf disguising the true origins of his characters by altering their sex.

The uneasy exchanges between Harold and Donald were many. Harold, who found his employer's shambolic approach to any semblance of organisation almost impossible to bear, in return irritated Donald by loudly clearing his throat to capture his attention, nearly always at a most inconvenient time. Donald was never noted for his patience and there were occasions when he responded vociferously, but despite these eruptions, Harold remained a valued and loyal employee of the practice for more than ten years.

Despite Harold Wilson's help with the office side of the practice, the veterinary workload became ever more demanding and it soon became apparent that it was too much for two men. An added burden for Alf was that Donald was branching out into other ways of earning money, spending increasing hours away from the practice.

Throughout his life, Donald Sinclair was a man with a multitude of interests. As well as shooting, fishing and hunting, he ran a pack of beagles, and later harriers, throughout the 1950s and into the 1960s.

One of his most enduring interests, in his later years, was pigeon racing. He maintained a very good loft of pigeons at Southwoods Hall, being acknowledged as an expert, with pigeon fanciers from all over the north of England asking him for advice. One day I asked him how he enjoyed his transition from horse specialist to a doctor of pigeons. 'Very much,' he replied, 'pigeons don't kick!'

As well as following these pastimes, he embarked on many different money-making schemes – some successful, some disastrous. His most successful was the growing of Christmas trees in the hilly land around Southwoods Hall which began more than thirty-five years ago and is still thriving today, years after his death.

His earlier business ventures, at the time when only he and Alf were in the practice, were less rewarding. In the late 1940s, with Audrey's help, he bought two farms, Bumper Castle and Low Cleaves near Thirlby, thus becoming a part-time farmer as well as a veterinary surgeon. His running of these farms was, characteristically, erratic and they both made losses. He would return to farming again in the 1970s, keeping a herd of suckler cows and calves at Southwoods, this time with a little more success.

In the late 1940s, as well as the running of the farms, he branched out with other more exotic ideas. One of these was the invention of an elaborate wire-mesh construction, designed to allow free-range hens access to a protected run where they would be secure from foxes. Donald's ingenious device, as well as barring the entrance of a predator, also prevented the hens from returning to the free-range areas outside. He dubbed his invention, of which he had high hopes, 'Sinclair's Patent Pop Hole'.

To his delight, he received an order for a large number of these devices. Having obtained the help of a local engineering works in manufacturing them, he transported them all down to Thirsk market place one Monday morning to clinch the deal with the purchaser.

Donald paced impatiently around his towering stack of ironwork but, despite waiting several hours, his 'customer' failed to arrive.

Alf remembered that day very well. It was late in the day when Donald, having reloaded his merchandise, drew up outside the door of 23 Kirkgate on his tractor with a mountainous pile of metalwork in the trailer.

'My God, Alfred!' he shouted. 'I've just about ruptured myself carting these bloody pop holes down here and the bugger hasn't even turned up for them! What am I supposed to do with all this lot now?'

The pop holes returned to Southwoods Hall where they rusted away gently over the course of many years. Undeterred, Donald was soon to try out some other ideas. One of these was the establishment of a mobile fish and chip shop, hopefully christened 'Enterprise Fisheries'. This potentially lucrative business travelled around the villages in the Thirsk area but, unfortunately, it did not live up to its name. Donald made heavy losses while his employees running the business did far better; they realised the potential, pocketed the proceeds and disappeared. 'Enterprise Fisheries', as with the quietly decomposing 'pop holes', would soon be forgotten.

Many have said that the partnership of Donald Sinclair and Alf Wight was a well-balanced one. Donald was always full of ideas – some good, some crazy – with Alf always there to hone them down to sensible proportions. Alf, throughout his working life with Donald, derived enormous amusement from his partner's escapades, but it was not always so funny at the time, especially during the busy period in the late 1940s, when Donald was often absent from the practice, pursuing his various activities.

Help was needed and, in July 1951, it arrived. A young man called John Crooks was the first of a long line of veterinary assistants to walk through the doors of 23 Kirkgate.

CHAPTER SIXTEEN

'It was rather wonderful to have an assistant, especially a good one like him. I had always liked him, but when I got a call to a calving heifer at three o'clock in the morning and was able to pass it on to him and turn over and go back to sleep, I could feel the liking deepening into a warm affection.'

These words, written by James Herriot in his final book, *Every Living Thing*, will have a special significance for many veterinary surgeons who have experienced the dubious privilege of leaving a warm bed to drive out to a cold farm in the early hours.

The arrival of John Crooks heralded a whole new meaning to Alf Wight's life. During his first ten years as a practising vet, he had had to be on call almost every night, and to be able to send someone else was a delightful and unbelievable experience. 'For the first time in my life, I had someone working for me!'

John was not only a competent veterinary surgeon; he was a likeable man and was popular with the customers. For Alf, those years of the early 1950s were happy ones. He and John became great friends and an atmosphere of laughter and good humour pervaded the practice. It was a period of prosperity, with their profession undergoing massive change as agriculture prospered and farmers became more educated. From the veterinary surgeons' side, high standards were expected – an ideal situation for a young, keen man like John Crooks.

John stayed in Thirsk for almost three years. He left in May 1954 to set up his own practice in Beverley, eventually achieving the distinction of becoming President of the British Veterinary Association in 1983. From his exalted position within the profession, however, he never forgot his humble beginnings in Thirsk, looking back on those days with Alf and Donald as some of the happiest of his life. His two employers gave him sound advice and tremendous support, so vital to a young person taking the first difficult steps in his chosen career. He felt so strongly about his time in Thirsk that when he left, he took with him a bottle of 'air' from 23 Kirkgate, hoping that it would infect his new practice with the refreshing and good-natured atmosphere he had enjoyed there.

John and his wife, Heather, remained great friends with the Wights, Alf becoming godfather to their first-born child, Annette. Many years later, when John became President of the BVA, he asked Alf to speak at the inaugural ceremony, at which Alf recalled his memories of John as t'yoong man', as he was called by the farmers. That was when Alf Wight, no longer the youngest man in the practice, suddenly realised that he was getting older.

The luxury of having an assistant transformed Alf's quality of life. Having savoured a taste of a more civilised existence, but still seeing his wife slaving in 23 Kirkgate, he became more determined than ever to get his family out of the big, cold house. On his many visits to the Yorkshire farms, he had been deeply impressed with the farm kitchens. They were not only warm, with fires or big cooking ranges dominating the room, but they seemed to be the nerve centre of the house where everything good seemed to happen. For a long time, he had dreamed of a comfortable house with a big, warm kitchen, he and his family seated cosily around the table. It was a vision so different from the spartan, icy surroundings they had endured for so long.

Although he had earned well for the past five years, Alf had saved very little. Quite apart from the cost of simply feeding and clothing his family, he had taken on additional financial responsibilities; I received private education at Ivy Dene Preparatory School while my mother had enjoyed the help of some busy little women in her uphill task of keeping the house in order. Having begun his professional career with no money behind him, Alf faced the task of looking for a new home with virtually no capital to his name.

Undeterred, he soon had his eye on a house in Stockton Road in Thirsk. Pleasantly situated and just the right size for the family, it was exactly what he was looking for. It was due to be auctioned in the Golden Fleece Hotel and, armed with positive thoughts and very little money, Alf attended the auction with a fierce determination that the house was going to be his. It was an experience he would never forget. The bidding rose to more than £3000, a sum he could only dream about, but with the sweat standing out on his forehead, he doggedly persisted in bidding, so desperate was he to get his family out of the cold, stone-flagged Kirkgate house. Finally, with the tension in the room rising by the second, and with only him and one other contestant left in the bidding, Alf could take no more. His iron resolve suddenly evaporated and he conceded defeat. He left the Golden Fleece a drained and beaten man.

The experience left its mark on him. As he was leaving the hotel, he glanced in a mirror but hardly recognised the ghastly visage framed within it – a gaunt, pale shadow of the man who had strode into the auction with such high hopes. He felt one hundred years old. This incident remained so firmly in his memory that he recalled it in *Every Living Thing*. How would he have felt had he been able to look more than thirty years into the future, when the sum of £3000 would be small change to him?

The loss of that house, in fact, turned out to be providential. Very soon afterwards, and after many hours of bartering, he bought a plot of land in Topcliffe Road on which he had his own house built. This house, costing £1000 less than the other, was not only a better house, but was one built to his and Joan's specification. With his stronger standing in the practice having enabled him to obtain a mortgage for £2000, he could now look forward to some comfort for the family in the years ahead. He called his new house, into which we moved in the winter of 1953, Rowardennan, after a favoured and beautiful spot by the side of Loch Lomond. It would be our home for the next twenty-five years.

I remember the day we moved in, my overriding memory being one of draught-free rooms and wall-to-wall carpeting. There was no central heating but, compared to 23 Kirkgate, it was the warmest, cosiest nest imaginable. The kitchen was Alf's greatest joy and was dominated by an Aga cooker, an impressive, solid bank of warmth that he would worship for the next twenty-five years. Alf, the rumpled figure in his dressing-gown, as he clutched his morning cup of tea and his toast and Marmite, would have reason to bless that Aga for many winters to come.

1953 was a year of happiness and achievement for Alf. He now had his own house, both his children were being educated in an excellent primary school, and the practice was doing well enough to support an assistant. His quality of life had taken a turn for the better.

One sad incident, however, occurred shortly following the move to Rowardennan; our little dog, Danny, was killed on the main road outside the house. He was, by then, fourteen years old, with a hard body and a heart that beat with the regular, strong rhythm of that of a young dog, but his one physical infirmity was deafness. He never heard the car that ended his life but his death was mercifully swift. We had regarded Danny as indestructible but the combination of unfamiliar surroundings and his inability to hear traffic was his undoing.

I remember my father coming into our bedroom to tell Rosie and me that Danny had met his end. We cried unashamedly. He had been regarded as a member of the family and it took us weeks to fully realise that our bushy little friend was no longer trotting by our sides.

Alf quickly realised that to travel to the farms without some canine company in the car was unthinkable, so he did what he always told his customers to do following the loss of a pet – he found another. Donald was running a pack of beagles at the time, in which there was one very small bitch that was regarded as the runt of the pack. As she had difficulty in keeping up with the rest, Donald was only too pleased to present his partner with a replacement for Danny. This appealing little creature, whom we called Dinah, thus became the second dog to travel the long miles at Alf's side.

Dinah was the opposite of her predecessor; her life revolved around the food bowl. After demolishing her meal within seconds, she was always ready for more and she utilised her greatest asset to get it. This irresistible little hound had a sweet face with liquid brown eyes which, once turned upon us, totally demolished our stern resolve not to over-feed her. She invariably joined us at mealtimes and, with my grand-mother, Lal, being the most vulnerable to Dinah's charms, a steady supply of juicy titbits would drop down to the strategically positioned little dog. This high living resulted in Dinah becoming very fat, despite the regular exercise she received while out with Alf. He repeatedly exhorted his mother-in-law to stop feeding Dinah, but the old lady was completely under her spell, resulting in Alf Wight, the vet, having to live with the ignominy of owning one of the fattest dogs in Thirsk.

Dinah, who walked for miles with us, was regarded, like Danny, as a member of the family and we were terribly upset when she died in 1963 at the age of eleven, through inadvertently consuming some rat poison; her insatiable appetite had contributed to her downfall.

James Herriot wrote about his first canine passenger in his fourth book, *Vet in Harness*, referring to him as a beagle named Sam.

Having him with me added so much to the intermissions I granted myself on my daily rounds. Whereas in offices and factories they had tea breaks, I just stopped the car and stepped out into the splendour which was always at hand and walked for a spell down hidden lanes, through woods, or as today, along one of the grassy tracks which ran over the high tops.

This thing which I had always done had a new meaning now. Anybody who has ever walked a dog knows the abiding satisfaction which comes from giving pleasure to a beloved animal and the sight of the little form trotting ahead of me lent a depth which had been missing before.

Sam the beagle is an example of James Herriot's habit of making a composite character out of one or two others. Sam is, in fact, Danny and Dinah rolled into one.

Such was his feeling for the canine race, Alf never understood how anyone could live without a dog, let alone walk without one. One day, he and I were exercising Dinah along the side of the Codbeck, a popular route with the dog walkers of Thirsk. A man whom neither of us recognised strode by, whereupon my father said to me, 'That's a suspicious-looking character! I wonder what he's up to?'

'Why do you say that?' I asked. The man looked fairly normal to me. 'What's suspicious about him?'

He gave the retreating figure another glance and smiled. 'He hasn't got a dog!'

All good things come to an end, and in the spring of 1954, Alf was very sorry to learn that John Crooks was leaving to establish his own practice in another part of Yorkshire. He would see John depart, to be replaced by another young veterinary surgeon – a pattern that would be repeated many times across the portals of 23 Kirkgate.

James Herriot talks about only three veterinary assistants in his books – John Crooks (to whom he gave his real name), Calum Buchanan (real name, Brian Nettleton) and Carmody (who is described as a student in the third book, *Let Sleeping Vets Lie* but who, in fact, was an assistant named Oliver Murphy). There were, of course, many others. Over a period of forty-eight years to the present day, upwards of thirty young people have worked as assistants in the practice – all providing a rich variety of personalities.

James Herriot writes about his sadness at the departure of John Crooks and how this was tempered by the arrival of the unforgettable Calum, complete with his badgers and an assorted menagerie. Brian Nettleton, the real Calum, did not actually arrive until 1957 and there were, in fact, four other assistants in Thirsk in the meantime – men whom Alf never mentioned in his books.

The assistant who followed John was a young man called Jim Chadwick. Had my father ever written another book, he may well have figured in it. While researching my father's life, I came across some work he had put on disk for future reference, among which there is a great deal of material about Jim.

Jim Chadwick was a handsome young man who soon became a great favourite with the ladies. He was not only handsome but charming, and turned out to be a real asset to the practice. He was a very good veterinary surgeon but in his first few weeks lacked confidence, continually appealing to Alf to extricate him from sticky situations. He told me, years later, how grateful he was for all the valuable support he received during those first uncertain weeks.

Alf did not mind; he preferred to have a young man who was willing to listen and learn. I remember another assistant who adopted a different attitude. Believing he knew everything, he refused to heed advice from his more experienced employers. The result was some disastrous mistakes on the farms which gave Alf and Donald many sleepless nights.

My father's old friend Eddie Straiton, for whom I worked for fifteen months, had little time for newly-qualified assistants who thought they knew it all. He had a forthright way of expressing his views. 'I'll tell you what's wrong with such people,' he said to me one day. 'They don't know enough to know they know bugger all!'

Jim Chadwick, however, had the sense to know that he had a great deal to learn. I asked him to tell me about his time in practice at Thirsk.

'I learned more in six months with Alf Wight and Donald Sinclair than I did in five years at university. The practice of Sinclair and Wight was a model which, in later life, I have always sought to achieve. I have had two people that I have tried to emulate. One is J. G. Wright, Dean of the Faculty of Liverpool Veterinary School, the other is Alf Wight.'

Jim wrote about one incident which smacks of life in Skeldale House with the incomparable Siegfried.

'I never saw Alf Wight put out but Donald Sinclair had his moods. I can remember the dressing down I received when I dropped a glass syringe which, of course, broke. Imagine my delight when a few days later Mr Sinclair did the same thing. I did not think it politic to comment though I did see the twinkle in Alf's eye.'

With the TB Testing work increasing, the work load became such that another assistant was appointed – Ken Hibbitt from Bristol, who had seen practice with Alf and Donald as a student. He arrived in November 1954 and he and Jim Chadwick became great friends. His arrival meant that Alf could now dispense with night work completely – an almost incomprehensible luxury. The early 1950s were some of the happiest days of his life. As well as having the pleasure of spending time with his family, he was working with men he liked, while doing a job he found fascinating and rewarding.

Ken also wrote to me about his time working in Thirsk.

'Alf was a great person to see practice with and he was equally good with the new graduate starting a professional career. He did not restrict his young colleagues solely to TB Testing and dehorning and other routine jobs but gave them an opportunity to visit the more interesting cases without interference. On the other hand, he was always available for discussion and pleased to offer advice. If an animal died, he was sympathetic and attempted to boost the confidence of his disappointed colleague. I well remember losing a cow suffering with fat necrosis within the first few months in Thirsk and being reassured by Alf that I could have done no more. He pointed out that he could use a small field to bury all his failures.'

Although the two young men relished their time in Thirsk, they had to work very hard. They received only one weekend off in five, with out-of-hours work extremely common. When on call, they would be almost certain to be on the road.

Alf knew that Ken would not remain in Thirsk. He had the brain of an academic with an ambition to take up a post in teaching and research. He left in February 1956 for Bristol University, where he lectured in Biochemistry, and attained a Doctorate of Philosophy in metabolic disease.

Ken's departure meant that another assistant had to be found and, in that same month, Oliver Murphy arrived. I am sure that, should his name be mentioned to the older clients of our practice, they would not remember him at all, yet he is one of the few assistants upon whom James Herriot bases a story.

Oliver, a serious-minded young man who was also bound for an academic future, stayed only four months in the practice. Although having little idea of how to handle farm stock, and becoming involved in some frightful rodeos, he was a pleasant young man and the farmers liked him. They liked him because he was a trier; he never gave up. Alf used this to effect in his books, describing Oliver as 'Carmody' the student – the young man who stubbornly hung on to a rope attached to a rampant beast while being towed through oceans of manure.

Alf loved to hear funny anecdotes from his colleagues, and Oliver, despite his serious attitude to life, was not without a sense of humour. He returned from a farm one day, plastered in mud after a torrid session trying to catch some wild bullocks. He had met with little success chasing his patients around a fold yard, finally hanging by his legs from a beam with a lasso in an attempt to snare an animal as it thundered past! The huge beasts were all fired up and, had Oliver succeeded in catching one, he would probably never have been seen again. After a few futile minutes hanging upside down, he got a taste of some dry Yorkshire humour.

The farmer appeared beneath him and looked up into his face. 'Mr Wight doesn't do it like this!' he remarked, calmly lighting his pipe.

Oliver was only a transient assistant but he was in Thirsk long enough to leave a strong imprint in the mind of the future James Herriot.

Late in 1956, some dark clouds began to gather. Jim Chadwick wanted to remain in Thirsk but, as a married man with responsibilities, he needed some security. Alf liked him so much that he fervently wished he could make him a partner but, as Donald would not agree, Jim had no alternative but to leave, which he did in January 1957. I was only fourteen years old at the time but I remember how depressed my father was at losing his colleague – someone he felt he could have worked with happily for the rest of his life. He was in low spirits for many days but soon realised that life goes on, and he prepared himself for a fresh face, a new man to instruct in the ways of Sinclair and Wight.

Only days after Jim's departure, Alf stood on the platform of Thirsk railway station where he beheld Jim's successor alighting from the train. He stared disbelievingly at the tall figure with the black moustache and the dark, flashing eyes – a badger draped over his shoulder and a huge dog striding by his side. He had always known the veterinary profession to be wonderfully varied, as the old principal at the Glasgow Veterinary College, Dr Whitehouse, had promised – and this spectacle certainly confirmed it.

Brian Nettleton had arrived. Alf reckoned that the new assistant was going to be an interesting one if nothing else. He was right. Brian was to provide his employers with rich memories that would be reborn in the guise of 'Calum Buchanan', a character who would enthral millions of television viewers many years later.

I doubt that a single one of the older farmers in our practice has ever forgotten Brian Nettleton – 't' vet wi't badger'. Brian was a unique character but also a very fine veterinary surgeon, one of the finest to walk the corridors of 23 Kirkgate. He was not only a big, strong man who impressed the clients with his no-nonsense, practical approach; he was also a skilled surgeon who could perform delicate operations upon all species. He was meticulously clean and his neat wounds always healed rapidly. He had a wonderful rapport with animals, a great asset for a man in his profession. This impressed the clients, many of whom looked upon him as someone approaching a 'Dr Doolittle' character.

He visited a herd of cows at Ampleforth one day, where he treated many of them to bring them into season. Brian, unknown to the herdsman, had erroneously calculated the dose of the drug, administering to each animal ten times the recommended amount.

The herdsman was impressed. A day or two later when speaking to Alf, he said, 'Ah've never seen owt like it! 'E injected all them cows an' 't whole bloody lot came on. Ah reckon it were t' moustache as did it!'

There was a touch of the gypsy about Brian who seemed to be at home in the wild. I used to accompany him on early morning trips into the hills around Thirsk where we would observe a rich variety of wild animals – creatures I hardly knew existed before Brian gave me a peep into their dark and secret world.

He was one of the most popular assistants to grace the practice of Sinclair and Wight but, at times, he was also one of the most difficult. He had a personality which meant that anything approaching a routine lifestyle was alien to him; even such a basic pastime as eating was not followed regularly. On one occasion Alf observed Brian, who had eaten nothing the preceding day, demolish two whole fruit cakes, while I myself saw him consume two and a half roast ducks at one sitting. Brian's was a free spirit – one that seemed to be forever trying to break loose – and, gifted veterinarian though he was, he always seemed to be looking for something beyond just veterinary practice.

His singular approach to life was certainly not suited to the running of an organised practice. Preferring to get up very early, he asked Alf whether he could start work at six o'clock every morning and finish at three in the afternoon – a request which was not granted. He also had a habit of disappearing from the practice for long periods without anyone knowing where he was. He infuriated Donald by cooking large quantities of foul-smelling tripe for his badgers in the flat above the surgery, while foxes running around the garden and owls flying down the corridor of 23 Kirkgate did little to improve his employer's mood!

The practice cars had a rough time under Brian's usage. Not only did he test the engines to their limits as he flew from call to call, but his badgers created havoc in the back seats which virtually ceased to exist after a week or two. He returned one day with one front wing of the car completely missing. When he saw the look of horror on Alf's face, he broke into a smile and said, 'Oh, I'm sorry, Mr Wight. I was hoping that perhaps you wouldn't notice it!' Brian's abundance of charm meant that he always got away with it.

Despite these local difficulties, Alf was very fond of him and had mixed feelings when he eventually left in November 1958. Alf already had a highly unusual colleague in Donald Sinclair and, much as he admired Brian, the presence of two of them in the same practice had been very demanding. Nevertheless, it was a sad day for Alf when Brian left to take a job in Halifax, Nova Scotia. He had been one of the most interesting and popular veterinary surgeons to grace the practice – another unforgettable character to be imprinted forever in the mind of the future James Herriot.

Brian Nettleton may have upset Donald with his erratic lifestyle but the senior partner, in turn, tested the patience of a whole host of assistants who worked for him.

Donald was a man of unusually limited patience. His being incapable of remaining on the telephone for long, made it nigh on impossible for clients to convey their full message. Veterinary surgeons know all too well the frustration of having to listen to long monologues issuing from the earpiece. Donald had a very simple solution. Upon tiring of the conversation, which he invariably did very quickly, he would simply say, very gently, and in the politest of voices, 'Goodbye!' This invariably resulted in the assistant's arrival at the farm without some essential equipment to do a job that Donald had failed to note during the swiftest of telephone calls. A loud 'ear bashing' for the unfortunate young vet invariably followed.

Whilst he was always polite to the clients, he was not so courteous to members of his family. His brother, Brian, once told Alf that he had had the misfortune to telephone Donald when he was watching his favourite television programme.

Donald, as usual, had seized the telephone before it had had the chance to ring fully. The conversation had been brief.

'206! Who's there?'

'Brian.'

'*Dad's Army*'s on!' The receiver was banged down.

Another of his habits, when in the mood, was that of taking on a huge number of calls. Despite protestations from his colleagues, he assured them that he would complete them all. He, of course, did not and the assistant on call would have to mop up Donald's remaining visits during the evening.

Donald always got away with it. He would apologise profusely, invite the young man for tea, and be totally forgiven every time. His natural charm was his saving grace.

'You know,' Alf said once, expounding on his partner, 'everyone is born with some quality that helps them along life's road. With Donald, it is his natural charm. No matter what he has done, you just cannot be annoyed with him for long. For as long as I have known him, he has possessed the ability to have people running around working for him. I wish that I could say the same of myself!'

One of Donald's genuinely endearing qualities, however, was his attitude to children. This phenomenally impatient man displayed a total reversal of character whenever a small child was involved. He gave plenty of time to his own two children, Alan and Janet – with whom Rosie and I played for many hours around the huge, magical Southwoods Hall – and he showed no less patience with those of others.

I remember him talking one day to a client in our office, when he was abruptly interrupted by a little girl. She had just completed a drawing of a frog and was longing to show it to someone. She chose the right man in Donald Sinclair.

He turned away from the client, stooped down towards the child and said, 'How very interesting! Let me see.' He examined the drawing carefully while the little girl jumped up and down with delight. 'And what do you call this little frog?' he asked gently.

'Francis!' cried the child, jumping higher and higher.

'Francis Frog! What a nice name!' Donald said.

There followed an excited account about her frog while Donald listened intently. He then took the little girl by the hand and led her out into the garden to show her some flowers – having totally forgotten about his paying customer in the office. What an extraordinary man! He had little patience with his fellow men but he had all the time in the world for a small child.

My father had two other 'assistants' – my sister and myself, and we accompanied him frequently on his rounds throughout the 1950s. One way we were of genuine assistance was through our dedication to opening and closing gates. The modern farm has far fewer gates, most of which have been replaced by cattle grids, but in those days a considerable slice of the veterinary surgeon's time was spent leaping out of the car to deal with the gates. When visiting the Ainsley brothers of Nevison House, Alf had to climb in and out of his car fourteen times to open and shut the gates, every one of them held together with old string. It turned a visit to this farm into a marathon session, so much so that he wrote about the place with its ancient gates and deeply rutted track in the opening to *The Lord God Made Them All*.

Rosie took her task very seriously. When the time came for her to attend school in 1952, at the age of five, she was racked with worry lest her father could not cope on his rounds without her.

During my years at secondary school, when I had already decided to become a vet, and had begun a more serious appraisal of my chosen profession, I had the opportunity to study him at work. I noticed his conscientious and caring approach, and particularly enjoyed watching him calving and lambing, procedures he performed with extreme gentleness. He said many times that lambing ewes was easily his favourite job, one he could perform quickly as well as gently when the need arose. One afternoon, he was confronted with sixteen visits to lambing ewes; three hours later, he had completed them all.

Another animal he treated very skilfully was the pig. I had little doubt, as a teenager, that I had chosen the right profession, but the visits to pigs with my father tested my resolve to its limits. I was terrified of pigs.

In those days, with home-cured bacon still figuring prominently in the Yorkshire country person's diet, there were many local smallholders with ramshackle sheds at the bottom of their gardens that housed huge, fat sows. These formidable animals did not appreciate needles being driven into their bodies and were especially aggressive when their piglets required treatment. Large sows possess a fine set of teeth but my father, who seemed to have no fear of them, would enter their domain, armed simply with a board or an old broom and skilfully inject them, despite their savage barks of protest.

When the piglets needed attention, the sow would be tempted outside with some food and the door locked, enabling the vet to carry on with his work in safety. The pig has been described as a difficult animal to treat, one that 'responds vociferously to the mildest of restraint'. This is certainly true and piglets are endowed with stupendous vocal chords from the moment they are born. I spent many an hour in my youth, helping my father inject squealing piglets, while outside, the enraged mother sow, driven on by the deafening noise of her offspring, furiously attacked our shaky refuge. My sole aim throughout these ear-splitting sessions was to establish an escape route should the colossal sow blast her way into the building.

I remember my father once asking me to inject a sow when I was about fifteen years old. Quivering with terror, I shot the needle into her leg. The vast pig erupted from the straw with a roar and I vaulted back out of the pen, my needle still protruding from her thigh. I received a severe dressing down.

'Damn it, Jim!' he shouted. 'You'll never make a vet if you run away from your patient!'

'I don't want to lose a leg!' I replied. 'Have you seen the size of those teeth?'

'You have got to get in and out quickly!' he shouted. 'It's no good being frightened of the bloody things!'

Although a sympathetic man, he was quick to chastise me if he thought I was not 'framing' properly, and would grunt with frustration should I fail to catch a young bovine by the nose first time, or receive a sharp kick from a cow through faulty milking technique.

'Don't stand back off her!' he would yell. 'Get in close! You'll get your head knocked off if you stand back!'

He repeatedly drummed into me that I would look an utter fool on a farm if I could not handle the animals properly. His instruction certainly stood me in good stead in later years. In 1975, in the *Daily Express*, I was amused to see a photograph of James Herriot chasing a small pig. This was, quite obviously, purely for the benefit of the article. Alf would have been the first to say that there is no future in chasing pigs; they can run at amazing speeds and possess superb body swerves. The only way to catch them is by the deployment of cunning tactics.

My father and I often had to inject dozens of lively pigs at one time.

When confronted by a pink, squealing wave hurtling around a yard, he would corner them with a large gate. Once trapped in a tight corner, the pigs would scream loudly and he would say, 'Wait, they'll calm down in a minute.' He was always right. All at once the noise would stop and the pigs would freeze. He would then inject them all, using a multidose syringe, and hardly a pig would move. Simple.

Although mainly a farm-animal vet, Alf Wight had to turn his hand occasionally to horse work. He had had plenty of experience in his first years in Thirsk, docking the tails of foals and castrating wild colts, while the foalings on the huge heavy draught mares were especially taxing. Donald, who had a fine reputation as an equine veterinarian – and was the Thirsk Racecourse Veterinary Surgeon for over forty years – did most of the horse work, but Alf was no novice when called upon to treat horses.

Alf was never to become regularly involved with equine work, but when it came to treating family pets, it was a different story. As the 1950s progressed, with the amount of small animal work gradually increasing, I had the opportunity to observe him perform in this vastly different arena. Here, not only did he display his all-round expertise as a sound and competent veterinarian but, as with his life out in the farmyards and fields of Yorkshire, he came across some fascinating characters whom, years later, he would masterfully and humorously commemorate to print.

CHAPTER SEVENTEEN

During the years of the 1950s, despite the small animal cases taking second place to farm work in the Sinclair and Wight practice, Alf became highly regarded as a sound small animal clinician. He realised that this branch of veterinary medicine could become increasingly important in the years ahead, and that a sympathetic approach to his patients would be of paramount importance.

The dictum, 'It's not what you do, it's the way that you do it' – one that he repeatedly drummed into every assistant – was something he carried out unfailingly himself. This quality of care and compassion towards a case is as important today as it was all those years ago. An article appeared in the newsletter of the Royal College of Veterinary Surgeons in March 1992:

'James Herriot is the yardstick by which the whole profession is judged and while his veterinary science may be, by today's standards, painfully out of date, his veterinary art is not. Alf Wight's promotion of veterinary surgeons remains the envy of every other profession.'

He always thought carefully before he acted, and approached each case very thoroughly. Despite his sound clinical expertise, however, he never aspired to become a specialist in the field of small animal veterinary medicine. As new techniques came to the fore, he tended to leave this to the younger men in the practice; indeed, he remained suspicious of many of the modern anaesthetics, preferring to keep his patient conscious if at all possible.

He retained his deep respect for general anaesthesia well into the 1960s and 1970s, preferring to perform comparatively major operations on animals simply under local anaesthetic. He removed large mammary growths from bitches and operated many times on dogs with entropion – where the ingrowing eyelid undergoes corrective surgery – purely under local anaesthetic. He always derived especial pleasure after entropion operations merely from observing the dog's tremendous relief from pain and irritation.

There was one procedure at which he regarded himself an expert – the 'wrapping' of cats. Using nothing more than an old blanket, he could reduce a savage, snarling cat to a trussed-up sausage in a matter of seconds. He was especially proud of his expertise in this 'field of veterinary surgery' and I remember him saying to me one day after completing one of these lightning performances, 'I probably won't be remembered for much after I've gone, Jim, but at least you'll be able to say that your old man was good at one thing! He could sure wrap a cat!'

It was his sympathetic approach to his cases that, more than anything, won him so many fans amongst his clients, with no one appreciating this more than Miss Marjorie Warner and her little dog, Bambi. This lady and her appealing Pekingese, who lived in a fine big house in Sowerby, were immortalised in the early James Herriot books as 'Mrs Pumphrey' and 'Trickie Woo', and they were to become two of the most well known of all his characters.

Bambi Warner was a delightful dog who loved everyone – and how we loved him! Every time this thoughtful little animal took his holidays, which was frequently, magnificent hampers would arrive at our door, addressed simply to 'Uncle Wight'. These contained foods we had previously only dreamed about: caviar, pâté de foie, honey-roast hams, exotic preserves and many other mouthwatering delicacies. Whenever Bambi visited the Yorkshire coast, large boxes of Whitby kippers were delivered to our door; it is hardly surprising that Alf, who loved kippers, wrote so affectionately about Bambi and Miss Warner in his books. He made the most of this situation, never forgetting to send prompt letters of appreciation.

Unfortunately, he made two fundamental mistakes that almost resulted in the termination of these wonderful gifts. He addressed his first letter to Miss Warner herself. After Bambi had expressed his displeasure, Alf promptly rescued the situation by dispatching a grovelling letter of apology to the little Peke. His second mistake was to address another one to 'Master' Bambi Warner when the correct mode of address should, of course, have read 'Bambi Warner, Esq'. Writhing with guilt, he fired off another letter but this time received no response. These were worrying days for the family as weeks passed without the delivery of a single hamper! Happily, with the passage of time and several attentive visits to his little friend, Bambi forgave him and the stream of succulent hampers began again. Alf had learned his lesson; in future, Bambi would receive the deference his status deserved.

So vivid were the descriptions of Mrs Pumphrey and Trickie Woo in the James Herriot books, Miss Warner quickly realised that they were based upon her and Bambi, but she bore no resentment. Alf always had a genuine liking for the lady and her charming little dog, portraying her as a warm-hearted and passionate, if slightly 'over-the-top', dog lover.

Alf Wight, although a popular vet, was the first to admit that he could not please everyone. There were certain farms where, no matter how hard he tried, his efforts resulted in disaster. He called them his 'bogey farms' and would go to great lengths to avoid visiting them.

One day Donald said to him, 'There's a cow with a bad eye at Furness's, Alfred. It's in your direction so will you go there?'

'No,' he replied firmly, 'I'm sorry but I'd rather not. Every time I visit that farm, something drops dead! Frank Furness is a lovely man and, despite my record of decimating his stock every time I set foot on his farm, I think he still likes me. I have no wish to stretch his good nature any further.'

'But you are going past the door, Alfred. It's pointless to send someone up there specially. It's only a cow with a bad eye, and you've only to put some ointment onto it. Nothing can go wrong!'

Donald was right. It was nothing more than a mild case of New Forest Disease. Reluctantly, Alf agreed and visited the farm where he duly applied the ointment to the cow's eye. It had been a simple and straightforward case.

He received a telephone call the following day. The cow was no better; in fact, she was worse, and her joints were beginning to swell. 'What on earth have swollen joints to do with bad eyes?' he thought, as he sped back towards the farm.

The cow was, indeed, much worse. Not only could she barely walk, but her breathing was laboured, with a profuse discharge pouring from her nose. With grim determination, Alf tried all he knew to save her. He injected her with antibiotics; he administered steroids and fluids intravenously; he shot high doses of vitamins into her and, before leaving the farm, he personally blanketed her up to keep her as comfortable as possible. He returned home with one thought drumming in his brain: 'What has all this to do with a sore eye?'

Alfred Wight's hand of doom had struck again. The following day saw a massive deterioration, with his patient recumbent and sunken-eyed. The knacker man arrived the same day to put her out of her suffering.

With this experience having served only to strengthen Alf's conviction that genuine 'bogey farms' do exist, it was a long time before he set foot on that farm again. Frank Furness never blamed Alf and, years later, when the James Herriot books began to hit the headlines, he wrote a delightful letter of congratulations to him.

It was not only with the large animals that Alf realised a veterinary surgeon cannot win all the time. There was a lady in Sowerby who regarded him as an idiot – likeable, but nevertheless an idiot. Each time he treated her dog, something went wrong. In due course, the dog became terminally ill, suffering from renal failure, and she asked for it to be put painlessly to sleep. Realising that he was on delicate ground, he had elected to inject the barbiturate into the abdomen, rather than by the less easy – but more reliable – intravenous route of administration. To his dismay, the drug seemed to have no effect; thirty minutes later, the dog was still walking around the floor.

The woman turned on him. 'Mr Wight! Over the years that I have brought my dog to you, you have consistently failed to improve his condition. Now that I want you to destroy him, you can't even do that properly!'

As the 1950s progressed, some major small animal surgery was tentatively undertaken. Towards the end of this decade, Alf was performing cat and bitch hysterectomies, but more complicated cases were sent to a small animal specialist twenty-six miles away in Darlington. Denton Pette, an imposing, accomplished small animal surgeon, was to become one of Alf's greatest friends – one who would, many years later, be immortalised as 'Granville Bennett', first appearing in the fourth Herriot book, *Vet in Harness*.

The description in the book fits the real man perfectly. 'Not over tall but of tremendous bulk ... he wasn't flabby, he didn't stick out in any particular place, he was just a big, wide, solid, hard-looking man.'

Above all, Denton Pette was a man of enormous presence. His wife, Eve, who is still a close friend of my mother, once said that a friend of hers asked someone how she would recognise Denton, having never before met him. 'Just look for a square man!' was the reply.

As James Herriot, Alf wrote very affectionately about his friend, referring widely to Denton's capacity to enjoy himself to the full. This incredibly generous man was the first to buy everyone a round of drinks but, with his apparently indestructible constitution having an ability to endure hours of extravagant socialising without any perceivable ill effects, one needed to be in good shape to survive an evening with Denton Pette.

Alf and Joan enjoyed many memorable occasions in the company of Eve and Denton, with Alf frequently senseless at the end. I, too, would spend many enjoyable hours with the Pettes – like my father, almost invariably ending up glassy-eyed and incoherent. He and I were, many times, driven home by my mother after roisterous sessions with Denton and his friends. 'What would all the James Herriot fans think of their hero if they could see him now?' I remember my mother saying one night, as she smiled at the slumped figures in the rear seat.

Despite Denton's exhilarating social life, much of which I experienced during my time seeing practice with him as a student, he always appeared immaculate each morning, in beautiful suits and sparkling shirt cuffs. As I listened to his rich, soothing voice with the clients hanging on his every word, I realised that I was in the company of a highly successful man.

His surgical expertise was amazing. He had thick, stubby fingers that seemed to caress the tissues as he worked, and he operated with lightning speed. One day, when working in Thirsk, I took a small dog to him in Darlington for an eye operation. Denton was beginning a surgical list. When he told me that he had three hysterectomies to perform, I suggested that I wander round the town for an hour or so and return later.

'Not at all, laddie!' he replied. 'I'll be with you in twenty minutes!'

'But you have three bitch spays to do, Denton!' I exclaimed. These operations – full ovario-hysterectomies – take the average surgeon about half an hour to perform.

'Twenty minutes! We'll have some coffee first! Care to assist me?'

I then watched him complete the three operations in exactly seventeen minutes; if I had not seen it for myself, I would never have believed it. He was a wonderfully gifted surgeon – fast, yet gentle. As Granville Bennett, James Herriot would, very accurately, portray his friend as the talented, colourful and generous man we all knew. In the later years of the 1950s, while watching Denton at work, Alf realised he was taking a peep into the future, where the veterinary surgeon's day would become ever more involved in the treatment of family pets. Much as he admired

Denton's work, however, his more rural existence among the farmers of North Yorkshire was the one he still preferred.

As James Herriot, Alf Wight said many times that his life in veterinary practice was far harder in his early days than it was in the last two decades of the century. It may have been more demanding physically, but he was the first to admit that, in other respects, it was far less stressful. The modern veterinary surgeon treads a minefield, where one mistake can result in distressing legal procedures. His every move has to be carefully made lest he breaks one of an endless list of rules and regulations, while the end of the day is usually taken up with filling in never-ending forms. Paperwork sails into the modern vet's life in mountainous waves.

Alf's life in the heyday of his professional career was not so bedevilled and, in addition, he did not have the pressure of long hours consulting indoors, which is the norm for the modern vet. He spent hours driving to small family farms, with his typical working day, demanding though it was, often finishing at five or six o'clock with tea in the company of his family. At this hour, for the modern veterinary surgeon in a high-powered urban practice, his day can be just getting into its stride with a full waiting-room.

I observed the tremendous rise in small animal work in the 1970s and, even in a largely rural area like Thirsk, tea with my own family was a rare occasion indeed. This may well have been a factor in not one of my three children showing the slightest inclination to become a veterinary surgeon. When I look back on my father's life in practice during the 1950s, my abiding memory is of a sunburned figure in an open-topped car, his dogs by his side, driving from one case to another among some of the prettiest countryside in England. There is little wonder that he wrote about those days with such feeling.

Those days were equally enjoyed by his family for whom he always made plenty of time. My memories of the 1950s are of taking off into the hills around Thirsk, or up into the Yorkshire Dales, and walking for miles, becoming familiar with every corner of the country around our home. Visits to the seaside – Whitby, Scarborough and Marske – were a special treat. As we two children grew older, we would camp and stay in Youth Hostels with Alf, as well as play cricket, football and tennis. He was not just a father – he was one of us.

Shortly after moving into our new house in 1953, Alf bought an extra plot of land behind the house on which he built a tennis court. He described the nerve-jangling experiences of its construction in his final book, *Every Living Thing*, but the effort was worthwhile. We played countless hours of tennis on that court.

He and I had many marathon games. In my teenage years, I played a great deal of tennis and regarded myself as a fairly competent performer, going on to win the school tennis championship – but I could rarely beat him. Our games were closely contested encounters of rude energy versus class. He would control the game from the back of the court, firing strokes along the white lines, while I just ran and ran. At the end of the game, he would lay his hand on my sweat-soaked shirt and say, 'Never mind, Jim, you're improving all the time. You'll thrash your old man easily one day!' I never did.

As well as tennis, golf was a game that Alf played regularly throughout the 1950s and, with the practice being quiet during the summer months, he had the time for it. Joan was also interested in the game and became a very steady player. Amongst the many people with whom they played were a couple who became extremely close friends – Douglas Campbell and his wife, Heulwen. Douglas was a chartered surveyor who was introduced to Alf by Alex Taylor, who lived next door to him at the time. Douglas, a tidily-built man who was always neatly groomed and very correct, could lead one to believe that he was a rather serious-minded and straight-laced individual, but there was much more to him than this. His clipped, precise way of describing things belied an acute sense of humour; he liked a drink and a joke, and the more Alf saw of this smiling man with the infectious chuckle, the more he liked him. He and Joan became such friends with the Campbells that, as well as enjoying countless evenings and weekends with them, our two families went on holiday together in 1956.

It was Douglas who had provided moral support for Alf on that shattering day in the Golden Fleece when he had desperately, but unsuccessfully, bid for the house he had wanted so badly. Later in 1951, when Alf and Joan were drawing up plans for their new house, his professional expertise as a surveyor was greatly appreciated.

The Thirsk and Northallerton Golf Club, to which Alf and Joan belonged, was a club with a difference. Because this small, nine-hole course had been purchased by the club together with existing grazing rights, it was populated for the greater part of the year by sheep. The other animals that explored the course were dogs, and two members who made full use of this rather unusual concession were Alf and Harry Addison. In the eyes of the Golf Club Committee, Alf Wight may have been a nobody, but Harry Addison was most definitely not.

Harry Addison, our family doctor, is mentioned in the James Herriot books as 'Dr Allinson'. He assisted at the birth of myself and Rosie, and we all looked on him as a doctor who could do no wrong. The tall, bespectacled, balding man was not only the finest player in the club but, with a strong personality that commanded respect from everyone, there were few objections to the presence of his dog on the golf course. To be able to combine dog walking with a round of golf suited Alf very well and this happy state of affairs continued for many years, but it did not last for ever. Harry Addison, having suffered a heart attack, made plans to retire to St Andrews and, at around the same time, the club committee ruled that all dog walking on the course was hitherto forbidden.

Alf was very sorry when Harry left; he used to love watching the doctor playing the game so well, marvelling at the easy swing, followed by the little white ball sailing straight and true towards the green before fizzing to a stop close to the hole. But there was another reason to rue his friend's departure; Alf, the lowly 18-handicap golfer, having lost his powerful ally, knew there was little chance of arguing his case for the reinstatement of dog walking over the golf course. His regular golfing days were finished; when it came to a decision between walking dogs or playing golf, his loyal companions won hands down.

Looking back on those days, he realised that dogs on a golf course are not a good idea and he bore no resentment against the committee, but it was a shame that his playing days came to such an abupt end. He did at least have ten happy years playing a game that gave him enormous pleasure.

It was not only tennis and golf that soaked up Alf's spare time, nor the hours he spent with his wife and children. He never neglected his parents in Glasgow, and continued to visit them regularly as he had done since his earliest days in Thirsk. His mother also made sure that he never forgot the city of his boyhood, posting to Thirsk a long succession of savoury parcels containing Scottish food that was not obtainable in Yorkshire – mutton pies, sliced sausage, 'tattie scones', and black pudding with oatmeal. Alf still retained his love of the traditional Glasgow fare, and used to fall ravenously on these delicacies after a hard day's work around the farms.

As well as the food, his parents sent down the *Sunday Post*, a traditional Scottish newspaper that Alf read religiously. He enjoyed the accounts of the Scottish football matches, while the timeless cartoon antics of 'The Broons' or 'Oor Wullie' still brought many a tear of laughter to his eyes.

The short holidays in Glasgow were of great benefit to Alf. His rural surroundings in Yorkshire seemed a million miles away as he listened to the bustle of the busy streets, the cries of the street vendors, the blaring of motor horns and the almost melodious droning of the tram cars as they swayed along Sauchiehall Street and the other great thoroughfares that he knew so well.

The enjoyment of our family trips to Glasgow throughout the 1950s was frequently enhanced by the company of my father's cousin Nan, who was also godmother to Rosie and me. Nan, daughter of Auntie Jinny Wilkins, was the cousin whom my father saw most throughout his life; she was only thirteen years older than Alf and was like an elder sister to him throughout his younger days. She was an unforgettable character in the true tradition of the Bells. Despite consuming prolific quantities of alcohol as well as smoking phenomenal numbers of cigarettes, she lived to her mid-eighties. She once told us that smoking was one of her great pleasures in life, and that she had no intention whatsoever of trying to break the habit. 'After all,' she said, 'I've been rolling my own from the age of eleven so why stop now?'

Nan's husband was Tony Arrowsmith, a smiling benevolent man with a small pencil moustache, who spent a large proportion of his time firing off little jokes and wisecracks. Being married to Nan, he had it made: no matter the quality of the joke, Nan would laugh uproariously. Smoking had bestowed upon Nan a sharp, rasping voice with a grating laugh which we heard incessantly on those trips to Glasgow. Tony's wisecracks and the harsh cackles of Nan were a tonic for us all.

Apart from visits to Glasgow, Alf did not take his family on holiday until 1950 when the arrival of an assistant, together with the steady prosperity of the practice throughout the 1950s, meant that he had the time and the money to enjoy a family holiday every year.

In 1951, we had our first-ever family holiday at Robin Hood's Bay on the Yorkshire coast where we enjoyed the company of Alex and Lynne Taylor who were living nearby at the time. Two holidays in Llandudno in North Wales, in 1952 and 1953, were followed by a trip to the Lake

District in 1954. We stayed at Skelwith Bridge near Ambleside, where it rained mightily, but this did not stop Alf falling in love with the magnificent scenery of the Lakes and he returned there regularly for the rest of his life.

A visit in 1955 to Baronscourt in Northern Ireland, where Alex Taylor was then managing the Duke of Abercorn's estate, was followed by holidays in Scotland every year for the next five years. Two of those, to Ullapool and Skye in 1958 and 1959, were made especially enjoyable by the company of Jean and Gordon Rae and their family.

Gordon, who was an expert on natural history, enriched the expeditions into the hills with his tremendous knowledge of birds and wild flowers. My father was deeply impressed. Having had a city upbringing, and knowing little about the flora and fauna of his native land, he would listen with amazement as Gordon unfailingly identified each and every tiny flower.

Gordon was a fitness fanatic. While in Ullapool, he woke us up early to run down to the pier and dive into the sea before breakfast. My father, although keen on keeping himself fit, had by now adopted a less rigorous approach to maintaining his health; with the old days of the ice-cold baths having long since been abandoned, he politely declined to join us.

In those days, Alf and Joan never considered a holiday abroad; few people did in those days. In later years they did go abroad on several occasions, but they never enjoyed holidays more than those they took with their family and friends within the shores of their own country.

Alf looked back on the 1950s as some of the happiest years of his life. The practice was doing well, he had the pleasure of spending time with his family and, in addition, he regained those youthful habits of widening his horizons. He started several hobbies, some of them seriously, others less so.

One of the more transient crazes was that of deciding to live 'healthily'. He bought a book by Gayelord Hauser called *Diet Does It*, and was convinced that, should he follow the advice within its pages, he would be supremely fit for decades to come. Gayelord Hauser described four 'superfoods' that were to be eaten every day – foods that in those days were virtually unknown. Yoghurt, wheatgerm, vitamin yeast and Blackstrap molasses began to appear on the kitchen shelves and Alf consumed them doggedly, not always with recognisable enjoyment.

One day, as he was spooning black treacle into his mouth, he was reminded of an old farmer who had told him that he was fed by his employer on the cheapest food available – black treacle and dumplings. The old man went on to tell him that t' dumplings stayed inside yer fer about a week, an't treacle went straight through yer!' I don't know what effect this strange diet had on my father's digestive system but, whatever the reason, he dispensed with it after a few months.

His resolve in following Gayelord Hauser's regime was further tested on the days when he followed another of the guru's recommendations – that of having a 'fruit day'. This was a day when nothing but fruit was to be eaten, the idea being to 'cleanse and detoxify' the system. He would return for his lunch, famished after a morning around the farms, to sit down to a couple of apples and an orange while his family around him devoured plates of roast beef, Yorkshire puddings and potatoes, all smothered in rich brown gravy. I used to think that my mother gleaned satisfaction out of torturing him by producing these mouth-watering meals on his 'fruit days'. He, of course, cracked under the pressure and was soon joining the rest of us among our lakes of gravy.

Another craze he undertook in 1958 was the playing of the violin. He had always loved listening to music, and had joined the Thirsk and District Music Society the previous year, but now he decided that he would like to play.

The violin was always Alf's favourite instrument. He had all the great violin concertos on record, and admired in particular the famous performers like Alfredo Campoli and Jaschia Heifitz. Many years later, as James Herriot, he appeared on the radio show, 'Desert Island Discs'. He had no hesitation in choosing as his all-time favourite, the Violin Concerto by Elgar.

His excursion into violin playing lasted for two to three years. He played with Steve King, headmaster at the local school, and through their common love of music and sport, they became good friends. Steve played the cello and the two spent many hours playing duets as well as performing in the local school orchestra. Alf wrote to his parents in 1958 about his new hobby:

'The old fiddle is progressing fast and I have improved out of all recognition. I am now nearly as good as those poor blokes you hear in the streets. But I do love it! I grab the instrument at every opportunity and it is funny how quickly the room empties after I start sawing.'

He did not progress much further with the violin and he received little encouragement from his family. The violin needs to be played very well to sound acceptable, and there were some very scratchy sessions around the fireside on those winter evenings. With the veterinary practice becoming increasingly busy, it was hard to find the time to devote to his hobby and, although he enjoyed his short association with the instrument, it finally scraped to a halt in 1960.

For Alf, the 1950s were years of enjoyment and satisfaction but towards the end of that decade, a darker period was beginning. It gradually worsened, almost unnoticed, but an event in 1960 would precipitate him into the abyss of a nervous breakdown that lasted for almost two years. It would be the only period of my life when I could say I had a father I hardly knew.

CHAPTER EIGHTEEN

Friday 8 April 1960 began happily for Alf Wight. With his friend, Guy Rob, he left Thirsk for the international football match between Scotland and England at Hampden Park in Glasgow, to which they would be accompanied by his father. These visits were enjoyable and relaxing occasions. Alf would not only have the pleasure of seeing his parents again, he would be able to talk football with Pop, always one of their favourite topics of conversation.

The letters that Pop wrote to Alf and Joan invariably began with the formalities of asking after the family, telling in a short sentence or two how he and Granny Wight were faring – the remainder consisting of long accounts of football matches, views on the state of Sunderland AFC, or his latest opinions on the England cricket team. They radiated the words of a sports fanatic, and Alf's letters to his parents, although not quite so heavily weighted, were in a similar vein. Joan would read the first couple of lines of Pop's letters, but on seeing the start of a three- or four-page report of a match between Rangers and Celtic, would then hand the rest over to her husband.

His son's visits to Glasgow were the highlight of Pop's year and they were equally enjoyed by Alf who never tired of his father's company.

But that day in 1960 was to be a tragic one. On arrival at his parents' home in Anniesland Road, Alf was horrified to see a hearse outside the door. His father had died suddenly of a heart attack while he and Guy were en route from Thirsk. Instead of enjoying the great atmosphere of an England v Scotland match, he found himself making funeral arrangements, while poor Guy Rob caught the next train home.

This unexpected and shocking experience was a body blow – one that was to have devastating consequences. He had lost someone he loved dearly and, for more than a year afterwards, his emotions would carry him downhill into a state of deep and serious depression.

My mother, Rosie and I travelled to Glasgow for Pop's funeral and I remember the look on my father's face at the Maryhill Crematorium. He appeared to be completely bewildered, bravely fighting back tears, while all around him, people, myself included, were crying at the loss of someone we all loved. The emotional pressure on him at the time must have been incredible.

In a letter to his mother shortly after his father's death, he tried to raise her spirits while expressing his own feelings: 'I know how he must be filling your thoughts and of the awful emptiness you feel. I feel it too, as you will know. But, you know, I feel now a kind of companionship with Pop. When something comes up about football or anything else in which we were both interested, I feel I am discussing it mentally with him. These things are all a closed book to us but what is certain is that the love and the memories never die and are a comfort to those who are left.'

It is not surprising that Pop's sudden and shocking death hit Alf so hard; there was a tremendous bond of friendship and affection between the two men. Pop's death was a blow to me, too. I was seventeen at the time, and in September of the following year was due to stay with my grandparents at Anniesland Road while I attended the Glasgow University Veterinary School. One of my greatest regrets is that Pop was not there to share my university days – but it was much sadder that he was not alive to see the wonderful achievements of his son as a writer. He would have been a very proud man indeed, and no one would have devoured his books more avidly, or appreciated the skill of James Herriot more than Pop.

He would also have been proud to watch his son receive so many tributes from all over the world. Alf, too, had regrets that Pop never had the opportunity to read his work, but he thought that there was one tribute that his father would have been particularly pleased about.

One day, more than thirty years later, at the time when his fame and popularity were at their height, he was walking with Alex Taylor and they were talking about Alf's recent distinction of being made Honorary President of Sunderland Football Club. 'You know, Alex,' he said, 'old Pop would have loved to see my literary success but he would have considered *this* to be my greatest achievement!'

Pop's sudden death was the catalyst for sending Alf Wight spiralling into a nervous breakdown but it was not solely responsible; he had been deteriorating emotionally for some time before that event. Nervous breakdowns can be very difficult to understand and, in his case, there were many factors involved.

In some respects, Alf was ideal 'nervous breakdown material'. Following his recovery, people used to say to me, 'I'm surprised that your dad had a breakdown. He always seemed so calm and never seemed to let anything worry him.' This explains a great deal. He did seem to be in control of a situation but he was a man who hid his emotions – someone who would bottle things up rather than openly discuss his feelings with others.

He was a worrier, a private man who rarely allowed his deeper thoughts to surface. He worried about Joan and her slavish attitude to housework. He worried about Rosie and me, and whether he had done enough for us. He fretted about his parents; with Pop's job in the office not always secure, would they manage to cope if he was out of work? As he observed the slow but steady disappearance of grazing land around Thirsk, he began to feel concerns not only for the future of the practice, but for that of the veterinary profession in general. In years to come, would people still be getting up at ungodly hours to milk cows or would some clever person produce artificial milk more easily and cheaply? With no capital behind him, he depended entirely on the financial success of his business. Towards the end of the 1950s, when there were some rumblings of discontent among the assistants, he took on the responsibility of dealing with them with little help from anyone else. He did not discuss any of these problems with his family; his selfless nature decreed that he shared his secret hopes and fears with no one.

One thing that haunted him throughout the latter part of the 1950s was his children's education. My sister and I were attending the local school, despite my father's fervent wish that we should receive private education. His own parents had made sacrifices to send him to a fee-paying school and, deep down, he blamed himself for failing to give us a similar opportunity.

Having privately educated us throughout our primary years at Ivy Dene school, my father had been prepared to carry on paying tuition fees throughout our higher school years, but my mother had had other ideas. She was adamant that we were to be educated in Thirsk and her argument was strengthened by the fact that he would have been hard-pressed to find the money to pay private school fees. He could have afforded it by stretching his finances to the limit, and not to do so only compounded his feelings of guilt.

All this should never have concerned him. Thirsk Grammar Modern

School, superbly run by the headmaster, my father's friend Steve King, achieved remarkable academic results for such a small school. The high standard of teaching, allied to tight discipline, ensured that Rosie and I received a wonderful education but, despite our success there, my father still had that nagging doubt; had he done all he could for us?

His veterinary colleagues, Donald Sinclair and Gordon Rae, sent their children to fee-paying schools, as did many people of means in the Thirsk area. It seemed to him that he was one of the few men of professional status who used the local school. What if we failed to achieve? Would he ever forgive himself?

He watched our education very closely and when I fell behind in my second year I remember receiving a severe lecture from him. I think that, had I not pulled myself together and improved dramatically the following year, he would have bartered his soul to send me away to school.

Our education was not the only cause of his concern for our well-being. In those days, the possession of a dialect was regarded as a stigma; it could be a hindrance to progress in one's chosen profession. As a Yorkshire boy who spent his time with other Yorkshire lads, I developed an accent – one that worried my father so much that he sent Rosie and me to elocution classes in the nearby town of Ripon. My father was convinced that it was doing me good but I hated every minute; I made no progress, and he eventually conceded defeat. Things have now changed, with the possession of a dialect, quite rightly, no longer frowned upon but, in those days, he was convinced that my Yorkshire accent would hold me back. It was just another example of his determination to do everything within his power to ensure that he gave us a good start in life.

His concerns for the welfare of others did not stop with his immediate family. Since the day he qualified from Glasgow Veterinary College in 1939, Alfred Wight had carried the burden of the belief that he owed his parents a debt he would never be able to repay. From his very first poverty-stricken days as a young veterinary surgeon, he had not only regularly sent money to his parents, but had written to them conscientiously every week as well as visiting them, without fail, several times every year. His devotion to his parents was admirable, but it had its price.

In the years following his recovery from depression, Alf would realise just how much those feelings of having to repay his parents had affected him. I well remember the day of my graduation from the University of Glasgow Veterinary School in 1966. My mother and father, who had come up for the occasion, were staying with us in my grandmother's home in Anniesland Road. We were enjoying a celebratory drink when my grandmother said to me, 'Jim, never forget that you owe your father a great deal. He has made sacrifices for you. You owe him everything!'

I shall never forget the expression on my father's face, nor his comments to me immediately afterwards. He led me into another room.

'You owe me nothing! Do you understand? Absolutely nothing!' He spoke with an intensity that I found a little unnerving. Having known him so long as such a reserved and mild-mannered man, it was a new experience to hear him speak to me so directly. I did, indeed, consider that I owed him a great deal and said as much to him.

He paused for a second, without taking his eyes from mine. 'You owe me – and your mother – *nothing!*' He said no more.

As his illness worsened throughout 1960, I noticed my father begin to exhibit subtle changes in his behaviour as he imagined his darkest fears beginning to assume threatening proportions. One of the worst was his concern that my mother was interested in other men.

I remember my mother at the time as an attractive and – when in the mood – flirtatious lady who was, without doubt, popular among my father's many friends and acquaintances. He had, from their very first meeting in 1941, been totally besotted by her, and his imagining that she could possibly forsake him for another, was, I feel sure, a factor in contributing towards his illness. I remember him being distinctly unfriendly towards a man he thought was paying too much attention to her. This was not like the man I knew.

This period, when I was in the sixth form at school, was the only time that I felt distanced from him. He was continually pressurising me to comb my hair, shave regularly, speak properly and generally behave in a manner he thought appropriate. I felt that my father was needlessly dogging my every move and I resented it. My busy days at school helped in taking my mind off the problem and he, too, was working hard in the practice, with the result that we never openly fell out, but there was, for the first time in our lives, a gulf between us. I did not fully realise it at the time but I was observing a man who was treading on the brink of a total nervous collapse, carrying the worries of the world on his shoulders.

In the early summer of 1960, when his illness appeared to be worsening by the day, Joan, on advice from the doctor, took him to York for psychiatric treatment. It was a very hard time for her. She had to cope with a husband who was undergoing a gradual personality change, but she stood by him – despite some unreasonable behaviour that was totally unlike the man that she had married. He seemed to become hypercritical of her – just as he was of me – but she bore it all with fortitude. I remember feeling great admiration for her. I was old enough to know that there was something seriously wrong with my father as I tried to imagine the strain that she was under.

As a result of the electroconvulsive therapy he was receiving, his memory began to desert him. On the occasion of Rosie's birthday, we all went to the cinema in Ripon to see a Walt Disney film, *The White Wilderness*. My father seemed to enjoy the film but when I mentioned it to him next morning over breakfast, he looked at me as if in a dream. His eyes appeared to be focused on a point several miles behind my head.

'Film? What film?' he said. He had no recollection of the previous evening.

It has been suggested that repeated attacks of 'undulant fever' were responsible for Alf's depression. This was contracted through treating cattle with Brucellosis, a disease that was rife in the dairy herds of Britain in those days – causing abortion and stillbirths in cows and heifers. In common with many others in his profession, Alf removed diseased afterbirths from hundreds of affected animals, which resulted in his developing, on more than one occasion, symptoms of high fever and delirium. At such times, he took to his bed for days.

This disease has been described as a depressive one but it seemed to have the opposite effect on Alf. He became light-headed and happy, lying in bed while cracking jokes to which he, himself, would respond with wild and hysterical laughter, often listened to with ill-concealed amusement by his children. Years later, he was to write a chapter in *Every Living Thing*, in which he described the unusual symptoms that he experienced. These attacks were very short-lived and he always returned to work quickly. Fortunately, he did not suffer any long-term effects from the disease – unlike many of his professional colleagues who developed such symptoms as crippling arthritis or severe and lasting depression. It is difficult to disregard Brucellosis entirely as a contributory factor towards Alf's illness, but it cannot be held solely responsible for pitching his emotions into such a grievous turmoil. The causes were far more complex than that.

Despite his marked deterioration following Pop's death, he managed to hide his depression from others, with his colleagues at work having little idea that there was anything wrong. He put a brave face on everything but there were times when even he could not conceal the effects of his illness from his family.

In October 1960, he took Rosie with him to visit his mother in Glasgow. As they approached the city, quite suddenly he seized his young daughter's hand and held it tightly to the gearstick of the car. She was only thirteen years old at the time but she can still remember the look of tension on her father's face, holding her hand in a vice-like grip as he approached his mother's home. Was the memory of his father's death too much to bear or was there an inherent fear of his mother that was coming to the surface? After he recovered from his breakdown, he was to adopt a far more relaxed approach to his mother but as he drew near to his old home that day, Rosie's hand firmly in his own, there were certainly some very powerful and devastating emotions within him.

To his eternal credit, however, he kept his feelings from us as much as he could and, reading the letters he sent to his mother, there is no hint of the upheaval within his mind. He fought his illness in the only way he knew – he kept working. The practice was thriving and, thanks to the increase in TB Testing work, three assistants were working there through most of 1960. In the spring of 1961, however, two of them left. It was at a time when my father was very low and he found himself having to revert to night work again, working as hard as he had ever done in his life. This was probably therapeutic and helped take his mind off his escalating worries.

In a letter to his mother in March 1961 he wrote: 'This morning I was out on a sunny hillside outside Ampleforth lambing a ewe and just thinking what other job in the world could be so wonderful.' The ability to still appreciate his good fortune in having a job that he loved must have been a great comfort to him in those difficult times.

Despite his high work rate, he made time for his hobbies of gardening, tennis and playing the violin – and he never forsook his family. In 1960 we went on our annual holiday as usual, staying with Alex and Lynne Taylor who, by this time, were in Glenlivet in north-east Scotland. Nor did he forget his mother in Glasgow, continuing to write weekly letters to her, supplying advice and support during a period when she felt so low at the loss of her husband. He was still the caring father to us, and the loyal son to his mother.

In October 1960, Eddie Straiton, while on a visit to Thirsk to speak to the local veterinary clinical club, had noticed that his old friend was not well. Six months later, having heard that there was little improvement, he offered to come to Thirsk to work as a locum in the practice while sending Alf and Joan to his holiday house in Banalbufar on the island of Majorca – all of this at his expense. This generous gesture was one Alf would never forget.

That restful holiday in June 1961 was Alf and Joan's very first trip abroad. The complete change of surroundings, with the wonderful scenery and the warm hospitality of the local people, provided a turning point in his recovery.

I remember collecting my parents from Thirsk railway station on their return from Majorca. Having not seen my father for three weeks, I was shocked at his appearance. He had lost a great deal of weight, his inability to resist the delicious Majorcan fruit and vege-tables having had a stimulating effect upon his digestive system. He was wearing a large white sun hat which seemed to dwarf his scrawny body.

I walked up to him and shook his hand. 'How was your holiday, Dad? Great to see you back!'

The sunken eyes in the white face looked at me for a moment. He must have been thinking how well I looked. We had had a heat wave in Yorkshire and I had been playing tennis with Eddie as well as accompanying him around the practice in his open-topped sports car. I looked like the one who had been to sun-drenched Majorca, not the pale figure standing before me.

'Marvellous, Jim!' he said, and his gaunt face broke into a smile. I knew then that he was on the road to recovery. The eyes, though tired, had lost their distant look and there was a twinkle of that old glow of humour and affection that I used to know. He looked ghastly but I knew he was turning the corner.

He returned from holiday to discover that one of the assistants in the practice was ill and unable to work and, weak though he was, he returned to the time-honoured therapy for nervous illness – hard work. As the weeks went by, however, there were occasions when he lapsed back into his quiet moods, and this prompted us to persuade him to take another holiday.

He could afford to be away from the practice, as two more young assistants had been recruited by this time, and Rosie and I, together with one of her schoolfriends, accompanied him on a walking holiday in the Yorkshire Dales. This holiday, during which I watched him getting better every day, has remained one of my most memorable.

The exercise in the fresh air was a tremendous tonic. Instead of worrying about everything, he had to concentrate on the physical challenge of keeping up with younger people. We walked through Wensleydale, Swaledale and Dentdale. We climbed over high fells and marched along green river valleys. We stayed in Youth Hostels, where we slept the deep and refreshing sleep that follows days of exercise in the open air and, despite suffering pain from blisters and developing a swollen knee while descending Great Shunner Fell, he enjoyed every minute of it. As I watched him improve, mentally as well as physically, it was as though the pure Yorkshire air was cleansing his mind and washing away the worries that had plagued him for so long.

On 18 August, while we were still in the Dales, my A-level examination results were due. My father had worried for weeks about these, knowing that, should I fail, I would not gain admission to Glasgow University. The tension was high as I telephoned from the Moorcock Inn at Garsdale Head for my results.

The headmaster, Steve King, gave me the news. I had done better than I could ever have expected and I recall the joy on my father's face as we celebrated over a pint or two at the inn. Never again would he worry about his children's education. Later, Rosie went on to do even better and was offered a place at both Oxford and Cambridge Universities. Thirsk School had done us proud.

After that walking holiday in the Dales, Alf's recovery gained momentum. He would remain a private man for the rest of his life but rarely would he allow his emotions to get the better of him. He had been in a very dark place and had emerged from it a wiser man. When he looked back on those bad days, he realised that there had been little to really worry about. His family's health and his financial status had been sound, while the practice had been thriving without any dark clouds to obscure the future. Realising that he should have confided in us more, he became a Samaritan in the mid 1960s, spending many hours just listening to other people, allowing them to unload their worries onto him. It was something he, himself, should have done many years earlier.

People had helped him through his illness. My mother with her unflinching support, Eddie Straiton with his wonderful gesture of friendship and, in our own way, my sister and I in doing well at school and alleviating his fears; but one man deserves most of the credit – Alfred Wight himself.

It would have been easy to give up work but he refused to do so. He had hardly a single day off, labouring valiantly throughout what must have been a terrible time. I have always felt great admiration for the way that he fought his illness and beat it. There were days, towards the end of 1960, when we feared that he would never recover, but he did.

In the years ahead, there would be periods which were to provide him with real cause for concern, but he had learned a lesson. Never again would he allow his inner feelings to tear him apart.

CHAPTER NINETEEN

It was fortunate that Alf had emerged from his illness a stronger man. In the years following his recovery, there was plenty to occupy his mind, with many demands upon his financial status. Not only was the gradual replacement of grass fields by arable land continuing, but the remaining stock farmers were becoming more knowledgeable, with an increasing number of them treating their own animals. Alf accepted this as part of the inevitable march of progress within the farming industry but, with small animal work still very much regarded as a sideline, it spelt a reduced cash flow coming in to the business.

The practice continued to be busy, and his income remained one worthy of his professional standing, but there was still plenty for him to worry about.

One stress-factor in running the practice was the job of keeping a 'weather eye' on the performance of the young assistants. Donald and Alf always liked to employ new graduates; they emerged from the veterinary schools full of up-to-date information which they could impart to the two partners who, in return, could mould the young men into the ways of the practice, giving them the invaluable practical experience of working with two men who had learned a great deal over the years.

The acquisition of knowledge is not in itself enough to equip a person for a life in practice; a willingness to learn, and a liberal dash of common sense are vital qualities for a successful veterinary surgeon. Most of the young graduates adapted very quickly to their new life but there were a few who found it difficult.

There was always a good-humoured atmosphere at 23 Kirkgate which, most importantly, provided a happy environment for the young vets starting out on their new careers. The two partners had a list of 'rules' which they imparted to every assistant; although given very much with the tongue in the cheek, each one contained a grain of common sense.

In my student days of the early 1960s, I remember Donald taking me round the farms, expounding his Golden Rules. I can hear his voice as though he were sitting beside me.

'Always attend! I don't care if a farmer rings in the middle of the night for a visit to an animal that has been ill for six weeks, *you will attend*!' Donald, of course, was very rarely the one who was asked to do so.

'Be pleasant! When asking for a bucket of warm water, say 'please'. It's no good trying to talk down to a Yorkshire farmer. They appreciate common courtesy like anyone else.'

'Paint a black picture! If you say a case is going to recover, you could be in trouble if it doesn't!' No one was a finer exponent of this than Donald Sinclair.

'Always do *something*! Never leave a farm without injecting something! Give a shot of vitamins . . . anything!'

'Be positive in your approach, and give everything a name. Never say you don't know what's wrong!' This may seem a little ridiculous today, but there was some logic in the rule – especially years ago when dealing with some of the older clients. 'Don't send that apprentice onter my farm again! 'E didn't know what were wrong wi't cow!' was a cry heard more than once by Alf and Donald.

Donald finished his recitation with his final rule – one that he had, quite clearly, learned the hard way. 'Always park with the nose of the car pointing out of the farm!'

One day, he gave some advice to an assistant who had the unenviable task of judging at a horse show. This is one of the most thankless jobs that a vet has to perform – should there be twenty contestants aspiring to win one prize, unequalled potential exists for making nineteen enemies. Donald had some sound advice for him.

'Be positive!' he said. 'Be friendly but firm. Thoroughly examine every animal, and do not let anyone sway your decision. And keep the car engine running!'

Donald, quite rightly, always insisted on the adoption of a professional approach to the customer at all times. He stressed that smart attire, even though the job was a rough and dirty one, was essential. He was particularly upset when any of his employees failed to wear a tie.

I remember, one extremely hot afternoon, walking into the surgery wearing an open-necked shirt.

'Where's your tie, Jim?' he snapped.

'I'm sorry, Donald,' I replied. 'I've left it in the car.'

'I want you to wear a tie!' Donald said. He began to walk towards the door before suddenly stopping and pointing at me. 'You're a disgrace to the profession!'

These 'rules', light-hearted examples of the 'art' of veterinary practice, were something Alf had learned from the earliest stages of his career, but there was another art that he developed after his recovery from depression, that of learning how to relax.

Having always regarded lunch as the most important meal of the day, no matter how hard he was working, he usually found the time to enjoy it. It was during this daily break from work that he developed the art of 'cat napping'. In my working years of living with my parents, in the late 1960s and early 1970s, I watched him sit down after his lunch, close his eyes and fall, almost instantaneously, into a deep sleep that rarely lasted for more than ten minutes. He assured me that he awoke refreshed for the afternoon's activities, adding that some of the great men of history – among them, Winston Churchill – had shared this ability to snatch refreshing sleep in the middle of the day.

Above all, at that time of his life, he was a man more at ease with himself. Realising that, only a few years previously, he had been close to suffering a total, irreversible collapse, he could now see everything in perspective. His life in veterinary practice was by no means an easy one, but he was now able, more than ever before, to count his blessings.

Having, for so many years, regarded the company of a dog as a vital ingredient towards the enjoyment of his leisure time, Alf – following the untimely death of his beagle, Dinah, in 1963 – wasted little time in replacing her. Hearing that John Bumby, a farmer from near Topcliffe, had a litter of Jack Russell terrier puppies, it was not long before he and Rosie visited the farm. One of the puppies leapt towards Rosie and furiously began to lick her face. Minutes later, they left the farm with a tiny black and white ball of energy bouncing around in the car. He was to be called Hector.

Hector would be the first of James Herriot's dogs to appear with him in the many photographs taken during the early years of his fame as an author. He was a vital part of Alf's life and accompanied him everywhere on his daily rounds. He extracted maximum enjoyment out of life; he loved everyone and everyone seemed to love him. Upon Alf's arrival at a farm in his open-topped car, the sharp face of Hector was often the first thing the farmer saw. He was a dog who would not be ignored and he rarely was. Cries of 'Morning, Mr Wight! 'Ello 'Ector! By . . .'e's a grand little dog!' were a common start to a visit as the farmer fought off the pointed, friendly nose darting at his face.

Hector never missed a thing while on his travels. His favourite position, as he gazed eagerly out of the window, was with his front paws balanced on Alf's hand while he held the gear lever; no dog in the world could have changed gear so often as Hector!

He was the noisiest of all Alf's dogs. In the years when I worked from home, before I was married, I often followed my father's car on our short trip down to the surgery. I could see the silhouette of his head with, next to him, the outline of his small companion – paws on the gear lever and his little mouth opening and closing at regular intervals as he barked into my father's left ear. The racket in the car must have been terrific but, to my father, Hector could do no wrong.

Hector possessed a seemingly endless supply of energy. He would often be allowed out of the car at the farms where the large, resident farm dogs, sensing his open and friendly disposition, would play with him happily. These frantic sessions did not last long, however; I saw many a panting dog lying exhausted on the ground with a small black and white torpedo remorselessly tearing into him. An odd snarl or a trembling upper lip were signals to Hector that the game was over.

One game the farm dogs took very seriously was the escorting of visiting motor vehicles off the farm. These chases were the highlights of their day. My father and I often saw them slinking around during our visits, waiting for their big moment which, when it arrived, heralded frenzied activity. Our departures from some farms were tumultuous occasions. As soon as the car wheels were set in motion, packs of lean, hairy creatures would appear from everywhere to accompany us down the long farm roads, their faces a picture of taut concentration. This threat to his domain drove Hector frantic as he rocketed around the inside of the car, barking defiance at the dogs outside.

These frenetic episodes were not without danger to the dogs. They had a habit of darting in towards the car and biting the wheels, which sometimes resulted in serious injury. One way of cooling the enthusiasm of our assailants was a well-directed jet of water. This was my job; I would load up a multidose syringe and, at the precise moment, fire at the panting faces when they got too close.

It seemed to be very effective. On receipt of the cold blast of water, the dog would grind to a halt before running off dejectedly back to the farm. On occasions I felt rather guilty about this, especially when the dog shook its head before following this with a reproachful look as if saying, 'What did you have to do that for? We're only having a bit of fun!'

Those days of 'riding shotgun' with my father were a source of great entertainment from my earliest years. The farm dogs provided the action and, later, Hector supplied the soundtrack.

Although basically a sound little animal – and much in demand locally as a stud dog – Hector became virtually blind at the age of five or six. He suffered from a disease called Keratitis Sicca, a slowly progressive drying of the conjunctiva, resulting in a curtain of black pigment creeping across the eye surface. There are modern treatments for this disease now, but in those days, having little idea as to the cause, we could only attempt to ease the severity of his condition while watching helplessly as Hector's window on the world gradually became darker. Despite the pain and blackness, the little dog remained as vibrant as ever, peering expectantly out of the car and barking defiantly.

Hector was, without doubt, Alf's favourite of all the dogs who shared his life. Much has been written over the years of the many benefits of pet ownership, with countless examples cited of the positive effects upon the health of those who enjoy the company of a pet. No animal had a more exhilarating effect upon its owner than that bestowed upon Alfred Wight by Hector, whose insatiable and infectious zest for life provided him with the perfect therapy to follow his recent years of illness.

Well aware of his good fortune in having emerged relatively unscathed, he determined to enjoy his life again to the full. Always having believed that there was more to life than just work, he began, once again, to take an interest in the world around him. The early years of the 1960s were a time when he decided to see more of it.

In 1961 and 1962, he visited Russia and Turkey as official Ministry of Agriculture veterinarian in charge of shipments of pigs, sheep and cattle, during which time he kept a diary, later using some of the entries in *The Lord God Made Them All.* He was so intrigued by Russia that, on returning home, he began to teach himself Russian; he decided against learning Turkish. Following their holiday in Majorca in Eddie Straiton's villa, Alf and Joan revisited the island twice more: in 1965, they drove through France and Spain to reach the island, during which time Alf again kept a diary. In 1965, he attended night school in Thirsk to study Spanish.

Beginning to feel so much better physically, he not only began to play much more tennis again – even representing Thirsk at the age of forty-six when he and Rosie teamed up in a doubles match – but he took up skiing in the winter as an additional interest. All this, together with his unchanging pastimes of walking, gardening, reading and watching football, resulted in his life becoming, once again, one of multiple activities.

His old enthusiasm had returned. With his marriage sound, as was the health of both himself and his family, Alf's outlook on life had taken a remarkable turn for the better. As he eagerly threw himself into his work in the practice, his exhausting illness of such a short time before seemed but a distant memory.

Alf not only made time to spend with the practice's assistants, he was enormously helpful to me. In the summer of 1965, he made arrangements with Eddie Straiton for me to see practice with him in Staffordshire. It was an enjoyable two months during which I learned a great deal from Eddie who was a first-class veterinary surgeon. For part of my time there, Eddie took a break in Majorca while I continued to work with the help, when needed, of his neighbouring colleagues – and my father.

I was on the telephone to Thirsk every day, asking about the treatment for scouring pigs, lame cows and coughing horses. I asked for advice on calving cows, and how to treat batches of calves with pneumonia and, in every case, I received invaluable assistance. My father had enough work of his own and it must have been very trying, giving advice to a young, green student more than 150 miles away – but he did, and I hung on his every word.

On one occasion, I faced the prospect of having to administer an intravenous injection to a cow. Aware that serious complications could follow a faulty technique, I was worried. Yet again I rang my father for advice.

'Dad, I have to visit a cow with milk fever.'

'Is it down?' he asked.

'Yes. I suppose I will have to give it an intravenous injection?'

'You will!' he replied.

'Which vein shall I use? The milk vein or the jugular?'

There was a pause. 'The jugular is a cleaner area to work.'

'Which is the easier?' I asked.

He replied promptly. 'Hector could find the milk vein.'

After I had qualified from the Glasgow Veterinary College in 1966, I returned to work officially for Eddie Straiton, my first job as a veterinary surgeon. It was in the October of that year that I telephoned my parents from Staffordshire. As it was soon to be their Silver Wedding Anniversary, I wanted to know what the plans were for the forthcoming celebrations. At that time, I reckoned my parents' financial position to be more than adequate and I looked forward to joining the family and friends at whatever party was being arranged. I was to receive a surprise.

'I don't think we'll go anywhere special,' my father replied. 'It's pretty expensive to go out nowadays!'

I thought this a little strange. Twenty-five years of marriage is quite a milestone and deserves some recognition, but there was to be no candlelit dinner for Mr and Mrs Alfred Wight.

The reason was simple enough: Alf was seriously short of money. He had recently visited his accountant, assuming that he had £820 in the bank, but had received a severe shock. He had been informed that he owed the Inland Revenue £800, leaving him the grand total of £20.

On the day he received this sobering piece of news, he went to Elland Road football stadium to watch Leeds United play, having been invited by two young men who used to live opposite the surgery in Thirsk. Alf often spoke later of his feelings at the time. 'I was there, but I never saw the match. It was like a dream. I thought to myself, "My God! I have slaved away in that practice for more than twenty-five years and what have I got to show for it? Twenty quid!"'

It seems incredible that Alfred Wight, a professional man of some standing in the local community, could not summon up enough money to celebrate his Silver Wedding; but there were good reasons and many factors were involved.

Alf had earned well for most of his professional life, but not well enough to become a rich man. His words to me before I embarked upon my veterinary career were very true: 'You'll make a decent living as a country vet but you'll never make a fortune.'

Unlike many modern practices, his was, for most of his working life, an agricultural one. The hours he spent driving large distances in his car, although enjoyable, only brought in a limited sum of money. Today, the treatment of family pets and horses generates a high proportion of our practice income, but during the 1960s he still depended primarily on farm work.

Overheads were high. Staff had to be paid and there were cars to be run. The purchase of expensive drugs and the provision of accommodation for the assistants all added to the costs of running the practice, while the cheerless spectre of the tax man was never far away. Many modern, large practices are now run as successful businesses, employing full-time managers, but in those days, in common with the vast majority of their professional colleagues, Alf and Donald Sinclair ran the practice themselves. Neither was an astute businessman, and it must have been very tiring to turn their hand to paperwork at the end of a long day.

Alf was never good with figures and Donald was not much better. It was in 1976, when I became a salaried partner, that I had my first insight into the torrid sessions they endured with their accountant, Bob Rickaby. Alf liked Bob very much but he dreaded his annual visit, the theme of which varied little from year to year.

Alf and Donald used to sit around the old wooden table in the waiting-room, listening to the résumé of the financial year. Donald suffered from a delicate digestion, the symptoms of which usually surfaced during Bob's visits. He would always sit in a hunched position with his arms tightly wrapped around his stomach – leaning forward and groaning softly at every piece of bad news from the accountant.

Alf adopted a very different posture. He would sit upright, staring out of the window at the old garden, a fixed and distant expression upon his face, and dreamily saying, 'Y . . . e . . . s' in response to the accountant's questions.

I clearly remember my first occasion around that table. I was seated next to Donald, who had a large piece of cod protruding from his coat pocket. My father was staring glassily at Bob who, having explained in detail how he had arrived at the figures, asked him whether he had understood.

'No,' replied my father.

The accountant was very thorough, attaching great importance to his clients' understanding of their financial position. He took a deep breath, removed his spectacles before giving them a polish, and began slowly to explain it all again.

'Listen, Alf,' he said, replacing his spectacles while fixing my father with a patient stare, 'let me put it to you in the simplest possible way.

You go to the butcher and you buy two pounds of sausages . . . are you with me so far?'

'Yes.'

'Right,' Bob continued, 'the sausages are five shillings per pound, so you give the butcher ten shillings. OK?'

'Yes.'

'Good! Now, these sausages that you have bought have actually cost you more than ten shillings, haven't they?' said Bob.

'Why?'

'Because they have been paid for out of taxed income.' My father stared silently out at the garden. Bob looked at him closely before ploughing on. 'You have already paid tax on that money you handed over to the butcher. Do you understand the analogy with the subject that we were discussing?'

'No.'

Bob took another deep breath. 'Well, let's put it another way, Alf. The butcher asks for less than ten shillings –'

At this point, my father came to life. 'It's all right, Bob! Look, we trust you! Just carry on! You could boil me in oil and I would never understand these figures.'

Bob looked at the blank faces around the table. He hesitated before going on to another point. It was an unwelcome one. 'Very well. Now, let me see, ah yes. I'm afraid you owe the practice four hundred pounds, Donald.'

Donald gave a hollow groan and lurched forward in his chair. 'Why?' he asked, quite reasonably.

'You have overdrawn!'

Donald sat bolt upright. 'Bloody hell, Bob!' he shouted. 'You're always giving us bad news! Why can't you give us some good news for a change?'

Bob was unruffled. 'If you look at the profits, Donald, there *is* some good news –'

'Not for me, there isn't!' interrupted Donald, tightening the grip around his waistline. I could see from the expression on his face that his digestive system was in ferment.

Bob continued to explain that the practice was really 'not doing too badly', but that expenses had to be met, and that the taxman wanted his cut.

'Not too badly, you say?' said Donald. 'I think we are going out of business. We pay out huge bills and nothing is coming in. We are going under! What do you think, Alfred? Don't you think we are going to the wall?' He nervously fingered the fish in his pocket.

My father continued to gaze out of the window, but a fleeting spasm crossed his face. We sat silently for a few moments, trying valiantly to grasp the facts and figures.

'How much can I have, Bob?' Donald exclaimed suddenly. 'How much is my share?' I had the feeling that my senior partner's limited store of patience was almost exhausted.

'Well, after deducting that four hundred pounds, let me see ...'

'Never mind that! How much?!'

The accountant arrived at a figure while Donald rocked backwards and forwards in his chair. After receiving his answer he leapt quickly to his feet. 'I must go now! Audrey is waiting for this fish. Lovely to have seen you, Bob. Do give my love to Gwen! Goodbye!'

Our yearly financial consultation had just ended.

Despite neither Alf nor Donald being experts in the field of facts and figures, the practice continued to make a profit but many other things conspired towards limiting it, not least among them the thorny issue of bad debts. Obtaining money from many of the old Yorkshire farmers was an art in itself, with some of the clients owing the practice large sums of money for years.

I remember telling my father, over lunch one day, about my morning round.

'I met two grand blokes today, Dad! Full of laughs with hardly a care in the world.'

'Who were they?' he asked.

I told him. He gave a wry smile. 'You know why they are so happy?' he said. 'They receive a prompt service for which they pay me very infrequently. They receive totally free overdraft facilities from our practice.'

Alf loved his work but he never enjoyed the business side of it, such as sending out bills and chasing up bad debts. Many vets today enjoy the challenge of managing their own businesses, but he never did.

'Why can't I just drive around, doing the job I love and receive a sum of money at the end of the week?' he used to say. 'I don't want a huge amount, just enough to ensure that I can continue to enjoy my life. Apart from some security for my future, there is nothing in the world I really want that I haven't got already.'

In many cases, of course, the farmers had genuine difficulty in paying their bills – and there were many very good clients who paid promptly – but there is no doubt that the practice was severely disadvantaged by its outstanding debts.

It was not only some of the farmers who were slow to settle their accounts; a large proportion of small animal clients walked out of the surgery without paying. Many of them never paid at all and one can only guess how much the firm of Sinclair and Wight would have been worth had all the debts been settled promptly.

Neither Donald nor Alf were ruthless businessmen. Not only did they find it difficult to ask for money, they performed much of the work for vastly reduced fees. Old age pensioners, and anyone who had fallen on hard times, were given cheap, sometimes free, treatment. When a dairy farmer from Asenby near Thirsk died, leaving a widow and a very young son and daughter to run the farm, Alf did not charge them for his veterinary services for a whole year. This 'Robin Hood' approach (Alf and Donald were not alone among their profession in this respect), while being very admirable, contributed significantly towards limiting the practice profits.

It is not hard to understand why the old farmers were so reluctant to hand over their money; every penny they made was earned through sheer hard work. But every cloud has a silver lining and, years later as James Herriot, Alf had many a good story to tell about the York-shireman's reluctance to 'part with his brass'.

Another drain on the practice finances was the running of the motor cars. The assistants were provided with cars, and the golden rule seemed to be that they were driven at maximum speed at all times. These tormented little machines rocketed round the country roads, frequently shooting into ditches, somersaulting into fields or having the oil sumps torn off on the rough farm tracks. They were a very expensive item.

On one occasion in the early 1960s when I was on holiday from university, I was with my father in the office when suddenly outside I heard a tortured roar followed by a high-pitched squealing. I ran to the window but could see nothing. 'What on earth was that terrible racket?' I asked.

My father seemed unmoved. 'It's only Ron setting off on the morning round,' he replied. He walked over to the window and looked wistfully out on to the street. 'He'll be arriving at the first farm by now!' He was obviously resigned to it all.

Ron Reeves was a very able and popular assistant, but one who set a new record in the practice. He managed to put a smooth, shiny finish onto a brand-new set of tyres in just 3,000 miles of motoring.

A few years later, Alf bought a second-hand car, a grey Renault 16. Previously, whenever he had replaced his car, he had bought a new one, but other priorities, for example pension provision, were now diverting his financial resources along other channels. One thing comforted him; he would not have to take any more ribbing from the farmers.

This used to be quite embarrassing. Whenever he was seen in a new car, he would receive remarks such as 'By gaw! Look 'ere! Another new car! Veterinary job must be payin' ower well!' It was good-natured banter, but he still cringed when under attack. He thought he was safe in his second-hand car as he drove onto a farm one day. He was mistaken. The farmer's wife sprang out of the door to meet him, and she was in an aggressive mood. It was just his luck that he was visiting one of the very few unpleasant farmers' wives in the district.

'By, the whole country's talkin' about your bills!' she shrieked. 'An' look at this! Another new car! All got wi' the money from us poor farmers!'

My father was ready for her. 'Actually it's only a second-hand one. I can't really afford a new car nowadays.'

She looked at it for a moment before returning to the attack. 'Oh? So it's just a lot o' show on nowt, eh?' He said no more; he knew when he was beaten.

Despite everything, my father was doing well enough in the early 1960s to preclude his receiving a full local authority grant towards the funding of my university education. As that decade progressed, however, he saw a gradual downturn in the practice fortunes.

The amount of TB Testing – although still a major contributor to the practice income – began to slowly diminish as the number of stock farmers in the surrounding area declined. In the early 1970s, a new government scheme to eradicate Brucellosis would begin, meaning more revenue for country practices, but not only was that still a long way off, the big upturn in small animal work was yet to materialise.

To add to his worries, a veterinary surgeon had established a practice in the nearby village of Maunby. This was a difficult time for Alf and Donald as they saw some of their clients desert them, taking their business to the new vet. It was, also, a very revealing experience. Some of the clients who left were men whom Alf had considered to be personal friends; conversely, others whom he did not know so intimately remained loyal to Sinclair and Wight. Alf was a very thoughtful man at that time, and he would never forget those clients who remained faithful to the practice. The opposition did not last very long, departing in 1968, but some clients were lost to the practice for ever.

It is interesting to compare the practice accounts during the years of the 1960s. At the end of the decade, Alf earned £4,685, over £1,000 less than he had earned in 1960. Although inflation was not high during that decade, it was still very easy to forget that the value of money gradually diminished with the advancing years and that other gently rising expenses chipped away persistently at the practice profits. This was a time when Alf and Donald realised that their charges – whilst still regarded by some of the farmers as being too steep – had not risen in line with their expenses.

Although Alf was never adept at dealing with figures, he was always a sensible person, and this stood him in good stead during his years of financial uncertainty. Despite the many factors limiting his practice profits, he still managed to earn well; in 1966 – the year that he could not afford to celebrate his silver wedding – he managed to earn the respectable sum of almost £5,000. Why, then, did he have no capital?

There is a simple answer. He earned well but, rather than save it, he spent it. Alf was always a generous man who thought little of spending money on others; this, combined with the high cost of living that everyone experiences, was a major obstacle to amassing capital.

His own family benefited from his generous nature. My sister and I had the happiest childhoods imaginable. We were well fed, we had several holidays each year and, in our schooldays, rarely missed out on trips. If my father was ever short of money, we were never aware of it.

It was not only his children who benefited from his generosity. He strove continually to make Joan's life less demanding. Even though Rowardennan was a modern house and easier to keep clean than the big old Kirkgate house, he still paid women to help her. In 1956, he bought her a Morris Minor, the first of a succession of new cars.

After 1961, he had to fund my university education and, four years later, Rosie's as well, but one of the most revealing examples of his generosity was the financial support he provided for his parents. From the first days of working with Jock McDowall in Sunderland, when he was earning £3 a week, he sent money to them and, even during his time in the RAF, when he was receiving a paltry three shillings a day, money was on its way up to Glasgow.

There are references to this in his letters to them. In one from Sunderland in 1940, he wrote: 'Here's 30 bob from my pay; buy yourself 10 Woodbines, Pop old boy!' And from Thirsk in 1941: 'Funny how hard it is to save! I don't spend much and I've only given you folks £40 since I came. I do wish it could have been more.' In later years, as he regularly sent money to them, he referred to it as 'the pension'. It must have amounted to a fair sum over all that time; he rarely missed a week.

In 1958, he bought his parents' house in Glasgow. As rent-paying tenants, they were faced with the possibility that the owner was going to sell the house which would have meant their having to find a new home. It cost Alf £1000, a substantial sum at that time. The debt he felt he owed his parents was repaid many times over.

Alf Wight received nothing in the way of financial aid throughout his life and this, combined with his generous and responsible nature, goes a long way to explaining his lack of any capital at that time. His position was hardly surprising, and indeed was no worse than that of many of his professional colleagues of the day, with his lack of readily available money balanced by freedom from any form of debt, save for the mortgage on his house. Admittedly, he was a worried man when he learned that he had no more than £20 to his name in 1966, but he did not allow this to spoil a life that was both rewarding and brimming with a wide variety of interests.

One day, in the early 1960s, while on a visit home during my years at Glasgow Veterinary School, I came across a small manuscript in one of the drawers at Rowardennan. It was a short story called *Left Winger* and it was about football. I sat down then and there to read it. Having noticed my father's familiar scrawl superimposed over parts of the typewritten text, I then approached him with it.

'This is very good,' I said. 'Did you write it?'

'Yes,' he replied, almost apologetically. 'You really think it's good, do you?'

'I really do! Why don't you send it to a publisher or a magazine?'

'I have,' he said. 'Several.'

'And?'

'No one seems to want it.' He thought for a moment before continuing. 'But you think it's good?' He seemed singularly interested in my opinion.

'Yes, I do!'

He seemed satisfied and dropped the subject.

I knew that my father had been writing for a year or two, and presumed that he was continuing to pursue yet another of his 'crazes'. This latest hobby seemed to be one at which he appeared to be not only adept but one also that he was clearly taking a little more seriously than the others. I continued to believe, however, that – as with many of his other interests, – he would persevere with this new enthusiasm for a while longer before giving it up for something else. I was wrong.

CHAPTER TWENTY

'May I borrow one of your magazines, Joan?' Alf asked of his secretary one day, a slightly sheepish expression upon his face. Joan Drake, who had joined the practice straight from school in 1959, four years previously, considered that she knew her employer quite well. She had regarded him as a man who was at home drinking beer in the company of his friends, or standing on the packed terraces of football grounds, but definitely not the type to read women's magazines. It was a strange request and she looked at him a little more closely.

'I'll give it back to you as soon as I have read it!' he promised. Detecting the look of puzzlement on her face, he lowered his voice before continuing. 'I want to have a look at the short stories.'

Unknown to many, including Joan Drake, Alf's pastime of writing – for which he was obtaining information and ideas from every possible source – had, in fact, been occupying an increasing amount of his time for several years. Around the late 1950s, he had bought books on the art of writing and, in his spare time, had tentatively begun to tap away on his typewriter.

The idea of writing a book had been one of Alf's long-held dreams. I remember his talking about it during my schooldays and a letter written by Joan to his parents dated 2 October 1955 is very revealing: 'I must tell you that there is great excitement in the house as it's Alf's birthday tomorrow. Guess what I have bought for him – a typewriter! I'm sure he will be writing to you much more often now; he may even get down to writing that book he has been talking about for thirteen years!'

Although Joan had been listening to Alf's ideas for writing a book almost from the day they first met, it took him more than twenty years to think seriously of turning his dream into reality.

He had an excellent grounding in that he was extremely well-read, and was a dedicated and accomplished letter-writer. He had observed tremendous change taking place within his profession and he felt a burning desire to put it all down in print. He wanted to talk about the quirky characters he had met, with their fascinating, old-fashioned customs and remedies. He felt compelled to describe the old Yorkshire he had grown to love – a way of life that was fast disappearing – and he wanted to preserve it for others to enjoy. A humorous slant could be provided by his friends, Donald and Brian Sinclair, with whom he had had so many hilarious times.

It was following the recovery from his nervous breakdown that, with such fertile ideas, he began to write in earnest, but he soon discovered that it was not going to be as easy as he thought. After about eighteen months of chopping and changing his story, he came to the conclusion that he was going nowhere. His book, a succession of long sentences full of florid adjectives was, in his own words, like a 'schoolboy's essay and a poor one at that'. He had to think again.

The pages of Alf's very first attempt are covered in corrections and alterations; he must have spent countless hours re-writing the book. The end result was a somewhat jerky collection of stories about farmers and his veterinary friends, Donald and Brian, whom he called Edward and Henry Vernon. Some of the episodes are ones that were eventually to appear in his first published book, but they are a pale shadow of the work that was to appear years later.

It was while he was sadly taking stock of all his efforts that an idea came to him. His book was, in essence, just a collection of short stories, tenuously connected together. He had always been a great admirer of the art of short-story telling, with the stories of Conan Doyle, H. G. Wells and O. Henry remaining some of his all-time favourites. He decided temporarily to shelve the idea of a long book and try his hand at short-story writing. While on his rounds, as he listened attentively to stories on the car radio, he thought to himself, 'Surely I can do as well as that?' With renewed feelings of confidence and excitement, he began.

For around a year or so, he wrote stories about football, golf, various outdoor activities and human relationships in general. Having re-read them many times over, he thought that they were really quite good and that his style was improving. He was quite impressed with his efforts. With feelings of delicate optimism, he soon began to wonder what others might think of them. He decided to take the plunge and sent some of the stories to selected magazines and periodicals, as well as to the British Broadcasting Corporation. Perhaps he might get the odd one published.

*

It is widely believed that James Herriot wrote innumerable stories that never reached publication. In fact, there were not many. He was working hard in the practice, managing to write only in short bursts in his free time, and the result of his labours was no more than seven or eight stories. After his death, I found one in his study entitled *The Saint's Day*, a story that I had never seen before. This story, about the discomfort suffered by a middle-aged man while on a sponsored walk with his young daughter, took me a long time to read; I had to keep stopping to wipe the tears of laughter from my eyes.

I read the stories at the time with great enjoyment, but it seemed that not everyone agreed with my opinion. His efforts at getting his work published drew a blank. His stories came back to him by return of post and he became, as he said later, 'a connoisseur of the sickening thud that a manuscript makes as it falls through the letterbox'. Not only did no one seem to want his work, but he was even further disheartened by the total absence of any comments or words of encouragement. The stories of James Alfred Wight had completely failed to interest anyone; as a potential author, he was a nobody.

Alf said very little to anyone about his hobby. As he did not really expect to attain the heady heights of published authorship, he kept his rejections very much to himself. He was discouraged but by no means beaten. He enjoyed writing and he did not take it too seriously, tapping out his stories in his own time with no one to pressurise him – but, deep within him, feelings of intense frustration were growing. He genuinely believed that the stories he submitted were as good as many he had read or listened to on the radio. Realising that he must be doing something wrong, he returned to studying the art of writing.

One day, he returned for lunch to regale my mother with yet another funny incident that had happened to him on his rounds. 'It would be a good story for the book!' he said.

She looked at him and said, '*The* book, Alf? You have been talking about writing a book for the past twenty years. You'll never write a book!'

'Why on earth not?' he replied.

'It will soon be our silver wedding anniversary,' she countered, 'and you still have not written it. Men of almost fifty don't start writing books!'

He explained away the twenty-odd barren years by suggesting that he was not the impulsive type and needed time to assemble his masterpiece. His wife was unimpressed.

Her remarks, however, had stung him and, on that very same day, he had a revelation. He realised he should return to writing about something on which he was well-informed, not just topics that interested him. He was an expert on only one subject – veterinary practice. He had been on the right track at the start. He would unearth his old book and begin again.

The more he thought about it, the more excited he became. He had fresh ideas and bought more books on the art of writing, studying them all closely. He had many hilarious episodes firmly fixed in his mind and he felt sure that, this time, with a year or two of 'practising' behind him, he could make a good job of it. He sensed a new surge of enthusiasm.

He began writing this book around the autumn of 1965, taking about eighteen months to complete it. It was a slow process as he was working full time in the practice, including some periods of night work. Abandoning the use of impressive and complicated words, he completely rewrote several chapters of his original book, changing the story many times over until, by the early months of 1967, he felt that he could improve upon it no more. His simpler, conversational style was, he felt, far more readable than his previous one.

He had finished. He felt that this was not only a great improvement on his original effort but was a book that could be enjoyed by people of all ages. With a warm glow of satisfaction, he realised that he had completed one of his life's ambitions.

For a few weeks, he relaxed and enjoyed the feeling of achievement. He had produced a book that his family would remember him by, a nice little story for his grandchildren to read, and for a while he put it to the back of his mind. The practice was busy at the time – experiencing the rush of early spring lambing – and he had plenty of work to occupy him, but it was not long before he began to feel restless. There was still a nagging question that remained unanswered: 'Was his book good enough to interest a publisher?' He just had to know.

He was not very optimistic. With the rejections of his earlier work having been such a disappointment, he had little reason to expect better luck with this one. He thought long and hard about the next step.

Joan had a suggestion. Having thoroughly enjoyed the 'Doctor' series of books by Richard Gordon – amongst them *Doctor in the House* and *Doctor at Large* – which recounted hilarious incidents about the medical profession, she reasoned that her husband's book was in a similar vein.

Why not therefore send his manuscript to the publishers of those books? Alf was in full agreement and, having ascertained that they were published by Michael Joseph Ltd, prepared to post off the manuscript to the London publishing house.

Before he acted, however, he had another thought. He telephoned his friend Eddie Straiton, who had had several books published by the Farming Press and had contacts in the publishing world. Eddie was very keen to help, but rather than send the book to Michael Joseph, he suggested he should contact a friend called John Morrison who had worked with the large publishing firm of Collins.

Alf therefore sent his manuscript down to Eddie, who read it before passing it on to his publishing friend. John Morrison read and liked the book, got back in touch with Eddie who, in turn, suggested a meeting between the three men in London. This was huge encouragement for Alf. Someone of influence had read his book – and had actually enjoyed it!

In a state of great excitement, Alf travelled down to London to meet Eddie and John Morrison, lunching at a restaurant called La Dolce Vita in Soho. Here he heard John Morrison confirm his enthusiasm and say that he planned to pass the manuscript to Collins to consider it for publication. This was music to Alf's ears.

A few days after returning to Yorkshire, he received a heartening note from John Morrison, dated 27 March 1967:

Just a little note to confirm that your three-volume typescript was duly sent off by special messenger to the chairman of Messrs Collins in St James' Place which will ensure that it is read carefully and sympathetically. As I told you and Eddie, I greatly enjoyed your book. You have two of the most important qualities of a good story teller – a graphic power of description of nature and scene, and evocative character delineation . . . I do not read many novels these days and am not conversant with today's trends in this medium but I hope that there will always be room for something so natural and sound and healthy (wholesome) as your story!

John Morrison's optimistic attitude together with his small note – the first real pieces of encouragement outside of his own family that Alf had ever received – gave him a tremendous lift. With his book on its way to one of the biggest publishers in the land, he wondered whether, perhaps this time, he would meet with some success?

*

The book was written as a novel. On the first page of the manuscript, which the family still has, are written the words: 'The Art and the Science: A novel by J. A. Wight'. His hero is called James Walsh, and is loosely based on himself and his experiences in practice.

It is fascinating to compare this book with his earlier and later works. He included, as he had in his first attempt years earlier, flashbacks to his veterinary college days, introducing two other fictional veterinary characters, Hugh Mills, and the quiet and apprehensive Bernie Hill. Both these men qualified with Walsh and had little adventures of their own. Donald and Brian Sinclair were there and, for the first time, appear as Siegfried and Tristan, although still retaining the surname of Vernon from the original effort. A love story between Walsh and a farmer's daughter ran through the script.

It was a fine effort, revealing touches of descriptive flair that were to be the hallmark of the future James Herriot, and some of the funny scenes were well done. There were, however, too many leading veterinary characters for a not-very-long novel, while the story, which seemed to jump from one character to another, lacked continuity.

Alf waited hopefully for news from London. He waited a long time. Nothing happened. Rather than being downcast, he felt a twinge of hope. As his other efforts had boomeranged back to the house by return of post, he thought that perhaps the deafening silence meant that his book was receiving serious consideration.

At last, after six long months, he received a letter from John Morrison. In it, he learned that the manuscript had been passed to one of Collins' most highly-regarded readers, Juliana Wadham. She had given it a favourable report and had passed it back to the Collins editorial department where it had received 'serious consideration'. This explained the long wait, but the end result was another grim disappointment: Collins did not want to publish it. He had been rejected yet again.

John's letter of 11 September 1967, however, contained much to encourage Alf:

On my return from holiday, I found your typescript and the enclosed letters awaiting me. These, as I hope you will recognise, are immensely encouraging and explain the long delay in their writing on the matter. I hope you will now give full consideration to the suggestions made by Juliana Wadham and lose no time in putting these to effect!

Anyway, I hope you'll be happy to know that, in the opinion of several of the leading authorities in one of the biggest publishers in the world, you are well over half way to success as an author.

Enclosed with John's letter was one from the Collins reader in which she stated that, although she had enjoyed the book, the publishers, while considering it to have 'so much good material', had decided that 'it was not satisfactory as a novel'. But there was something else in that letter – some advice from Juliana Wadham that would be some of the finest that Alfred Wight would ever receive.

She asked him: 'Why have you written this as a novel? These stories are, quite obviously, based upon real incidents so why turn them into fiction? Why don't you re-write it in the first person as an autobiographical work? The stories will be all the more appealing to your readers if they realise they are ones that are based upon fact!'

My father read her letter again and again. The more he thought about it, the more sense it made, and he set about re-structuring his book with supercharged enthusiasm. It was a twist of irony that his very first effort, years previously, had been written in the first person, as Juliana Wadham now suggested!

In September 1967, when I was still working with Eddie Straiton, I received a telephone call from my father. He wanted me to join him in the Thirsk practice.

I did not really want to. I was having a great time in Staffordshire, and wanted to get some more experience before returning home at such an early stage in my career. I replied that I would give it serious consideration but that I was happy where I was, and my father – selfless as ever – did not pursue the matter.

Another call from my mother, however, changed my mind. The practice, at that time, was going through a difficult period and was reduced to a three-man outfit. This meant that my father, at the age of over fifty, was having to do regular night work, alternating on a one-in-two rota with the remaining assistant, Tony Kelly. My mother added that, with the financial position within the practice not as good as it might have been, my return would be a great help, especially as I could live at home, alleviating the problem of finding accommodation for a new veterinary surgeon. I returned to Thirsk in October 1967 which, as well as providing extra help for my father by taking on his night work, gave him more time to rewrite his book.

I have always found it intriguing that my father not only wrote his novel while working full time in the practice but, from August 1966, he had been on call every alternate night. He must have had amazing dedication to sit down and begin writing after a full day's work, a time when most people would have just wanted to put their feet up.

During my first few months working in Thirsk, I remember him restructuring his book. He did not have a study, but simply tapped away on his typewriter among the rest of us in the sitting-room. He wrote that book in front of the television, having the ability to shut off his mind and concentrate on the words in front of him, but if something interested him on the television, he would stop and enjoy it before effortlessly switching himself back into writing mode. Truly remarkable.

By the summer of 1968, Alf had re-written his book, this time a semi-autobiographical account of his first year in veterinary practice in Yorkshire. Although it was now written in the first person, many of the stories were ones that had appeared in his previous book. As before, the main characters were based on the Sinclair brothers. He changed the title from *The Art and the Science* to *If Only They Could Talk*.

This title was suggested to him in November 1967 by a client called Arthur Dand, a dairy farmer who lived on an uncompromising little farm at the foot of the White Horse near Kilburn. He was a farmer with a difference. He, too, was a keen writer and sent off parcels of his work to various publishing houses. Like Alf, he was meeting with little success. Whenever Alf visited Arthur Dand's farm, the visit was a long one as the two men compared notes and discussed their aspiring ambitions to become well-known authors. Alf always thought that Arthur was one of, perhaps, thousands of writers whose work, sadly, will never be enjoyed by the rest of the world. It was he, however, who provided the title for Alf's first book.

In July of that year, Alf re-submitted his much improved book to Collins. The book was sent on to Mrs Wadham, but little happened for a while as she not only had other reading commitments but was due to go on holiday to Ireland. She wrote to Alf in early September, assuring him that she had started the manuscript with the same amount of enthusiasm as she did the previous time and that she hoped to let him hear about it very soon. There was then a period of silence for three months. As before, Alf retained a ray of hope. Could they, again, be thinking seriously about publishing it? With the practice becoming busier again, he had plenty to occupy his mind but, in late November, his curiosity got the better of him and he posted off a letter of enquiry.

He received a prompt and courteous reply in which the publishers stated that they were sorry but their 'lists were full'. This was a polite way of saying that they did not want his manuscript. He had been rejected again which, after the initial disappointment, did not really surprise him. The length of time required for the reply, plus the fact that he had had to remind them about the manuscript, led him to ponder whether anyone had even bothered to read it.

Two days later, however, he received an apologetic letter from Juliana Wadham. She had read and greatly enjoyed the manuscript, but her enthusiasm had not been shared by Collins. Her letter, dated 29 November 1968, said:

I was appalled to hear, today, that you still haven't heard from Collins as I sent your book in several weeks ago. I really can't apologise too much as you have been so kind and patient and I, myself, as you know, am an enthusiastic supporter of *If Only They Could Talk*.

By now, I expect you will have heard that Collins themselves don't feel it is quite the book for their present lists ... I, personally, am very sad that Collins are not going to do it and I hope you have more luck in the future.

There was still a tiny glimmer of hope. His manuscript had been passed on by Collins' editorial department to an associate company, Geoffrey Bles Ltd in Doughty Street. Three weeks later, however, Alf received an all-too-familiar message; their lists were also full. At this point, he asked that his manuscript be returned to him direct. He later recalled, 'The thud that *it* made coming back through the door was the loudest of all!'

This rejection was, he felt, the final blow. He had had enough. He had to accept that he was a veterinary surgeon not a writer, and he finally admitted defeat. He had tried; he had tried very hard, but he had failed.

He still felt proud of what he had done. Quite apart from having written a book that could be passed down through generations of his family, he had had the satisfaction of having his work genuinely praised by John Morrison and Juliana Wadham, two highly-experienced readers who had no reason to enthuse over his little book other than that they thought it had real potential.

Alfred Wight had knocked on the door of the world of publishing but he had not managed to walk through. He had, he thought, done pretty well to have progressed so far but this was the end of the road. He put his sorry brown paper parcel into a drawer and immersed himself in the job that he was trained for, the one that he loved best – veterinary practice.

These were happy days in the practice. Tony Kelly, the longest-serving assistant ever to work for Sinclair and Wight, was a most likeable and reliable vet with a great sense of humour, and there was both hard work and plenty of laughter in our daily routine.

The rejected book lying in the drawer was the last thing on my mind. Watching my father laughing at some of Tony's latest escapades one day, I thought that he, too, had forgotten all about it and had finally cast off his ambitions to be a published author. With the figure in front of the television now no longer having a typewriter in front of him, I felt that this latest enthusiasm had had its day. Once again, I was mistaken.

One day in the spring of 1969, Joan said to Alf, quite out of the blue, 'Why don't you send your manuscript to Michael Joseph, as we were going to do originally?'

Knowing her husband well, she sensed that, even though his book had lain in a drawer untouched for weeks, he could not really stop thinking about it. With her words, yet again, having re-kindled the smouldering desire to get his manuscript published, he opened the drawer and took out his book.

He did not send it straight to Michael Joseph; he had another idea. Two years previously, Alf had bought a book called *Sell Them A Story* by someone called Jean LeRoy. In it, she advised that anyone who wished to have their work published should first approach an agent – and she would know because, according to the biographical note on the jacket flap, she herself was a literary agent.

Until this time, Alf had not seriously considered sending his book to an agent, but suddenly the idea seemed a very good one. He located *Sell Them A Story* on his crowded bookshelves, took it to bed, and began to read it again. Alf found the book inspiring and, as he read it for the second time, his ideas took a new turn. Not only would he send his manuscript to an agent, he would send it to none other than the author of that little book, Jean LeRoy herself.

As he lay in bed that night, he must have wondered whether he would ever meet with success. As a veteran of so many rejections, he was not too optimistic but, believing that his book was easy to read and contained material that could be enjoyed by people of all ages, he still felt hopeful.

It was a fateful spring day in 1969 when Alfred Wight opened the drawer and lifted out his tattered manuscript. As the well-travelled parcel sped on its way to Miss Jean LeRoy, c/o David Higham Associates, 76 Dean Street, Soho, London, questions flashed across his mind.

Would the amusing stories about Donald and Brian Sinclair that his friends and family had heard about for so many years ever reach a wider audience? Would the agent read his book and, if so, would she like it? Would she consider it worthy of publication? This time, he would not have to wait long for his answer.

CHAPTER TWENTY-ONE

One April morning, barely a week after he had sent off his manuscript to Jean LeRoy, I came down for breakfast to find my father seated at the table. His hands were trembling as he fingered a letter that had just arrived.

He looked at me and said, very quietly, 'Jim, I can't believe it but my book might be published! After all these years! I just can't believe it!'

He handed me the letter. It was from David Bolt, a director at David Higham Associates, saying that he liked the book 'enormously' and considered it would have every chance of reaching publication.

This was a revelation. After so many rejections, Alf had received a positive response – and within such a short time. It was beyond anything he had dared to hope for. The letter included an invitation to visit the literary agency in London, which happened to be extremely convenient as he was already going down to the capital to see the football match between England and Scotland at Wembley. As Alfred Wight watched Scotland take on the 'auld enemy' that day, he had more than just football on his mind.

On its arrival at the David Higham offices, Jean LeRoy had taken the manuscript home, and almost immediately had started to read it. After only one or two chapters, she had realised that she was in the company of an unusually gifted writer. The author's wonderful descriptions of Yorkshire, his vivid characterisation, the humour and the easy, readable style, had convinced her that she was in possession of something special.

Jean LeRoy was thrilled with what she had read, and walked excitedly into the David Higham offices, waving the manuscript and exclaiming, 'This is a find!' As she personally handled newspaper and magazine rights rather than selling to publishers, she passed Alf's manuscripts to David Bolt. He too was greatly enthused, and felt sure they could be on to a winner. A letter to the unknown author was soon on its way to Yorkshire.

At the meeting in London, where Alf met both Jean LeRoy and David Bolt, he was told that they felt very positive about the book, and had the ideal publishing house in mind.

'Which one is that?' Alf asked.

'Michael Joseph,' replied David Bolt – the very publisher to whom Joan had suggested Alf should send the first manuscript, over three years previously.

When the manuscript of *If Only They Could Talk* arrived at the offices of the publishing company of Michael Joseph Ltd in Bloomsbury, centre of London's publishing world, Mrs Anthea Joseph, deputy chairman and one of the company's editorial directors, did not read it straight-away. This was not unusual. Manuscripts of all descriptions flowed through the doors of Michael Joseph each day, with the ones sent in by agents meriting more attention than those arriving unsolicited from hopeful members of the general public. Only a fraction of the manuscripts received would achieve publication. Although any manu-script arriving from David Higham Associates – an agency Anthea Joseph rated highly – would be considered carefully, the company had published, in the previous decade, three novels with a veterinary background, and Anthea was not certain there was room for any more in a similar vein. These three books – *A Vet's Life, The Vet Has Nine Lives* and *Vets In The Belfry* – were by an author called Alex Duncan which was, in fact, a pseudonym used by the thriller writer Madeleine Duke, whom the company also published.

Anthea Joseph passed the manuscript of *If Only They Could Talk* to her part-time secretary, Jennifer Katz, to read. Young people in editorial departments often took manuscripts home to read and report on; it was one way of adding to the notoriously low salaries paid to junior publishing staff. Jennifer took it home for the week-end and, like Jean LeRoy, returned to the office on the Monday morning, waving the manuscript in the air and exclaiming, 'We *must* publish this book! It is the *funniest* book I have read for years!' Such was her enthusiasm that Anthea Joseph duly packed it into her briefcase, along with four or five other manuscripts she had to read, and took it home.

Anthea Joseph, widow of the company's founder, was an extremely astute publisher and she could 'smell' a good book when she met it – whether the book was literary or commercial. At the following week's editorial meeting, she consulted with her colleagues: could they publish another book with a veterinary background, starting off a new author from scratch? Dick Douglas-Boyd, sales director at the time, was certain they could.

However, there was one other factor which may have contributed towards the destiny of *If Only They Could Talk*. Some years later, Anthea Joseph told Alf that it was the words of Clarence Paget, then editorial director of Pan Books, that had helped her make the decision to go ahead and publish this unknown vet from Yorkshire. Clarence and Anthea were long-time publishing friends and would often lunch together to talk about the authors they jointly published, Michael Joseph in the original hardback edition and Pan Books in the subsequent paperback edition. A rising star for both publishing houses at that time was Dick Francis.

Clarence was a publisher held in high regard by Anthea and it is very probable that during a lunch Anthea would have mentioned 'the vet from Yorkshire' and her concern whether, following the three Alex Duncan books, there would be room for another with a veterinary background. It appears that Anthea sent Clarence part of the manuscript for his opinion since, according to Alf, he had returned it to her almost immediately, stating very emphatically, 'You could have a real seller there!'

This story has been viewed with some scepticism by those connected to the publishing world. Anthea Joseph was a very shrewd publisher, and it is highly debatable whether she would have needed the advice of anyone else. Nevertheless, Alf was convinced of the veracity of the story. One thing is certain: Clarence Paget as well as Anthea Joseph would forever occupy a special place in his memory: two more of the many players whom Alf regarded as having tilted fortune his way in that long game of chance on the road to success.

Alf Wight's fingers went into trembling mode again as he opened another letter from David Bolt at David Higham Associates. This letter, written on 18 June 1969, informed him that his book was definitely going to be published. The contents made sweet reading:

Dear Mr Wight
          IF ONLY THEY COULD TALK (J. Walsh)
I'm delighted to say that we've had an offer from the very first publisher we tried, the excellent house of Michael Joseph. I had Anthea Joseph, the deputy chairman, on the telephone this morning and after a little discussion settled on the following terms, subject, of course, to your approval. . . . As you

may know, Joseph are particularly good with 'animal books' and ought, I think, to do very well with this one.

We settled, didn't we, on the pseudonym 'James Herriot' after you discovered that there is, in fact, a James Walsh in practice?

Receiving this letter was one of the greatest moments of Alf's life. Having always loved browsing through bookshops from his years as a boy in Glasgow, the thought of seeing his own work on the shelves gave him shivers of excitement.

He was shortly invited to London again, this time to meet Anthea Joseph. He found her a charming woman, and the two of them developed an instant liking for each other. They met for lunch, at which Anthea Joseph told him how much she had enjoyed his book, as well as telling him about other similar authors the firm had published. As David Bolt had said, they had successfully published books with an animal or medical theme: apart from Alex Duncan, there was Paul Gallico, Richard Gordon and Monica Dickens. As she progressed to explaining the contract and how money would be paid as an advance against future royalties, Alf began to like her more and more.

There had been one decision that he had had to make quickly, one to which David Bolt had referred in his letter. Alf could not use his real name – Alfred Wight – as this would have been construed as advertising; the Royal College of Veterinary Surgeons were very strict about this in those days. Any form of advertising was regarded as unprofessional conduct and Alf obviously could not afford to be suspended or, possibly, struck off the Veterinary Register. He had had to choose a pseudonym.

To find a name that he liked had been a strangely difficult task. He had got used to 'James Walsh', the name he had used for his original novel – and he had submitted the manuscript of *If Only They Could Talk* under that name – but now, with publication a reality, he had to re-think. There was already a 'James Walsh' in the Veterinary Register.

On the evening of 11 February 1969, while watching a fifth round Football Association cup tie on television between Birmingham City and Manchester United, he had noted that the Birmingham goalkeeper was called Jim Herriot. My father, who was continually thinking of ideas for a pseudonym, had liked the name; it was an unusual one and he had reached, yet again, for the Veterinary Register. To his surprise, there were no veterinarians with the name of Herriot. He had marked the name down for possible future use, little dreaming that the name of Birmingham City's Scottish international goalkeeper, who played six times for his country, would one day become world-famous. On that February evening, Alf Wight's search for a pseudonym had come to an end.

Years later, in 1988, a Glasgow newspaper, the *Sunday Mail*, ran an article on the origins of Alf's literary name, bringing the original Jim Herriot, who was then working as a builder in Larkhall, Lanarkshire, to visit the surgery in Thirsk. He was not a keen reader but had watched the television series of the books. He had had no idea that the famous Yorkshire vet had borrowed his name, and was astonished that the celebrated author was excited at the prospect of meeting him.

The two men got on famously. On meeting his namesake for the very first time, Alf Wight extended his hand with the timeless words, 'James Herriot, I presume!' Football, of course, was discussed at length, and my father gave the ex-goalkeeper a signed book; Jim Herriot, in return, gave him one of his Scottish international football jerseys – a gift that remained a treasured possession.

Throughout his years of fame, Alf was amused to receive letters from some of his fans enquiring whether he could be related to them. People with the name of Herriot, fully believing it to be his real name, were hoping that the famous author was a long-lost cousin.

One particular incident in 1972 amused him. His second book had just been published when he was approached by one of the local Thirsk solicitors.

'I hadn't realised that you were so intelligent!' the man said.

'What do you mean?' Alf asked.

'Just that!' carried on the solicitor. 'And a scholar with a deep knowledge of medieval history as well.'

'Oh yes?'

'Certainly. I'm very impressed that you chose the name of Herriot.'

'Oh . . . yes?'

The man continued. 'I'm amazed that you knew that a "herriot" was the best calf in the herd that the feudal lord exacted from his serf every year. What an inspired choice!'

Alf gave the man a knowing look. 'Well, there you are!' he said. 'Don't you be so quick to judge a person in future.'

For his first book, Alf Wight received £200 as an advance from Michael Joseph, half on signature of the contract on 5 August 1969 and the other half due on publication. This advance would be set against royalties of 10% of the book's published price for the first 2,000 books sold, rising to a maximum of 17½% should the book become a best-seller. At his first meeting with Anthea Joseph, she had explained to him that advances for first books by unknown authors were rarely high; it was not so much the outlay in advance they had to consider when taking on a new author, but the fact that the book would take up a place on the publishing list and would need time and care spent on it by all the departments.

It was indeed a modest amount but he fingered that first cheque in wonderment. He was soon, however, to receive a far bigger boost to his financial status. In November, Jean LeRoy negotiated the sale of the serial rights to the influential newspaper, the *London Evening Standard*. The book was to be serialised, prior to publication, in a newspaper with a huge circulation in London and the home counties.

Alf thought that he had entered the world of fantasy when he received a telephone call from his agent informing him of the deal that had been struck. The newspaper was to pay £36,710 for the serial rights – a sum that would be considered good today, but thirty years ago was monumental. I was there when he received the call and saw him nearly fall off his chair. To a man who had had only £20 four years before, it was unbelievable. On that day, with grim words like 'mortgages' and 'overdrafts' soon to be spectres of the past, he reckoned that his financial worries were over for all time.

I remember my father's happiness at the time as he began to feel that people were on his side. He had had to make many decisions in his life, but that of employing an agent was surely the very best. He often said to me, 'I love to think of all those people beavering away on my behalf, taking all the decisions and negotiating deals, while I sit up here in Yorkshire and just carry on writing!'

Alf Wight remained loyal to David Higham Associates throughout his career, never forgetting the good work they did for him. David Bolt, the agent who sold the first book to Michael Joseph, left the firm at the beginning of 1971 to establish another agency and, realising the potential of James Herriot, wanted Alf to move with him. Fully aware of how much David Bolt had helped him, this was a difficult decision, but Alf opted to stay with the firm rather than the individual agent. From that time onwards, his agent at David Higham was Jacqueline Korn, who dealt with every James Herriot book and continues to handle his literary affairs to this day. Sadly, Jean LeRoy – the author-cum-agent who had been so instrumental in kick-starting Alf's literary career – died in 1970. She was never to see the phenomenal rise to success of the little-known vet who had sent her his frayed manuscript on that fateful day in 1969.

The serialisation of *If Only They Could Talk* by the *Evening Standard* in the spring of 1970 was a time of high excitement. I remember the thrill my father felt as he read the copies of the newspaper, seeing his work actually in print for the very first time.

He would receive mountains of fan letters during his life but he never forgot the very first one. It was from an elderly man living in the East End of London who had read the first episode in the newspaper. This was the incident in the opening chapter where James Herriot spends hours calving a cow in the middle of the night. After finally completing the job in a state of exhaustion, the farmer asks him whether he would like a drink. To the reply of 'That's very kind of you, Mr Dinsdale, I'd love a drink,' James Herriot receives the curt response, 'Nay, I meant for t' cow!'

I remember my father telling us about that episode at the time it actually happened, and we had all found it very funny. James Herriot's very first fan, however, was not so amused. The letter was barely literate but it exuded pure outrage. The shaky writing was deeply imprinted into the paper: 'If I'd been you, I would've chucked that bucket of water (bloody) over his head!'

If Only They Could Talk was published in April 1970 and 3,000 copies were printed. It sold steadily and, later in the year, another 1,000 came off the press. This was by no means spectacular but it was good for a first book by an unknown author.

Alf could not resist looking in the local bookshops to see whether his book was being prominently displayed. He was disappointed. Very few copies seemed to be on view and, in many cases, it was placed in the children's sections. Brian Sinclair, who was delighted to be portrayed as Tristan, was very supportive. He, often assisted by John Crooks – Alf's first veterinary assistant – went into every bookshop, he could find, switching the book onto the best-seller shelves to help the sales!

This eager support from Brian contrasted sharply with the attitude displayed by Donald, whose response to the release of *If Only They Could Talk* – from the first day of publication – had been one of almost total silence. The two brothers, sharing many qualities through their singular behaviour, were, in other respects, so very different.

Alf looked for references to his book in the review pages of numerous newspapers and magazines but without much success. However, despite the lack of publicity, he was a man still hardly able to believe his good fortune in becoming a published author, and was more than satisfied.

One person who loudly extolled the virtues of the book was his ebullient cousin, Nan Arrowsmith, in Sunderland. Not only was she the most fanatical lover of animals of all Alf Wight's relatives – always possessing at any one time a noisy menagerie of assorted dogs and cats – but she and Tony ran a bookshop in the town and she looked forward eagerly to selling his book. Half of Sunderland must have known that her cousin was now an author.

One day, a young sales representative walked into the shop. 'You may be interested in this new book,' he said, showing her a copy of *If Only They Could Talk*. 'Some old vet has written down his experiences. It's all been done before, but it may be worth stocking a couple of copies or so?'

He could not have anticipated the dramatic response. 'Let me tell *you*, young man!' Nan exploded, blasting cigarette smoke into his face. 'James Herriot is *my* cousin and he is *not* old! He's nobbut a lad! And I'll tell you something else – his books are going to be best-sellers and I personally will sell hundreds. You mark my words, you cheeky young bugger!' The long grating laugh that followed helped to put the startled sales rep at ease.

It is not surprising that many people saw the potential of that first book. It is written in an easy-to-read, conversational style, with vivid characterisation woven into the poignant descriptions of a bygone way of life. Above all, the book conveys a warm feeling to the reader, with an abundance of humour and astute observations into that most fascinating of subjects, human nature.

It is revealing to compare this polished final product with the earlier book that was rejected in 1967. There is no doubt that Alf had made huge strides in the art of writing within the space of only two years.

In Chapter 8 of *If Only They Could Talk*, Siegfried takes James to a farm to perform a post mortem. He forgets his knife and has to borrow a carving knife from the farmer's wife.

This story was included in the original novel, and the following is an extract:

'When he arrived at the house he found that he had forgotten to take his p.m. knife and decided that he would have to borrow a carving knife.'

In the published version, it is told differently:

'We arrived at the farmhouse with a screaming of brakes. Siegfried had left his seat and was rummaging about in the boot before the car had stopped shuddering. "Hell!" he shouted, "no post mortem knife! Never mind, I'll borrow something from the house." He slammed down the lid and bustled over to the door.'

The flat narrative of his earlier effort is replaced with a graphic illustration of the character of his eccentric partner. The stories of Siegfried and Tristan in *If Only They Could Talk* are so masterfully reproduced in print that I enjoyed reading about them even more than hearing them first hand.

During the years at the end of the 1960s, when my father was re-writing his book, I was only dimly aware of his dedication and determination. None of us really expected that he would become a published author and, anyway, being young, carefree and finding my own feet in my new profession, I had other things on my mind. I was pleased that my old man was enjoying his hobby but I showed little interest in the final product. That is, until he showed me the letter from David Bolt.

Realising that he must be a better writer than I had thought, I read the manuscript. I read it purely for enjoyment – the way it was meant to be read – and I enjoyed it primarily because it *was* very funny. The fact that I knew most of the characters within its pages made it all the more fascinating.

I could see my father was pleased that I had read the book and he repeatedly asked me for my opinion on it. Throughout his literary career, he seemed to attach great importance to his family's views on his work and, from that time onwards, I read every one of his manuscripts prior to publication. I provided a fair amount of material for him; he was always on the look-out for fresh stories and a proportion of them, even in the first two books, were based on my own experiences. He had an ear for any little incident, with the storyteller's ability to turn it into an enjoyable tale.

After my father received his letter of acceptance from the publishers, I wanted to tell people about his success but he felt differently. Years before, he had asked us to keep quiet about his writing, and he re-emphasised his wish that I tell no one.

'I don't want anyone to know about this,' he said to me.

'Why not?' I asked. 'It's a great achievement.'

'Well, I wouldn't like some of the characters in the book to recognise themselves,' he replied.

I was surprised. Most of them came over as appealing personalities; also, some were so vividly described that I was sure the real people would recognise themselves anyway.

'Everyone will know that "Atom" Thompson is Phin Calvert in the book,' I said, 'and Miss Warner is unmistakable as Mrs Pumphrey!'

My father winced. 'Not if I keep denying it! These people may not like to be portrayed as they have been. They probably won't read it anyway, but please don't say a word.'

He had set the book in the Dales, whereas nearly all the stories occurred around Thirsk. He also placed everything in the period before the war and gave his date of qualification as 1937 rather than 1939; this was to put anyone off the scent in case they tried to find out who James Herriot really was. 'I want to continue to be known as a vet round here, not as an author!' he said.

This cautious outlook was typical of his character. His primary concern may well have been that he did not hurt the feelings of others, but there was also a certain logic in this secretive approach to his success; some of the more old-fashioned Yorkshire people could be very prickly if they thought that someone was having a chuckle at their expense.

In retrospect, it seems laughable that Alf Wight should have gone to such great lengths to preserve his anonymity, but he did – never losing the instinct to keep secret the true facts behind his stories. For the next twenty years, he repeatedly asserted that his first books contained incidents that had occurred before the Second World War, and that the characters within them were either very old, or even dead. In fact, many of the stories had their origins in comparatively recent events. He stuck stubbornly to his statement, as though hoping that his true identity would remain a secret, and that no one about whom he had been writing would be offended by their portrayal in his books.

An amusing incident occurred in the mid 1970s – long after his cover had been blown. Old Mr Smedley, from the village of Coxwold, berated him one day in the surgery for *failing* to include him in any of his books! Alf Wight's fear of upsetting the Yorkshire folk may well have been groundless.

CHAPTER TWENTY-TWO

Alfred Wight was not the only one to be pleased with the sales of *If Only They Could Talk*. Anthea Joseph was delighted and asked him to consider writing a sequel which, she felt, would add impetus to the popularity of the first book. She soon heard that her new author was on his way already; he had enjoyed writing his first book so much that, by January 1970 – three months before the publication of the first – he had already completed 40,000 words of a new one. With plenty of material at hand and his confidence riding high, he was now fully locked into the 'hobby' that had fascinated him for so long.

The completed manuscript of his second book, called *It Shouldn't Happen to a Vet*, was in the hands of Anthea Joseph in February 1971. The contract – for which he received an advance of £300 – was signed on 22 March 1971, and the book was published in January 1972. Once again, to the delight of my father and his bank manager, the *London Evening Standard* serialised the book prior to publication. This book received far more publicity than the first, and was reviewed in various papers and magazines.

One review in the *Sunday Express* of 23 January 1972, by the then literary editor, Graham Lord, meant a great deal to Alf. Lord's glowing appraisal of the book did wonders for Alf's morale who was convinced that this one review, in a widely-read paper, gave him one of the biggest breaks of his literary career. My father, ever the appreciative man, contacted Graham Lord to express his thanks and was to remain grateful to him to the end of his days.

John Junor, the editor of the *Sunday Express*, liked the book so much that his paper, from 1974 through to the 1980s, was to serialise all the James Herriot books prior to their publication, bringing them to the attention of millions of readers and giving the sales a tremendous boost. John Junor, who was brought up very close to Alf's Yoker area of Glasgow, was a man with whom Alf corresponded for years, always maintaining that the *Sunday Express* editor was a very influential figure in helping him along the path to success.

Another factor that aided the increased sales of the second book was the adoption of a very different dust-jacket. The jacket of *If Only They Could Talk* – showing a young carthorse rearing up while being held by a young boy – had bestowed the aura of a children's novel on it, and was probably the reason for the book being put into the children's department in the bookshops. Michael Joseph, realising their mistake, commissioned a jacket illustration from the popular artist 'Larry' and also asked him to produce a cartoon for each chapter opening, which emphasised the book's humorous content. Not only did 'Larry' go on to illustrate the next four James Herriot books, but he also produced a new dust-jacket cartoon for *If Only They Could Talk* which appeared on the second and subsequent reprints of Alf's first book.

Eight thousand copies of the second book were printed, a very big increase over the first book, showing Michael Joseph's confidence in their author from Yorkshire. James Herriot was not yet a household name but his books were selling well; he was on his way.

It Shouldn't Happen to a Vet is a very similar book to the first one, with the mixture much as before – plenty of humour, a genuine insight into a fast-disappearing way of life and some dashes of pathos thrown in, too. Like its predecessor, it has the ability to move the reader to tears of both joy and sadness. Alf quickly saw the potential for a third, maybe even a fourth book, and decided to introduce another character who could run through the subsequent titles. He brought in a little love interest, and Helen Alderson, who was based upon Joan, enters James Herriot's life for the first time.

The book opens with a chapter on Mr Handshaw. James Herriot visits a recumbent cow that he considers, after treating her for several days, will never walk again. He advises humane slaughter. The farmer does not take his advice, but keeps her for several weeks, after which the cow suddenly jumps to her feet. This was a great triumph for Mr Handshaw who had 'put one over' on the professional man.

The real Mr Handshaw, a man by the name of Billy Goodyear, is still alive and, only recently, one of the practice's young assistants paid a visit to his farm.

'He's an interesting old fellow!' the assistant said to me on his return. 'He told me a story about your father.'

'Oh yes?' I replied. I could guess what was coming.

'He said that your dad treated a cow years ago and said "it would never get up n' more". He kept it alive, against your dad's advice, and it got up!'

Billy Goodyear never let my father forget about the cow that would 'never get up n'more' and I sometimes wonder what Alf Wight would have thought, had he known that the farmer would still be basking in that moment of glory, years after his death.

It Shouldn't Happen to a Vet illustrates another aspect of James Herriot's writing – that of his altering the characters by changing their sex, or making one composite personality out of several others.

In chapter 7 of the book, a character called Mr Worley appears. He is a man who is completely devoted to pigs. His whole life revolves round them, and there is nothing he likes better than sitting by the fire, 'talking pigs'.

The 'real' Mr Worley was based upon a lady called Mrs Bush who ran a country inn at Byland Abbey near Thirsk. She kept Saddleback pigs in the yard behind the inn and she loved every one of them. She liked my father as she was convinced that he, too, loved her pigs. I am not quite so sure about that. Not only were Mrs Bush's black and white sows pretty formidable creatures, especially at farrowing time, but she had the awkward habit of calling us out in the early hours of the morning to attend to them. In her eyes, however, he was a real 'pig vet'.

One evening, Alf had an unnerving experience while having a quiet drink at the inn. Mrs Bush approached him and said, 'Ooh, Mr Wight, I did enjoy reading your book. And I liked the chapter about that man and his pigs!'

A thin film of sweat appeared on Alf's brow. Surely she had not recognised herself? 'I'm glad you liked it, Mrs Bush,' he replied.

'I know exactly how he felt!' she continued.

'Do you really?'

'Aye. D'you know, Mr Wight . . . it could've been me!'

The second book ends with a wonderful story – one whose origins I remember very well – that illustrates, perfectly, the unique character of Donald Sinclair. Siegfried, while escorting some upper-class, influential people to the races, meets an old friend and becomes inebriated after which, following the loss of his car keys, he has to borrow his friend's filthy old vehicle to transport his outraged guests away from the race-course. The final touch of farce is provided, as usual, by Siegfried who is watched in disbelief by the unsmiling occupants as he attempts to clean the car window with a dead hen!

*

In the following five years up to 1977, Alf produced four more books, an impressive feat for a man working full time as a veterinary surgeon. As in those long years when he was writing the short stories and novels, he worked in the living-room, right in front of the television. By now he found it no hardship to settle down at the end of a working day, with the stories flowing effortlessly from his typewriter. Having watched him put in a full day's work in the practice, I used to stare in amazement at the contented figure tapping away. He had one great advantage; he genuinely loved writing, unfailingly regarding it as a hobby rather than a profession.

From 1973 onwards, everything that he published received enthusiastic reviews before climbing rapidly to the top of the best-seller lists. His third book, *Let Sleeping Vets Lie*, a title suggested by Joan, was published in April 1973. This book, like the previous two, was serialised by the *Evening Standard*, and it hit the ground running – immediately becoming a best-seller. Michael Joseph printed 15,000 copies which disappeared off the bookshelves with lightning speed. The reader is introduced to more characters, including Ewan Ross, the neighbouring vet for whom James Herriot T.B. tested endless cows, and Carmody, the student. There are endless tales of the Yorkshire farmers with their funny ways, and the gentle love story between James and Helen winds through the book, finally resulting in their marriage and honeymoon in the Yorkshire Dales.

The opening chapter is about a formidable dog belonging to Joe Mulligan, a deaf old Irishman. In real life, he was a man called Mr Thompson, and the dog was one that no vet in his right mind would dream of approaching. This enormous animal – known simply as 'Thompson's dog' – sparked waves of high tension along the corridors of the surgery whenever he walked through the door.

One day, Alf was walking his little Jack Russell terrier, Hector, across the fields near Thirsk, when he beheld the misleadingly benevolent face of 'Thompson's dog' shambling along beside the old man. To his horror, Hector began to gambol around the huge animal. The big, shaggy creature displayed little more than mild interest towards the small black and white form that was swarming all over him, but my father was still concerned. Old Mr Thompson could see the consternation on Alf's face. 'Don't worry, Mr Wight,' he shouted, ''e only eats Alsatians!'

On 18 April 1973, at Michael Joseph's new offices in Bedford Square, the official publication of *Let Sleeping Vets Lie* was celebrated. So pleased was the publishing house of Michael Joseph with their increasingly popular author that, besides throwing the special publication party for him, they had – two months previously – already contracted him to write three more books, for which they paid a total advance of £5,250. These were still early days and the figure was not a generous one, but to Alf Wight, with his ever accelerating sales over the next few years, this would turn out to be of little significance.

One of the benefits of having a now-famous father was the frequent attendance at many excellent parties, together with the meeting of hordes of interesting people. New friendships were forged at these functions, commonly enhanced by the presence of liberal quantities of alcohol. This first publication party was right up to expectations. Many of the family's friends were willing participants. Denton Pette (later to be depicted as Granville Bennett), Brian Sinclair (Tristan, of course) and their wives were there, (Donald Sinclair remained at home to manage the practice), as was Eddie Straiton, as well as my future wife Gillian, who had been invited as a close friend of Rosie's. Gill, unfortunately, having under-estimated the alcoholic content of the drinks that seemed to be poured into her glass in never-ending quantities, spent the latter part of the evening in a moribund state in the ladies' cloakroom.

Full of remorse the following day, she wrote an abject letter of apology to the author. His reply is one that she has kept as a treasured memento:

My dear girl, I hasten to assure you that your feelings of remorse are entirely unnecessary and, in fact, there is something ludicrous in apologising to me, the veteran of a thousand untimely disappearances and as many black and hopeless dawns. I see you describe yourself as a 'sordid little heap in the Ladies'. Well that's a good description of me but for 'Ladies' read 'Gents' or 'Friend's back room' or 'Back seat of car' or, in one case, 'Corner of tennis court'.

Let me further assure you that your 'awful behaviour' was probably not even noticed by a roomful of people who had punished the champers for a couple of hours, then waded into the vino for a similar period. It remains rather a blur to me.

I dimly remember the two Michael Joseph men making rather incoherent speeches of thanks to which, they tell me, I made a slurring twelve-word reply. I honestly don't remember and that goes for a very drunken Tristan and most of the others.

But I do remember meeting you right at the start and that was lovely! Much love, James Herriot

Gill received another souvenir of that memorable evening. 'Larry', the cartoonist whose brilliant illustrations brightened each chapter of the books, was also a guest at the party. On hearing that Gill was a doctor, he drew her a cartoon depicting a needle on the end of a massive syringe being thrust into an equally imposing backside. The drawing was completed in a matter of seconds, a feat watched with amazement by Alf; to him, painting or drawing – like mathematics – were pursuits that would forever remain shrouded in mystery.

I have cause to remember that evening as it was then that I heard, for the first time, Brian Sinclair giving a strident rendition of his 'maniac laugh', that my father had described to us so often. After the party was over and we were beating our uncertain way back to our hotel, he suddenly let loose. As I listened to the London streets echoing to the sinister, primeval cries, I felt exceedingly grateful that the man causing them was none other than old 'Uncle Brian' himself. At heart, he had changed little since those wild days in Thirsk so many years ago.

The fourth book, *Vet in Harness*, was published in 1974 and was another immediate success, this time with an initial printing of 20,000 copies. The reader is introduced to the larger-than-life Granville Bennett while, in chapter 25, a village cricket match on a hopelessly sloping and uneven pitch is described. Alf, always a great cricket fan, was very proud to receive a letter from Sir Leonard Hutton, whom he rated as one of the all-time great Yorkshire and England batsmen. He had obviously enjoyed the chapter. Dated 26 February 1976, it read:

I have just read your new book. May I congratulate you on the cricket match; it reminded me so much of one or two of my earliest matches in Yorkshire.

Thank you so much for making two dark February evenings so enjoyable. I know the people so well whom you have spent your life amongst. We have them in cricket, too.

This was where Alf scored. His books were not just a collection of stories about animals and vets. His professional experiences were a backcloth to a description of so many different walks of life; there was something in them to interest everyone.

As he kept generating more books in the early 1970s, Alf's confidence grew. He had attempted the art of introducing flashbacks in the novel that was rejected in 1967, but he returned to this technique for his next two books, *Vets Might Fly* which was published in 1976, and *Vet in a Spin* which appeared on the booksellers' shelves in 1977. So successful was he now, that 60,000 copies of *Vets Might Fly* were printed by Michael Joseph and they flew off the shelves within a very short time.

These two books hark back to his time in the Royal Air Force and he returned to those earlier days with much greater skill in the use of flashbacks than in his previous attempts. By this time, he was a household name, with his books entering the best-seller lists within a couple of weeks of publication. As each new book was published, it acted as a catalyst for the sales of the preceding titles and, by the mid 1970s, he had sold hundreds of thousands of copies in hardback together with millions in paperback.

Paperback books, of course, sell more copies than the more expensive hardback editions. In the 1970s, Michael Joseph – along with many other publishers at the time – did not have a regular paperback partner with whom they shared profits. They would sell paperback rights to any number of paperback houses, Penguin Books, Pan Books and Corgi being some of the leading names.

With the shelf-life of a commercial hardback book rarely being more than six months nowadays, the paperback edition usually follows a year after the hardback is published – often coinciding, if the author is prolific, with the next hardback. In the 1970s, however, the hardbacks usually continued in circulation for much longer and, with a higher income from the hardback rather than a part-share of a lower-priced book, the gap between hardback and paperback publication was often two years.

Michael Joseph, therefore, were in no rush to sign a contract for *If Only They Could Talk* with a paperback publisher and, in the event, they sold the first two books at the same time to Pan Books. The contract between Michael Joseph and Pan was signed in June 1972, six months after the publication of *It Shouldn't Happen to a Vet*; the serialisation of the two books and the favourable reviews and media interest would not have gone unnoticed by Pan. The leading player in negotiating this contract was none other than Clarence Paget who, in 1969, had encouraged Anthea Joseph to take a chance with the 'unknown vet from Yorkshire'.

The first two books were published in tandem by Pan in November 1972, with 60,000 copies of each being printed. It would prove to be a wise move by Pan. The sales accelerated throughout the following years as the successive books were published in paperback until, by early 1979, Alf found himself the recipient of no less than six 'Golden Pan' awards. Each of his first six books sold more than one million copies in paperback – an achievement equalled only, at that time, by Ian Fleming, the author of the hugely successful James Bond books.

Alfred Wight, although a man who had carved out his life with his own hands, was quick to acknowledge any help he had received in attaining this heady success. The dedications in his earlier books reflect his gratitude.

In the first book, the dedication is to Eddie Straiton. Alf never forgot that it was he who had introduced him to the former Collins executive, John Morrison, who in turn had passed his manuscript on to that publishing house. It was, in effect, the advice of the Collins' reader, Juliana Wadham – to transform his original novel into a semi-autobiographical account of his life – that was a major turning point in his fortunes. Juliana Wadham was responsible for the addition of that magic ingredient to James Herriot's work; the fact that his memorable stories were based upon real-life incidents.

The dedication in the second book – to the Sinclair brothers – reflects the appreciation of his good fortune in having spent much of his life in the company of those colourful characters who had provided him with incomparable material for his stories.

In the third book, he acknowledges his wife. In her own way, Joan had contributed more than anyone in helping him on the road to success – not only by gently goading him into writing his first book and then encouraging him to persevere with getting it published, but by providing a happy and stable family environment. One of his favourite sayings was that he wrote his books, not alone, but 'in the bosom of my family'. Joan, through her enduring support of her husband, was mainly responsible for his family life being a contented and happy one.

The dedication in the fourth book, to his mother in Glasgow, is testimony to his undying gratitude to the woman who, during those difficult years of the depression in Yoker so many years before, displayed astonishing determination that her son would be a success in the world. She was, of course, extremely proud of her son's achievements, so much so that she began to accost people in the street with the words, 'Now, you know who I am, don't you? I am James Herriot's mother!' On her correspondence, too, she would no longer sign her name as Hannah Wight – just 'James Herriot's mother'.

The dedications in the fifth and sixth books (the former to his beloved dogs, Hector and Dan, the latter to Rosie, Gill and me) were in appreciation of some of those with whom he always maintained he spent many of the happiest times of his life.

By the mid 1970s, James Herriot's books had become established best-sellers in Great Britain, but it was not only his astonishing success in his own country that bemused him. Long before this, his reputation had spread beyond its shores. With his prodigious book sales abroad having resulted in their being translated into most of the world's major languages, he had become known as the 'World's Most Famous Vet', but it was his massive popularity in one country that had been largely responsible for rocketing him to international fame. Nowhere was he held in higher esteem than in the United States of America.

CHAPTER TWENTY-THREE

One Wednesday afternoon, some time in the late 1970s, I was aware of a great deal of noise in the waiting-room of 23 Kirkgate. The small animal side of the practice was beginning to expand to such an extent that it now accounted for a high proportion of our income, and it was good news that the waiting-room was so full.

'It looks as though we're going to have a good surgery today, Dad,' I said. 'That room is heaving!'

My father put his head round the door and looked inside. He strode back into the office with an apologetic smile. 'Don't get too excited, boys,' he said. 'I've just counted two hamsters, one Yorkshire Terrier and forty-five Americans!'

This invasion by tourists of our modest little premises was becoming commonplace. The name of James Herriot had become so famous that thousands from all over the world flocked to Thirsk to see his veterinary surgery. As well as from Great Britain, they travelled from Europe, Canada, Australia and even Japan – but by far the greatest number came from the United States. It seemed that he had become an icon on the other side of the Atlantic.

Alf Wight had always liked the American people. Long before he became famous, he had been attracted to their open friendliness and love for life.

'The Americans like us,' he often used to say. 'Lots of other nations don't, but they do. I like people who like me!' As his stratospheric sales in the United States continued, his affection for the people of that country deepened.

Alf never forgot the debt he owed the Americans, always endeavouring to see every one that had paid him the compliment of travelling so far to see him. As these intrusions into their working day could be a nuisance to the other veterinary surgeons in the practice, he set aside two afternoons a week to talk to the visitors and sign their books. The queues down Kirkgate on Wednesday and Friday afternoons were enormous, especially during the summer months.

These book-signing sessions went on for many years and we all became used to the throngs of tourists pouring into the waiting-room. I often watched, with amazement, the excitement on the faces of these people as they shook hands with my father. He meant more to them than just an author whose work they admired; he was someone they felt they knew personally through his warm and compassionately written stories.

Alf, who always considered himself to be a very ordinary man, could never really understand this adulation. He said to me on many an occasion, 'Here's me, an ordinary "run of the mill" vet and all these people are flocking to see me as though I was the new Messiah!' Some who travelled to worship at the 'shrine' of 23 Kirkgate were fellow veterinarians with a string of degrees to their names; Alf used to say that he felt a fraud to be treated with such respect. Despite his bemusement, he was, indeed, someone special, with many of those fortunate enough to meet him regarding the occasion as one of the highlights of their entire lives.

I gained a great respect for many of the fans who came to see him. A large number, understanding that ours was a working business, did not intrude; they would simply approach the building and photograph it. Others who came inside displayed astonishing generosity. After signing their books, my father would invite them to give a donation to a local charity that he supported; this was a stray dog sanctuary – the Jerry Green Foundation Trust – that had a branch near Thirsk. On several occasions a £50-note was found when the little red box was emptied. It was not only James Herriot himself who profited from his incredible success.

In an address to the Harrogate Medical Society in 1974, Alf tried to explain the American people's fascination for his work: 'I think that the American people like my stories because they are reaching out for the simple things which they, in their materialistic and urbanised society, have lost: old, unspoiled Yorkshire and a way of life so different from their own.'

Through his warmth, understanding and compassion for both his patients and fellow men, James Herriot, in effect, humanised his profession, and the many fans who travelled the thousands of miles to see him found that the real man behind the caring image was every inch the gentleman they imagined him to be.

The tidal wave of admiration from the other side of the Atlantic was one that could, so easily, have never happened. As with his publishing achievements in Great Britain, it was through a small twist of fate that he got his first foothold in the United States, and one man, more than any other, was responsible for establishing James Herriot's enduring grip on the American public's imagination. His name was Tom McCormack.

McCormack was the chief executive of the New York publishing house, St Martin's Press. He flew to London in the summer of 1970 on a buying trip, hoping to acquire some books that would have good potential sales in the United States. He was desperate for something spectacular since St Martin's was struggling to keep afloat. Unless a best-selling author could be found to turn around the fortunes of St Martin's Press, there was a real possibility that the company would have to close down, with the loss of many jobs.

While in London, he arranged a meeting with David Bolt at David Higham Associates, one of many such meetings he had during his visit. An agent would always try to interest visiting American publishers in books in which they held American rights, where they had a responsibility to the author to try to place the book in America. David Bolt would have discussed a number of the company's clients with Tom McCormack and when he handed him a copy of *If Only They Could Talk*, it would not have been with any great hope since the book was very British and an unlikely one for the American public.

If Only They Could Talk had not been published long and its sales had not caused any ripples in the pool of London publishing. Tom McCormack looked at the book distastefully: not only was it small (Americans like to read big books, preferably about Americans, and at that time were not very interested in short British books), he did not like the jacket which he thought gave it the impression of being a children's book. He liked the title even less, and when he learned that it was written by some unknown vet from Yorkshire, his interest evaporated. Common courtesy, however, dictated that he did not throw the book back at David Bolt so he packed the unexciting little volume into his case and took it back home. Three years earlier, James Herriot's work had lain around in London, completely forgotten, and the same fate was to befall it in New York. It lay, unopened, in the chief executive's house for a full three months.

He may never have read the book but his wife, Sandra, picked it up one evening and began to read it. It was not long before she voiced her opinion. Turning to her husband, she said, 'You gotta read this – and if you don't publish it, you booby, I'll kill you!'

In the face of such compelling words, he had little choice but to read it himself. With every passing chapter, his excitement grew as he began to realise that he was enjoying the work of a master story-teller; by the time he had finished reading the book, the germ of an idea had become established in his mind. Could this be the author he had been looking for?

As the weeks went by, the idea grew into a firm resolve that the rest of the United States was going to read the book, too. In the years to come, he would have cause to bless the forceful advice from his wife on that memorable evening in New York.

My family has always admired Tom McCormack for his unwavering determination in getting that first book published. He was so convinced that he had a potential best-seller, he was prepared to stake his whole career on its success. He saw this man, James Herriot, as the possible saviour of his ailing firm – but he had some enormous obstacles to overcome.

The first was that the book was too short; if he were to win over the American public, he needed a book twice the length. Early in 1971, however, his prayers were answered. He contacted Claire Smith of the Harold Ober agency in New York – the American associate of the David Higham agency in London; she too had been trying to interest American publishers in *If Only They Could Talk*, but with little success. When Tom McCormack approached Claire Smith, she told him that she had heard from London that the vet had completed another book. This was exactly the news that Tom had been waiting for. As soon as he could, he obtained a copy of the book from the David Higham agency in London. After enjoying it as much as he had the first, he saw that the two books could be combined into one volume.

Tom still had a problem; he wanted the book to have a more definite ending – something that the second book, like the first, did not have. Through David Higham Associates, he contacted Alf, very tentatively asking if he could write a finale to the book – one where James Herriot marries Helen, in order to give the story a satisfying conclusion. He wondered what the strange vet in distant Yorkshire would make of such a request, but he was not to be disappointed. Alf, intensely excited at the prospect of his books being published in America, was only too happy to oblige and, in Tom McCormack's words, 'He wrote three chapters, gave us a wedding, and an ending that chimes as gloriously as *The Sound of Music*.'

Rosie proposed a title for this new book, *ILL Creatures Great and Small* while, coincidentally, someone at St Martin's Press had come up with the title *ALL Creatures Great and Small*. Alf was keen to use Rosie's title, but Tom preferred to adopt the more traditional title. There was no argument and Tom got his way; these were exciting days and, bemused as he was by the enthusiastic approach of his new-found publisher in America, Alf was willing to cooperate in every way that he could. In later years, when he had become an established best-selling author, he had the confidence to stand his ground when Tom wanted to alter parts of his stories, but in those early days, he toed the line.

On 17 September 1971, as Alfred Wight signed the contract with St Martin's Press for *All Creatures Great and Small*, he could hardly believe his good fortune; but no one could have anticipated just how momentous that signature would turn out to be.

1972 was a hectic year for Tom McCormack, during which he had to overcome another huge hurdle – convincing everyone at St Martin's Press that the memoirs of the first two years in the professional life of an obscure vet in faraway Yorkshire could possibly become a best-seller. Having finally persuaded his colleagues, he next had to convince the booksellers to support it. He began a 'campaign of enticement, intimidation and force-feeding'.

He threw everything into the marketing of the book. Six thousand copies of the first chapter were printed and given away to selected librarians, bookstores and reviewers. A money-back guarantee was offered to anyone who was not delighted with the book, little ivory animals were sent to major bookstores as a gimmick to draw their attention to the book, while Tom wrote personally to all the major reviewers. In his letters he described the reading of the book as a 'rich and joyful experience', while saying of James Herriot and his work, 'he conveys a love of life that seems thoroughly justified. No book I've worked on in fifteen years of publishing has given me more pleasure.'

Despite this energetic marketing campaign, advance sales were disappointing, with only 8,500 copies of the book in the shops two weeks before publication. Tom, however, remained convinced that if only a leading reviewer would read it, like it and give it a good review, then the book would take off. The vast American public, he felt sure, needed only a taste of *All Creatures Great and Small* before they would want more; all he asked was that someone would give it to them.

This was a brave venture from a man who had put his whole future on the line. The failure of this book – on which he had pinned so many hopes – could have serious consequences for both himself and his company. As publication day approached, Tom McCormack crossed his fingers and waited.

All Creatures Great and Small was published in November 1972 to a profound silence from the major reviewers. Tom was bitterly disappointed. Was there anyone else in the United States of America, he wondered, who shared his appreciation of the writing of this man, James Herriot? Was he the only one in the vast publishing industry who saw the author's potential? Had he made a massive mistake in risking his future on the work of the unknown Yorkshire veterinarian? He waited, desperately, for a tiny glimmer of hope.

It was not long before his questions were answered. On 12 November, while reading the *Chicago Tribune*'s 'Sunday Book World', he felt a surge of excitement. On the front page of this enormously influential newspaper was a review of James Herriot's book. The review, by a man called Alfred Ames, radiated superlatives.

'If there is any justice, this book will become a classic of its kind. . . . With seemingly effortless art, this man tells his stories with perfect timing. Many more famous authors could work for a lifetime and not achieve more flawless literary control.'

This was the break Tom McCormack had been waiting for. This one review set in motion a host of others. Anatole Broyard wrote in the *New York Times* on 14 December: 'James Herriot, a British veterinary surgeon, is one of those rare men who know how to appreciate the ordinary . . . He's a veterinarian, that's what he is, and when his right arm is free, he's a helluva writer as well.'

By January 1973, the reviews were pouring out. The *Houston Chronicle* headed its review: 'Superlatives aren't enough. This book is absolutely super, a rarity, magnificently written, insightful, unforgettable. If you have ever loved a friend, human or otherwise, this is the book for you.'

These reviews provided the spark to ignite a sales inferno that swept across the United States of America. The book was on *Time* magazine's best-seller list by early January 1973, and that of the *New York Times* later that month. James Herriot's fame soon spread from coast to coast and, within one year, his book had been selected by book clubs, serialised in magazines and published as a condensed book by Reader's Digest. Within a few months of publication, the paperback rights were bought by Bantam Books, and after two hundred thousand were sold in hardback, a further million followed in paperback – 1973 was a truly phenomenal year, for both James Herriot and Tom McCormack.

The name of James Herriot had been propelled into millions of households within weeks of publication. Tom McCormack had gambled and he had won. He had spent over $50,000 in promoting the book but, as he was to acknowledge later, 'If it weren't for a man named Alfred Ames, it all might have turned out different.'

Despite the staggering success of his new author, Tom McCormack did not rest on his laurels. Sales of *All Creatures Great and Small* had hit the market like a typhoon – one he had no intention of allowing to abate. What better way was there, he thought, of ensuring this than by inviting James Herriot himself over to the States on a promotional tour?

Alf, although excited by all the publicity he was receiving, felt that his primary allegiance was to the practice and, with the busy time of lambing fast approaching, his initial reaction was to refuse the invitation. There were only four vets in the practice at that time, but we assured him that it was too good an opportunity to miss, so in late February 1973, he visited America for the first time.

The trip only lasted a week but it pulsated with action from beginning to end. There were long successions of television appearances and book signings, interspersed with tours around the sights of New York, with visits to exotic restaurants and cocktail parties. To a man used to the steady life among the even steadier Yorkshire people, it was like a dream.

When he returned home, my mother and I asked how it had all been. He replied, 'Utterly fantastic – but I'm knackered!' The high life in America had been a truly wonderful experience but he was pleased to be back in Yorkshire. Much as he had enjoyed his time in the United States, he assured us that he would never do another promotional tour.

It was not to be. Throughout the summer of 1973, sales of the paperback were so massive that he finally agreed to do a second tour in the autumn of that year, this time organised by Bantam Books. The tour lasted three weeks and was even more exhausting than the first. Joan accompanied him on this second trip but they had little time to themselves. They flew to several big cities and the tour was, again, a long procession of book signings and television appearances. It seemed to Alf that every room in the United States had a television – every one of which appeared to be switched on permanently – and his face must have been seen in millions of homes, morning after morning.

During phone-in sessions, he was asked questions about skunks and alligators (animals rarely seen in the surgery of Skeldale House), he argued with people about the ethics of religious slaughter (Alf always hated to discuss emotive subjects that could result in explosive argument) while, all the time, there was the pressure of an ever-tightening schedule that had to be adhered to.

He returned from this second trip totally drained. After a few days recovering from the ordeal, he put down his memories of the tour.

. . . To a book signing session in New York where a queue of fans brought not only their books but their pets, too. They deposited shaggy creatures on the table with requests like, 'You gotta sign this to Fluffy, Dr Herriot.' Some of the names were unusual. Naming a pair of hamsters Hermann and Lucius struck me as a little bizarre, but the feeling of wonder wore off as I autographed books to cats called Hamburger, Sweet Feets, Pancake, Noo-catt Noo-catt, Popcorn and there was a canary in the queue, William Byrd. The dear Americans! Warm-hearted, generous and even more scatty over their animals than we are.

I had only one respite in the entire three weeks, one blessed Sunday when I awoke to find no appointments fixed. It was in San Francisco and, outside my bedroom window, the Californian sun poured down on the Golden Gate bridge spanning the blue waters of the bay to the mountains beyond. I knew I should be out there tasting the delights of this most beautiful of cities but I lay motionless hour after hour staring glassily at the ceiling. And yet I have survived. The floors have stopped moving, my cheeks have stopped twitching and my stomach has almost agreed to make peace and let bygones be bygones. Still, the parting thought remains. I love America and its people but I'm not going back, just yet . . .

It took Alf several weeks to recover. He returned with bronchitis, cystitis and severe phlebitis in both his legs and, for a while, he took on the appearance of an old man. This, he vowed, had been his last promotional tour, and it was. Over the next five years, his subsequent books were combined into two further volumes for the American market, both storming the best-seller lists and remaining at the top for weeks. His sales did not need the boost of any more personal appearances.

Let Sleeping Vets Lie and *Vet in Harness* were combined into one volume, *All Things Bright and Beautiful* which was published in September 1974. *Vet in a Spin* and *Vets Might Fly* were amalgamated into *All Things Wise and Wonderful* and this hit the market in September 1977. Both came out to glowing reviews followed by tremendous sales.

Alf never showed any inclination to return to the United States. He loved to meet the American people – and his affection for them never wavered – but he was content to see them on his own ground. Over the years, he must have shaken hands with many thousands of tourists as they flooded into his part of Yorkshire, but he never allowed his massive popularity to overwhelm him. As far as he was concerned, his celebrity status made no difference to his attitude towards the many friends and acquaintances he had made over his years in Thirsk. This aspect of his character, one that was greatly appreciated by the local people, would be reflected in their constant protection of his privacy in the face of so many visitors. He was still regarded in the local community as Alf Wight, not James Herriot – something he had wanted since those very first days along the road to fame.

It was fortuitous that, as well as this level-headedness, his sense of humour did not desert him since he was occasionally reminded that his writing did not please everyone. In 1977, he wrote in the magazine *Pedigree Digest*:

The letters, like my visitors, are mainly complimentary. I read them with my morning tea and it is a good start to the day to learn that I have given pleasure to many people in many ways. The letters which touch me most deeply are from people who are ill or who have suffered bereavements and who tell me that I have made them laugh and helped them to face life.

But nothing is perfect and even the letters have their other side. It makes me choke over my tea when I am suddenly accused of an 'obsession with drink and profanity' or out of the blue I am told that my books 'reek of male chauvinism'. The Americans in particular castigate me for 'taking the Lord's name in vain' based on what I had thought to be an occasional innocent 'My God' in my writings.

One or two visitors expressed disappointment upon meeting him. On the covers of the American editions, James Herriot was depicted as a handsome young hulk but Alf, of course, was around sixty when the hordes of tourists began to invade Thirsk. Some of them, expecting to see a younger man, received a surprise. He wrote about one such incident in the magazine *Pedigree Digest* in 1977:

Many readers of my books come along to the surgery expecting to see a dashing young vet of twenty-five. When they are confronted by a grizzled sixty-year-old they often find it difficult to disguise their dismay.

Most of them are diplomatic about this but one lady was disconcertingly forthright. 'You know', she said, 'it was so funny when I introduced my daughter to you this afternoon. She thought she was going to meet a young man and she got a dreadful shock when she saw you!' Fortunately, this information was imparted to me in a pub and I was able to reach for a quick restorative.

He was finding that fame can bring its own problems but he accepted this quite calmly. I remember his handing me a strange letter from a displeased reader. After I had finished reading it, he gave me a resigned smile with the words, 'You can't win 'em all, boy!'

Such sharp little wounds to his ego, however, were few and far between as his popularity continued to accelerate throughout the 1970s but, despite this, Alf continued to maintain as low a profile as possible, politely but firmly declining all the many invitations to revisit the United States. Ironically, it was his friends and family who gleaned far more enjoyment and satisfaction from holidays there.

In the late 1970s, Brian Sinclair – who was now famous as Tristan – toured America on several occasions, speaking about his friend James Herriot. He received wonderful hospitality from his hosts, many of whom were veterinarians, like himself. Brian used to meet Alf regularly in those days, regaling him with stories about his American experiences, and Alf would rarely return from these meetings without another humorous anecdote.

One of his favourite memories was that of Brian recounting a social occasion at which there was a Scotsman dressed in full Highland regalia. He was wearing a magnificent kilt, hanging in front of which was a highly-coloured, hairy sporran. This splendid human being was approached by a pleasantly inebriated woman. She had heard of the mysteries that lurked beneath a Scotsman's kilt and was fascinated by the dangling sporran. She pointed at it unsteadily and, in a slurred

45. James Herriot author meets the other James Herriot who lent him his name

46. After a hard day's work as a vet, Alf would write his books on a portable typewriter in front of the television in the evening

47. The in's and out's of a vet's life . . .

48. Arthur Dand, farmer and
fellow author, with Alf

49. The fury of the chase: pigs are almost impossible to catch in the open

50. Dick Francis and Donald Sinden with Alf at the Authors of the Year party

51. Anthea Joseph, Alf's publisher, and Lady Kaberry at a *Yorkshire Post* literary lunch

52. Signing books for farmer Austin Bell of Wethercote in his front room

53. The queue in W. H. Smith, Harrogate, 1977

54. How many animals need attention tonight, or is it *all* books?

55. The queue waits patiently for the doors of 23 Kirkgate to open

56. The ultimate honour: at Buckingham Palace after receiving the OBE in 1979

57. Simon Ward and Lisa Harrow played James and Helen in the first film. This shows them after their considerably more splendid wedding than the real couple (*right*) had thirty-two years previously

58. In the second film, John Alderton played James Herriot, again opposite Lisa Harrow. Colin Blakely (*right*) played Siegfried

59. Partners in more senses than one: the television actors stand behind their true-life counterparts. Christopher Timothy and James Herriot/Alf Wight; Robert Hardy and Siegfried Farnon/Donald Sinclair, and Peter Davison and Tristan Farnon/Brian Sinclair

60. Alf with Christopher Timothy in the garden of 23 Kirkgate

61. Christopher Timothy with the clapperboard during the filming of an episode of 'All Creatures Great and Small'

62. With granddaughters Zoe and Katrina

63. With Sunderland F. C. fans on
King's Cross Station in London

64. After the memorial service at York Minster: the author, Chris Timothy,
Joan, Robert Hardy and grand-daughter Emma Page

voice, said, 'Now tell me, truthfully, what exactly *do* you carry in your scrotum?!'

It was not only Brian, but many other friends, who benefited from the high regard in which Alf was held in America. On trips over there, whenever they mentioned that they were from Yorkshire, the name of James Herriot almost invariably arose. It was one that bonded many friendships across the Atlantic.

Tom McCormack and Alfred Ames – two men who played vital parts in helping Alf to his success – were held in very high esteem by the family. Tom and his wife Sandra met Alf and Joan several times over the years during their frequent visits to Great Britain, while the Alfreds – Ames and Wight – and their wives were to meet in Yorkshire in August 1988. That vital and influential review in the *Chicago Tribune* so many years before remained fresh in the minds of both men.

Alf Wight was a man who always appreciated those who had helped him and, in return, Tom McCormack never forgot the Yorkshire vet whose writing helped put his firm back on a safe footing. In October 1995, eight months after Alf's death, he and Sandra made the special journey from America to pay their respects at the memorial service in York Minster. It was to be his final gesture towards the author to whom he said, all those years ago in 1973, 'Beyond the money, you do bring Sandra and me a personal pride unmatched by anyone else we publish. You are exactly the kind of man one comes into publishing for.'

Despite fans from all over the world thronging the waiting-room at 23 Kirkgate, Alf never allowed this world-wide adulation to unseat his sense of priorities. He had been twice to America where he had been treated like a hero. He was an international celebrity, with his financial worries now behind him, but he was still exactly the same man that I had always known. Not only did he speak very little about his achievements, but his attitude to his family, friends and local people remained completely unchanged.

Around 1977, I remember approaching him for some advice about a problem in the practice. I apologised and said, 'I shouldn't really be bothering you with this, Dad. You are a best-selling author now. You shouldn't have to worry about the practice any more.'

He replied swiftly, 'I don't care how many million books I have sold, the welfare of this practice will always be more important to me!'

The explosion of publicity surrounding his literary success was beyond anything that any of us could have imagined but, during those exciting years of the 1970s, he was still, first and foremost, a family man and a veterinary surgeon.

CHAPTER TWENTY-FOUR

A period of ten years had seen a dramatic upturn in the fortunes of Alfred Wight. The 1970s opened with the publication of his first book, followed by undreamed-of success and subsequent financial security. The beginning of the previous decade had started with the sudden death of his father, succeeded by a period of nervous exhaustion and escalating worry. There is little wonder he frequently referred to that period of his life as the 'horrible sixties'.

I asked him one day how he thought his life would have turned out had he not been so successful as an author.

'I would have carried on working full time,' he replied. 'I had a modest pension on the go, lots of little insurance policies and would probably have sold the house to buy a bungalow somewhere in Thirsk. I would have floated away into an obscure retirement, probably every bit as happy as the one I am enjoying now!'

These were not empty words. My father, never one to regard money as a means to an end, rarely exhibited the lifestyle of a rich man. His high earnings, however, did allow him some luxuries that he had previously been unable to afford. In April 1977, he bought Mirebeck, a bungalow situated under the Hambleton Hills that was to be his home until his final days. He was able to buy rather more expensive cars, he and Joan went on holiday abroad, and he did not need to think twice about taking his friends out for dinner; apart from these comparatively modest indulgences, his way of life remained largely unchanged.

It would be an exaggeration, however, to say that he was disinterested in his new financial status. He gained great satisfaction out of helping others and, especially in the final few years of his life, gave away large sums of money to various charities and to several of his friends. Rosie and I, especially, had great cause to be grateful for his generosity in assisting us with such vital outgoings as buying houses and the funding of our children's education. A more helpful and thoughtful father would be hard to imagine.

As well as satisfaction, he derived considerable amusement out of his improved financial position, not least upon observing the deference that was accorded him in some circles. Whenever he walked into his bank, the attitude of the manager and staff towards him was in sharp contrast to the reception he used to receive in his younger days. On one occasion back in 1950, after Joan had lost her engagement ring, he bought her a replacement which did little to lessen his overdraft at the bank. Mr Smallwood, the manager of the Midland Bank in Thirsk – and someone who regarded Alf Wight, with his never diminishing overdraft, as something of a liability – was not amused. He summoned Alf to his office.

'This just will not do, Mr Wight!' he said. 'It will not do! A man in your position cannot squander money on luxuries. I don't want you ever to repeat such a reckless action without consulting me beforehand.'

After his literary success, Alf had many a smile while recalling this incident. Gone were those days of slinking into the dreaded inner sanctum of the bank manager's office to cower beneath the stern reprimands from the man in charge of his life.

Although he tried hard, throughout his celebrity years, to maintain his comparatively modest way of life, it was not possible to stay out of the limelight completely. His position as one of the most popular authors in the country required his playing a full part in supporting the momentum of the James Herriot industry. However, this was something that, especially in the early years of his fame, he often enjoyed.

Dick Douglas-Boyd, the sales director at Michael Joseph, was someone whom Alf and Joan got to know well over the years. Whenever a new book was published, there were inevitable requests from booksellers for signing sessions and Dick would usually attend these to ensure everything went smoothly. In fact, he and Anthea Joseph used to vie for the pleasure of travelling from London to be with Alf, Anthea usually winning the literary lunches or dinners. With everyone so interested in his rise to fame, Alf found himself thrust into the world of after-dinner speaking; it was something he never really enjoyed but, with such an interesting story to tell – and an equally interesting profession about which to talk – he was soon in great demand.

One function he really enjoyed was the annual 'Authors of the Year' reception, run by Hatchards, the famous booksellers in London's Piccadilly. At these parties, he met the crème de la crème of that year's authors – like him, the ones who had made the tills rattle the most. He often recalled the first one he attended, at New Zealand House in London. Alf could hardly believe the upturn in his fortunes. As he and Joan stood on the Martini Terrace, the top floor of New Zealand House which looks out over Trafalgar Square, Westminster and the lights of the City, they sipped champagne while rubbing shoulders with such celebrities as H. E. Bates, Jilly Cooper, Antonia Fraser and Spike Milligan. Alf and Joan attended many Hatchards' parties over the years, and on one occasion were introduced to the Queen and Prince Philip. They always enjoyed meeting the other authors and some very famous personalities, the majority of whom used to greet them like old friends. They also learned that the public images these people sometimes portrayed could be a misleading reflection of their real selves.

One politician whom they regarded with less than a friendly eye was the Labour Prime Minister, Harold Wilson. The fact that his government was plundering Alf's income through punitive taxation did not improve his opinion of him. 'He may be a clever man,' he said, 'but I don't trust him an inch! I wouldn't buy a second-hand car from Harold!' Edward Heath, the leader of the Conservative Party, was, in Alf's opinion, a far more genuine and upstanding man than the Labour leader. How he wished that Heath, not Wilson, was in charge of his country.

Then, at one of the 'Authors of the Year' receptions in the mid-1970s, he met none other than Harold Wilson himself, and I shall never forget my father's later remarks.

'I met Harold Wilson! What a grand little man!'

'I thought he wasn't one of your favourite people,' I replied in amazement.

'He comes from a similar background to myself,' my father continued enthusiastically, 'and he is a dog lover and a football supporter! We had a rare old chat together. Do you know, he is just the sort of man I like! I could have spent all night talking to him.'

Alf's income from the practice during the first years of the seventies was still welcome. He did not become a really wealthy man until 1976, and it was not until the following decade that he could consider himself a millionaire.

His accountancy files for that period make interesting reading. In 1972, he earned less than £2,000 from his book sales. This rose to £3,578 in 1973; then there was a big jump to £37,252 in 1974. It is true that he earned additional sums from, for example, newspaper serialisation rights, but his earnings in those opening years of the 1970s, for a man needing to establish a secure future for himself, were not enough to enable him to work part-time.

One of the reasons he was not quite as affluent as others imagined him to be, was that he was not receiving the full income from his phenomenal sales in America. On the advice of his accountants, he spread his earnings over a number of years rather than taking it as it was earned, so mitigating the tax burdens that were beginning to assume ever-increasing importance. Through not receiving the income from the sales of his books at the time, much of the money that was generated was, instead, diverted into other accounts, some of which, months or years later, would prove difficult to unlock when he actually wanted the money.

This was not the fault of St Martin's Press but it did cause Alf considerable worry. His agents, David Higham Associates, were in constant touch with St Martin's, attempting to clarify the situation, but there was a considerable delay before the money that was rightfully his was lodged in his bank account. The continuing viability of the American publishing house was something that, understandably, gave him cause for concern; should it become bankrupt, there was every chance that his huge earnings in the United States would disappear without trace. Happily, the fortunes of St Martin's Press improved, and as the 1970s progressed, his money eventually found its way across the Atlantic.

In 1976, his income from book sales soared to £165,000 but he had another problem to contend with by then. A Labour Government had been elected and the Chancellor of the Exchequer, Denis Healey, was famously said to declare his intent to 'Squeeze the rich until the pips squeaked'. James Herriot's pips made plenty of noise around that time. Alf had to pay a top rate of tax of 83%, together with the hardly credible figure of 98% on investment income.

The tax bills that my father received make horrendous viewing. He said to me many years later, after having paid millions into the coffers of Her Majesty's Treasury, 'There are two words in the English language that are music to my ears – Tax Free!' No wonder.

He and his accountant fought long battles with the local tax inspectors – surely some of the most unpopular people in the land. His every little move to avoid tax legally was stubbornly contested by the men from the Inland Revenue. He was not surprised to learn that his opinion of them was shared by many of his customers.

While visiting one of his clients, John Atkinson, Alf noticed that the farmer appeared to be a little preoccupied, and remarked that he did not seem his usual self.

The farmer replied, 'One o' them tax fellers is comin 'ere ter talk ter me.'

'That could be awkward, John,' Alf said, with some feeling.

'Aye, it's a bad job! Ah doubt ah'll 'ave ter snarl 'im down a bit!'

The tax man certainly 'snarled' Alf Wight down throughout his years of success, but he refused to resort to complicated ways of avoiding tax. He and Joan did, however, visit the tax haven of Jersey in 1974. Had he remained there, whilst benefiting from the island's favourable tax laws in operation at that time, he could have realised a considerable sum which he could have legally brought home.

'Are you going to live there for a year?' I asked him on his return.

'No, Jim, I'm not,' he said.

'Surely it's worth shacking up there for a while? There is a lot of money at stake.'

'If I earn £100,000 and I pay tax, I am still left with nearly £20,000,' he replied. 'That is still one hell of a lot of money, and quite enough for us. No, I'll stay here and pay up! I am now nearly sixty years old,' he continued. 'The remaining years I have left are very important to me. I love living in Yorkshire among my friends and family – and Jersey is a long way from my football team! Tell me this, how do you put a price upon one whole year of your life?'

Two years later, his accountant, Bob Rickaby, exhorted him to consider other legal ways of avoiding the astronomical tax bills. Bob was involved in mountainous heaps of correspondence with accountants in London who specialised in the tax affairs of high earners. Their advice was tempered by the fact that my father doggedly refused to live abroad. Other best-selling authors such as Leslie Thomas, Richard Adams and Frederick Forsyth were all residing overseas to limit the effect of the taxman's teeth, but Alf Wight insisted on staying where he was.

Many other ingenious schemes were put forward by the London accountants – varying from buying large tracts of forestry to owning racehorses. One way of limiting the tax burden was by setting up trusts that would benefit his relatives several generations down the family tree. This was an efficient means of tax avoidance but it meant that his immediate family would hardly benefit from his earnings.

'Why should I give my money to someone I am never going to

know?' was his response. 'I can just picture some young person, years from now, fingering my money and celebrating the memory of an unknown great, great grandpappy Wight! No, I would rather pay more tax and give a little of what is left to the family that I know.' Not surprisingly, I agreed with him.

One way that he did achieve a little tax relief was by putting my mother and me onto the payroll. My mother helped with his increasing piles of correspondence while I read his manuscripts as well as providing him with several incidents for his stories. The tax man fought this tooth and nail – and we were only allowed a very small sum – but at least it was a minor victory in his continuing war against the punitive taxation laws.

In desperation, one of the accountants said to him, 'Look, there are only two really best-selling authors still living in this country – you and Jack Higgins. Why not telephone him and find out how he tackles this problem?'

Jack Higgins had achieved phenomenal success with his novel *The Eagle Has Landed*, and Alf seemed to remember that he was living somewhere in South Yorkshire. He eventually managed to discover his address only to receive a brief, taped message on the telephone to the effect that Mr Higgins was now in residence on the island of Jersey! He, too, had failed to defeat the Inland Revenue.

Alf's determination never to live overseas, with the resulting payment of colossal sums to Her Majesty's Chancellor, meant that it would be many years before he could call himself a seriously wealthy man.

He said to his accountant, Bob Rickaby, one day, 'I get masses of letters asking me to donate money to good causes and fund scholarships for veterinary schools. They must all think I'm a millionaire.'

'You could have been,' replied Bob, 'but by living in this country you have written five books for the tax man and one for yourself!'

To his credit, Alf did not let his failure to amass huge sums of money worry him. His agent, Jacqueline Korn, said to me recently that, of all the best-selling authors whose literary affairs she has looked after, he was the one whose fame altered his lifestyle the least.

Although Alf had been pitched into the world of the celebrity, the vast majority of his time was still spent as a veterinary surgeon in Thirsk. The practice of Sinclair and Wight, in the early 1970s, was busy, and still only a four-man operation. It would have been impossible to run the business with any fewer, and Alf worked full time for the following ten years, right up until 1980 when more assistance was acquired. By then, he was almost sixty-five years old, and was entitled to take his foot off the pedal a little.

He and I always got on well together and there were occasions when I was grateful for his compassionate approach to his younger colleagues. In those early years of the 1970s when I was living at home, he observed on many occasions my delicate condition after an evening on the town. As the telephone was by his bedside, he took the night calls when I was on duty. I always heard the ringing in my room – an unwelcome noise it was in the early hours of the morning. He had two ways of answering these calls. His usual response was, 'Very well, *we'll* be out' – in which case I knew it would be me crawling out of my bed. On the odd happy occasion, however, I would hear him say, 'Right, *I'll* be out.' This meant that he had felt sympathy for his wayward son, and would soon be on his way to a cold farmyard while I buried my head deeper into the pillow. These are some of my fondest memories of a merciful father.

I did not always get off so lightly. On one occasion, he was scanning the list of work for the day. 'Let me see, now,' he said, thoughtfully. 'There is a visit to Felixkirk to see a poorly calf, and what have we here? Oh yes, a trip to Ainsley of Nevison House to castrate twenty large bulls.'

'Which one do you want me to do?' I asked tentatively. Ainsley's beasts were noted for their huge size and lightning response to any form of interference.

'I'll just get my crystal ball,' he replied, cupping his hands around the imaginary object. 'Yes, James, I see good old Nevison House . . . and, yes, there is a scene of high activity. I see flying feet, I hear bad language and . . . yes . . .' he continued, looking directly at my face, 'I see a bearded figure!'

There was always plenty of humour in the practice as my father enjoyed watching his young colleagues learning the tricks of the trade. One day, one of our assistants, while visiting a group of young pigs suffering from a disease called 'Bowel oedema', had injected two particularly badly affected ones that had been exhibiting severe convulsions. Several days passed without his learning the result of his treatment, and this concerned him.

'Don't ask!' advised Alf. 'A silence means they are either better, or they are dead.'

The young veterinary surgeon who was, naturally, itching to know what had happened, saw the owner of the pigs shortly afterwards, an elderly, bent man, walking along the street. He approached him.

'Now then, Mr Braithwaite!' he said. 'How are those pigs of yours getting on?'

'Nicely, thank yer,' replied the old man. 'Doin' right well!'

'Oh good,' said the assistant, with some relief.

Mr Braithwaite took his pipe out of his mouth and looked at the young vet. 'Them two you injected died, but 't rest are awright!'

On hearing the story, my father retorted, 'I told you not to ask him!'

His advice to me in my early days as a veterinary surgeon was of paramount importance. While I was full of the latest theoretical knowledge, he had the advantage of years of practical experience – and there were plenty of lessons to be learned.

On one occasion in 1970, Alex Talbot (the other assistant in the practice at the time) and I were operating on a Labrador. This big, friendly dog had the unfortunate tendency to consume large quantities of socks, shirts, old trousers – in fact, anything that was soft enough to pass down his enormous gullet.

These unscheduled eating episodes were frequently followed by emergency operations to remove the offending substances and he soon became one of our most valued customers. On this occasion he had feasted upon a long piece of highly-coloured cloth and, having opened his abdomen, we had made several incisions into his intestinal tract but could not remove the cloth in one piece; it seemed to be firmly anchored somewhere. The operation was beginning to assume epic proportions when my father walked in.

'What's the problem, boys?' he asked.

I explained, through clenched teeth, that we had opened up several holes in the dog's digestive system but that the cloth was still tightly anchored.

He looked at the gaping wound and the perspiring faces of his two young assistants before opening the dog's mouth.

'This is interesting,' he said quietly and began to extract, very gently, a long piece of colourful material out of the animal's mouth. There seemed to be no end to it as he continued pulling. When he had finally finished, he tossed the entire heap nonchalantly into the waste bin.

'There was some string attached to the cloth and this was wrapped around his tongue. I don't think you will have any more trouble!' He walked quietly out of the room to a deafening silence. It had taken him less than one minute to solve the problem.

'Why hadn't we thought of looking in the dog's mouth?' I thought to myself. Alex said nothing for several minutes. Suddenly, he swore savagely – twice – and continued suturing.

These were good days in the practice. Business was improving and, with it, the profits. There was an increasing flow of dogs and cats through the old house at 23 Kirkgate, and the farm side of the work had also taken an upturn, with a new scheme to eradicate Brucellosis from the cattle population of the United Kingdom well under way. This meant that there was plenty of work for us all.

My father was observing a great change in his profession as more modern drugs and treatments began to strengthen the veterinary surgeon's armoury. However, in Donald Sinclair, he still had a partner on whom the passage of time seemed to have had very little effect. Just as in those far-off days of the 1940s, Donald's fertile brain was continually thinking of ways to earn extra income. One day in the hot summer of 1975, he approached my father and myself with his latest scheme. With the farm stock thriving outside at pasture in the warm sunshine, there was very little work for us. Donald was restless.

'Alfred! Jim!' he exclaimed. 'We should be doing something rather than hanging around! We have wages to pay but the assistants are standing around doing nothing. It won't do! I have an idea!'

My father's eyes narrowed. Knowing his partner of old, he wondered what sort of wild ideas were ricocheting around in his brain.

Donald continued with an analysis of the practice finances. 'Alfred, I have calculated that unless we are making thirty pence a minute, we are going to the wall. We'll go under unless we start to get busy!'

A spasm passed across Alf's face. He had heard this so many times before but it still managed to twist his stomach into a knot. 'Right, Donald,' he said, 'what do you suggest?'

'We'll start a dog trimming parlour! Think of all those hairy dogs in Thirsk, dragging themselves around in this heat. It will give them a new lease of life.'

There was a pause as my father took it all in. He exhaled slowly before shooting a swift glance in my direction. 'Okay, Donald,' he replied. Despite my father's clear lack of enthusiasm, we all found ourselves, two days later, in the consulting-room with Mrs Warham's hairy little Pekingese on the table and Donald clutching some huge horse clippers.

The session began badly with Donald ramming the clippers into the ancient electric socket on the wall. This was followed by a loud explosion which delayed matters while a bemused electrician repaired the damage under Donald's impatient stare. We were soon under way again.

We watched in amazement as Donald hacked furiously at the hairy little creature. The old clippers made a tremendous noise as great clumps of hair flew around the room. My father occasionally tried to tender some advice but his partner was in full cry. Within minutes, the little dog was stripped bald save for his head and tail, and he presented an unusual sight. Isolated tufts stood up from his pink skin rather like cacti in a desert, while the removal of the hair from his rear end threw his hitherto concealed testicles into bold relief.

Donald stood back to admire his work. 'How about that, Alfred?' he asked, a trace of uncertainty in his voice.

My father took a while to reply. The dog appeared to be totally unconcerned but I could sense that my father felt a little differently. He stared, mesmerised, at the apparition in front of him. It no longer bore any resemblance to the canine species.

'Fine, Donald,' he said, slowly and deliberately. '*You* will return the dog to its owner, won't you?'

I was, unfortunately, present when Mrs Warham came to collect her freshly-groomed pet. She gazed, open mouthed, at the little creature before her. The bald, spiky body was in stark contrast to the tufty tail with the bright red testicles bulging beneath. The eyes shone happily from the depths of the hairy face. Mrs Warham burst into floods of tears.

Sinclair and Wight's dog-trimming business drew to a sudden close but there was a satisfactory ending to the story. The summer of that year turned out to be an extremely hot one and Donald's little patient, bereft of so much hair, enjoyed the best summer of his life – and went on to grow a wonderful new shining coat. Donald had been right; his first and only customer did, indeed, receive a new lease of life.

The fact that some things altered little was quite refreshing for Alf, as he was under pressure to adapt to the ever-changing aspect of his work as a veterinary surgeon. Realising he had to move with the times, he kept well abreast of developments within the large animal side but left the more sophisticated small animal work to his younger colleagues. However, despite his assertions that he was never a 'real small animal vet', I was always pleased when he assisted me in performing an operation; his abundance of common sense and care for the patient, together with his deep mistrust of general anaesthesia, ensured that he never took his eyes off the patient's respiratory rate. As a veterinary surgeon, when in the company of animals both large and small, I always found his presence a reliable and comforting one.

Although he had a great deal to learn from his younger colleagues, we in turn had much to learn from him. We soon realised that many of our customers were far more impressed with a man of experience than one full of 'book learnin''.

In turn, Alf never forgot that it was his life among the farming community that had provided him with much of his material, and would continue to do so. His veterinary work throughout the 1970s took on extra meaning as, with his mind now switched onto writing, he was continually looking for new material, asking me or other members of the practice to jot down anything interesting that had occurred on the daily rounds. His first six books contained many incidents that actually happened around this time, rather than in the years either side of the war when he set the stories.

To remember incidents, he relied simply on 'headings'. There are notebooks full of these headings in his virtually illegible handwriting. He did not, as already mentioned, keep a regular diary; these simple headings were all he needed to remind him of the many interesting or funny incidents that he might incorporate into his books, and he referred to them continually as he wrote.

Alf repeatedly maintained that his celebrity status meant very little to the local people of Thirsk but, when one considers the average Yorkshire person's reluctance to display his feelings openly, it is likely that he may have been mistaken. There is no doubt that a large proportion of them – farmers included – were not only well aware of his achievements but derived pleasure themselves through his worldwide acclaim. The fact that they rarely exhibited their opinions on his success suited Alf very well. He often said how lucky he was to have spent most of his working life amongst them. During his years of literary fame, whenever he appeared under the spotlight, he never seemed fully at ease. I observed him many times on television, wearing the vague and uneasy look of someone who wished that he were elsewhere. The fact was that he was not comfortable when under the media glare; it was something he never fully enjoyed. Alf Wight was at home among the farmers of North Yorkshire and his oft-repeated expression, 'I am ninety-nine per cent vet and one per cent author' was one spoken from the heart.

All of this contrasted sharply with the open admiration expressed by his adoring fans from further afield. One day, an American visitor had accompanied Alf to a farm and said to the farmer, 'What's it like having such a world-famous author as a vet? It must be great! Yeah?'

The farmer displayed no emotion. ''E's just one o' the boys round 'ere!' he replied.

This is exactly how Alf wanted to be known. He did not seek deference from those people he had known for so long. 'The farmers round here couldn't care less about my book-writing activities. If one of them has a cow with its 'calf-bed' hanging out, he doesn't want to see Charles Dickens rolling up!'

This casual approach to his fame by the local people was illustrated by an incident that remained etched in his memory. In 1974, when Alf had four published books to his name, BBC Television cameras descended on Thirsk. They were there to film for the 'Nationwide' programme – and the object of their attention was James Herriot and his meteoric rise to fame. The film crews were there all day. Zoom lenses homed in on him as he calved cows, cameras were held inches from his face as he drove from farm to farm, and the premises at 23 Kirkgate were festooned with all the latest in modern technical equipment and what seemed like miles of cable. It was a long and tiring day.

It was well into evening surgery when the director finally said to Alf, 'Mr Wight, would it be possible – just to round everything off nicely – to interview one of the interesting old characters that you talk about in your books? Can you think of anyone?'

'There happens to be a man in the waiting-room who would fit the bill perfectly,' replied my father, pleased to be able to take a break from the exhausting schedule. 'His name is Mr Hogg, an engaging chap, and a well-respected breeder of sheepdogs.'

Not only was Mr Hogg, a farmer from nearby Kilvington indeed, something of a character, he was also a good talker. He revelled in his appearance in front of the cameras, and the director got more than his money's worth.

When the interview had finally ended, the farmer sidled up to the director and whispered quietly into his ear. 'I 'eard that yer wanted ter talk to a local character. Is that right?'

'Yes,' replied the director.

Mr Hogg's voice sank to a whisper. He pointed a soiled finger towards Alf. 'Yer should 'ave a word wi' Mr Wight. 'E's a very interestin' feller!'

'Oh yes?' said the director.

'Aye! In fact, Ah'll tell tha summat!' He put his face even closer to the director's ear. 'Don't let it go no further, like, but . . . just between you an' me . . . Ah've 'eard 'e's written a couple o' books!'

In tandem with the literary success, there were many happy occasions in the first half of the 1970s. In September 1973, Rosie was married and twelve months later it was my turn to leave the family home. I was thirty-one years old and I think my parents were pretty relieved that I had finally taken the plunge. Having been living at home for almost seven years, they were beginning to think that I was going to be a permanent resident.

One of the happiest events occurred in May 1973 when our beloved football team, Sunderland – against all the odds – beat Leeds United in the FA Cup Final. This, the most coveted prize in the English game, had last been won by Sunderland way back in 1937.

Alf travelled to Wembley with his old friend Guy Rob, and I well remember the smiling, swaying figure staggering back home that Saturday night. In 1990, he wrote about that memorable day in a newspaper article:

'When the referee blew the final whistle at Wembley and I found myself dancing with my arms round a distinguished-looking gentleman in a camel coat who was a total stranger, I felt that from that moment on I could die happy.'

Alf derived enormous pleasure and satisfaction from his literary achievements, but nothing would thrill him more than watching that tremendous victory for the red and whites.

There were other less happy events. In June 1972, Joan's brother, Joe Danbury, died in hospital following a protracted illness. This distinguished and good-natured man was liked by everyone and his death was a severe blow, especially to Joan.

Then, on the last day of December 1973, Alf's great friend and colleague, Gordon Rae, died. Despite his dedication to physical fitness, Gordon had developed severe arthritis in both hips, followed by a series of heart attacks. His death was felt keenly by both Alf and Joan. Their weekly Thursday outings to Harrogate were a little darker without Gordon's open and laughing face. He was one of the most likeable men Alf had had the privilege of knowing.

At his funeral, Alf and Joan recalled their impecunious days of the 1960s when, unable to afford the cost of dinner out to celebrate their silver wedding anniversary, Gordon and Jean Rae had saved the day. As Alf had also just had his 50th birthday, he was asked where he would like to spend the occasion. 'The Double Luck Chinese restaurant!' had been his immediate response. The occasion was to be modest, but both enjoyable and delicious – and one that would, for ever, be fondly remembered by Alf and Joan.

Joan's mother, Laura Danbury, who had lived with us for so many years, outlived her son, Joe, but by only three years. In the final twelve months of her life she was confined to a nursing-home in Ripon. She was almost blind and my wife, Gillian, used to read her extracts from my father's first books. The old lady would lie back in bed and listen attentively to every word that was said. She always thought the world of her son-in-law and she loved his stories as well.

Alf, in return, had a great regard for his quiet and gentle mother-in-law who, even a day or two before her death, had the complexion of a young girl. He often said to me, 'Before you think of marrying someone, have a good look at her mother. More often than not, she will turn out to be like her!' Perhaps he had gazed long and hard at Laura Danbury before marrying Joan all those years ago in 1941.

Another less than happy event occurred in 1975 when Rosie divorced her husband, Chris Page. She moved back to Thirsk with her baby daughter, Emma, and her life soon began to improve as she began work as a doctor in general practice in the town. She received enormous help from her parents in raising Emma who spent most of her childhood in the company of her grandparents. The four of them spent many holidays together, the majority of them in Alf's, and Rosie's, favourite surroundings – the lochs and mountains of north-west Scotland. When Emma was older, they travelled abroad on holiday, but the magic of Scotland always had a special place in their hearts.

One of their favourite haunts was the Ardnamurchan peninsula, the most westerly point of the British Isles. This is a quiet and lonely spot but, when the weather is kind, it is an area of haunting beauty, with magnificent white beaches, and views out towards the islands of Rhum,

Eigg and Skye. Alf had always loved the wild and lonely places of Britain, and each time he stood on the beach at Sanna Bay, staring across the sea to the mystical blue peaks of the Cuillins of Skye, he felt a particular thrill that no other place in the world could give him.

This was a peaceful retreat where he felt a million miles from the media pressure. He was always grateful that his fame as an author, rather than a star of the screen, meant that he went largely unrecognised. He was, therefore, somewhat surprised one day, while on holiday in Scotland, to be approached by a man.

It was in 1986 and the book *James Herriot's Dog Stories* had recently been published. On the jacket of this book is a picture of him with his Border Terrier, Bodie, and Rosie's yellow Labrador, Polly. The man walked up to him and said, 'Excuse me, but wid ye be, by any chance, James Herriot?'

'As a matter of fact, I am,' he replied, 'but how on earth did you know? I didn't think that my face was well known?'

'Oh no, it wisnae you I recognised,' continued the man. 'It wis the twa dugs!'

Alf Wight's face, especially in the earlier years of his success, may not have been known to many but, in 1973, just as the Herriot band-wagon was gaining momentum, his fame was to receive a boost which would ensure that his name would become familiar to millions more. A film based on his books was going to be made. This would be followed by a second one, and a television series which would be shown all over the world. James Herriot, the reluctant celebrity, was soon to become a star of the screen.

CHAPTER TWENTY-FIVE

'You know Simon Ward, the actor who played young Winston Churchill in the film we saw recently?' my father said to me one morning in 1973.

'Yes,' I replied.

'Well, he's going from strength to strength,' he continued. 'He's going to play another famous person in his next role.'

'Who's that?' I asked.

'Me!'

Within six months of his first success in America, the idea of turning the best-selling books into a film became a reality. The film, called 'All Creatures Great and Small', was sponsored by Reader's Digest and was made originally for American television. It was released in this country in the spring of 1975.

The idea of seeing himself and his friends portrayed on the big screen thrilled Alf. 'Just think of all those famous stars performing *my* work!' he said. His feelings at the time were ones of pride mixed with incredulity. Apart from Simon Ward playing himself, Anthony Hopkins, who later was to become a major international star, played Siegfried, Brian Stirner was Tristan, while the part of Helen was taken by Lisa Harrow.

During the shooting of the film in 1974, we visited the film sets on several occasions to watch the actors at work. Alf felt a twinge of disappointment when he learnt that the chosen location was the North York Moors rather than the Yorkshire Dales, but this did little to dampen his excitement as he watched, almost disbelievingly, his past come to life before his eyes. He had no desire to become involved with the production of the film. He approved the scripts but declined to act as veterinary advisor – a job taken on by a colleague from York, George Sutherland.

Alf was especially delighted with the performance of Anthony Hopkins, who brought out the warm and effervescent nature of Siegfried perfectly. He thought that Simon Ward, too, was ideally cast as the slightly bemused young vet, pitched into the company of so many singular characters. He was intrigued by Lisa Harrow as she bore a marked resemblance to Joan in her younger years.

These were heady days, but unfortunately not everyone approved of the way they were depicted. After visiting the film set near Pickering with Alf, Brian and their wives, Donald Sinclair declared he was not happy about his portrayal. Never was the unpredictability of 'Siegfried' more vividly illustrated than at that time.

One morning, shortly after they had been up to watch the shooting of the film, I walked into the office at 23 Kirkgate to find my father seated, ashen-faced, at his desk. It was obvious that something had upset him deeply. He turned to look at me and his voice trembled as he spoke. 'Donald is going to sue me, Jim!'

His words rendered me speechless for several moments. 'Sue you? Why? What have you done?'

He stared out of the window as he often did when grappling with his feelings. 'He does not approve of the way that he has been played in the film. I knew that he didn't like the way that he came over in the books, but I never thought that it would come to this. After all we've been through together!'

I felt a surge of anger and disbelief. 'I would give my right arm to be shown to the world as Siegfried Farnon,' I retorted. 'He is portrayed as a generous and warm individual, an interesting and fascinating man. His unpredictability shows up, but we all know that that is exactly what he is like!'

My father said nothing, but I was fired with indignation and continued to vent my feelings. 'You have been a great friend and support to him for years, and he threatens to *sue* you? And it's no good his saying that the way he has been described is exaggerated, just ask any of the farmers round here! You have *under*portrayed him if anything. If he tries to sue you, I'll be the first to jump on the stand and give the real facts!' My words tumbled over each other as I let him know exactly how I felt. Like my father, I have never been outwardly aggressive, but Donald's threat infuriated me – especially as I had rather envied his being portrayed as he had been.

My father held up his hands. 'Just calm down, will you, Jim? I've been thinking about this for some time. Why do you think that Donald is such a peerless character? I'll tell you why – it's because he doesn't realise he is! It's all very well everyone else having a good laugh at his extraordinary behaviour but he genuinely doesn't believe that he is eccentric. I think perhaps he feels I'm making fun of him and it's understandable that he's upset. You know what he's like, he changes his mind with the wind direction. It may all blow over so don't say anything to him, all right?'

I realised that my father, who knew his partner as well as anyone, was probably quite right, but I had my final say. 'Donald should feel proud to be associated with such a memorable character as Siegfried Farnon!'

This flare-up from Donald had been brewing for some time. Three or four years previously, when he had first set eyes on *If Only They Could Talk*, he had remained tight-lipped. This was in striking contrast to his brother's reaction. Brian was delighted to be known as Tristan, and discussed his new role enthusiastically with Alf whenever they met, but in all the years that I knew Donald, I never once heard him speak about the books of James Herriot.

Alf did. The only time that he ever heard his partner refer to his work was when he said to him, one day after reading the first book, 'Alfred! This book is a test of our friendship!'

This had upset Alf, but now his greatest fear had materialised – that his writing would not only hurt someone but that he would be taken to court over it. Even worse, it was one of his oldest friends who was raising objections.

I remember him saying to me at the time, 'I have lain awake these last two nights wishing that I had never written the bloody books!'

The threat of legal action from Donald was a risk that the film company had had to take. At the outset, he had refused to sign a licence issued by the producers, Tallent Associates of New York, allowing them to 'make any changes in, deletions from or additions to any account of my life and to fictionalise and dramatise the account as the producer may deem necessary'.

Brian had signed his disclaimer without a murmur but Donald had felt differently. In his opinion, it would give the producers a free hand to depict him in the film as they wished, and for a man who resented his part in the James Herriot phenomenon, his reluctance to sign is hardly surprising. He had been upset when the producers risked the consequences and had gone ahead without his agreement, but when he saw the portrayal of himself on the film set, his long-felt, simmering feelings of disapproval boiled over.

Alf acted quickly. He immediately telephoned not only Brian, but their sister, Elsa, who lived in the south of England. Having explained the situation, they both offered Alf their full support, agreeing that the depiction of their brother was not exaggerated in any way. Elsa was a great fan of the Herriot books and was so indignant that Donald was objecting to the character of Siegfried that she warned her brother forcibly that there would be dire consequences should he attempt to take the matter further. Whatever she said appeared to work and filming continued.

Donald exploded again the following year, when he read some of the reviews of the film which described Anthony Hopkins' performance as the 'eccentric bachelor' and the 'excitable Siegfried', but never again was the threat of litigation to cloud the relationship between the two men.

In Donald's defence, I firmly believe that he would never have actually sued my father. He was always a man whose next move was impossible to predict and, despite this confrontation over his portrayal as Siegfried, he always had a deep respect for his partner.

In all the time that I knew Donald, I never really understood how he felt about the publicity surrounding the 'Herriot explosion'. Shortly after his threat of legal action, he and Audrey were present at the end-of-film parties that everyone enjoyed with the actors and producers, and they seemed to be thoroughly at ease.

In the following years, when thousands of tourists invaded the surgery, Donald would frequently take it upon himself to give them a guided tour of the premises and the old garden. Was this the same man who had confronted his partner about the books and films which he said he disapproved of so strongly? The inimitable Siegfried Farnon was every bit as unpredictable in real life as James Herriot had shown him to be.

After this episode, Alf trod very warily when writing about Siegfried, toning down his character considerably in future books. I thought this was a great shame and I told my father so at the time. I had always reckoned Siegfried to be the pivotal character in the books, one whom the many Herriot fans had grown to love. Tom McCormack, of St Martin's Press in New York, agreed. He wrote to Alf in 1974:

'I think you can honestly tell your partner that the million American readers who have come to know him through *All Creatures* are immensely fond of him. Next to James and Helen, he is easily the favourite character in the book. Surprisingly, his combustibility is a much more attractive thing than any blandness and sobriety that might replace it . . . I'd urge strongly that the American edition be allowed to retain the lively and explosive Siegfried we've all grown so fond of.'

Throughout their years together, Alf was always the driving force in the practice to whom Donald often turned for advice, even on personal matters. There was no real need for him to bow to Donald's wishes in any way but, at the back of his mind, he felt a stab of guilt. I remember his saying to me at the time, 'We all have a laugh at old Donald and his ways but perhaps it's a bit different for him, being on the receiving end of it all?'

Alfred Wight had upset one of his oldest friends and he was going to see that it did not happen again. From then on, the character of Siegfried was considerably played down in the books.

One thing that softened the blow a little for Donald was that he, Brian and I received a small percentage of the money from the film royalties. This was a legal measure to avoid tax, my father arguing that we had contributed towards providing the material on which the original stories were based. The taxman did not allow any substantial amounts to filter down to us but, nevertheless, it was a welcome addition to the yearly budget. Alf felt that any amount, no matter how small, was better in the pockets of his friends than adding to the already considerable sum that was fattening the purse of the Inland Revenue.

This injection of cash was repeated with the next film, and we received regular little cheques right through the television series into the 1980s. As a newly-married man, I was highly appreciative of this extra money, and Brian, too, was delighted to receive these welcome boosts to his economy, as a letter written to Alf in May 1980 reveals. The style shows that he had changed little from those fantasising days of his youth:

Salutations Schistosoma,

I have just received a simple printed letter from David Higham and his limited Associates, enclosing another simple cheque for £597.38.

A blessing on you, kind and noble sir – this means that I and my kin can revel in the hot groceries once more and I can indulge my craving for Tetley's Bitter Ale to my belly's content.

We must meet again soon, to taste the dishes of Cathay, so nobly served in Wetherby Market Place.

Yours as ever,

Wolf J. Flywheel

*

The first film received good notices and a second one was planned. This one, called 'It Shouldn't Happen to a Vet', was shot in 1975 and had its Gala Première in London's Shaftesbury Avenue on 8 April 1976.

Reader's Digest again sponsored the film and the producer, as for the previous one, was David Susskind. This time, to Alf's delight, the film was shot in the Yorkshire Dales around his most favourite areas of Wensleydale and Swaledale. Apart from Lisa Harrow who played Helen once again, there were different actors playing the main characters. John Alderton – already popular with the British public for his many appearances in 'Upstairs Downstairs' – took the part of James Herriot. Colin Blakely played Siegfried but, in this film, there was no Tristan character.

While John Alderton provided a more forceful James Herriot, with a flash of humour always evident, Colin Blakely's role as Siegfried was more subdued than the portrayal by Anthony Hopkins. Although he brought some wonderful comedy to the part, there was hardly a trace of the spontaneous eccentricity that was the hallmark of the real man. This was partly because Alf insisted on some changes since he was not prepared to upset Donald again. After reading the scripts in advance of shooting, he was adamant that the peaks and troughs of Siegfried's character be smoothed out.

Joan and Alf approved of all the actresses who played the part of Helen in the films and television series, but Lisa Harrow was their favourite. She never forgot her role in the Herriot films and kept in touch with Alf and Joan for years afterwards.

As before, we went to watch the shooting on several occasions, and all agreed that the background of the wild fellsides and dales added an authenticity that was missing from the first film. Alf was particularly pleased that the scenery of the Yorkshire Dales was going to be shared with so many others.

Many of his friends went with him to watch the filming, Brian, Denton Pette – and Donald, too. Denton was intrigued to observe Richard Pearson's portrayal of his own character, Granville Bennett. At the time, Denton owned an MGB and the boot of the car had been lovingly converted into a bar, stocked with a fine selection of beers and spirits. The actors and film crew were not slow to avail themselves of Denton's extraordinary hospitality, and Rosie remembers arriving one day above Keld in the upper reaches of Swaledale, to be greeted by a smiling Denton with the words, 'Rosie, my dear! A small aperitif, perhaps?'

On these trips into the Dales, there was someone else who appreciated the odd tipple from Denton's 'mobile pub' – an old friend and colleague of his, and Alf's, called Basil Aylward. Basil, the veterinary surgeon from Richmond in lower Swaledale, was the veterinary advisor to the film – Alf having again declined to play any major part in its production.

The mischievously-smiling Basil, a *bon viveur* in a similar mould to Denton, was another colleague in whose company Alf laughed continuously. One of their favourite meeting places was the Black Bull at Moulton, near Richmond, where many a good tale was told over a few beers and the magnificent seafood that is the speciality of the house.

Basil, a born raconteur, was able to recall a seemingly endless store of highly entertaining tales of mishaps and calamities which typify the life of the veterinary surgeon. It is the disasters which befall our colleagues that are so much more interesting to listen to than their triumphs, and this open admission of his own fallibility was an endearing feature of Basil's personality.

In his fourth book, *Vet in Harness*, James Herriot describes an incident in which he travels with Granville Bennett to a veterinary society meeting in Appleby. They drive over the moors in a violent snowstorm but, amazingly, arrive safely. After the meeting, he and Granville – fortified with good food and fine ale – return at incredible speed over the wild, snowbound road, only to discover the following morning that the road on which they had just travelled was reported to have been blocked for days!

It was, in fact, that redoubtable pair, Basil and Denton, who made the white-knuckle ride to Appleby and back, and it was after hearing about it from Basil one night that Alf took out his notebook and marked the incident as one to form the basis of a good story in a future book. This is another example of his using author's licence; the story did not happen as he told it but, as with so many others, it was based upon a real incident.

'It Shouldn't Happen to a Vet' was another box office success. As excellent family viewing, it was a change from the increasingly violent films that were being released at the time. Although Alf, in fact, enjoyed many films in which sex and violence were the prominent feature, he was still pleased that this wholesome film was one to which the whole family could be taken safely.

Donald seemed to approve of the way that he was portrayed this time. We were all very relieved, especially as one scene in the film compares Siegfried with Adolf Hitler, describing him as a 'mad sod!' Alf seemed to be more upset about this than Donald who, after completion of the film's shooting, threw a big party in Southwoods Hall for all the cast and several of his friends. Donald was in great form at the party, laughing and chatting with everyone. Who could have forecast the throwing of such a party when, two years earlier, he was threatening his partner with litigation?

John Rush, the agent in charge of film and television rights at David Higham, in common with many others, always thought that the Herriot books were not ideal material from which to make a feature film and that, being episodic, they were far better suited to a television series.

Before the making of the first film, he had tried unsuccessfully to interest television companies, but it was not until after the release of the second film that the idea for a television series was put into place. David Susskind, the American who owned the right to produce any spin-off series following the films, eventually sold his interest to the BBC and, in 1977, a new group of actors assembled in the Yorkshire Dales. James Herriot's stories were to be filmed yet again, but this time, they were to be beamed into the homes of millions.

The books and films had made the name of James Herriot famous but the television series, 'All Creatures Great and Small', turbocharged his popularity. It was after this series that the number of tourists visiting Thirsk rocketed to unbelievable proportions. His famous characters had now infiltrated people's sitting-rooms and they liked what they saw.

Once again, Alf took a back seat when it came to being involved in the production. He approved the scripts – many of which followed the storylines of the books closely – but nothing more. He was quite content just to pay regular visits into the Dales to watch the actors at work. Jack Watkinson, the vet in Leyburn, acted as veterinary advisor in the Dales, while, with much of the studio work being shot in the Midlands, my father's old friend, Eddie Straiton, provided the professional expertise.

The part of James Herriot was played by Christopher Timothy. Up until this time, he was not well known to the public but it took only one or two episodes on the television to propel him to stardom.

Chris Timothy developed a lasting respect for Alf Wight, a man he felt proud to have played. He was diffident about meeting him for the first time but, after his first introduction on the film set in the Dales, was soon put at his ease.

While fishing in Swaledale one day, and sensing a tap on his shoulder, he turned round to face a man he did not know.

'Are you Chris Timothy?' asked the stranger.

'I am,' replied Chris.

The man continued in a quiet Scottish burr, 'Well ... I am your alter ego.'

Chris liked him from that first meeting and he never lost his affection for my father, whom he described many years later, as a 'private, totally approachable, totally delightful, up-front guy'.

For their part, of all the stars Alf and Joan met during those intoxicating years, Chris has been the one who has kept in touch with the family more closely than any other. He continues to visit my mother whenever he is nearby, and often sends letters from abroad whenever his acting engagements take him further afield. Chris, who has appeared on many factual programmes about James Herriot, has been incredibly supportive of anything that has involved the man to whom he feels he owes so much. His role as the famous vet, one which gave an enormous boost to his career, is something he has never forgotten.

I shall always remember his unflinching cooperation when asked to speak at my father's Memorial Service in 1995, together with the wonderful performance he gave when reading the passage from *Vet in Harness* about that great composite character, 'Biggins'. Chris was pleased we had chosen that particular episode since he had become friends with the actor who played Biggins in the series, who had himself sadly died prior to the Memorial Service.

If Chris Timothy was a comparative unknown before assuming the mantle of James Herriot, the actor who played Siegfried – Robert Hardy – most certainly was not. He was already an established and much-respected performer and, as well as having experience as a Shakespearean actor to his credit, his versatility was such that he had stepped expertly into the roles of such diverse personalities as Winston Churchill and Benito Mussolini.

I remember my first meeting with Robert Hardy. One afternoon in the surgery in 1977, I was surprised to see a figure in a white coat, counting tablets into a bottle beneath the disconcerting stare of Donald Sinclair. Seconds later, Donald seized the bottle.

'No, no, Tim! I've already told you! These tablets are for dogs only! You *never* give these to cats!' I wondered who this unknown, brow-beaten employee of the practice could be? I looked more closely at him. 'Good heavens, it's Robert Hardy!' I said aloud.

His smiling face turned towards me and Donald introduced us. 'I am very pleased to meet you,' he said. 'Call me Tim. That is how I am known to my friends.' I took an instant liking to him.

With filming having only recently begun, he was spending a few days at Southwoods Hall with Donald to give him the opportunity of studying his character. It proved, not surprisingly, to be a most illuminating experience and his time was obviously well spent because his portrayal of Siegfried, a character whom he came to love dearly, was brilliant. Although he bore no physical resemblance to the real man, he captured his impulsive character perfectly and his performance passed the severest possible test – the approval of the Yorkshire farmers who knew the real Siegfried so well. 'By! That feller teks auld Sinclair off well!' was a cry that I heard countless times.

Donald and Robert Hardy became the best of friends over the years but, true to form, Donald did not approve of his television portrayal. Almost twenty years later, in 1996, I had the pleasure of seeing Tim Hardy on the top of the White Horse Bank, near Thirsk. He had come to open officially the White Horse Preservation Society, an organisation dedicated to the upkeep of the famous White Horse that had been cut into the hillside above the village of Kilburn over a hundred years ago. He gave a short but revealing speech in which he reminisced about his role as Siegfried.

He had approached Donald one day and said, 'You have never really approved of my portrayal of you, have you?'

Upon receiving the predictable response, he had countered, 'Very well, who *would* you have liked to have played the part?'

'Oh, someone with manners. Someone like Rex Harrison!' Donald had unhesitatingly replied.

'From that moment on,' said Tim, 'I knew I was a dead duck!'

Robert Hardy's feelings for his part in the series are revealed in a letter to Alf dated New Year 1978:

'The first of our interpretations of your marvellous work goes out on Sunday 8th and I hope, and hope, you will like it . . . the joy that I've already had in being part of it all is like nothing else I've ever experienced.'

Carol Drinkwater, who played Helen, and Peter Davison as Tristan, were ideal in their parts. Carol brought a lively sexiness to her part and Peter stepped most convincingly into the role of the likeable but feckless Tristan.

Alf thoroughly enjoyed the series. The producer, Bill Sellers, ensured that the stunning scenery was displayed at its best throughout and, in choosing the village of Askrigg in Wensleydale, he brought the fictitious town of Darrowby to life. This village was certainly in Alf's mind when he originally set his books in the Dales back in the late 1960s; the grey buildings surrounded by the fells, with the dry-stone walls snaking down from the high ground, are straight from the pages of James Herriot's books. After the series began – the first episode was shown on 8 January 1978 – thousands of tourists invaded Askrigg and Wensleydale. They may have been a nuisance to some, but they certainly boosted the economy of the Dales for many years.

Another feature of the series was the excellent acting from the extras. Some of the farming characters were brilliantly represented and, as Alf said, 'could have stepped straight out of the old farm buildings that I used to know'.

Johnny Byrne, the scriptwriter, did a most skilful job in transposing the writing of James Herriot to the spoken word, and many of the scenes rang with authenticity. One of Alf's favourite episodes concerned the vets' uphill struggle in extracting money from some of the old farmers. He said to me, the day following the screening of the episode, 'Did you see that one, last night? It brought back a few memories, I can tell you!'

For many, the series became addictive viewing. An extract from the *Western Daily Press*, dated 30 January 1978, illustrates the high regard in which it was held:

Churchgoers in the village of Lowick, Cumbria, have been blessed with the chance to worship all things bright and beautiful – and then go home to 'All Creatures Great and Small'. For the tiny Lakeland church has been given a special dispensation to hold its Sunday evening service earlier than usual so the congregation can get home in time to watch its favourite television programme.

Since the series started, there had been a decline in the numbers attending Evensong and those that turned up complained of missing the start of the programme.

Such was their popularity, forty-one episodes were shown over the following five years, and they very quickly became compulsive viewing for a huge proportion of the population, with estimates running up to 14 million viewers.

Alf's own opinion of the television series appeared in the *Yorkshire Evening Post* in 1981:

Not only did it capture the essence of what I had tried to say, but also the central characters were absolutely splendid ... they were us come to life. I watched it faithfully.

Human nature being what it is, I probably watched Chris Timothy a little more closely than I did the others. I always saw myself as the rather diffident figure – not exactly a 'grey' figure but not a particularly colourful one – caught between two flamboyant, thoroughly zestful characters. Christopher Timothy perfectly captured that air of diffidence.

James Herriot had, by the early 1980s, become not just a famous international name, he had become an industry. He had sold millions of books in hardback and many millions more in paperback. The television series had made his name a household word and was transmitted to countries all over the world – right through the 1980s with repeats into the following decade. The area of North Yorkshire that he had made famous had assumed a new name; it had become known as 'Herriot Country', with tourists visiting Thirsk and the Yorkshire Dales in their thousands. With his books having been translated into so many languages, fans came from all corners of the world.

Alf, while having to admit that he greatly enjoyed meeting so many people from overseas, preferred to spend most of his time away from the spotlight. Not only had he bought, in 1977, his house in Thirlby where he and Joan were secreted away from the thousands of prying eyes but, in 1978, he acquired a cottage in the village of West Scrafton – a cluster of grey stone houses and farms, lying on the southern side of Coverdale and surrounded by wild fells and moorland. It was here, where he could merge into obscurity among his beloved Yorkshire Dales, that he found total peace – where, in the morning, he would awake to a silence broken only by 'the sound of the bleating of sheep or the cry of the curlew'.

He and Joan stayed in the West Scrafton cottage regularly, in all weathers and at all times of the year. Here, he would walk his dogs endless miles over the green tracks while drinking in the sweet, clear air of the high dales. There was nowhere he would have rather been.

It was an idyllic spot in the summer, but in the darker months of the year, West Scrafton could show a different side to its nature. One late October afternoon, he was walking his dogs along the road towards the neighbouring hamlet of Swineside. His head was lowered to protect himself from the driving rain, screaming in from the surrounding moors. On the road, he met one of the local farmers, surrounded by cows and elegantly attired in a torn mackintosh, around which was an ancient hessian sack held in place with a piece of string. The road was running with water and mud.

The farmer paused in the lee of one of the stone buildings before raising his weather-beaten face to Alf. He shouted above the noise of the wind. 'Afternoon, Mr Wight!'

'It's not much of a day!' yelled Alf in response.

'Nay, you're right!' continued the farmer, looking around him at the desolate scene. 'You're 'avin' a bit o' holiday up 'ere, eh?'

'Yes, just having a nice break from the practice.'

The farmer scrutinised the damp figure before him. Everyone in the village knew who he was; they all knew he had the means to spend his holidays on sun-drenched beaches in exotic locations. The farmer had spent almost his entire life working in the village, and a hard life it had been. Many people are entranced by the beautiful scenery of the Yorkshire Dales, but those who try to make a living out of the place can sometimes take a different view.

The farmer looked again at the rippling puddles in the road, the rapidly darkening sky and the filthy wet dogs standing expectantly at Alf's feet. He looked him steadily in the face before turning to set off after the mass of cows. A puzzled look passed over his features as he paused for a final word. 'Why der yer come 'ere?'

Whilst not really enjoying the massive publicity that surrounded him, Alf was, in fact, making matters worse for himself; he was still seated in front of the television with his typewriter. He did it for neither fame nor fortune; he simply loved writing. With lists of 'headings' secreted away in the drawers of his desk, there was still plenty of material.

Between the years of 1978 and 1981, two more books appeared. One of these was to sell more copies in hardback than any of his previous six and was largely responsible for the never-ending coachloads of tourists pouring into his part of England. This book – one that he almost never wrote – was destined to become his greatest best-seller. It was called *James Herriot's Yorkshire*.

CHAPTER TWENTY-SIX

One day in 1978, my father called me to his house in Thirlby. 'Jim,' he said, 'I want to ask you something.' I always knew when he was going to mention something important; he spoke slowly and quietly with a slight trace of uncertainty.

'Michael Joseph would like to produce a picture book of those parts of Yorkshire I have made famous through my writing. It would be accompanied by a text, written by me. They want to call it *James Herriot's Yorkshire*.'

His eyes were now focused directly on mine as he continued. 'What do you think of the idea? Do you think that my words alongside photographs would interest people?'

I felt somewhat flattered that this established best-selling author valued my opinion, but I was not really surprised. Although not without confidence in his own ability, he continually sought suggestions from others – maintaining until the end of his life that he was simply 'an amateur at the writing game'.

I thought for a few moments. 'No, Dad. I don't think that it's a good idea at all.'

'Why not?'

'Why should someone from, say, California, want to look at some pokey little corner of Swaledale?' I replied confidently. 'These places bring back great memories for us, but I can't see the fascination in them for anyone else. Forget it. It won't sell.'

'You don't think so?'

'No.'

'Perhaps you're right.' He lapsed into thought and dropped the subject.

He must have listened to me because he told his publishers that he had serious misgivings about the project. However, their persuasive arguments finally won the day, and Alf agreed to go ahead. This beautifully illustrated book, the inspired idea of Alan Brooke, then editorial director at Michael Joseph – and whose concept received wholehearted support from Alf's editor Anthea Joseph – went on to become a mega best-seller, far exceeding all his previous books. It became the 'essential companion' for the thousands of fans from all over the world who flocked to see those 'pokey little corners' of Yorkshire that I had confidently predicted would hold no interest for them.

The dubious quality of my advice was emphatically illustrated some sixteen years later. In 1995, four months after my father's death, Rosie and I took part in a BBC television programme about outdoor activities called 'Tracks'. Part of this weekly programme described those walks that were particular favourites of selected celebrities and, for James Herriot's favourite, we had chosen to film the programme in the upper reaches of Swaledale.

This wild and unspoilt area figures largely in the Yorkshire book. He loved it for its beauty and loneliness but we were not alone for long on that occasion. I was astonished to see a coach disgorge a throng of American tourists who strode purposefully past us, many of them clutching their copy of *James Herriot's Yorkshire*! Sixteen years after publication, it still held its fascination for so many of his fans.

This book was published in 1979 and is totally factual. Such was its success that it became the trailblazer for many look-alike publications, including *Wynford Vaughan-Thomas's Wales*, *Poldark's Cornwall*, *Catherine Cookson's Northumberland* and the highly popular series of books by the enigmatic fellwalker, Alfred Wainwright. My father loved reading Wainwright's books; he wrote simply, but with great feeling, for the high country of the British Isles, especially the Lake District and Scotland, and I feel sure that had he and my father met, they would have had much in common.

The superb photographs in *James Herriot's Yorkshire* were taken by the freelance photographer, Derry Brabbs; it was his first book and its tremendous success was to make his name. He was to go on and illustrate many more of the books that would follow in its wake, including the Wainwright series.

Derry was chosen in a somewhat bizarre fashion. Nowadays, photographic agencies would be asked to submit the portfolios of their major clients but not so in 1978. Michael Joseph decided that a Yorkshire-based photographer would be best, for obvious reasons: not only would he or she be close at hand, but would already understand the vagaries of the Yorkshire weather. The firm's managing director, Victor Morrison – who, with his considerable flair for design, oversaw the book's production – had a secretary whose husband was a freelance photographer.

He was consulted and suggested that a simple way to start would be to check the *Yellow Pages* directories for Yorkshire, under the heading PHOTOGRAPHERS, and see what emerged. Victor Morrison did just that and compiled a list. Derry Brabbs, having the luck to have a surname starting with B, was approached first of all – and the search for a photographer ended there.

James Herriot's Yorkshire is lavishly illustrated with photographs of places that evoked many happy memories for Alf. The pictures of Wensleydale brought back images of the hard, early years helping his old friend Frank Bingham, at a time when he had first set eyes upon the magic of the Yorkshire Dales. There is an account of a Youth Hostelling holiday when I and a schoolfriend, Ian Brown, walked with my father through Wensleydale and Swaledale. Such was the popularity of the book, that this walk has been traced by many people and has become known as the 'Herriot Way'.

The vivid photographs of the Thirsk area, the place where the vast majority of the stories had their origins, and where my father brought us up along an uncertain but happy road, had especial meaning for him.

The North York Moors and the Yorkshire coast are not forgotten. Derry Brabbs's pictures of the old Grand Hotel in Scarborough made Alf shiver as he recalled his days in the RAF, drilling on the beach and sleeping in the cold, windswept dormitories. On a softer note, he fondly remembers the town of Harrogate, his haven of escape every Thursday afternoon at a time when he was working day and night to establish himself as a veterinary surgeon.

Every section of the book stirred memories, some of them hard but all of them happy. 'But what I see most clearly on my map,' Alf wrote in the book's introduction, 'is the little stretch of velvet grass by the river's edge where I camped or picnicked with my family. I can see the golden beach where my children built their castles in the sand. These are the parts, when my children were very young, which stand out most vividly from the coloured paper. These, indeed, as I look down on my Yorkshire, are the sweet places of memory.'

James Herriot's Yorkshire is about the recollections of a best-selling author. To his family, it meant a little more. It invoked memories of a father who ensured that we were able to share his happiness in those days when we were young.

*

By 1979, over 12 million books by James Herriot had been sold, and Alf had little more to prove to his publishers, but writing had become a way of life and, in 1981, his seventh book of stories was published. This book, entitled *The Lord God Made Them All*, took him over four years to complete but there were reasons for this. Not only had he written the text for *James Herriot's Yorkshire* since the last volume of stories, *Vet In A Spin* published in 1977, but the new book was much longer. This was primarily for the American market with its insatiable demand for 'big' books, and enabled St Martin's Press to publish *The Lord God Made Them All* at the same time as the British edition. They had, of course, had to wait to publish *Vets Might Fly* until *Vet In A Spin* was published, so they could produce one big volume, *All Things Wise and Wonderful*.

The new book became an instant best-seller on both sides of the Atlantic, and such was James Herriot's popularity in the United States that over half a million copies were sold there in hardback alone.

Although I and many of my father's close friends have always regarded his earliest books as our favourites, this one contains some wonderful material, and like the others, brings to life a whole host of new and fascinating characters.

In chapter 15, he describes his treatment of a dog with demodectic mange, belonging to Sister Rose. This character was based upon a woman called Sister Ann Lilley, from the Friarage Hospital in nearby Northallerton. She was closely involved with my father's favourite animal charity, the Jerry Green Foundation Trust, and she ran several small dog sanctuaries of her own. She is someone for whom Alf had great respect. It is a sad story ending in the death of Amber, a beautiful golden retriever, to whom, in real life, my father had become very attached. *The Lord God Made Them All* is another book that illustrates not only the triumphs but also the heartbreaks that punctuate the life of every veterinary surgeon.

The period in which the book was set had moved on, and now included stories about Rosie and me – who were both given our real names. Extracts from James Herriot's books were reproduced in countless periodicals and magazines, primarily in Britain and America, and there was one chapter in *The Lord God Made Them All* which proved to be the most popular of all.

The story tells of James Herriot's attendance at a concert at which his young son was performing. I was about eight years old when the concert, organised by my piano teacher Miss Stanley, took place in the Sowerby Methodist Chapel. The concert was a succession of recitals by her young pupils and they all performed admirably – all except me. I made two disastrous attempts at a little piece called 'The Miller's Dance' before, to wild and relieved applause from the assembled parents, I finally succeeded at the third try. The effect on my father's nervous system was devastating.

The hilarious description in the book is one that I have read many times, and I can understand why it is so popular; the tension of watching one's offspring performing in public is something with which many a parent must identify. James Herriot's harrowing experience of witnessing his child transforming a nice little concert into a farce is one that many must dread.

Years later, when my father was asking me if I remembered the incident, and I replied that I didn't think I had ever been so frightened, he replied, 'Well, it might have frightened you, but it very nearly killed me!'

I had always felt a little guilty about my reluctance to practise the piano, and thus waste the cost of the lessons, but at least it provided my father with material for a chapter that became one of the most popular he ever wrote.

On reading his manuscript prior to publication, I found as usual the humorous stories the most enjoyable, especially his account of saving his own life in the face of an enraged bull by smashing the creature repeatedly over the nose with an artificial vagina – but there is, of course, far more to his writing than this. *The Lord God Made Them All* is a book that, once again, illustrates James Herriot's understanding of human nature – it is a book not just about animals and veterinary surgeons, but about the everyday emotions that everyone experiences.

The spectacular triumph of *James Herriot's Yorkshire* had not gone unnoticed by the Reader's Digest Association. Having published much of James Herriot's work in their condensed books on both sides of the Atlantic – and sold millions of copies – they approached Michael Joseph with the idea of producing an illustrated volume of selected stories from the James Herriot books. Alan Brooke, Michael Joseph's editorial director, together with Alf's editor, Jenny Dereham – who had succeeded Anthea Joseph following her tragic death from cancer early in 1981 – came up to Yorkshire with representatives of the Reader's Digest, to talk my father into the idea of the book. He was soon won over. This book, published in 1982, was called *The Best of James Herriot*.

Apart from the introduction, Alf had comparatively little original work to do for this book. It was a compendium of his stories, and Alf had final approval of the content. Interspersed amongst the stories were sections which covered different subjects connected with Alf, Yorkshire and the veterinary profession. These sections were superbly illustrated with a mixture of historical photographs of the places about which he wrote, new colour photographs of the incomparable Yorkshire landscape, and a multitude of line drawings. Readers interested in a post-war cow-drencher, a Swaledale sheep, or the intricacies of a dry-stone wall would find it all in this book.

Alf always regarded this as a wonderful book, beautifully produced, and a treasure trove of information for every James Herriot fan. 'Just look at this book!' he said shortly after he received his first copy. 'This will make a terrific gift. I'm sure it will sell well!'

I refrained from giving my opinion this time. He was right; it was another best-seller – one with which my father was particularly proud to be associated.

The final years of the 1970s and the earliest ones of the 1980s marked the zenith of the James Herriot success story. They were golden years during which everything he did resulted in astounding success. He had written eight worldwide best-selling books, the television series had projected his name into the living-rooms of millions of households and he had, by that time, attained complete financial security. For a man who had started with virtually nothing, it was a staggering achievement.

However, with the welfare of his family and friends meaning a great deal more to him than material success, inevitably there were one or two unhappy events, the effects of which would, for a time, outweigh his feelings of intense satisfaction over his literary achievements.

As a true animal lover, the death of his noisy but lovable little dog, Hector, was a shattering experience. At the age of fourteen, Hector was having difficulty eating. Suspecting a cancerous condition of the oesophagus, Alf took him to Denton Pette for a second opinion, where his worst fears were realised. Denton had no alternative but to say it would be kindest to put him to sleep. Alf, totally desolated, staggered from Denton's surgery before climbing into his car for the long, quiet journey home. Denton, observing his friend's obvious distress, suggested that Hector be buried in his own garden – an offer to which the distraught Alf readily agreed. The little dog, to this day, lies in Eve Pette's garden in the village of Aldborough St John.

One of the most difficult tasks confronting the veterinary surgeon is that of having to end the life of a dearly loved pet; it can be a traumatic experience for both owner and veterinary surgeon. This was the first time that Alf had had to make the decision to end the life of one of his own animals; having found himself in the unenviable position of so many of his clients for whom he had had to perform this delicate service, it gave him an even greater understanding of their feelings.

Hector's death was one of the most emotionally draining experiences of Alf's life, but the passing of his little companion did not mean that he was without a dog; he had Dan, a black Labrador, who was originally my dog. In 1967, when I returned to work in Thirsk from my first job in Staffordshire, I brought Dan with me, and he and Hector took to one another straightaway. They soon became inseparable, riding everywhere together in my father's car.

Like Hector, Dan became a much-photographed member of the canine race. He appeared in many magazines and newspapers when the name of James Herriot was becoming well known, and is the dog staring up expectantly at Alf on the cover of *James Herriot's Yorkshire*. This was a typical pose for Dan; his whole life was one of chasing or carrying sticks and the photograph on the cover shows him staring intently at one held in Alf's hand. His car was constantly littered with an assortment of Dan's sticks and the big, black dog covered endless miles alongside Alf, always with a stick in his mouth.

He was very different in character from Hector, maintaining a dignified silence in the passenger seat of the car, as he surveyed the scene around him with noble indifference. There was one occasion, however, when Dan revealed a deeper side to his character.

A journalist from the Far East had come to interview Alf for a magazine article. They had driven around the countryside with Dan in the back seat, before stopping at a pub for lunch. On their return to the car, they were shocked to discover that Dan had torn into pieces the notes the journalist had left on the car seat. This was completely out of character – the only time in his entire life that he had shown any destructive tendencies. Did the big dog know that in parts of the Far East, people ate dogs? And was this his way of lodging his protest? Never again would Dan display such behaviour.

Dan's companionship was a great comfort following Hector's death, but it would be less than four years before Alf had to face, again, the distress of losing a dog. One day in 1981, after weeks of agonising over such a difficult decision, he asked me to put Dan to sleep. With the old dog having been weakening for some time with advanced arthritis of the hips, Alf had tried everything to help him, but his time had come. Dan lies buried in the field behind my father's house.

Many argue that, once having lost a pet, it is impossible to find another to take its place. Alf, who wasted no time in acquiring another pet, thought differently. Many dogs occupied different stages of his life; every one had its own distinctive personality and each one left its own particular memories.

It was during the decade following the mid 1970s that James Herriot's massive contribution, not only to the image of the veterinary profession, but to the feeling of well-being within the community as a whole, was fully recognised. With his writing having brought pleasure to millions, honours began to be showered upon him. It is well-nigh impossible to enumerate every recognition of respect that was bestowed on Alf Wight, but some of them were particularly special.

It was a proud moment for all the family when we saw the New Year's honours list in the newspaper on 30 December 1978. We had known in advance that my father was to receive the Order of the British Empire in recognition of his services to literature, but to see it in print was particularly thrilling.

It was an unforgettable experience when Alfred Wight received his honour from the Prince of Wales at the ceremony in Buckingham Palace at the end of the following February. As I looked at him, I cast my mind back almost twenty years to the time he began writing stories simply because it was something he had always wanted to do. Who would have thought that those unpretentious but charming accounts of life so long ago in far-off Yorkshire would have led to James Alfred Wight shaking hands with the Prince of Wales?

It was, also, a memorable evening the night before. Courtesy of Pan Books, a splendid party had been arranged for us – and for those with whom my father was connected in the world of publishing. As we quaffed never-ending glasses of champagne that helped to forge effortless friendships with total strangers, I remember thinking what a wonderful life it was, being the son of such a famous man.

True to his character, he talked very little of this honour, proud though he was to receive it. One day, many years later, after writing another colossal cheque to the Inland Revenue, he said to us, 'I think I know the reason why I received the OBE. By remaining in this country and paying so much tax, I must have been largely responsible for the continuing solvency of Her Majesty's Government!'

He was, however, to receive some compensation. An elegant envelope arrived one morning in October 1979. An equally impressive piece of paper within, from Buckingham Palace, said that Her Majesty the Queen requested the honour of the company of Alfred Wight for lunch. I remember goggling at the invitation while he simply said, 'I don't think I can decline this one, do you?'

The family, understandably, was intrigued to hear all about it and bombarded him with questions on his return from the Palace.

I asked him if he had sat next to her.

'No,' he replied. 'They stuck some minor individual between myself and the Queen.'

'Who was that?' I asked.

He smiled gently. 'The Governor of the Bank of England.'

As he lunched in the magnificent dining-room, a footman at attention behind every chair, his memory flickered back almost fifty years to the penniless young vet, seated in his tiny car in the Yorkshire Dales, chewing at his cheese sandwiches.

On this occasion there was no clear water from the moorland streams to complement his meagre lunch; instead, he drank a number of the finest wines. He made sure that he did not consume too much, which was a wise decision since, eventually, he was summoned to a private audience with the Queen. He found her to be a most approachable and delightful person with a sharp sense of humour and an infectious laugh. My father told us that she had said that his books were some of the few that had made her 'laugh out loud'.

It is understandable that she would have enjoyed the books of James Herriot. Not only would the humour have appealed to her but she is, of course, such a genuine animal lover.

On his departure from the Palace, he observed the other guests stepping into a succession of chauffeur-driven limousines. He was about to hail a taxi when one of these prestigious vehicles glided up to offer him a lift. It was none other than that 'minor individual', who was in fact Sir Robert Clark, chairman of Hill Samuel and Co. He was a most likeable man who provided my father with the perfect conclusion to a memorable day.

The following evening, I was having a drink with my father and two of his farming friends, Billy Bell and Gordon Bainbridge, in the Three Tuns Hotel in Thirsk. Many subjects were discussed but not once did he mention his day out at Buckingham Palace. James Herriot the author was, once again, Alf Wight the vet.

On another occasion, in June 1983, he was again in the company of royalty. He and Joan were invited to a private dinner given by Dick and Mary Francis in honour of the Queen Mother. Dick Francis, author of many best-selling books about the world of horse racing, was one of the famous people Alf got to know well and he was probably one of his favourites – a modest and charming man with whom he kept in touch throughout their almost parallel climb up the ladder of fame. Both men were published by Michael Joseph and Pan; both had Anthea Joseph and then Jenny Dereham as editor.

In July 1979, he received an Honorary Doctorate of Literature from Heriot-Watt University in Edinburgh. On his return from the ceremony, he seemed almost stunned to have received it. 'I felt a little out of place,' he told us, 'among so many intellectual giants. Me, the simple little country vet!' A photograph of the ceremony shows that characteristically vague and bemused expression on his face.

Almost five years later, in March 1984, he received a special British Tourist Authority Award for 'Helping to create a greater awareness throughout the world, of Britain's attractions'. At a ceremony in London, Sir Henry Marking, the BTA chairman, said: 'The name of James Herriot seems to leap out from every bookstall and every TV screen in the world . . . I am sure James Herriot never thought of himself as a travel promoter but "Herriot Country" is now well and truly established on the international tourist map, ranking in appeal alongside "Shakespeare Country" and "Burns Country". Through his work, James Herriot has helped to bring new prosperity and employment to a great county already so rich in literary heritage, history and beauty.'

Alfred Wight had certainly boosted the economy of North Yorkshire. Such was his fame by now, that small businesses began using his name. 'Herriot' cafés, guest houses and hotels sprang up to make good profits out of the tourists who continued to pour into the area. An advertisement for one hotel particularly amused him. A part of its brochure read, 'Welcome to "Herriot Country", the home of the world's most famous vet . . . No pets.'

Alf derived great satisfaction out of this boom in the tourist trade. Although some of the local people were not too pleased that their part of the world had become such a focus of attention, and turned an unfriendly eye towards so many strangers invading their patch, Alf often said, 'I have put money into a lot of pockets around here and that has to be a good thing.'

Others agreed with him. In April 1984, he was the first winner of the Yorkshire Salver – awarded in recognition of services to Yorkshire and its people. He received his award at a ceremony in Leeds and was nominated for 'Putting Yorkshire on the international map and bringing tourists, trade and employment as a result.'

Alf Wight was proud to receive such awards but some that gave him the greatest thrill were those bestowed on him by his own profession. As early as 1975, he had been made an honorary member of the British Veterinary Association and, seven years later, on 8 June 1982, he received his Fellowship of the Royal College of Veterinary Surgeons. This recognition, from the profession of which he was always particularly proud to be a member, meant a great deal to him. The words delivered that day by the College's President, Peter Hignett, were very perceptive:

'The Veterinary Profession owed Alf Wight a considerable debt of gratitude . . . not only because he had presented the profession to members of the public as a concerned and caring body of men and women but because he had never at any time sacrificed the respect of his colleagues for the popularity of public acclaim. The profession is proud of him and the way he has conducted himself in a situation which would have turned many a lesser man's head.'

In 1984, he received an honorary degree of Doctor of Veterinary Science from the University of Liverpool with, again, the emphasis being on his contribution to the image of his profession.

This tremendous enhancement of the popularity of his profession had been recognised very quickly by veterinarians in the USA. The American Veterinary Medical Association had honoured him as early as 1975, and he was particularly pleased to read a review of his work, in that same year, by Professor Eric Williams of the Oklahoma State University College of Veterinary Medicine.

Professor Williams, who was a veterinary practitioner in his native

Wales before emigrating in 1961, highlighted one aspect of James Herriot's writing – the authenticity of his accounts of veterinary life. This was something with which veterinarians all over the world could identify. In his review of *All Things Bright and Beautiful*, Professor Williams wrote:

'Here is a brilliant, honest, lucid day-by-day-and-night, exposition of the triumphs and despairing moments of veterinary practice. . . . James Herriot's honest revelations come as a much needed tonic and reassurance to a world which appears to be going mad when daily we are faced with crime, scandal and vanishing moral standards. I am overjoyed that my colleague portrays so well the bonds of trust and friendship with his clients which are the basis for a successful professional life . . . to aspiring veterinarians, here is a superb thesis on veterinary practice.'

Eric Williams remained a staunch supporter of my father and his effect upon the profession. For many years, he was the Editor of the *Bovine Practitioner*, the official journal of the American Association of Bovine Practitioners. In 1982, Alf was the very first recipient of honorary membership of that association. Although proud to receive such an honour he, as we expected, declined to visit America for the presentation – but it still took place. A delegation of the association, including Eric Williams, came to Yorkshire and presented Alf with his honour at the Three Tuns Hotel in Thirsk.

How he enjoyed that evening! He was able to swap experiences with his colleagues from the other side of the Atlantic and listen to the successes and failures that are common to veterinarians the world over.

Alf received countless offers to travel around the world and receive the many honours that kept coming his way but, by the beginning of the 1980s, he began to feel overwhelmed by his ever-increasing fame, and politely either refused them or received them in absentia. He even declined to appear on the front page of the enormously influential *Time* magazine – something that could have propelled his fame to even dizzier heights. He stuck to his regular excuse that he was 'one per cent author and ninety-nine per cent veterinary surgeon'.

From 1980, Sinclair and Wight was a five-person practice. With Alf's workload being lighter than it had been, he had plenty of time, had he so wished, to rush round the world furthering his image. The real reason for his reluctance was that he had had enough. He was determined to prevent the relentless publicity taking him over and he wanted, quite simply, to be left alone. Nothing was going to change his way of life, and it was his success in maintaining this ideal that was largely responsible for his continuing happiness in the face of an avalanche of publicity that could so easily have overwhelmed him.

Now Alf Wight, the retiring family man, was coming to a decision that would disappoint millions of his fans. He declared in 1981 that he would write no more books.

It was becoming impossible to completely dodge the spotlight. Everyone knew who he was. Tourists poured into the surgery while ever-bigger waves of fan mail were stuffed through his letter box. One envelope was addressed to 'James Herriot, Darrowby, Scotland'; it homed in on the unwilling celebrity like all the others.

In a newspaper article in July 1981, following an exhausting promotional tour of Britain after the publication of *The Lord God Made Them All*, Alf made the following statement:

'I feel I just have to escape. I'm nearly sixty-five and all I want is a bit of a rest. I've never been one for the limelight and now, all I want is to get back to normal. I want to spend more time with my grandchildren. I want to start enjoying again the things I used to enjoy, gardening and walking. I want to get involved again in the thing I do best, my work as a vet. At this very moment, the very mention of writing makes me want to scream.'

His massive literary success had brought him a sense of deep satisfaction but, for someone who did not enjoy the attendant publicity, it was becoming a burden. Life at home among his family and friends, and around the farms of North Yorkshire, was closer to his heart.

Alfred Wight fully appreciated the tremendous benefits writing had bestowed upon him but he was acutely aware of something else; he had been a happy man long before James Herriot walked into his life. He was, indeed, grateful for all James Herriot had done for him, but the time had now come to show him the door.

CHAPTER TWENTY-SEVEN

One of the greatest benefits bestowed upon Alf Wight by his friend James Herriot – financial security – was enhanced by the election to power of a Conservative government in 1979. Its lower levels of personal taxation meant that Alf could retain a higher proportion of his earnings so, by 1981, he could consider himself a millionaire.

He was not an inspired businessman but, more importantly, he had common sense. He had no desire to stretch his financial horizons to the limit, while words like 'Off-shore Investments' and 'Split Capital Trusts' meant little to him. A distrust of the stockmarket, coupled with a cautious approach to investing money, led to his missing out on the great share bull market of the 1980s, but he lost little sleep over this. He retained his distrust of 'smart deals' and 'unbeatable offers' until the end, and a favourite expression was 'Beware glossy brochures!'

He certainly derived a great deal of pleasure out of his money and was very generous with it. From as early as 1977, he worked in the practice for only £2,000 per year – a change that benefited not only myself, but Donald Sinclair, too. In one year, after deducting car expenses from his practice profits, he was left with little over £1,000 to show for a year's veterinary work.

Bob Rickaby, his accountant, was aghast. 'Alf, you have worked for a whole year for the practice and you have earned no more than you did in 1946!'

His response was to simply shrug his shoulders. 'Don't worry about it Bob. I couldn't care less!'

Never a greedy man, he was, throughout his life, amazed at the lack of generosity he sometimes observed in others. Although unable to identify with it, he could see the funny side.

I remember him telling me, many years ago, of a visit he made to a shop in Thirsk to buy some fireworks. He asked for some rockets.

Another customer overheard his request and leaned towards him. 'Don't buy rockets, Mr Wight,' he whispered, 'they 'ave a good selection o' Roman candles an' some right good Catherine wheels, at good prices an' all!'

Alf was mystified. 'My kids love to see rockets soaring into the sky. Anyway, what's wrong with the rockets?'

The man eased in closer. 'Why, everyone else can see 'em!'

Alf could now do the things he wanted, without wondering whether he could afford it. More holidays and meals out with friends figured very prominently. The Thirsk area abounds with fine eating places and Alf always enjoyed his food. Having a cosmopolitan taste, he frequented a wide variety of restaurants but he was never happier than when seated in a Chinese or Indian restaurant having already consumed a few pints of good Yorkshire ale at a nearby pub.

Two of Alf's greatest friends, Alex Taylor and Brian Sinclair, brightened his life during the 1980s. In 1981, Alex retired from his job in the north of Scotland and, three years later, he and Lynne decided to spend their retirement near Thirsk. Alf was delighted; to have his oldest friend living so close was a wonderful bonus.

Alex's company was a constant source of enjoyment. From their very first days together in Glasgow, he had always had the capacity to make Alf laugh and, with Joan and Lynne being such good friends, this they all continued to do for ten more years.

Another who never failed to paralyse Alf with laughter was, of course, Brian Sinclair, James Herriot's Tristan. Following Brian's retirement in 1977, the two of them met almost every Thursday afternoon in Harrogate. Gordon Rae's death in 1973 had cast a shadow over my father's Thursday afternoons, but the appearance of the smiling face of Brian among the crowded bookshelves of W. H. Smith – their favourite meeting place – added, once again, that extra touch of pleasure to those visits to his favourite town. Over several cups of coffee, they would reminisce back to the old days in Thirsk, and Alf would revel in the endless funny stories from Brian's seemingly inexhaustible repertoire.

One person who especially lightened Alf's life at this time was his daughter. Never were two people closer than Rosie and her father. Since she lived next door, it was natural they should spend a great deal of time with each other – and they had much in common. Holidays, both at home and abroad, hundreds of miles of dog-walking and regular visits to football matches were favourite occupations. Rosie supplied a constant source of interest and conversation to brighten his days and, in the last years of his life, she – with her mother – would provide him with tremendous support.

Alf stated that one reason for turning his back on the limelight was a desire to spend more time with his grandchildren. By 1981, he had four of them. Emma, Rosie's daughter, was born in 1975, and my son, Nicholas, in 1976. The dedication in *James Herriot's Yorkshire* is to both of them.

My daughter, Zoe, arrived in 1980 and my third child, Katrina, in 1981. *The Lord God Made Them All* is dedicated to Zoe, and Katrina received her recognition in *James Herriot's Dog Stories*.

Alf saw far more of Emma than his other grandchildren. Rosie, as a single parent, received tremendous assistance from her parents in raising Emma, who grew to regard her grandfather more as a father. He was a truly dedicated grandfather and had great patience with her as a small child – walking for miles to pick wild flowers, or reading to her from countless storybooks.

He derived, as many grandfathers do, great pleasure from his grandchildren. All my children are very musical, and I am sorry that my father, who had such an appreciation of music, could not have lived a little longer to hear their performances on the piano, cello and trumpet. He did, however, have the satisfaction of hearing Nicholas play the piano, shortly before winning the St Peter's School music prize, and he heard Zoe playing the trumpet in a school orchestral performance of the Grand March from *Aida*.

On the way home from that performance, he kept repeating, 'Was that *really* Zoe playing those clear notes?' I could not help feeling a little grateful to my children; through their playing, the pleasure they gave to their grandfather compensated somewhat for the agony he had had to endure, listening to the comical attempts from his own son all those years ago.

In 1981, another character bounced into Alf Wight's life – a self-willed, whiskery-faced Border Terrier called Bodie. After the death of his black Labrador, Dan, no time was wasted in finding another four-legged companion and Bodie, Alf's last dog, was one with a personality all his own. Alf, who had always admired the Border Terrier as a breed, was a happy man on the day he finally owned one.

Bodie, always regarded as a bit of a show-off, was a very photogenic dog who posed rather like a ham actor in the many photographs taken of him with Alf. The tendency to display a haughty superiority over others of his kind was illustrated many times – especially on meeting other male dogs when he would sail into the attack without a second thought. For the first time in his life, the world's most famous vet needed a lead before he dared to venture forth with his dog.

Another reason for the lead was that this unpredictable little creature could take off into the distance with alarming suddenness. I remember, one late October afternoon, walking with my father, Bodie and my own little Heeler bitch over the wild moorland at the head of Coverdale. Suddenly, Bodie – without any warning – took off like a rocket and disappeared.

After a full half-hour, we were still desperately shouting his name – strangled cries of 'Bodd ... ee! ... Bodd ... ee!' issuing from our cupped hands. Darkness was almost upon us as I scanned the bleak horizon, hearing only the sound of my father's voice which, by then, was no more than a hoarse croak, We had just about given up hope when I finally spotted a small brown form zooming around the opposite hillside in the gathering gloom. I ran over and was able to catch him as he was demolishing a decomposing rabbit.

Bodie's greatest pal was Rosie's dog, Polly, a sweet-tempered yellow Labrador who has, like her effervescent little friend, appeared on many photographs with James Herriot. Bodie was the perfect gentleman towards Polly, always allowing her first grab at the biscuits that my father carried in his pocket during his many walks with the two dogs. Looking at Bodie standing patiently beside Polly, it was hard to believe that this was the hooligan who tore into every male dog unfortunate enough to cross his path.

In his later years, Bodie's energy consumption dipped dramatically and he became bone idle, refusing to go on his daily walks. He was not, however, allowed to become a total degenerate; Alf carried him under his arm on the outward half of his walk leaving Bodie little choice but to return home under his own steam.

Despite these antisocial traits, he was a most appealing dog and his whiskery little face accompanied Alf everywhere. He would sit patiently with him for hours – under his chair while he wrote in his study, or by his side as he watched television. Although frequently referring to his little friend as 'a bit of a screwball', Alf loved him dearly.

Bodie, who outlived his master by eighteen months, was a much appreciated companion for Joan in the period following Alf's death. In 1996 he developed kidney failure and I had the sad task of putting him to sleep. As I did so, I could not help casting my mind back to my father's very first dog, Don, who also succumbed to kidney failure, fifty-three years previously. Alfred Wight's first and last dogs – two different characters in their own way, both of them difficult at times, but each one a loyal and wonderful companion.

Alf stated on a television programme in 1990, 'Vets can be just as silly about their own dogs as the fussiest of our clients!' This statement certainly describes Alf Wight himself. A large proportion of his life was dedicated to the well-being of his own dogs; whenever outings or holidays were planned, their welfare always received first consideration. Only under the most extreme circumstances would he board any of them in kennels, and the only hotels in Great Britain that Alf and Joan would stay at were ones that catered for dogs. Almost everywhere they went, a hairy face or two was invariably in attendance.

Throughout his years in practice, he was told many times by his clients, 'You'd better get this dog better, Mr Wight. My missus thinks a lot more about him than she does of me!' Being a dog lover himself, he could see the grain of truth in the statement. James Herriot writes movingly about the unique bond between people and their pets. The real man, Alf Wight, could have stepped out of any one of those stories.

By the mid 1980s, the practice of Sinclair and Wight was undergoing massive change, with the small animal work becoming increasingly important. By this time, Alf, who was almost seventy years old was, not unnaturally, finding it difficult to keep up with modern techniques, and left the more complicated treatments to his younger colleagues. He was still extremely interested, however, and would watch operations he had no intention of attempting himself. Despite the realisation that he was beginning to lose touch with the rapid advances within his profession, he still had his following among the practice clients; his thoughtful and caring approach to every case – the timeless attribute of the popular veterinary surgeon – was appreciated as much as ever.

Something else in the practice was timeless – Donald Sinclair. Now that Alf was no longer dependent upon veterinary work for a living, he could take a more relaxed view of his partner's eccentricities at 23 Kirkgate.

One afternoon, during an unusually quiet day, Donald said to him, 'Alfred, I don't know why we pay all these young assistants. Life is not so hard as it used to be, and I could run this place single-handed.'

Alf raised his eyebrows. He knew his partner well but this sounded something special. 'Single-handed? Are you quite sure about that, Donald?' he replied, well aware that veterinary practice was one of the most unpredictable of professions.

'Absolutely, Alfred! There is certainly no need for *you* to come in tomorrow. Take a day off!'

'Are you really sure?'

'Yes, Alfred, go home!'

The following morning, the practice of Sinclair and Wight was desperately short of staff. Early-morning emergencies had meant that the other two assistants and I were out on call, and to complete the picture, our secretary was off with flu. At ten minutes to nine, Donald Sinclair calmly walked into a quiet, empty veterinary surgery.

The 'single-handed' vet was soon to have some company. Within minutes, the office of 23 Kirkgate was transformed into a maelstrom of activity, with a long succession of customers filing in through the door while, to add to the noise, the telephone roared into life as repeated emergencies flowed into the practice.

We kept the diary of that day as a special memento and it makes interesting reading. In the space of about half an hour, over twenty telephone calls were logged, in addition to the several patients in the surgery needing urgent attention. The calls included lambings, broken legs, a horse to put down, a foal with a torn eye, several cases to stitch and, all the time, the office continued to fill with people and animals – one of which, a crazy Afghan dog, barked wildly and incessantly. The writing in the day-book becomes increasingly spidery and illegible as the pages are turned. The one-man show was under pressure.

It was not long before the telephone rang in Alf's house. He could almost sense the tension as he lifted the receiver.

'Alfred?' there was a desperate quality in his partner's voice.

'Yes, Donald?' he replied.

'Come down – *now*!'

'Why, Donald? Is it busy down there?' The sound of shouting and barking dogs could clearly be heard.

'*Busy?!* The place is going mad!'

'Are you alone? Is there no one to help you?'

The voice rose to a shriek, 'Not a bloody soul!'

These were days of reflection for Alf. He was observing the gradual disappearance of veterinary practice as he used to know it. The small family farms were steadily going out of business, to be incorporated into larger estates, and the old stone houses bought up by wealthy people to be converted into fine, modernised homes. The old Yorkshire that he knew – the way of life he had preserved in print – was on the way to becoming history.

One of Donald Sinclair's stock phrases was 'I do not like change', but there was little that Alf and he could do about the march of progress within both the veterinary profession and the farming industry. They were especially sad to see the steady replacement of the old cow byres with modern milking parlours; more efficient perhaps, but cold and austere. Both men remembered with affection the delicious sensation of warmth on walking into a cow byre on a cold winter's day, with the rows of contented cows, the gentle chink of the chains around their necks, and the sweet, delectable smell of hay. But Alf knew this was a nostalgic picture that was fast becoming a thing of the past.

There were some timeless relics in the surgery that were soon to be destined for replacement. One day, while in the office at 23 Kirkgate, my wife Gill pointed towards the window. 'Those curtains!' she exclaimed in a loud voice.

She was referring to the old 'red' velvet curtains that had hung beside the office window for almost forty years. They were tattered and frayed, with part of the fabric so thin that it was possible to see straight through them out onto the street beyond.

My father was seated at the desk. 'Curtains?' he replied slowly.

'Yes! They are utterly appalling!'

'Oh?' He gazed affectionately at them for a moment. He had spent so many years in their company that it seemed unthinkable to replace them. Her comments, however, had struck home and they were soon heading for the bonfire.

He told me about this shortly afterwards. 'Gill's absolutely right, of course,' he said. 'They were pretty awful, but they were old friends to me. They were here when I first came to Thirsk all those years ago!'

He paused a moment before pointing to our telephone exchange box on the shelf next to the desk. 'It's that thing over there that worries me far more than the old curtains!'

'Why's that?'

'It's about three inches from my ear when I sit at the desk and I don't trust it.'

'Why?'

'It hums . . . and it's hot!'

The days of the telephone box, too, were numbered. The practice of Sinclair and Wight had begun to enter the modern age.

His life in practice was changing by the day, but it was the passing of many of his old farming clients – men, women and their families, that he had come to know so well – that was especially saddening. As the years rolled by, it was easy to forget that he, too, was getting older.

One day, he was standing outside the surgery with a farmer as a funeral procession passed by on its way to St Mary's at the end of Kirkgate. 'There goes poor old Tom! I'm sorry to see him go,' he said quietly.

'Aye,' replied the farmer. He then turned gloomily towards my father and said, 'They're pickin' 'em out of our pen now, Alf!' Alf had always looked very young for his years, and had a youthful outlook upon life, but this chastening expression gave him food for thought.

A less sombre reminder of the advancing years hit him shortly afterwards. One afternoon in 1982, a woman flagged him down as he was driving home through his village. He opened the car window. 'Mr Wight,' she said, 'it's about the old folks party in the village hall.'

'Why, yes, of course,' Alf responded, reaching into his pocket for some money. He had always supported this occasion. 'Just hang on a minute and I'll give you something towards it.'

The woman produced two tickets. 'Nay, I don't want no money! These are for you. Enjoy the party!'

Alf Wight had, for as long as I can remember, always referred to his parents and other elderly people as 'the old folks'. Now, he was one of them.

In general, Alf had enjoyed good health throughout his working life but, with the passing of time inevitably starting to assert itself, he began, when he was about sixty-two years old, to experience angina attacks. As several of his relatives had died of heart attacks, these symptoms were a source of considerable concern but, as it turned out, none of us need have worried; the angina was not to prove the threat we had imagined.

A few years later, in the summer of 1981, he experienced the agony of renal colic. These attacks, initiated by the presence of large kidney stones, were the most excruciating experiences he had ever endured and, for a long time, a bottle of painkilling tablets was his constant companion. He suffered pain intermittently for about a year before the problem was eventually resolved.

He spent a week in hospital at the time of his worst attacks, but he was always convinced that he cured it himself by flushing the stones from his system one evening in the Three Tuns Hotel in Thirsk – assisted by the intake of large volumes of McEwans Export ale.

It was not only Alf's health that was under siege in 1981. Both Donald and Brian were experiencing serious problems of their own and Donald's was of his own doing; he stepped in front of a speeding motor cycle in Thirsk market place and suffered a severe fracture of the lower leg.

He was admitted to the Friarage Hospital in Northallerton where the sister in charge of the ward soon informed Alf that his partner was, without doubt, the worst patient she had ever had. Considering the chaos he engendered in the practice over the years, I can well believe that was true.

I visited him one day in hospital. I had been beside his bed for no more than a minute before he said, 'Thanks for coming, Jim. You can go home now! Goodbye!'

True to his impatient nature, Donald discharged himself from the hospital very quickly. He purchased an automatic car, and stomped around the practice carrying an enormous plaster cast on his leg for almost a year. A simple thing like a broken leg was not going to prevent 'Siegfried' from enriching the atmosphere of 23 Kirkgate.

If Donald's experience had been inconvenient, Brian's was far more serious. He began to lose weight in 1980 before eventually being admitted to hospital for tests, but he continued to deteriorate steadily throughout 1981. I visited him early in 1982 in St James's Hospital in Leeds, and was appalled to see his condition. Gone were the chubby cheeks and the twinkling eyes; instead, I saw a gaunt, sunken-eyed skeleton – someone I barely recognised. As I drove home that day, I wondered whether I would ever see Uncle Brian again. The outlook was bleak; no one had been able to diagnose his condition and all treatment had failed. These were desperate times for his family; Brian's wife, Sheila – like Brian, a very close friend of Alf and Joan – could only watch helplessly as her husband continued to waste away before her eyes.

Donald, horrified, watching his brother visibly fading, was convinced that he was going to die. One morning, he strode purposefully into the surgery.

'Alfred!' he said. 'I have had a word with Sheila and I'm going to Leeds to bring Brian home!'

'Why?' Alf asked.

Donald was in sombre mood. He thought a great deal of his younger brother, and the past weeks had been an ordeal. 'He's getting no better, he's going to die, and I want him to die at home . . . with dignity.'

At that time, a consultant had been specially drafted in to help in the diagnosis of Brian's illness. My father's response was immediate. He, too, was deeply depressed by Brian's dreadful condition but he felt that Donald was wrong.

'He is your brother, Donald, and it is your decision, but I think you are making a mistake.'

Donald paced around the floor, wrestling with his dilemma, but his mind was made up. 'No, I can't stand watching him going to nothing. He's coming home!'

Alf was never one to interfere, but the life of one of his greatest friends was at stake and he had to say more. 'He's only got one chance, Donald, and it is in that hospital. This new consultant just might come up with something. If Brian comes home, he will definitely die. Please leave him where he is. It's his only hope.'

Donald, racked with emotion, said no more and left the room.

Donald Sinclair was a man with strong convictions – and was never one to listen readily to others. There was just one man, however, to whom he would sometimes listen, and that man was Alfred Wight. Having, from their very earliest days together, had a high regard for his partner's opinions, he once again took his advice. Brian stayed where he was.

No one really unravelled the mystery of Brian's condition (thought to be an obscure pituitary gland disorder) but shortly after that conversation in the surgery, a broadside of drugs was thrown at him, following which, remarkably, he began to improve. The drugs were gradually withdrawn as he got better but he had to remain on steroids for the rest of his days – a small price to pay for several more happy years.

Another of Alf's great friends whose health had given cause for concern was Denton Pette. Having suffered a stroke in 1977, from which he never fully recovered, he died in July 1981. Eve and Denton were some of the first to be asked to the many dinners and celebrations following Alf's success as a writer, Denton's open and cheerful countenance being a vital contribution to their enjoyment. Both Alf and Joan felt his death keenly.

Shortly before Denton was taken ill, he and Alf watched a fiercely contested football match between Sunderland and Middlesbrough. Being a fanatical supporter of Middlesbrough – and an equally dedicated hater of Alf's club, Sunderland – we often wondered whether the excitement of that occasion had contributed towards his stroke.

Denton was another of those great characters who crossed Alf's life and, as Granville Bennett, will be remembered with great affection by many Herriot fans. Alf wrote of his great friend in the *Veterinary Record*, 'He was a true friend to a host of people who will remember him with gratitude for the happiness he brought into their lives.' He did, indeed, bring happiness and laughter into many people's lives.

In 1981, Alf's regular visits to Glasgow drew to a close. For over ten years, he had spent either Christmas or New Year with his mother – and he and other members of the family visited her often at other times of the year. In the summer of that year, however, she was moved down to a nursing-home in Harrogate and was there until her peaceful death the following December. As Alf stood at her funeral, his mind swept back to myriad memories of his mother who had sacrificed so much to ensure that her son realised his ambition to become a veterinary surgeon. She had been a force to be reckoned with in her time but she left us all with memories of gratitude and respect.

Her pride in the achievements of her son had led to many embarrassing moments. 'Now, you know who I am?' she would say to total strangers. 'I am James Herriot's mother! Let me introduce you to him. Alf ... Alf ... ?' Like his father before him, Alf would have quietly disappeared from the scene.

It is beyond the scope of this book to describe the many hilarious episodes concerning my grandmother, but the old lady who looked after me so well during my university years is remembered by the whole family with great affection.

Alf Wight may have been at the very height of his success in the early 1980s, but the loss of those close to him at that time, together with his own bout of ill-health and Brian's serious illness, were a constant reminder that time was passing by. As he looked back over the previous ten years of achievement, he had reason to feel proud of what he had done; and as such a careful and compassionate man, he had – apart

from the brief upset with Donald over the characterisation of Siegfried
– managed to achieve his success without hurting the feelings of others
in any way.

From his very beginnings as a writer, Alf's primary concern was that
he should not upset his friends but, in 1981, he was reminded again that
the trappings of fame can take on an unpleasant guise when he fell out
with his old friend, Eddie Straiton.

In the summer of 1981, Eddie was summoned to appear in front of
the Disciplinary Committee of the Royal College of Veterinary Surgeons
on a charge of bringing discredit on the profession. He had stated on BBC
Radio's 'Jimmy Young Show' that he had 'raced' his young assistants to
see who could neuter a cat the fastest and that, during one race, he had
inadvertently opened up one supposedly female cat only to discover
that it was a tom.

With Eddie having always been an extrovert character, this story was
meant as a humorous aside but there were those who did not see the
funny side of it. On 29 September 1981, he found himself, not for the
first time, standing before the Disciplinary Committee. Some character
witnesses would clearly have helped Eddie's case and an obvious one
was Alf Wight – one of Eddie's oldest and most respected friends – but
Alf had declined to appear on his behalf.

In Graham Lord's biography of James Herriot, it says that Eddie
claims that the reason Alf did not support him was because he was due
to be made a Fellow of the Royal College of Veterinary Surgeons – an
extremely high honour in the British veterinary profession – and that
he did not want to jeopardise this in any way.

I am greatly saddened that Eddie could think so poorly of one of his
most loyal friends; one who had stood by him steadfastly through an
eventful and sometimes controversial career. Not only was Alf not
informed of his impending honour until two months *after* Eddie's
disciplinary hearing, but he would never have sacrificed the interests
of one of his friends for the purpose of adding yet another honour to
his already impressive list.

Alf, in fact, disapproved of Eddie's remarks about the 'spay race'. He
considered that his friend – by asserting that he could neuter a cat with
lightning speed – had demeaned the skills of his profession. Knowing
well that spaying a cat is not always the simple and straightforward
operation that many believe it to be, he felt that Eddie's remarks
had been in poor taste. However, Eddie Straiton had been a staunch

supporter of the profession in the past, and Alf would have appeared on his behalf to stress his many admirable qualities had he not been, at that time, tormented with the pain of renal colic.

Eddie, deeply upset over Alf's hesitation in offering him his support, and under immense pressure not only from the impending disciplinary hearing but also from the imminent death of his wife from terminal cancer, allowed his feelings to spill over with the use of some very strong words. His impulsive and misguided accusations very sadly inflicted irreparable damage on a friendship that stretched back to their days together in Glasgow.

I well remember the effect of Eddie's words on my father. Through no fault of his own, Alf Wight was being accused of insensitivity and selfishness by one of his oldest friends. Feelings of intense hurt and disbelief were followed by anger and a determination that he would never have anything to do with Eddie again.

Eddie quickly realised his mistake. More than one letter of apology arrived on Alf's doorstep but my father was unrepentant. I remember arguing with him at the time, reminding him that they had been friends for so long, but I was unable to influence him. Once something was fixed in his mind, he could be a very difficult man to reason with.

As the years rolled by, I am happy to say that his attitude softened towards Eddie and they resumed correspondence. Eddie's hurtful accusations, however, were the ultimate reason for Alf Wight's refusal to appear at the disciplinary hearing in 1981.

The years from 1981 to 1985 were a non-productive time for James Herriot the author – during which he savoured the rest from the pressures of writing – but the size of the 'James Herriot Industry' decreed that he could never completely return to the relative obscurity of veterinary surgeon and family man. His name was now too big. Fan mail continued to pour into his house and, with the name of James Herriot producing visions of pound and dollar notes for many, he was under gentle but constant pressure from his main publishers in England and America to produce another book.

Alf had little interest in how much money he, or other people, would make out of his return to the typewriter, but writing by now was in his blood. He was all too aware of the massive changes he had observed within his profession and the heartfelt desire to preserve that old way of life in print was beginning to assert itself again.

'I consider that I am a very fortunate man,' he said. 'I have lived through the golden years of veterinary practice – without doubt, the best years.' The new age of rules, regulations and paperwork did not appeal to him, and a deepening nostalgia for his rapidly disappearing world was to result in his sitting, once again, in his study, tapping out more stories.

I remember this as a time of concern for my mother. Realising that her husband was not getting any younger, but also aware that she could not stop him pursuing the interest that had now become ingrained in his soul, she urged him to refrain from the deadlines of delivery dates and to take things a little more slowly.

During the glitzy years of the 1970s, at which time she often accompanied him on his public engagements, many people believed that she was the dominant force of the pair – displaying an apparently unenthusiastic attitude to his success. Knowing him better than anyone, and fully acquainted with his sensitive nature, Joan was simply trying to protect him from the avalanche of publicity that she feared would have a detrimental effect on him. In doing so, she conveyed a false impression of the relationship between her and her husband. Throughout their long marriage, it was he who made all the major decisions in the family.

Realising that Alf could never fully turn his back on writing, she was not really surprised when, in 1986, he allowed himself to be persuaded to write some material for a new television series of 'All Creatures Great and Small.' He had, in fact, written a few stories already – the list of 'headings' for ever at his side – and this latest approach was enough to rekindle his eagerness to begin writing again in earnest. The result of this was, eventually, the publication in 1992 of his final book, *Every Living Thing*. James Herriot was, once again, standing by the side of Alfred Wight.

CHAPTER TWENTY-EIGHT

In the years between his finally finishing *The Lord God Made Them All* in 1980, and beginning serious work on *Every Living Thing* in 1988, Alfred Wight wrote no other books. Despite this, several new ones were to appear under his name during that period. As well as *The Best of James Herriot*, which was published in 1982, *James Herriot's Dog Stories* was published in 1986, together with a succession of children's books that came out throughout the 1980s, the last one being produced in 1991.

The book of dog stories was a compilation taken from the previously published books. The introduction is of particular interest as it is the only time that James Herriot gave his many fans an insight into his life as a young man at Glasgow Veterinary College – where the dog was regarded in those days as a species of minor importance, and the cat was hardly ever mentioned! How different it is for the veterinary student of today.

For the children's books, as with *Dog Stories*, Alf had little to write. Each one was a story taken from the earlier Herriot works – brightly illustrated to appeal to the younger generation. In consultation with his editor, Jenny Dereham, some of these stories were quite heavily re-written, with the more explicit veterinary descriptions considerably toned down and the stories trimmed or stretched out to the appropriate length. They were an inspired idea. Each one was based on a specific character – Blossom the cow, Oscar the cat and Bonny the cart-horse amongst them. One of the books, *The Christmas Day Kitten*, was an international best-seller. James Herriot's gift of bestowing endearing qualities on these engaging creatures, together with the colourful illustrations by the talented artists, Peter Barrett and Ruth Brown, guaranteed their success.

As the children's books began to appear, Alf received countless letters from his many young fans, as well as drawings of their favourite animal characters. James Herriot's easy style appealed to all readers, from the discerning professional reviewer down to the young child in primary school. His fan club truly encompassed all readers great and small.

Two of those stories have special significance for me, as it was I who was responsible, many years previously, for providing the material within them. *Moses the Kitten* was the first in the series for children, and was published in 1984. It originated from a visit I paid to Terry Potter's farm at Baldersby near Thirsk. I had just completed my work on the farm when Ted, the pigman, said to me, 'Come over 'ere. Ah've summat ter show ther!'

He took me over to a pen in which there was a huge sow suckling an enormous litter of shiny, pink piglets. It was not this scene of utter contentment that impressed me the most, however; I was astonished to see that one of the piglets in the row was black!

'Ah bet yer've never seen a pig like yon little youth!' said Ted. ''Ave a closer look!'

The 'piglet' was, to my amazement, a cat – and a fairly well-grown one, too. 'Ah found 'im wanderin' about t'buildings 'alf dead wi' cold an' Ah thowt Ah'd give 'im a chance an Ah put 'im ter this auld sow,' said Ted. 'Look at 'im now! By! 'E 'as done well!' The sleek, black coat was one of the finest I had ever seen on a cat. The creature gave me a cursory glance before elbowing his way deeper into the row of fat, feasting piglets.

I recounted this experience to my father over lunch. He suddenly stopped eating and sprang upstairs for his notebook. 'Another story to add to the James Herriot collection,' he said, after returning to his knife and fork.

Another of the children's books, *Blossom Comes Home*, had its origins on the farm of my father's old friend and client, Arthur Dand. Arthur showed me an old cow that was quite obviously past her productive life. She had been a wonderful cow in her time but her overgrown feet, protruding hip bones and sagging udder displayed stark evidence of a lifetime of high milk production.

Arthur had always been very attached to her but, one day, having realised that he could no longer afford to keep her, he had reluctantly come to the decision to send her for slaughter. As he gazed after the wagon that was taking his old friend away on her final journey, she put her head out of the back of the trailer before emitting a long and plaintive cry. The sight of the old cow, staring out for the last time at the pastures she loved, was too much for Arthur. He leapt into his car, raced after the slaughterman's wagon, flagged it down and, within minutes, Blossom was back home.

'She may be no use to me any more,' he said to me, 'but she's going to spend the rest of her days right here!'

After I told this story to my father, the notebook was, once again, produced. 'Keep feeding me the information,' he said, 'and I'll do the rest!'

A farming friend of mine told me, a year or two ago, 'It's a "numbers game" now.' He was absolutely right. Gone are the days of calling cows Buttercup and Bluebell; they are simply part of an enterprise driven on, as with most things, by money. In today's commercially dominated world there is less room for sentiment although that is not to say that the modern farmer is without feeling for his stock.

I was to observe an example of the close bond between the farmer and his animals on a recent visit to a hill farm.

The visit – to a farm in the Hambleton Hills to put down an old cow – was an unusual one. As the farmer took me over to her, he requested that I perform the job as painlessly as possible. She was lying on a bed of straw, unable to rise, and she presented a pitiful picture. Her taut, wrinkled skin, gentle, grey face and pure white eyelashes – all hallmarks of a very old animal – caught my attention immediately. As she turned her head slowly towards me, she seemed to be appealing for help, but I knew that I could do little for her.

'This auld girl is twenty-two year auld,' said the farmer unsteadily. 'She's been a grand cow in 'er time an' Ah want 'er to go quietly.' He paused a moment as he composed himself. 'Can yer inject 'er to put 'er away? Ah don't want 'er to be shot.'

Shooting is a swift and humane way to destroy an animal but he was adamant that she received an injection, despite the fact that this would render her carcass unsuitable for dog meat, let alone human consumption. It was a most unusual request.

'Of course, George,' I replied, 'but you do realise that this means you will receive absolutely nothing for her?'

'No matter,' he replied, walking over to the old animal and stroking her head gently. His voice trembled with emotion. 'She owes me nowt! Yer don't mind if Ah don't watch, der yer?'

His eyes filled with tears as he turned away to walk into the house. As the old cow collapsed back onto the straw after the injection, I felt that I had suddenly stepped back into James Herriot's world – and visions of Blossom the Cow swam before my eyes. The 'numbers game' had not completely taken over, not quite.

Although not actually writing more books at this time, Alf was never allowed to forget that he was a famous author, and he still spent a large part of his time in the Kirkgate surgery signing books for his many fans. Years of this activity eventually resulted in his developing arthritis in his hand and, in the last few years of his life, he spent time at home signing, at his own pace, countless self-adhesive labels that his admirers could stick into their books.

Occasionally, during long signing sessions in the surgery waiting-room, he had to politely decline requests for wordy dedications. One day, following yet another such session, he returned to the office, smiling.

'Most people are quite satisfied with "Best Wishes, James Herriot",' he said, 'but one guy has just asked for "To Ray, Elsie, Kevin, Holly and Louise on your first ever visit to Yorkshire. With very best wishes, James Herriot, Helen, Siegfried and all the rest at Skeldale House!" I made the excuse that the old hand would probably seize up half-way through!'

The new television series of 'All Creatures Great and Small', for which he began to write new material in 1986, proved to be every bit as popular as the previous one; it ran on into 1990 and finally ended with a 'Christmas Special' in December of that year. The only change in the cast was the introduction of Lynda Bellingham, who played the part of Helen in place of Carol Drinkwater. She, like the previous two actresses who had portrayed Joan, stepped into the role perfectly.

This series did not ring with quite the same authenticity as the earlier ones. Having virtually exhausted James Herriot's original material, extra writers were needed – with some of the later episodes only loosely based upon his stories. Nevertheless, they were, as with the previous series, a great success – and were watched and enjoyed by millions.

New characters appeared for this series, many of whom were to reappear in Alf's final book, *Every Living Thing* – a title suggested by his American publisher, Tom McCormack. This book, published in 1992, was one my father thoroughly enjoyed writing. Not only did he now have a word processor to assist him – to quote his favourite expression at the time, 'How did I ever manage without one?' – but he told very few people that he had intentions of writing another book. This meant he could proceed in his own time without the pressure of any deadlines.

'I don't want anyone looking over my shoulder holding a contract,' he told me. 'I can write this book in my own time, so please don't tell anyone what I am doing!'

It took him, in fact, over four years to complete the book, finally unleashing the news to his publishers in 1991. This was received with delight, as well as surprise, and the book, like its predecessors, soon shot into the UK best-seller lists.

He had some arguments with Tom McCormack about several of the chapters which Tom wished to change – but he was, by now, such a confident author that he allowed very little tampering with his original manuscript. Despite these minor disagreements, the result was a book that sold 650,000 copies in hardback in America in the first six weeks, and remained on the *New York Times* best-seller lists for almost eight months.

Every Living Thing introduces the reader to Calum Buchanan, 'the vet with t' badger, and based on the real-life character, Brian Nettleton, Alf's memorable assistant. Brian was such a fascinating personality that Calum figures in eleven of the fifty-two chapters and his vibrant character strides through the pages of the book, bringing back many happy memories for all of us who knew him.

Sadly, Brian was never to read about himself in *Every Living Thing*. More than twenty years after leaving the practice, he came back to see us in Thirsk, where we were delighted to be reacquainted with the piercing dark eyes, the flamboyant moustache and the ageless enthusiasm of a man who had changed little over the years. We were so pleased to have had that opportunity to have spoken to him; less than one month later, Brian was tragically killed in a car accident in Canada. It is good to know that, in Calum Buchanan, he will live forever.

Another assistant who appears in *Every Living Thing* was my father's very first one, John Crooks. In this single case, he used John's real name – an indication of the lasting respect and friendship the two men enjoyed for so many years.

I, too, come into the book, and it was a revealing experience for me as I read it, wide-eyed, for the first time. In chapter 7, he writes about Rosie and me accompanying our father on his rounds when we were small:

She always ran to get things for me while Jimmy invariably walked. Often, in the middle of a case, I'd say, 'Fetch me another syringe, Jimmy,' and my son would stroll out to the car, often whistling, perfectly relaxed ... And I have often noticed that now, when he is a highly experienced veterinary surgeon, he still doesn't hurry.

After reading this, I began to analyse myself, and quickly realised that my father was quite right! Excepting occasions when a sudden burst of activity is desperately needed, I have never been one to hurry along life's road, but it was not until I read this chapter that I was aware of this aspect of my character. Donald Sinclair must have had a similar experience, many years before, when the character of Siegfried Farnon first sprang out at him from the pages of *If Only They Could Talk*, and I was reminded of the old quotation from the Scottish poet, Robert Burns – one of my father's favourites: 'O wad some Power the giftie gie us, To see oursels as others see us!'

There have been occasions when people have stated that James Herriot was 'a writer of *fiction*', questioning the veracity of some of the stories and claiming that Herriot had simply used well-worn jokes to his own advantage.

In chapter 26, there is a story about a character called Arnold Braithwaite. He is a boastful man who regales everyone in the local pub with stories of the many celebrities whom he claims to know personally. No one, of course, believes him but Arnold has the last laugh when, at the end of a hockey match in Darrowby, several of the players, many of them internationals, walk over to shake Arnold by the hand.

This story is based on a memorable individual by the name of Harry Bulmer. Harry was often to be found propping up the bars of Thirsk where he always had a good audience for his seemingly exaggerated anecdotes. He was regarded by most of the locals as a 'right romancer', with very few believing his pretentions to be on first-name terms with countless celebrities. There was one story he often told about the time he lent his bat to Len Hutton whose own had broken during an innings of a Test Match at Headingley. Harry gleefully reported that, when the great batsman returned the bat, after successfully scoring over a hundred runs, he had done so with the words, 'Thanks, Harry! That's a lovely bit of wood you have there.'

There was, however, a surprise in store for the locals who continually poked fun at him. A major hockey match was due to be played at the Thirsk Athletic Ground and Harry assured everyone that he knew many of the players, some of them internationals from other parts of the country. Everyone thought that Harry would be exposed for the story-teller they believed him to be but, on the day of the match, there was more than one open mouth as several of the players approached him after the game with cries of 'Look! It's Harry! How are you, Harry?' No one laughed quite so hard at Harry's stories following that day at the Thirsk Athletic Ground.

Alf, in fact, enjoyed Harry's company. He was a man with a great knowledge of cricket and football – subjects that Alf never tired of discussing. There is a photograph, taken in the Three Tuns Hotel, of Harry – his head back and mouth open – regaling everyone with yet another fantastic tale. Standing by his side is Alf, eyes wide with delight. One can almost see him making a mental 'heading' for his notebook.

The story of Arnold Braithwaite in *Every Living Thing* – one that has been described as simply being based on a hoary old joke – is just another example of the factual basis behind James Herriot's stories. Not only would Alf have been the first to acknowledge that many of his stories were embellished – and that he changed the dates of a number of the incidents within them – but he accepted with equanimity the fact that there was a significant number of people who were unimpressed with his writing. To be referred to as a writer of fiction, however, is something to which he would most certainly have taken exception.

Throughout the second part of the 1980s, Alf was able to observe, from a comparative distance, the onward roll of the 'James Herriot Industry'. Despite the Herriot-mania all around him, he succeeded in adopting a very low profile and, apart from devotedly signing thousands of books for his fans (to whom he always felt very grateful), his involvement with the celebrity status was minimal. He spoke little about it; indeed, he could sometimes appear to be almost bored by the whole thing.

He had additional opportunities to make big money by allowing his name to be used to endorse items such as pet feeds, but he would not countenance the idea. Displaying sparse interest in anything that smacked of commercialism, that old glazed look would come over his eyes whenever any strategies for making more money were suggested to him.

One of the most striking features of my father's character was his 'vagueness'. On many occasions when I was speaking to him, his glassy expression betrayed a mind that was racing away elsewhere. Some subjects that particularly failed to interest him could send him spinning off into a virtually hypnotic state within seconds, and it could be a frustrating experience trying to re-establish contact.

One thing, however, that was always guaranteed to erase any film in front of his eyes was the mention of football – especially anything to do with Sunderland Football Club. Having become a season ticket holder, he rarely missed a home game, and the club were quick to realise that they had a major personality as a supporter.

In 1991, having bought some shares in the club, he received a letter. It was one that meant a great deal to him. The directors were offering him the honorary position of Life President of the club 'in view of your lifelong support and loyalty and your assistance and contribution in so many ways . . . You will be entitled to two free directors' box seats, car park and the use of the 100 club for all home games . . . We believe that you certainly deserve this recognition.'

He regarded this honour as one of the most satisfying he had ever received, but he declined the free seats in the directors' boxes, preferring instead to cheer his team along from among the crowd as he had always done on countless happy occasions throughout his life.

His football team always provided him with wonderful entertainment. They were never a boring team, with almost every match seeming to have some significance as they continually strived for either honours or sheer survival at the end of every season. In 1992, he had the great satisfaction of seeing Sunderland again perform in the FA Cup Final at Wembley. He arranged seats at the stadium for a party of his family and friends where, despite the team losing to Liverpool, everyone enjoyed a memorable day out.

The club has now moved to a brand new stadium in Sunderland, where the chairman, Bob Murray, and his directors, have set aside a room within it called 'The James Herriot Room'. Pictures of Alf Wight adorn the walls, one photograph depicting his own football-playing days at Glasgow Veterinary College. The club has not forgotten the famous author whose pleasure at the success of his team on the football field was never to take second place to that engendered by his astonishing literary achievements.

After his death, a tribute appeared in the north-east newspaper, the *Sunday Sun*, ending with the words: 'For here was a genuine football man who truly understood the agony and the ecstasy of being a Sunderland supporter. A caring, compassionate man who loved all creatures great and small ... and all creatures red and white.'

More honours were heaped on him during the late 1980s and early 1990s. In 1987, the Humane Society of the United States decided to make an annual award, in his name, to a person selected by the society for conveying concern and compassion for animals.

In April 1989, he was invited to address the World Small Animal Veterinary Association Congress that was to be held that year in Harrogate. This was a great honour that he could not refuse – and it was conveniently close to home – but he was full of trepidation about speaking in front of so many of his learned colleagues from all over the world. He rose to the occasion and, true to his character, delivered a speech full of modest references to his own life as a veterinarian. His self-effacing speech did little to prevent his being the star of the show. When it came to expertise and knowledge of the latest techniques in modern veterinary practice, he was, indeed, among his betters that day but, as every veterinarian there realised, Alfred Wight's own contribution towards the image of his profession was unequalled.

This was summed up by the highly respected American veterinarian, Dr Stephen Ettinger. He stated in a television interview around that time: 'Without any doubt, James Herriot is the most famous veterinarian in the world and, perhaps, the most respected. He has shown the world that the veterinarian is the gentle doctor.'

In 1992, Alf became the first recipient of the British Veterinary Association's new Chiron Award for 'exceptional service to the veterinary profession' although, by then, he had retired from veterinary practice. At the end of 1989, feeling that he had little to contribute to the everyday activities within the practice – and suffering the indignity one day of being helped out of a pig pen by two youthful farm lads – he considered it might be time to call it a day. Finding it increasingly difficult to keep pace with the huge changes occurring within his profession, he knew that he was making the right decision.

He was, by then, seventy-three years old and had completed almost fifty years working as a veterinary surgeon. There had been times of triumph and disaster, days of happiness and despair but, above all, there had been years of working at a job that had never failed to fascinate him.

Donald Sinclair, although five years older than Alf, steadfastly refused to retire and continued to 'work' on until 1991, but that year, he suffered a stroke which effectively ended his days at 23 Kirkgate. Incredibly – although perhaps unsurprisingly – Donald, who was admitted to hospital, paralysed down one side of his body, discharged himself nine hours later. He made a complete recovery from that stroke and, within a few months was, aged over eighty, once again walking about in the hills above Southwoods Hall.

Donald, living so close to Alf, was always around to brighten his life, as was Alex Taylor, but the late 1980s had seen the demise of more old friends, among them, one of his greatest: Brian Sinclair.

On 13 December 1988, Brian, who had been suffering for some time from circulatory problems, succumbed to a heart attack. Brian, who had always rejoiced in his portrayal as Tristan, had been one of Alf's closest friends and it was a bleak day for him when he learned that he would never again look on his open and laughing face. It was a mournful occasion for us all as we attended his funeral in Harrogate where many tears were shed for such a popular and respected man.

I remember, so well, my father talking about his great friend shortly after his death. He spoke with great feeling about the man with whom he had spent so many uplifting hours of fun and laughter.

'Brian may have been a practical joker for most of his life,' he said, 'but, beneath that hilarious veneer, was a sound and dependable man. A true friend in every sense of the word.'

Brian's death was a blow to so many people. A day or two after he died, I went to see Donald at his house and expressed my sorrow at his brother's death.

He looked away from me before gazing out at the rolling hills around Southwoods Hall. 'Thank you, Jim,' he replied. 'It's a bugger, isn't it?'

He lowered his head and wept quietly. As I consoled him, I realised that those frightful shouting sessions of the 1940s, described so vividly in the books of James Herriot, had surely hidden Donald's true feelings for his wayward but so engaging younger brother.

They were sad times for me, too, to see my father's friends fade away but December 1991 would be a month his family would never forget. It was when we learned that the days of Alfred Wight were numbered. For this man – with whom, over a period of more than fifty years as a father, friend and professional colleague, I had never had a cross word – the end was in sight.

CHAPTER TWENTY-NINE

Early one Friday morning in December 1991, I received a telephone call from Malcolm Whittaker, the consultant surgeon at the Friarage Hospital, Northallerton. He had some bleak news to convey.

The previous month, Alf had suffered a severe rectal bleed while walking in the field behind his house and, following some tests, had eventually been admitted to hospital for an operation. During the pre-operative examination, Mr Whittaker had noticed a small lump in Alf's groin.

'What is that?' he had asked.

'I think it is just a benign lipoma, Malcolm,' Alf had replied.

The consultant had not been so sure. 'How long has it been there?'

'Oh, for several months.'

Having felt again around the nameless growth, Malcolm Whittaker had suggested a little further investigation. His suspicions had been well-founded. Upon analysis, the 'harmless lipoma' had proved a far different proposition. It was, in fact, an adenocarcinoma – a secondary cancerous spread from some primary source within the body which, after tissue-typing, was thought to be the prostate gland.

All this was transmitted to me over the telephone that day and it hit me like an express train. Having been informed that my mother and sister had already been told, I asked the consultant the obvious question.

'How long has he got to live?'

'It's difficult to say,' replied the surgeon, whose voice then acquired a lighter note as if trying to lift my feelings, 'but he could have as much as three years.'

Having thanked Malcolm for his call, I sat down at the table and buried my head in my hands. Tears ran down my face as I tried to grasp the reality of the situation. Three years! I kept thinking of the time span, hoping fervently that it would be longer.

In retrospect, we should have suspected something like this, as Alf had shown symptoms of prostatic problems for some time. He had begun to have difficulty passing urine some five years previously and, around 1988, had started passing blood. His prostate gland had been investigated, found to be enlarged and attempts made to remove it. Biopsies taken at the time, however, showed no sign of malignancy, and we had assumed it was just a benign enlargement. Our optimism, however, was now dashed.

I visited him at his home, Mirebeck, shortly after I had received the dread news. He seemed to have taken it very calmly and was hopeful that the treatment he was about to undergo could stave off the cancer for a considerable period of time.

'It's wonderful what can be done nowadays,' he said. 'I'm just going to carry on enjoying myself and looking forward.' We were delighted with his optimistic approach but Rosie, being a doctor, knew the harsh facts. Three years was the *most* that we could hope for.

Before leaving Mirebeck that day, I glanced back into the sitting-room. As I looked at him, seated in front of his word processor whilst putting the final touches to *Every Living Thing*, I wondered whether I would have had the courage to launch straight back into work should I have just received such fearful news. He had begun his long battle against cancer in the only way he knew; he was going to keep busy and continue being active for as long as he possibly could.

He was put onto a series of monthly Zoladex injections, and both chemotherapy and radiotherapy started. Throughout 1992, he did not appear to deteriorate much, although the radiotherapy and the Zoladex made him feel sick for a while. This stoical acceptance of his condition, together with the apparent stabilisation of the symptoms, gave us hope that, perhaps, the cancer could indeed be beaten.

He gave Joan a terrible fright early in 1993 when, having suffered a sudden cardiac arrythmia followed by a cerebral anoxia, he lost consciousness and collapsed on the floor of the kitchen. Having immediately rung Rosie, she was then at a loss as to how to help him. She cradled his head in her arms which, in fact, could have resulted in his death by further restricting the blood flow to his head. The prompt arrival of Rosie, who laid him out flat on the floor, saved the day, after which, following a short stay in hospital, he made a complete recovery.

In fact, 1993 was quite a good year for Alf, with the satisfaction of seeing *Every Living Thing* continuing to prove just as successful as his previous books. Later that year, however, having begun to experience symptoms of the carcinoma spreading, he found himself in hospital again where he underwent yet another operation. This was the beginning of grimmer times ahead – a time when we realised that the cancer, having kept a misleadingly low profile for almost two years, was beginning to show its true colours.

The brave veneer that he put on his condition cracked only once, in the autumn of 1993, when my mother rang me to say, 'Please come up to see your father. I am at a loss to know what to do with him.'

This was an unusual call. My mother had, very admirably, borne the burden of watching her husband slowly deteriorate, rarely asking for any assistance, but he had become so severely depressed that she now felt powerless to help him. As I sat with him that day, I was reminded of the bad times over thirty years before, when he had suffered his great depression. He now looked at me, once again, with eyes that were a million miles away.

The position was very difficult for Rosie and me. We tried to cheer him up by talking about his hugely successful life, and the joy that he had given so many people, but we were looking into the eyes of a sensitive and private man, a sincere and deeply caring person with a complex personality which, despite our close relationship with him for so many years, we had never managed to fully comprehend. There had always been a part of my father that I had never really reached and, as I looked at him that day, I knew that I had little chance of unlocking the secret emotions that were troubling him. He had kept his innermost feelings to himself for so many years; why should he release them now?

He assured us that the cause of his despondency was not the fact that his days were coming to an end. I could well believe this. Although without any strong religious faith to help him through those difficult times, he had not only always been a selfless man whose concern for the welfare of others transcended any thoughts of his own well-being, but he, himself, had no fear of death. During his short speech on the occasion of his Golden Wedding anniversary in 1991, he had spoken of his good fortune in having enjoyed such a fascinating and fruitful life, dominated by good health and a supportive wife and family, and that, whatever the future held for him, life had already dealt him a more-than-generous hand. Realising that he still held that philosophy – and that he faced his future with a calm inevitability – I knew that the cause of his present depression was far deeper than just the bleak prospect of his worsening health. Those same mysterious emotions that had always simmered beneath the surface were, once again, exerting their influence.

'What *is* the matter, Dad?' I asked. Well out of my depth, such a banal and basic question was delivered more in hope than expectation.

He continued staring out of the window and I remember his answer well. 'I have this feeling of profound and overwhelming melancholy.' He would say no more.

As an illustration of his deeply sensitive nature, I remember his giving an interview to Lynda Lee-Potter of the *Daily Mail*. Having had a few drinks beforehand, he gave her an unusually frank interview in which he poured out his feelings, expressing especially his intense and lasting love for Rosie and Emma. On reading this in the paper, he was deeply upset. He said that he could not remember releasing his feelings so effusively; it was certainly not in his nature to do so.

It was a full two years later before I fully realised how much this had affected him. I had driven him, my mother and Gill up into the Dales for the day and he and I were walking along a green track high above Summerlodge in Swaledale. In those final years of his life, there was nothing he liked better than being driven across to the Yorkshire Dales; he would sit quietly looking at the places that must have rekindled so many happy memories and, despite his advanced condition, he would always insist on getting out of the car for a moment or two to take in the wild scenery and drink in the fresh, clean air.

On this particular day, it was a short walk; with the cancer, by then, having a firm hold upon his body, he could move only with difficulty. Suddenly, he stopped and put his finger to his lips.

'Jim, I want to ask you a question,' he said, looking down at the winding valley of the river Swale, far below. I said nothing, but allowed him to continue.

He did not look directly at me as he spoke. 'Tell me . . . have you ever felt that I thought more about Rosie than you?'

I hesitated, as the question had taken me completely by surprise. There followed a silence, broken only by the sound of the wind coursing across the high moorland. I looked straight at him but he continued to stare into the distance, waiting quietly for my response.

'Such a thought has never even crossed my mind, Dad,' I replied.

He nodded his head but no words escaped his lips. The subject was never to be raised again.

As we climbed back into the car, I thought to myself, 'For how long has he been tormented with this? How much of an effort was it to ask that question?'

1994 was a bad year. We watched him lose weight steadily as his condition became worse, and many were shocked at his appearance during the final year of his life.

From the very first day that the cancer had been diagnosed, he expressed a wish that we should tell no one about it, but it did not take a qualified doctor to know the cause of his weight loss in those last few months. It was as though he was still trying to keep his troubles to himself – but everyone knew by then.

He received a bad setback in June 1994. A sheep had strayed into his garden and, in trying to escape, shot past him and knocked him to the ground. Alf sustained a fracture of the femur and, once more, he found himself in hospital where he underwent an operation to pin his leg. It was another period of severe pain and one that he could well have done without. I have always admired the way he bore the distressing conditions that afflicted him in his last few years. Not only did the invasive cancer induce severe pain, but he had to endure the post-operative distress following each operation. He had managed to steer clear of hospitals for so many years but, at that time, he seemed to be in and out of them regularly.

For reasons that I am unable to explain, the melancholic feeling that descended on him in 1993 did not last long, and the final three years of his life were certainly not ones entirely of gloom. He acquired satellite television which proved to be a boon. He watched hours of sport – especially cricket, football and tennis – and, in addition, he was able to enjoy many of the old comedy programmes that were re-shown. His favourite comedians were a joy for him during his years of pain, and still managed to bring tears of laughter to his eyes.

Despite the dark rumbling clouds of cancer, his outlook on life remained generally very positive as he continued to occupy himself fully. The continuing barrage of fan mail certainly kept him busy and he tried to reply to all the letters that arrived at the house. He walked, gardened and read, just as he had done all his life.

His mind remained very alert and he continued to take an active interest in the world around him. Not only were his favourite newspapers read every day from cover to cover as he maintained his lifelong interest in current affairs, but he continued reading books almost until the end. When I went to see him a few days before he died, he was reading one of his all-time favourites, *The Historical Romances of Sir Arthur Conan Doyle*.

'What a wonderful book this is,' he said. 'I have read it umpteen times and it still grabs me! That is the mark of a great writer.'

'I think that *your* books have grabbed a few people as well, Dad!' I replied, wondering whether he realised that his books, like those of one of his most favourite authors, had been and would be, read over and over again and that many of his fans regarded him, too, as a fine writer?

I am not sure that he did. Throughout his life, he always said he was just an average writer who had struck lucky. Rosie and I went to see him regularly, and in the last few weeks of his life, he was often to be found stretched out on the sofa watching the television, but he always gathered the strength to get to his feet. When we left, he always came to see us off with the words, 'Thanks for coming.'

Thanks for coming?! It was as though he regarded our visits as a duty we felt that we had to perform. We both told him that his company was, and always had been, very special to us; whether this self-effacing man really believed us or not, we shall never know.

His failing health did little to slow down the onward march of the 'James Herriot Industry', and in 1993 a video, 'James Herriot's Yorkshire', was produced. It featured Christopher Timothy in some of James Herriot's favourite locations, and 22,000 copies were sold by Christmas of that year. The health of James Herriot may have been declining but his name stood as strongly as ever.

The video was launched at a private showing in Leeds that October, where the title of 'Honorary Yorkshireman' was conferred on Alf Wight and Chris Timothy. As my father was not well enough to attend the reception, I accepted the honour on his behalf. He was very proud to have been recognised by his adopted county – one that he had done so much for.

In 1994, his book *James Herriot's Cat Stories* was published. This book was like the earlier *James Herriot's Dog Stories* in that it contained chapters taken from all his previous books, but otherwise it was very different. For a start, it was a small book and very short. The reason for this was simple – Alf had not written many stories about cats. Jenny Dereham at Michael Joseph read through the first seven books and found only five or six stories which would be suitable; the rest, she said, had a tendency to be about splattered cats arriving on the operating table after being hit by cars. Since the stories were to be illustrated throughout in colour, these were not very suitable. When she heard that Alf was writing one more book, *Every Living Thing*, she asked if he could possibly write some 'nice' cat stories which could go into the later compilation. Alf, as always, helpfully agreed.

Although a great lover of cats, Alf only ever owned a few and then for short periods; this meant that he referred less to them in his writings than to his dogs. He had them as a boy in Glasgow, and he and Joan once had a sweet little tabby called Topsy but, after her premature death, they did not get another for over ten years until Oscar arrived.

Oscar was a stray who turned up on the doorstep of Rowardennan but he was with us for only a few weeks before he simply disappeared one night, never to be seen again. Alf endured the agony, like so many of his clients when their own cats disappeared, of being left with the heart-rending uncertainty of their final demise. He later wrote a story about a cat called Oscar (which was also turned into one of the children's books) and he gave the story a happier ending.

No more cats were to share Alf's life until, in his final few years, two little wild strays took up residence in the log shed behind their house in Thirlby. After months of patient coaxing, he finally managed to get close enough to stroke them, but they never became house cats as Bodie pursued them relentlessly. These two, named Ollie and Ginny, made star appearances in both *Every Living Thing* and *James Herriot's Cat Stories*.

Cat Stories had exquisite water-colour illustrations by Lesley Holmes. It was a runaway bestseller, especially in the USA where it sold more copies than any other previous James Herriot book, staying on the *New York Times* best-seller list for almost six months. After Alf's death, two companion volumes were published: *James Herriot's Favourite Dog Stories* and *James Herriot's Yorkshire Stories*. Both were again illustrated by Lesley Holmes, who not only portrayed the animals so well but captured the magic of the Yorkshire landscape.

Towards the end of 1994, Alf received what was to be the last tribute paid to him prior to his death. It was also one that meant a great deal to him.

In November, he received a letter from the Dean of the University of Glasgow Veterinary School, Professor Norman Wright, in which it was proposed that the new library in the school be named the 'James Herriot Library'. It was in recognition of his services to the profession and the letter went on to say that the Veterinary School was very proud that James Herriot was a graduate of Glasgow and could they have permission to use his name? Deeply moved by this proposed dedication, he replied in his letter of acceptance: 'I regard this as the greatest honour to ever have been bestowed upon me.'

He had many tributes paid to him throughout a distinguished veterinary and literary career, but his response to this final appreciation revealed an undiminished affection for the city in which he spent the formative years of his life.

As well as this final tribute from his old Alma Mater, visits to Sunderland to watch his football team served to lighten his flickering last few weeks. Despite his rapidly failing strength, he insisted on following the fortunes of his team – his last visit being in early 1995, only one month prior to his death. He needed constant support when making his way painfully to his seat in the stand, and Joan expressed great concern that he might suffer a final collapse, but Rosie was very positive about it.

'It is a great thing that he still wants to go,' she told her. 'At a time like this, we should give him as much pleasure as possible and, anyway, should he die at Roker Park, what better place to end his life.' We knew that he had not long to go and I have often thought, since his death, that had he not died at home, he would have approved of ending his days in the company of the red and white stripes – and less than a mile away from Brandling Street where he first looked upon the world all those years ago in 1916.

Right up until a few days before his death, he refused to give in – remaining determinedly mobile by walking around the house and garden every day. I have strong feelings of consolation that, remarkably, he was a bed-ridden invalid for no more than two days. If ever a man fought cancer with fortitude, it was my father.

Many people helped him through his illness. He was so grateful to the doctors and nursing staff at the Friarage Hospital that he gave a very substantial sum of money towards the acquisition of a scanner for the hospital, in appreciation of the wonderful treatment he had received.

Joan, of course, was the person who helped him more than any other. She bore the distress of watching him slowly but surely deteriorate, managing the vast majority of the work in tending to his needs. From their first days together, she had supported him through good times and bad – most of them good – but never would her devotion to her husband shine more brightly than during those final, dark months of his life.

Alex and Lynne Taylor, too, played their part in brightening his days while Donald Sinclair still managed to make him smile as he had done, unconsciously, since they first met all those years before.

The last thing he ever wrote was the foreword to a small booklet about the White Horse Association. It was at the request of one of his friends, a farming client called Fred Banks, who was president of the association. The famous White Horse, which had been cut into the hillside above the village of Kilburn in 1857, is a vivid landmark which, together with the Whitestone Cliffs, formed a majestic background to Alf's work in veterinary practice for almost fifty years. He wrote the foreword only three days before he died, saying in it:

I had spent only a few days in Thirsk when . . . I had one of my most delightful surprises – my first sight of the White Horse of Kilburn. I find it difficult to describe the thrill I felt at the time and it is something which has remained with me over the years. As a young man, it was one of my favourite outings to take my young children to sit up there on the moorland grass and savour what must be one of the finest panoramic views in England; fifty miles of chequered fields stretching away to the long bulk of the Pennines.

Alf's love of writing, and his willingness to cooperate with so many requests, had lasted up until his final days.

In late January 1995, on one of my visits to his house, I was alarmed at his appearance. He was always a man who hid his pain from others, but he could not conceal it this time. He told me that he had an excruciatingly sore point in his back. There was little to see, but to touch the area provoked an agonised response.

The last time that I had seen something similar was many years before, when I had visited my old Chemistry master, John Ward, who was suffering from lung cancer that had finally spread to his spine. He was in tremendous pain and died only a day or two after my visit.

As I spoke to my father that day, I could not help but notice the similarity and I knew that the end was near. I left his house with one thought on my mind – a fervent hope that he would not have to suffer for much longer. He had been through some bad days and it could only get worse.

I did not have to wait long. On the evening of Tuesday, 21 February, unable to remain on his feet, he was confined to his bed. A syringe pump, delivering morphine into his system, helped to ease the pain.

I visited him that evening but his usually lively conversation was absent. Heavily drugged, he could only talk slowly and unsteadily but still managed a smile or two as Alex Taylor reminded him of some of the countless funny times they had shared in their youth.

He deteriorated steadily throughout the following day and soon could no longer speak coherently. I remember, having at one point sat gently on the side of his bed, being startled to see him gasp and grimace with pain. Knowing how stoically he had borne his disease for so long, I wondered what sort of horrendous assault his body had endured to generate such a reaction.

I saw him alive for the last time on the evening of 22 February and I knew the end was very close. I shot out to a farm visit the following morning before visiting him again, but he was dead before I arrived at the house. My mother, Rosie and Emma were by his side when he died.

As I looked at him that morning, I felt utterly alone. The shock of his death was not as severe as the one I had received over three years earlier when I first knew he had cancer; instead, I felt nothing but an overwhelming sorrow, and I knew that my life would never be quite the same again. On that morning of 23 February 1995, the world lost its best-loved veterinary surgeon. His family, and those close to him, lost a great deal more.

CHAPTER THIRTY

Within twenty-four hours of my father's death, letters of condolence began to arrive on his family's doorsteps. My mother received literally thousands, while Rosie and I had hundreds to read. They came not only from close friends, but from clients of the practice, local people who had felt privileged to know him personally, former assistants who had worked at 23 Kirkgate, many members of the veterinary profession and, of course, admirers of his work from all over the world. With so many, including those who knew him only through his writing, feeling that they, too, had lost a great friend, we were not alone with our thoughts at that time.

As he would have wished, the funeral – conducted one week later by the Reverend Toddy Hoare in the nearby village of Felixkirk – was a quiet family affair. As well as the immediate family, only Donald Sinclair, his daughter Janet, Alex and Lynne Taylor, their daughter, Lynne, too, and Eve Pette, Denton's widow, were present. A small service was conducted afterwards at the crematorium in Darlington.

On the day after he died, the James Herriot Library was due to be opened at the Veterinary School in Glasgow. I had agreed, at the time that it was proposed to him three months before, to accept the honour on his behalf.

When they heard the sad news, the Veterinary School suggested that the ceremony be postponed, but I felt that it was something that I had to do. This was the last honour he had received – and one that had meant so much to him. It presented me with an emotionally challenging task but I had a feeling of great pride when I saw my father's portrait looking, almost poignantly, across the library and out of the window to the Campsie Fells where he had spent so many happy hours in his youth.

On either side of the plaque in the James Herriot Library there are two photographs, one of Alfred Wight and the other of Sir William Weipers – two very famous graduates who made enormous contributions to their profession. I have often wondered what my father would have thought, all those years ago as an insignificant student at

Glasgow Veterinary College, had he known that one day he would be pictured alongside the man he had so admired? I feel sure that he would have been a very proud man had he lived just those few more days to have seen it.

My low spirits following my father's last days were not improved by the death, shortly afterwards, of Donald Sinclair. Donald had had an emotionally turbulent few months. The death of my father had hit him so hard that he could not summon up the courage to speak to me until a full week later. When he did, it was in typical fashion. The telephone rang in my house and when I lifted the receiver, a voice said, simply, 'Jim?'

'Yes, Donald?' I replied.

There was a long pause, which was unusual for such an impatient man. When he spoke, his voice was unsteady. 'I'm fed up about your dad.'

I had no chance to respond. The telephone went dead. It had been the briefest of conversations but I knew how he felt – and what he had tried to say.

Worse was to come Donald's way. His wife, Audrey, who had been failing for some time, died that June, three and a half months after my father. Donald had been totally devoted to her throughout their fifty-two years together and, following this devastating blow, he seemed like a lost person, drained of all his humour and vitality.

One day not long after Audrey's death, he walked into the surgery in Kirkgate and stood beside me as I operated on a dog. He had always been a startlingly thin man but, on that day, he seemed to have shrunk to almost nothing. That gloriously volatile aura of eccentricity was absent as he stood quietly, observing me at work. The wonderful character I had known for so many years bore little resemblance to the old man at my side, and I felt a pang of sympathy as I glanced at his face – one that betrayed an air of loneliness and hopelessness.

Suddenly, he broke his silence. 'Jim, do you mind if I come and live here?' he asked quietly.

'These premises belong to you,' I said, 'so you can do what you like.'

'I have always wanted to live in that top flat. Looking over Thirsk to the hills – the one where your mother and father had their first home,' he continued.

'Yes, there is something very nice about the flat,' I replied. Although

I knew that Donald had become depressed living alone in Southwoods Hall, I hardly expected him to move house at such an advanced age.

'I'll move in tomorrow,' he said, and disappeared as suddenly as he had arrived. It was the last time that I saw Donald Sinclair alive.

The following morning he was found, at Southwoods Hall, in a coma. He had taken an overdose of barbiturate, leaving a scribbly note indicating his desire not to be resuscitated. His children, Alan and Janet, were soon by his side and, after five days of heartache and uncertainty, he finally passed peacefully away.

Surprisingly, for such a mercurial man as Donald, his death was, in some ways, predictable. Many years ago, when I first joined the practice, Donald had once talked to me about his enthusiasm for voluntary euthanasia, with the conversation eventually becoming focused upon death and final resting places. For a young man of twenty-four, it was a rather disconcerting subject.

One of Donald's acquaintances had recently suddenly died at a Rotary Club luncheon, and I had said to him, 'It's not a bad way to go really. He was a good age and he died at his favourite pastime – eating!'

'I know a better way,' Donald had said.

'Oh? And what is that?'

'Shot in the back of the head, at ninety, by a jealous husband!'

He had continued our slightly morbid discussion with, 'When I die, Jim, I would like to be buried at Southwoods in that field below the pine wood near the third gate, the one that looks up to the hill.'

'I think that would be a splendid place,' I had replied.

'Do you really think so?'

'Yes, I do!'

I have never forgotten his spontaneous reply, 'I'll save you a place next to me!'

Donald did not die at the hand of a jealous husband; his own hands were to finally end his life as he remained true to his lifelong dedication to voluntary euthanasia.

In July, a memorial service for Donald and Audrey was held in Thirsk church, followed by refreshments at Southwoods Hall. I felt heavy-hearted as I gazed around the grounds of the fine old house where I had spent such good times but, as my eyes rested upon that grass field below the pine wood at the foot of the hill, I could not help smiling as memories of Donald flooded back. He had been one of the most engaging, as well as impossible, men I had known. The traumas that we experienced while trying to persuade him to retire when well over eighty are still fresh in my mind, and many people have said that no one but Alf could have worked with him for so long, but he did have many special qualities.

Only weeks before my father died, I had been listening to him reminiscing about his life with Donald. I asked him how he had coped with Donald's eccentricities over all their years together, and he paused before replying.

'I don't really know,' he said, 'but I can tell you this. We had a hell of a lot of laughs together and, from the first day I met him, I knew that he would never stab me in the back.'

He became immersed in thought again before continuing with his appraisal of his unforgettable partner. His face broke into a smile. 'Where else would I have found such a wonderful character to weave into my stories?'

My own overriding memories of Donald are of a man who would never do anyone a wrong turn, a loyal colleague who did not speak a single disparaging word of his fellow professionals, and one with that endearing quality of total humility. He would regale us all, not with his successes, but his failures, and I remember his words, 'If there are mistakes to be made, I have made them. Listen to me and you will learn a lot!'

Above all, I remember a man forever surrounded with an aura of humour and laughter, and whenever I think of him, I am smiling – just as my father did throughout his many years spent enriched by the company of one of the most colourful and entertaining men he had ever known.

Although my father's quiet and unassuming funeral was something that he himself would have wished for, we realised that many others, besides his own family, would want the opportunity to pay their final respects. With these thoughts foremost in our minds, the memorial service for James Alfred Wight was planned during the summer of 1995 and, on 20 October, eight months after his death, the service was held in the magnificent setting of York Minster. This occasion was a memorable one, not only for the moving service and the glorious music, but for the humour rather than the sadness that pervaded the Minster that day. It was truly a celebration of a life that had meant so much to so many.

Chris Timothy and Robert Hardy both gave virtuoso performances reading extracts from James Herriot and P. G. Wodehouse. I gave an address, Rosie's daughter, Emma, gave a reading, and Alex Taylor delivered a moving tribute to his oldest friend. My daughter, Zoe, played the trumpet during the ceremony, as part of the St Peter's School brass group, part of which included a fanfare on the theme music from 'All Creatures Great and Small', especially composed by the St Peter's School Music Master, Andrew Wright.

Two thousand three hundred people attended the service. There were representatives from the Royal College of Veterinary Surgeons, the British Veterinary Association and many other professional bodies. His associates from the publishing world were represented, as well as countless friends, clients of the practice, and former assistants who had learned so much from him in those first uncertain steps in their careers.

Fans of his books came from all over the country, from Scotland to the south coast of England – many to honour a man who, simply through his writing, was someone they felt they really knew. My father had remained astonished by his success until the very end of his life and I, too, found the occasion at the Minster almost too much to grasp. I felt privileged to have had a father who had achieved so much from modest beginnings – one to whom so many people had poured into York Minster to pay their respects.

No one, of course, felt the death of my father more keenly than my mother. She had not only lost a husband whom she had loved dearly, but one with whom she had shared a happy and fulfilling life. The quiet house after his death was something that she – as with so many other widowed people – had to learn to live with. Fortunately, in Bodie, the Border Terrier, she still had someone to look after, but this ceased when I put Bodie to sleep eighteen months after my father's death.

My mother, however, is not alone. My father was almost never without a dog, but the only animal that still stalks around his house is a tortoiseshell cat called Cheeky. Around the time I had the sad task of putting Bodie to sleep, this gentle little creature arrived on the doorstep completely uninvited. I have always regarded this as a remarkably providential incident and my mother has proved to be every bit as soft with her animals as her husband had been.

This fortunate cat, as well as being fed as well as Alf Wight had been, has a centrally-heated porch in which to sleep. The man who installed it could not quite believe what he was doing. 'I've been asked to do some funny things in my time,' he said to me, 'but central heating . . . for a *cat*?'

In March 1996, the veterinary practice of Sinclair and Wight moved from 23 Kirkgate to new premises on the outskirts of Thirsk. The old house may have had a certain charm but with its long winding corridors, lack of space and inadequate parking facilities, it had become a liability. We, literally, had to move to survive.

The famous ivy-covered front with its red door, however, has been preserved as a memorial to James Herriot. In 1996, the local authority, Hambleton District Council, purchased the premises and have converted it into a visitor centre under the title of 'The World of James Herriot'. Skeldale House will live on for many years to come and it is a fitting tribute by the people of North Yorkshire to one of its most distinguished adopted sons.

I have been asked many times whether my father would have approved of such a massive venture being undertaken in his name – especially as he always tended to shun publicity. He was always grateful for the low-key approach to his success by the local people, but they have revealed their true feelings for him in their overwhelming support for the project. I know that he would have been greatly moved by this gesture of appreciation and respect.

The innumerable tributes paid to Alfred Wight since his death reveal that respect and affection in which he was held by so many throughout the world.

One, from the *Chicago Tribune* – the newspaper that was so influential in igniting the name of James Herriot across the United States of America in 1973 – echoed the feelings of so many people. Mary Ann Grossman wrote:

People often ask me about my favourite author, probably expecting me to wax eloquent about Proust or Shakespeare, so I used to be a little embarrassed to honestly reply, 'James Herriot'. But not any more. After spending a wonderful weekend re-reading Herriot's books, I realized that his writing has everything; finely-drawn and colorful characters, empathy for humans and animals, a good story set in a gentler time, humor, respect for uneducated but hard-working people and an appreciation of the land.

But there's something else in Herriot's writing that I can't quite articulate, a glow of decency that makes people want to be better humans. I guess we'd call it spirituality these days, this profound belief of Herriot's that humans are linked to all animals, whether they be calves he helped birth or pampered pets like Tricki Woo, Mrs Pumphrey's lovable but overfed Pekingese.

Alf's own profession did not forget the massive contribution that his writing had made in enhancing the image of the veterinary surgeon. His very first veterinary assistant, John Crooks, wrote his obituary in the *Veterinary Record* in March 1995:

James Alfred Wight, under his pen name James Herriot, was without doubt the world's best known and best loved veterinary surgeon. Others better qualified than I, will, no doubt, write of his literary prowess and of his immense contribution to the veterinary profession, as shown by the honours showered on him throughout the world. These accolades he accepted with great pleasure yet total humility.

The last time we met, only a few months before his death, he expressed genuine, slightly bemused astonishment at his phenomenal literary success. I treasure our last conversation which was all of veterinary matters, of difficult cases and hilarious situations. Although he qualified in the pre-antibiotic era, Alf quickly adapted to new medicines, new anaesthetics, new surgical techniques and laboratory procedures. When I joined the practice in 1951 I found it totally up to date. He had small, sensitive hands and was especially skilled in obstetrical work. Although not long in the arm, it was amazing with what facility he dealt with difficult calvings in the large shorthorn cows common in the 1950s. One farmer said to me, 'Aye, 'e got us a grand live calf – but 'e near 'ad to climb in to get it out!' He handled animals with gentleness and firmness. He loved his work.

The world will remember a brilliant and modest writer who made his profession famous. Those of us who had the privilege of working with him, and those who had the privilege of having their animals cared for by him, will remember him for what he most aspired to be – a highly competent and caring veterinary surgeon.

I know that my father would have approved of these words. Throughout his years of literary fame, he persistently regarded himself as primarily a veterinary surgeon, but the praise heaped upon him was always in reference to his achievements as a writer. John's appreciation of his friend as a vet – a view shared by many others – would have meant a great deal to him.

Alf Wight – and his alter ego, James Herriot – was, indeed, loved by many, but it is important to remember that he was only one of countless veterinarians the world over who are every bit as caring and compassionate as he was. He had, however, that extra quality – the gift of the born raconteur which resulted in his becoming the best ambassador the veterinary profession could have ever hoped for. It was through his writing that he displayed to the world the veterinary surgeons' dedication and concern for their patients – in effect, humanising his profession in a world becoming increasingly motivated purely by profit and efficiency. As a veterinary surgeon, he was just one of many others who shared his fine qualities.

As a writer, however, he stood alone. The warmth and affection that he felt for others, animal and human, flowed from his pen as though writing were an outlet for the emotions that he felt deeply but could never fully unleash. It is within the pages of James Herriot's books that the real character of Alfred Wight is to be found.

It could be argued that being the son of such a man could have posed serious problems in trying to live up to his example – but it has not. Alfred Wight never cast a shadow over his family. Far from being in awe of his massive success, his modest approach to it ensured that I have felt nothing but pride in the achievements of a man whom I considered simply as a great friend and father rather than a world-famous personality.

If my father had a gravestone, I would inscribe upon it the advice that we, as his younger colleagues, heard from him time and again: 'It's not what you do, it's the way that you do it.'

I am unable to inscribe this lasting tribute to him as he has no headstone; instead, his ashes are scattered among the moorland grass at the top of the Whitestone Cliffs from where a huge area of his beloved North Yorkshire can be seen. Rosie suggested this spot and it is entirely fitting for his final resting place. I have stood here for many an hour, looking at the places where my father played out a great slice of his life. His practice, where he toiled manfully among all creatures great and small, is stretched out below, as far as the distant Pennines which first captivated him in those far-off days in 1940. Thirsk, where he brought up his family, and Thirlby, his home for the last eighteen years of his life, are clearly visible but, above all, it is a fresh and clean part of

Yorkshire with a breath of the wildness and freedom that was so close to his heart.

My father described this stretch of Yorkshire as having the 'finest view in England'; for a man with such feeling for the beauty of the country around him, there could be no better place to lie.

I return to that spot many times when walking my dog, and only last week I sat there with her – just as my father had done countless times with his dogs. As I gazed out at the patchwork of fields stretched below, I had feelings of sadness and nostalgia.

The world that James Herriot wrote about has all but disappeared and the countless family farms which James, Siegfried and Tristan visited in their rattly little cars are now few in number. Almost all of the fascinating old Yorkshire farmers that James Herriot immortalised are now dead and gone, together with the hard-working bands of farm men with whom he spent many happy hours.

Large cultivated fields, splashed with the colour of modern buildings, have partly taken the place of the greens and browns of hedges and old farmsteads but, apart from this, the picture of 'Herriot Country' laid out before me was not very different from the one I knew as a boy. As well as sadness, however, I had feelings of gratitude; how many men can claim to have had a father who left such great memories that could be shared with so many?

My memories that day, however, were not of James Herriot the author, but of Alfred Wight, the father. Following his death, one of his fans sent me the famous prayer by Henry Scott Holland, Canon of St Paul's Cathedral (1847–1918). The words are moving ones and bring great comfort to those who grieve at the loss of a loved one. The first and final sentences of the prayer seemed to have especial significance at that time:

'Death is nothing at all. I have only slipped away into the next room ... Why should I be out of mind because I am out of sight? I am waiting for you, for an interval, somewhere very near, just round the corner. All is well.'

As I sat that day with the 'finest view in England' stretched before me, I did wonder whether I would ever see my father again. I would give a great deal to be able to do so. I have so much to say to him and countless questions to ask. I do not know and I can only hope.

There is, however, one thing of which I am certain. James Herriot, the unassuming veterinary surgeon who enthralled millions, was no fictional character. There was a man I knew, who possessed all the virtues of the famous veterinarian – and more. A totally honest man whose fine sense of humour and air of goodwill towards others ensured that he was respected by all who knew him. A man on whom, after his death, a Yorkshire farmer delivered his final verdict: 'Aye, he were a right decent feller.' That man was James Alfred Wight.

INDEX

refresh yourself at penguin.co.uk

Visit penguin.co.uk for exclusive information and interviews with
bestselling authors, fantastic give-aways and the
inside track on all our books, from the Penguin Classics
to the latest bestsellers.

BE FIRST

first chapters, first editions, first novels

EXCLUSIVES

author chats, video interviews, biographies, special
features

EVERYONE'S A WINNER

give-aways, competitions, quizzes, ecards

READERS GROUPS

exciting features to support existing groups and
create new ones

NEWS

author events, bestsellers, awards, what's new

EBOOKS

books that click – download an ePenguin today

BROWSE AND BUY

thousands of books to investigate – search, try
and buy the perfect gift online – or treat yourself!

ABOUT US

job vacancies, advice for writers and company
history

Get Closer To Penguin . . . www.penguin.co.uk